Hispanic Baroques:
Reading Cultures in Context

HISPANIC ISSUES • VOLUME 31

Hispanic Baroques:
Reading Cultures in Context

Nicholas Spadaccini

AND

Luis Martín-Estudillo

EDITORS

Vanderbilt University Press

NASHVILLE, TENNESSEE

2005

© 2005 Vanderbilt University Press
All rights reserved
First Edition 2005

This book is printed on acid-free paper.
Manufactured in the United States of America

The editors gratefully acknowledge assistance from the
College of Liberal Arts and the Department of Spanish
and Portuguese Studies at the University of Minnesota.

*The complete list of volumes in the
Hispanic Issues series begins on page 323.*

Hispanic Baroques : reading cultures in context / [compiled
by] Nicholas Spadaccini, Luis Martín-Estudillo.
  p. cm. (Hispanic issues)
  Includes bibliographical references and index.
  ISBN 0-8265-1498-7 (cloth : alk. paper)
  ISBN 0-8265-1499-5 (pbk. : alk. paper)
  1. Spanish literature—Classical period, 1500–1700—
History and criticism. 2. Baroque literature—History and
criticism.
  I. Spadaccini, Nicholas. II. Martín-Estudillo, Luis.
III. Hispanic issues (Vanderbilt University)
PQ6064.H57 2005
860.9'11--dc22
                                                    2005004455

HISPANIC ISSUES

Nicholas Spadaccini
Editor-in-Chief

Antonio Ramos-Gascón and Jenaro Talens
General Editors

Nelsy Echávez-Solano
Luis Martín-Estudillo
Associate Editors

Fernando Ordóñez
Assistant Editor

Contents

◆ **Introduction:**
The Baroque and the Cultures of Crises

Nicholas Spadaccini and Luis Martín-Estudillo

The present volume deals with various formulations and uses of a concept—the Baroque—which in recent times has undergone a series of recyclings and permutations at the hands of literary/cultural critics and artists from various fields and academic disciplines. Baroque, Neobaroque, and Ultrabaroque are related concepts which have also been used to define certain social and cultural manifestations from the early modern period to late and post-modern times. Current interpreters of the Baroque in its latest reincarnations have pointed to some striking parallelisms between these disparate periods by invoking the notion of *horror vacui* and alternative ways of understanding complex realities. Thus, whether one emphasizes the "containment" side of the Baroque (José Antonio Maravall being its major exponent in connection with the dominant culture of seventeenth-century Spain) or its "transgressive" or liberating aspects (as has been the case with most Latin American voices on this question), what they seem to have in common is an awareness that these phenomena must be understood within the larger frame of epistemic and/or social crises. Interestingly, in recent years there has been substantial emphasis on the notion of a "baroque reason" and the rejection of traditional dichotomies and established norms, even in reference to the context of the earliest Baroque. Mabel Moraña (in this volume) addresses precisely the transgressive nature of its various adaptations within Latin America but also cautions that one must deal with its functionality within different historical and cultural contexts. Thus, she examines the logic of baroque disruptions, reappearances and transformations through the notions of "difference" and "ruin." Its latest permutation—the Ultrabaroque—is said to reflect an attitude that facilitates an exuberant representation of the "processes of transculturation and hybridization" (270) and is tied to a poetics which revindicates a historical memory, one that recalls the exhibitionist violence of colonialism.

Nowadays, the term "Baroque" seems to have overcome the negative connotation that it once had. Its etymology is still debated: it has been related to a syllogism of the discredited Scholastic philosophy, to an irregularly shaped pearl, and to a granitic rock. In the mid-1700s, when it began to refer to the arts of the previous century, "baroque" was understood as "ridicule pousée à l'excès" (ridiculous to the excess) (Diderot in Wölfflin 23) and opposed to classical norms. Yet, partial recuperations of the concept were on the way: at the beginning of the nineteenth century, the Schlegel brothers saw the great Spanish playwright Pedro Calderón de la Barca as a Romantic author *avant la lettre*. It was precisely in Germany where a more moderate and comprehensive study of the Baroque was initiated, one that understood it as an evolution of the Renaissance, even if this development was considered by many as being "measureless" or "infamous."

A substantive change in the perception of the Baroque was propitiated by the publication of Heinrich Wölfflin's *Renaissance und Barock* (1888) which saw it not as a degeneration of the Renaissance but as an autonomous, valid style. Wölfflin placed its origins in Counter-Reformation Rome and considered it to be "free" ("developed without models") (23), and, most of all, "painterly" (29). Later on, he proposed a total of five dichotomies ("forms of representation") to distinguish classical art from the Baroque: linear vs. painterly; plane vs. recessional; closed vs. open form; multiplicity vs. unity; and clearness vs. unclearness. Despite efforts at a revaluation of the Baroque, as late as the 1920s it was still possible to find pejorative criticisms such as Croce's statement that "quel che è veramente arte non è mai barocco, e quel che è barocco, non è arte . . ." (what is truly art is never baroque, and what is baroque, is not art). This negative assessment is not generalized and, in fact, will become a minority view as the Baroque is rediscovered by various generations of artists, cultural critics, and collectors in fields as varied as poetry, performance, cinema, interior design, architecture, haute couture, etc. (Calloway).

There is another concept, that of "Mannerism," which is often found in association with the "Baroque," especially in art history. These two concepts often overlap as Arnold Hauser shows when he argues that the conflict between the two styles "is more sociological than purely historical" (94). Mannerism is said to be

> the artistic style of an aristocratic, essentially international cultured class, the early baroque the expression of a more popular, more emotional, more nationalistic trend. The mature baroque triumphs over the more refined and exclusive style of mannerism, as the ecclesiastical propaganda of the Counter Reformation spreads and Catholicism again becomes a people's religion. The court art of the seventeenth century adapts the baroque to its specific needs; on the one hand, it works up baroque emotionalism into a magnificent theatricality and, on the other, it develops its latent classicism into the expression of an austere and clear-headed authoritarianism. But in the sixteenth century mannerism is the court style par excellence. (94–95)

Hauser applied his theory of historical materialism to define the art of this period as the expression of Catholic, anti-Reformation propaganda, focusing on the Church's use of art and literature as symbolic weapons to guide and co-opt the masses. At the same time, the aristocracy is said to have adapted this art for its own use and enjoyment thanks to its spectacularity and richness. Hauser's view of the associated concepts of Mannerism and Baroque relates to stylistic as well as to ideological features.

Wylie Sypher, on the other hand, understands them as two stages of Renaissance style, with Mannerism being characterized by "formal disintegration" and the Baroque by "formal reintegration." Sypher maintains that Mannerism has its own rules, among which he mentions a "diagonal or mobile point of view, disproportion, imbalance, thwarted verticality, funnel space [. . .] and tensions that were accommodated rather than resolved." Thus, baroque art would be "a reaction against the unstable, involved, and over-ingenious structures of mannerism" (184) which are extravagantly and exuberantly resolved, performing a "mighty katharsis by spectacle, by an expressive power" (185). Hernán Vidal (in this volume) challenges the arbitrariness with which concepts such as "Mannerism" and "Baroque" are constructed and goes on to focus on the manner in which the artistic production of the seventeenth century connects to social and political developments. The operative concept in his analysis is that of "military revolution," the development of massive armies (land and naval forces) which triggered the changes associated with the birth of Modernity. To the extent that the Baroque is viewed as "a category of imperial administration," he complements Maravall's focus on institutions and ideas to explain and interpret its culture.

Interestingly, the irruption of postcolonial studies seems to have given new impetus to the debate regarding the Baroque both as aesthetic category and as historical/cultural problem. This is seen in the discussions that center on decolonizing critical agendas. Thus, in a recent volume on colonial Latin America, one of the editors explains his project in this fashion:

> What this book does is, precisely, the opposite of *criollismo*: an in-depth study of the peculiarities of Latin American colonial situations that take into account its consequences for the situations of social injustice of the present; a study that holds the historical agents that created that social injustice responsible and that does not forget the memories of the colonial subjects demonized or repressed by hegemonic power. (Verdesio 9–10)

Despite the certainty with which this statement is made, the author does acknowledge the work of critics such as Mabel Moraña for understanding that "the Baroque esthetic trend served, depending on the authors, either the cause of the consolidation of the colonial status quo or the resistance to it" (4). Regardless of where critics fall within the political spectrum, and despite their specific critical agendas, it is clear that the Baroque as a category of analysis still holds sway in literary/cultural studies, particularly in connection with Latin America. Moreover, as we point out later in this introduction, the concept of Baroque is still engendering new terms to describe and interpret new realities.

In a prior volume of Hispanic Issues, Alberto Moreiras reflected upon the understanding of the Baroque as a "field of identitarian expression concerning the peculiar Hispanic experience of modernity" (207) and challenged the well-known interpretation of Roberto González Echevarría, which sees the Baroque "as a mark of continental identity" and locates it "metonymically in the so-called Boom of the Latin-American novel" (212), while, in fact, not going beyond the Colonial Baroque or "its status as regional ideology at the service of the constitution of the local as a differential/mimetic/identitarian apparatus of social capture" (212). Moreiras not only distances himself from what he calls regionalist, identitarian paradigms, but specifically embraces the concept of the Neobaroque, which for him implies an "interruption of the principle of regionalization" and a kind of passage or "pilgrimage toward the outside" (210). The Neobaroque is mobilized in the name of a "freedom of thought" (218) marked by interruption in line with the foundational work of Severo Sarduy and José Lezama Lima (225).

   In the 1950s, Lezama Lima had spoken of the Spanish American Baroque as the art of "counter-Conquest" and as an urban and intellectual phenomenon close to the spirit of the Enlightenment—a frame for new "formas de vida y de curiosidad" (46) (ways of life and types of curiosity)—while Severo Sarduy would later identify the Baroque with an epistemic break (especially reflected in a revolution in astronomy) and would argue for a restricted semantic field, "un esquema operatorio preciso, que no dejara intersticios, que no permitiera el abuso o el desenfado terminológico de que esta noción ha sufrido recientemente y muy especialmente entre nosotros" (1386) (a precise operative scheme, without interstices, which would not allow for the abuse or the lack of accuracy that this notion has suffered recently, particularly among us). Sarduy was probably referring to broad definitions such as Alejo Carpentier's, for whom America had always been baroque. But Sarduy's main contribution to the debate was his notion of a neo-baroque *retombée* (a relapse or achronic causality) marked by the appearance of a crisis in our understanding of the universe and expressed through an art of irregular, inapprehensible forms: "un neobarroco en es-tallido en el que los signos giran y se escapan hacia los límites del soporte sin que ninguna fórmula permita trazar sus líneas o seguir los mecanismos de su producción" (1375) (an exploding Neobaroque in which signs spin and escape toward the limits of the medium, without any formula that could trace its lines nor follow its production mechanisms).

   Sarduy's arguments were to open a rich debate about the similarities between our age and the seventeenth century and have found much echo in the fields of literary/cultural studies even beyond the Spanish-speaking world. For example, the Italian semiotician Omar Calabrese adopted Sarduy's idea of a baroque relapse and concluded that "many important phenomena of our time are distinguished by a specific internal 'form' that recalls the baroque" (15). Calabrese attempts to describe the morphology of an anti-classical "social aesthetics" and, like Sarduy, identifies connections between contemporary science and art, although he avoids establishing a relationship of causality between them. Moreover, as Moraña indicates, correctly, in this volume, "Calabrese dismisses, in a radical manner, the historicity and contingency of all cultural production in order to establish a transmediatic and transcultural perspective that approximates phenomena and fields of knowledge that, in fact, are only related by their semiotic behavior and their contemporaneity" (250).

Freedom and Containment

In recent years literary and cultural theory has dealt with how power relations are part of a dynamic process that exceeds its negative attributes when it is seen only within the seemingly oppressive domain of the "State." Some of Foucault's ideas on this issue have become common currency, especially the assertion that power "doesn't only weigh on us as a force that says no but that it traverses and produces things, it induces pleasure, forms knowledge, produces discourse. It needs to be considered as a productive network which runs through the whole social body, much more than as a negative instance whose function is repressive" (60–61). Similarly, others have argued for a "dialectic of control" in social systems (Giddens 145), contending that "all power relations . . . manifest autonomy and dependence 'in both directions'" (149). The reversible order of this scheme seems to be advanced as an expressed critique of Max Weber's conception of bureaucracy which holds that, within bureaucracies, formal authority relations are accepted consensually at all levels of the organization, so that controlling bodies and their subjects work together. Interestingly enough, this same type of critique of "trickle down" power relations has been leveled against Maravall's interpretation of baroque culture.

Following general lines of thought which argue for the reciprocities of power relations, and keeping in mind Maravall's well-known interpretation of the Baroque as a "conservative," "guided," "urban" and "mass-oriented" culture, we will examine different types of texts from the Spanish 1600s for the purpose of showing that while a homogeneous subject may indeed be posited through a variety of cultural and artistic products oriented toward "mass" consumption (especially certain types of theatrical performances, sermons, festivals, chapbooks, and so on), the possibility of alternative positions cannot be excluded. Such alternatives are implied in the subject's awareness that power relations involve reciprocity. In Maravall's case it must be said that despite his basic emphasis on ideas and institutions and, therefore, on the exercise of power from above rather than a focus on subjectivity on a more concrete level, his writings also make clear that one cannot understand the complexities of Spanish baroque culture without taking into account the discrepant voices that are raised against its conservative programs.[1]

While literary/cultural critics often question Maravall's notion of *dirigismo* (social guidance) to explain how in the 1600s the monarcho-seigniorial segments of Spanish society worked to maintain the prevailing system of privileges, they continue to rely on his extraordinary work of synthesis to examine along socio-historical lines various types of texts of the Spanish 1600s within that immediate context of production/reception (Romero Díaz, R. de la Flor). From our perspective, Maravall's interpretation of the Baroque seems to be especially useful in dealing with the impact of certain "mass-oriented" cultural products of the 1600s. One could mention the sacramental and secular plays that were staged in the thousands in the urban centers of Spain, as well as the performances of sermons by famous preachers on sacred occasions and spectacular displays connected with religious and/or secular celebrations (catafalques, triumphal arches, elaborately decorated altars, processions, and various other visual and/or auditory effects, including illumination and pyrotechnics). In fact, Maravall's general interpretation is further sustained by a conservative line of picaresque narratives that espoused, at least on some level, the repression of social and moral deviance.

The case for Spanish baroque theater as a vehicle for social and political propaganda is well known and has been argued by various scholars (Maravall, Díez Borque, and Noël Salomon) in conjunction with the popular *comedia* of the early 1600s whose manifesto was Lope de Vega's *Arte nuevo de hacer comedias en este tiempo* (New Art of Writing Plays in Our Time) (1609). Let us consider for a moment Cervantes' implicit criticism of Lope de Vega for having acquiesced to the demands and tastes of the *vulgo* (a non-discriminating "mass" consumer) and the realities of the marketplace where producers and the entire commercial and regulatory circuit of the theater favor the kind of formulaic plays that were composed by Lope and his school of playwrights. Cervantes' critical position on this matter is made clear in several of his well-known texts, among them *Don Quijote* (I, 48), *Ocho comedias y ocho entremeses* (1615) (Eight Comedies and Eight Interludes), the *Adjunta al Parnaso* (1614) ("Addendum" to *Voyage to Parnassus*), and in some of the plays written toward the end of his life, among them *Pedro de Urdemalas* (Peter, the Great Pretender), a three-act play, and "El retablo de las maravillas" (The Magic Tableau), a one-act farce, to mention the most prominent examples. The "Addendum" to *Voyage to Parnassus* carries a brief dialogue between a certain Pancracio and an interlocutor named Miguel (de Cervantes) that speaks eloquently to this issue:

Pancracio:	¿Y agora tiene vuesa merced algunas comedias?
Miguel:	Seis tengo, con otros seis entremeses.
Pancracio:	Pues, ¿por qué no se representan?
Miguel:	Porque ni los autores me buscan ni yo les voy a buscar a ellos.
Pancracio:	No deben de saber que vuesa merced las tiene.
Miguel:	Sí saben; pero como tienen sus poetas paniaguados y les va bien con ellos no buscan pan de trastrigo. Pero yo pienso darlas a la estampa

para que se vea de espacio lo que pasa apriesa y se disimula o no se
entiende, cuando las representan. Y las comedias tienen sus sazones
y tiempos como los cantares.

(Pancracio: And now [tell me], do you have any *comedias* [available for sale]?
Miguel: I have six of them with six other interludes.
Pancracio: Then why aren't they being represented [on stage]?
Miguel: Because producers do not seek me out nor I them.
Pancracio: Surely they must not know that you have them.
Miguel: Yes they do know; but since they have their own protégés and do
               fine with them, they do not look for problems. But I plan to have
               them published so that one might see slowly [on the printed page]
               what moves quickly and is either concealed or not understood
               when they are represented [on stage]. Moreover *comedias*, like
               songs, also have their seasons and occasions.)[2]

Cervantes understands that his kind of conceptual theater was out of step
with the expectations of producers, actors, and audiences. We also see in this
quotation that he reflects two attitudes toward the act of reading: one hinging
on spatial development in time (theatricality) and the other based on narrativity
in a strict sense (Spadaccini and Talens, *Through the Shattering Glass* 46). For
Cervantes, theater is a system of representation and an institutional apparatus
with its own conventions and mediations which "produces action, time, and
meaning through a time imposed on the audience moment by moment" (47).
On the other hand, theatricalized narration provides the discriminate reader
with a mental space of interpretation that precludes the type of closure imposed
by the accepted canon of the staged performance (47).

Cervantes' position on this issue provides a stark contrast to that of Lope
de Vega, who expresses reluctance at having his plays appear in print for fear of
being subjected to misunderstanding and unfavorable scrutiny in the privacy of
the reading rooms. Unlike Lope, Cervantes displaces his plays from the public
stage, away from the impressionable *vulgo* and onto the printed page in search
of a thoughtful reception. In fact, the implications of theater as spectacle is a
recurring motif in much of his writing, and in plays such as *Pedro de Urdemalas*
and *El retablo de las maravillas*, this very question is inscribed in their respective textual spaces, thus challenging the reader to reflect on the fictional status
of theater and the manner in which it functions ideologically. Moreover those
plays speak to the manipulative uses of the new popular theater and how the
vulgo's perceptions are mediated by the material conditions of the stage with

its ever greater reliance on special effects (*tramoyas*), a recognizable character typology, constant twists of the plot, extraordinary emphasis on action rather than characterization, the repetitive uses of certain themes (among them, the harmony of country life, the social and political integration of the rich peasant, and the stability of the traditional honor code), and the ultimate resolution of conflict often through the intervention of the Monarchs or their representatives. In fact, it is the repetitive character of these "mass-oriented" products that propel the spectator onto the realm of the familiar, facilitating a non-discriminating reception (Horkheimer and Adorno; Maravall) as Cervantes knew well in opposing his theater to the formulaic *comedia nueva* of the beginning of the 1600s.

The notion of a non-discriminating, "mass" reception which Cervantes attributes the theater-going public of the *comedia nueva* is also useful for a discussion of the baroque sermon and the *auto sacramental* (sacramental play). Regarding the former, it is well known that preachers used rhetorical devices and dramatic ploys to captivate audiences, as we learn from a certain Fray Ángel Manrique (1613), a contemporary of Cervantes, who stresses that the oral performance allows the preacher to give "vida a lo que decía con la voz, con las acciones, con el modillo de decir, con los meneos; pero en el papel es imposible escribirse nada de esto" (cit. by Barnes-Karol 76) (to give life to what he is seeking to convey, through his voice and actions, his manner of saying things, and the movements of his body; whereas on paper it is impossible to write any of this). There is also evidence that preachers sought to profit through the use of representational techniques that were common to the new popular theater. Thus, toward the end of the seventeenth century (1698) a certain Francisco Caus was to describe one of his colleague's sermons in this manner: "con ser tan contrario de las comedias, se portaba en este exercisio como los comediantes. Estos, para llamar gente, y tener ganancia, suelen disponer en el Teatro algunas apariencias, que llaman Tramoyas, a cuya novedad se junta tal vez mayor discurso que para un sermón, y con esto aumentan su grangería" (Even though it [preaching] is so contrary to the theater, he behaved in this exercise as actors do. Actors, in order to attract audiences and make a profit, commonly use scenic effects called *Tramoyas*, which, because of their novelty, draw perhaps bigger crowds than sermons do, and, in this way, they increase their earnings) (Ledda, cited by Barnes-Karol 57).

Another interesting document along these lines is a treatise written by the jurist Gaspar Gutiérrez de los Ríos whose *Noticia general para la estimación de las artes, y de la manera en que se conocen las liberales de las que son mecánicas y serviles...* (1600), deals among other things with the connection between the art of painting and drawing with rhetoric and dialectic:

> No es poca también la emulación que tienen estas artes con la Retórica. Porque si para ser perfectos los Oradores han de ser diestros y esperimentados en el estilo del dezir, grave, mediano, humilde, y mixto, correspondiendo siempre a la material que se trata: de una manera en las cartas, de otra en las historias, de otra en los razonamientos, oraciones y sermones públicos: de una manera en las cosas de prudencia, de otra en las cosas de dotrina: si deven assí mismo demostrar todo género de afectos de ira, misericordia, temor, o amor, y passarlos a los oyentes, para poder persuadir e inclinarlos a lo que se dize. (Calvo Serraller 79)

> (It is not little the emulation that these arts (painting and drawing) also have with Rhetoric. For if in order for the Orators to be perfect, skillful, and experienced in the style of saying—serious, moderate, humble, and mixed—corresponding always to the material at hand: in the letters one way, another in the histories, still another in the reasonings, orations and public sermons: one way in matters of prudence, another in doctrinal ones: they must likewise demonstrate all types of impressions: ire, mercy, fear, love, and transfer them to the listeners in order to persuade them and incline them toward what is said.)

According to Gutiérrez de los Ríos, the audience will be moved by the ensemble of representational skills with which the preacher conveys the message.

Other documents from the period underscore the importance of painting over printed texts for the illustration of religious history and values as well as for the preservation of secular authority. Thus, in a memorandum to King Philip III by a number of court painters, ca. 1619, it was stated that, "la pintura, que en un instante nos muestra y hace capaces de lo que por lectura era fuerza gastar mucho tiempo, y hojear muchos libros, siendo en ellos dicho con multitud de palabras, con mucha erudición y teología para declararse, y muy posible, después de todo, quedar menos entendido de mucha gente" (Calvo Serraller 165) (painting, which in an instant shows us and teaches us what would, of necessity, have taken much time leafing through and reading many books, since what is stated in them is said with many words, with much erudition and theology for the sake of clarity and which, in the end, might be less understood by many people).

The various quotations included above proffer a distinction between the text that is represented on stage or through pictorial images and the one that is read; between the possible mediation through linguistic and kinesic signs on the part of the preacher or through spectacular depictions on the part of the painter and a reception through reading that is of necessity more cerebral and less susceptible to emotion. The sermon sought to teach and persuade the faithful in line with the principles of the Counter Reformation. This same idea was to guide the Catholic painter, according to Francisco Pacheco in his *Arte de la Pintura* (1649), in which there is an explicit mention of the parallelism that exists between the work of the painter and that of the preacher. His ideas about the mission of painting must be understood within the context of Counter Reformation culture, since the Council of Trent had defended the use of images to promote devotion and to strengthen worship. Pacheco compares the painter's labor to that of the preacher in that they both worked at the service of Church and faith. As such they had a common goal: to persuade the populace. In the case of a canonical painter such as el Greco, it has been demonstrated (R. de la Flor, *Barroco* 117) that his *Toledo: Plano y vista* (1610–1614) "purifies" the image of a city contaminated by the presence of non-Christian, Semitic elements. This idea connects perfectly with Maravall's interpretation of the Baroque as a culture of guidance and control.

Baroque secular and religious celebrations allow people to partake of the splendor and spectacle associated with key institutions of the Spanish state: the Church and the Monarchy. Thus, the elaborate representation of sacramental plays on the feast of Corpus Christi gave visibility to the concept of transubstantiation as well as to other teachings of the Catholic Church. At these public spectacles the audience would be expected to be engulfed in a sea of emotion and be guided toward an affirmation of faith (Brad Nelson, in this volume, analyzes Calderón's *El gran mercado del mundo* to underscore the inscription of certain tensions within the text and the possibility for a different kind of reception). This very idea is conveyed by the great Mexican Creole writer, Sor Juana Inés de la Cruz, in a short dramatic panegyric ("Loa") to the sacramental play *El divino Narciso* (The Divine Narcissus) which, according to the text, was destined to be represented in Madrid. In the panegyric, the allegorical character called "Religion" speaks in metaphors but simultaneously undertakes the representation of the story through visual images with the aim of converting native subjects through their senses. In the respective examples of sermons and sacramental plays, an audience became absorbed into a power network that was an expression of God's will, while in the case of the early Lopean *comedia,* the symbolic identification was often with the King and was effected through an honor code that demanded absolute obedience.

The conservative energies within the Baroque can also be felt within a moralizing line of picaresque narrative whose archetype is Mateo Alemán's

Guzmán de Alfarache (1599, 1604), an extraordinarily popular novel, a best seller which went through some twenty-six editions in the seventeenth century and the publication of some fifty-thousand volumes. In this particular narrative, the alliance between Church and State in disciplining and punishing the deviant *pícaro* is manifested throughout the text, but most especially in part II, where the sermon becomes the dominant narrative structure. The narrator's apologia for traditional order is summarized in the idea that salvation can be achieved within one's social position ("sálvase cada uno en su estado").

In general we might say that *Guzmán de Alfarache* and several other picaresque narratives of the early Baroque propose a totalizing conception of morality in relation to an individual who is depicted as breaking the very rules which the aristocratic and ecclesiastical State expects him to obey. Fiction, then, serves to represent the essentially moral nature of reality as well as the possible outcome of a world without rules. Thus various manifestations of transgression such as sorcery, witchcraft, prostitution, thievery, abuse of charity, and countless other forms of delinquency became embedded in the cultural and political discourses of the time. Picaresque literature provides a mapping of the cancerous underclass that roamed the cities in order to expose the dangers posed by those "unhinged" individuals to the urban groups (including merchants) that had the most to lose from their illegal activities. In another picaresque novel, *La hija de Celestina* (1612) (Celestina's Daughter), Madrid, "the mother of all people," becomes part of Elena's ecosystem, a place of riches and temptations to be exploited; the anonymity that the city provides facilitates her contact with individuals of various ranks who are tricked by her into believing that she possesses spiritual gifts and healing powers. Her activities include prostitution which, in the end, contributes to her demise: after it is discovered that she has killed her pimp, she is garroted by the authorities, stuffed in a barrel, and thrown in the Manzanares river. But not before she returns stolen property to her victims and undergoes a spiritual conversion! This conventional ending à la *Guzmán* corresponds to a discursive integration of different spheres of society.

A sample of literary texts from the Hispanic baroque period point toward a broader and more problematic understanding of power relations. One of the most interesting figures to have dealt with the complexities of such relations is the Jesuit thinker Baltasar Gracián whose *Héroe* (1637) is emblematic along these lines insofar as it makes clear that individuals and groups bring a kind of capital (*caudal*) to every transaction (Primor II, "Cifrar la voluntad"). To the extent that such capital becomes someone else's object of desire, the actions of one's potential antagonists must be anticipated through an understanding of their mental processes. This relationship of power may be viewed as productive insofar as the individual is involved in an exchange that allows for the possibility of gaining practical knowledge, the kind that may be used in defense of the self. For this individual there emerges a break between knowledge viewed as an instrument or as a product of power relations and knowledge seen as an absolute explanation of oneself, grounded outside of concrete social relations (Sánchez and Spadaccini).

Let us recall that in many baroque texts, the concept of *virtù,* in which an individual is a producer of his own genealogy, undergoes a transformation. That production now depends upon the use of practical knowledge framed by prudence (Maravall, *La cultura* 138 ff.), by one's ability to exercise a discursive constraint. This prudent use of knowledge allows one to navigate through the perilous waters of deception in which individuals are isolated and subjected to predators. This very idea is captured in Gracián's Aphorism 181 of his *Oráculo manual y arte de prudencia* (Art of Worldly Wisdom), which advises: "Sin mentir, no decir todas las verdades" (Don't lie, but don't tell the whole truth). One of the reasons for suppressing truth is the unpredictability of its reception and the possibility of exposing oneself to personal harm:

> No hay cosa que requiera más tiento que la verdad, que es un sangrarse del corazón. Tanto es menester para saberla decir como para saberla callar. Piérdese con sola una mentira todo el crédito de la entereza. Es tenido el engañado por falto y el engañador por falso, que es peor. No todas las verdades se pueden decir: unas porque me importan a mí, otras porque al otro.

> (Nothing requires more skill than the truth, which is a letting of blood from the heart. It takes skill both to speak it and to withhold it. A single lie can destroy one's reputation for honesty. The man deceived seems faulty, and the deceiver seems false, which is worse. Not all truths can be spoken: some should be silenced for your own sake, others for the sake of someone else.)

In the world of the court as represented by Gracián, survival depends upon techniques of representation which call for the management of truth in order to avoid bitter disillusionment or what is graphically called a bloodletting of the heart ("sangrarse del corazón"). Survival and ultimate success hinge upon a careful negotiation of one's relations with others within clearly established parameters, and only those who practice a strategy and technique of prudence can control their own destinies ("arte para ser dichoso" [the art of success], aphorism 21). This self-control is opposed to spontaneity or to the giving of oneself to passion. Through his aphorisms Gracián proposes an economy of language and behavior and a controlled, self-defined individual through a highly pragmatic action which leaves nothing to chance (Sánchez and Spadaccini). For good reason Gracián's aphorisms point to the importance of rhetoric as a discipline to manage public life. Within the context in which his writings were received in baroque Spain, the idea for the reader was to assimilate patterns of behavior that could help one take advantage of the rules of an established social order without seeking to transform them (Spadaccini and Talens, *Rhetoric and Politics*). The highest form of practical wisdom was to understand the demands of public "opinion" within the structure of a court that now included professional bureaucrats, statesmen, artists, and various moneyed groups and then master the proper techniques of public representation, in other words, theatricality. (See Ordóñez Tarín in this volume on the contradictory relationships between institutions and intellectuals such as Gracián and Quevedo; see also Egginton's problematization of Gilles Deleuze's philosophical hypothesis about the Baroque through a reading of Gracián's *Criticón*).

There are various other narratives of this period that stress a practical view of morality. This can be seen in a witty picaresque novel that challenges directly the moral assumptions propagated by the popular *Guzmán de Alfarache*. In Francisco López de Úbeda's *La pícara Justina* (1605), published soon after the appearance of the second part of Alemán's novel (1604) and just prior to the publication of the first part of *Don Quijote* (1605), the dual structure of *Guzmán de Alfarache* is maintained only in appearance. The somber voice of Guzmán, the converted *pícaro*, now gives way to an ironic and playful account of a life of deviance and the creative steps taken by Justina to improve her lot. In this particular picaresque narrative the baroque city again becomes the center of attraction and it is within that space of exchange that her morality is shaped by individual action. Such action is expressed through parody of the official discourse on poverty and charity as her notion of giving (and taking) is of a contractual kind, with none of the theological trappings assumed by the official discourses of Church and State. Justina also rejects any apprehension of reality that relies on sight, for it can numb the mind and cast prudence aside. True love is defined by Justina as exchange and, as such, it resides in the hands rather than in the heart. The world is seen through her hands which become the emblem of the individual's control of the self in the practical sphere of social intercourse: "amor que sale primero a los ojos y a los meneos que a las manos, no creo en él; manos muertas y ojos vivos es imaginación y quimera . . . Reniego del amor, si ése es amor" (446) (I do not believe in the kind of love that manifests itself to the eyes rather than to the hands—says Justina—Dead hands and live eyes are love's imagination and chimera . . . If that is love, I reject it). Justina's self-definition and initiatives are precisely what the totalizing, moral narrator of *Guzmán de Alfarache* wishes to suppress (Sánchez and Spadaccini). A different understanding of power relations may be gathered from an analysis of colonial texts in that the so-called "Barroco de Indias" tends to impugn those discourses that deprive the Other of a voice. Important figures such as Sor Juana, Sigüenza y Góngora, and Espinosa Medrano (El Lunarejo) claim an American identity forged in a vital space that encompasses a variety of languages and cultures. For these Creole intellectuals "alterity and identity are the two sides of the same collective experience and of the same project, one that struggles to make possible the utopia of the American being as a socially differentiated subject" (Moraña, *Relecturas* v). At the same time it is important to underscore the fact that baroque colonial writing is defined not only by its contestatory orientation but also by its propagation of hegemonic discourses. This can be seen, for example, in the "Loa" that precedes Sor Juana's *El divino Narciso* and in Sigüenza y Góngora's *Theatro de virtudes políticas* (Theater of Political Virtues). (For an analysis of the contestatory voice of intellectuals such as Cervantes and Inca Garcilaso on the colonial question, see Suárez in this volume).

In the case of the Creole *letrado* Sigüenza y Góngora there is a clear attempt to distance himself from the encomiastic messages that were usually inscribed in the triumphal arches constructed to welcome figures of power and authority. In his case he was to organize the reception of a Viceroy (the Count of Paredes and Marquis of la Laguna), who was coming to Mexico from the metropolis. The *Theatro* underscores the irony and resentment of a Creole intellectual against the metropolis' attempt to impose its cultural and political models. For Sigüenza y Góngora, the very idea that a bureaucrat was to be received as a Caesar exposed the Empire as an empty mask. For his part, he preferred to invoke old Mexican warriors whom he contrasted to the faceless bureaucrats who were arriving from Madrid. Sigüenza y Góngora's suggestion is that the addressee of the triumphal arch did not understand the allegorical significance of the monument, for he had not had contacts with indigenous cultures and, in any case, suffered from a lack of interpretative capacities. Sigüenza y Góngora perceives this emptiness and supplements the image of the monument with an elocutive explanation inviting the Viceroy to seek counsel and consult "con su pueblo todos y cada uno de los asuntos de este arco" (189) (with his people any and all matters included in this arch). The homage to the Viceroy thus becomes a pretext by Sigüenza y Góngora to distance himself from the arch's purpose to embody metropolitan power.

In the case of Sor Juana, she utilizes the "Loa" to reflect upon the vitality of native cultures and the impossibility to assimilate the Other through violence. For this reason "Occidente" (one of the allegorical characters) will say that violence will not force her to forget her roots: "no me podrás impedir/que acá, en mi corazón, diga/que venero al gran Dios de las Semillas!" (387) (you cannot prevent me/that here, in my heart, I say/that I adore the great God of the Seeds). In the "Loa" the ideas advanced by the allegorical character "América" (speaking to "Religión") indicate that the repression of indigenous cultures cannot be fully successful as long as they have a will to preserve their own past. The "Loa" makes clear that the violence perpetrated on the Indies has been done in the name of God, despite the fact that the institutional discourses of Church and State are not always comprehensible to native Amerindians. In these verses, the discourse of Empire is summarized through the allegorical voices of "Religión" and "Celo" who speak of conquering and assimilating the Other to the Same. Yet, "Religión" is cognizant of the fact that the cooptation of native subjects needs a different strategy. Sor Juana manages to distance herself from the propagandistic designs of the *auto sacramental*, a genre which, in line with pos-Tridentine ideology, seeks to eliminate any divergence of thinking in order to advance Church doctrine. (For a discussion of Sor Juana's complex theological views, see Marín in this volume).

The "Loa" reflects on the nature of the *auto sacramental* as an instrument to strengthen faith, making visible on stage what would otherwise only reach the faithful through auditive means, that is, through the preacher's rhetoric. Theater, then, was seen as a vehicle having great potential for propagating religious and social messages. Yet, it is also clear that Sor Juana rewrites the mystery of transubstantiation through the insertion of native elements, giving us a glimpse of a new, Creole America which has acquired a new language and, with it, the power to question and debate. It is an America that will continue to speak on the road to independence (Jara and Spadaccini).

The subversion of dominant discourses regarding the colonization of the so-called New World is not exclusive of Amerindian intellectuals. In fact, even a figure such as Luis de Góngora (Spain's greatest baroque poet), whose work Sor Juana and Sigüenza y Góngora knew well, manages to express his reservations regarding the process of conquest, the greed of the colonizers, and the violent subjugation of native peoples. This is precisely what we see in Góngora's *Soledades* (vs 366–503) (Solitudes) where the pilgrim listens to the testimony of a shepherd who participated in the colonial enterprise. Góngora's criticism is embedded in a highly metaphorical and experimental language which had contributed to his reputation as a kind of prince of darkness.

Interestingly, the extraordinary experimentation with language that is the hallmark of much of Spanish baroque literature also involves a definition of the reader in the tension between containment and freedom. (For a discussion of the notion of "author" and the creation of the literary field see Gutiérrez in this volume). This may also be seen in Cervantes' fiction where reading emerges as a demystifying activity, one which goes beyond the simple linguistic properties of discourse to discover that those properties "announce the authority and social competence of speakers" (Bourdieu 63).

From a rhetorical standpoint, one of the techniques used by art and litera- ture to persuade was to implicate the reader/spectator in the work itself. In Cer- vantes, perhaps more than in any other Spanish writer of his time, the audience is rescued from this type of cooptation as a separation of reality from literature is effected within fiction. Moreover his self-critical texts confront dialectically the life experience of the reader and, in so doing, reject the sort of ideological manipulation that was being promoted through the mass-oriented culture of his time.

In this discussion of containment and freedom in the Spanish Baroque, we return to Cervantes, for he had the pulse of his age as few other Spanish creative writers did. His texts bring to the reader's attention the specific registers that contextualize the act of communication and challenge the reader to reflect upon the reliability and authority of the speaker. With respect to the picaresque, he rejects the totalizing voice of the reintegrated *pícaro* (the voice of social and moral authority) and invents characters who shape their own destinies through dialogue; while in reference to the official theater of the early 1600s, he under- scores the manipulative uses of art in the creation of a model of life. Finally, his writing brings to the foreground the questions of gender and ethnicity as expressions of how to give voice to the repressed Other. He brings to his cre- ative project an uncanny understanding of the mechanisms and uses of specifi- cally defined cultural artifacts and the manner in which they are constructed and received by different kinds of audiences. His texts activate the "reader," calling attention through irony to the conventions that help to propagate the myths of official culture. The post-Cervantine novella of Gonzalo de Céspedes y Meneses, Juan Pérez de Montalbán and María de Zayas y Sotomayor may also be seen as cultural spaces for the confrontation of contradictory discourses in urban settings (see Romero-Díaz in this volume).

We have attempted to sketch out various representations of power rela- tions during the early period of the Spanish Baroque focusing on the idea that containment and freedom are not mutually exclusive concepts. The success of any guidance had to contend not only with an appropriate receptivity on the part of subjects who were being guided but also with those who were creating their own spaces of resistance: those who relied on self-guidance.

Baroque and Modernity

Descartes believed that one of the three main goals of philosophy is to help in the guidance of life (*Principia Philosophae*, 1644). Cartesianism was adopted in many parts of Europe as an alternative to a decadent Scholasticism, and although Descartes's works were included in the *Index* of prohibited books in 1663, liberal Dutch universities continued using them. It was precisely in the Netherlands where Baruch Spinoza developed a philosophy which entailed a moral and personal search of vital wisdom along lines comparable to those of Descartes and Gracián. Their rationalism tends to suppress the passional, that is, any element that could interfere with the pragmatic achievement of the individual's goals. Martin Jay speaks of a multiplicity of visual cultures founded on three different "scopic regimes of Modernity" which constitute historically defined ways of seeing. The dominant one in the modern era is Cartesian perspectivalism, which can be identified with the Renaissance (Albertian) notion of perspective and Descartes's idea of subjective rationality. In the words of Jay, this regime "was in league with a scientific world view that no longer hermeneutically read the world as a divine text, but rather saw it as situated in a mathematically regular spatio-temporal order filled with natural objects that could only be observed from without by the dispassionate eye of the neutral researcher" ("Scopic regimes" 118). A less prevailing regime is the one modeled by the Dutch "art of describing" or Northern nonperspectival tradition of the map and its lack of insistence on the boundary of a window frame, opting for the continuum of the painted surface with the world beyond the frame. Finally, a regime that has been especially attractive for postmodern thinkers because of its "subversion of the dominant visual order of scientific reason" (*Downcast Eyes* 47) is that of the Baroque with its distorted, unfocused, vertiginous opticality and its rendering of the visual field from multiple viewpoints.

While much of the discussion about the Baroque today focuses on the notion of the irrational, one must also acknowledge its more explicitly rational side. Accordingly, in recent years there has been a great deal of discussion about the existence of a "baroque reason" which would emphasize excess, plurality of views, and corporality. For Roland Barthes, the baroque semantics is the topos of the impossible, modeled on the oxymoron. It would also entail the rejection of the great classical dichotomies that oppose subject and object, real and unreal, masculine and feminine. For Christine Buci-Glucksmann, "contrairement à toute métaphysique du sujet et du Cogito comme présence à soi dans la re-présentation, la vision—celle de saint Paul—dépossède le sujet de lui-même, le désapproprie, l'absente en une série de métamorphoses, de sorties hors de soi" (*La folie du voir* 118) (Contrary to all metaphysics of the subject and of the *Cogito* as presence in itself in the re-presentation, the vision—that of St. Paul—dispossesses the subject from himself, it disappropriates him, it makes him absent through a series of metamorphoses, of exits from the self).

Buci-Glucksmann has developed an interpretation of the Baroque and of contemporary culture around the axis of what she considers to be "le grand axiome du baroque: Être, c'est Voir" (92) (the great axiom of the Baroque: to Be is to See). In an interview given toward the end of 2000 on the occasion of an exhibition called *Triomphes du Baroque* (Triomphes of the Baroque) dealing with the work of contemporary "carnal artist" Orlan, Buci-Glucksmann relies on some of the notions that she had explored in *La folie du voir* (The Madness of Seeing) to stress the polarity of the Baroque, one of jouissance vs. one of death; one of fullness or plenitude (as in the case of Leibniz or Deleuze) vs. one of emptiness or void (Borromini's spiral, for example); one of glory or power such as Bernini's vs. the Baroque of the martyr (Sigismond). The Baroque is seen as a special moment within our monotheistic Western culture (a culture of "the fall and the elevation" [26]): "it's a dualist culture, and what's interesting in the feminization of culture is the refusal of this dualism. The baroque is a moment within Christianity, and even within the counter reformation, which will introduce the double and will hybridize the low into the high and the high into the low" (26–27) thus pointing to the Baroque's potential for rejection of established norms. (García Pabón in this volume studies *criollo* narratives of the seventeenth and eighteenth centuries to explore the particular responses to the intersection of life and death and its relationship to their subjectivity).

In the late twentieth century the Baroque was to emerge as a crucial concept for a comprehensive understanding of Modernity. The appearance of the concept of Neobaroque and the insistence by many contemporary artists on finding affiliations with the cultural production of the seventeenth century have contributed to the acknowledgement of its importance. Already in the 1920s, Walter Benjamin realized that his project of developing an "archeology of the modern" had to go through an analysis of the major elements that constituted the imaginary of the seventeenth century. He was to come to the conclusion that the Baroque—and Modernity at large—were essentially melancholic, with Hamlet and Baudelaire being the greatest exponents of this condition. (For a discussion of the Baroque and melancholy, see R. de la Flor in this volume). Thus, in his *The Origin of German Tragic Drama*, completed in 1928, Benjamin's conception of Modernity did not depend only on Enlightenment reason; he recognized that certain factors deny the rationality of the process of historical construction and, in so doing, he pointed to the impossibility of stable totalities and absolute truths.

The image that Benjamin used to illustrate that process was that of the *ruins*. The tragic events which developed during and immediately after his lifetime would sadly confirm the convenience of such an icon. Commenting on Benjamin's work, the Spanish philosopher Ana Lucas was to observe that "baroque theater had staged a representation of the world that becomes 'ruin,' but it has been only nowadays when we have finally confirmed the ruinous character of our whole reality. Instability, polidimensionality, mutability, and fragmentarity are baroque traits which Benjamin detected in Modernity and which have now exploded, invading all aspects of cultural and social reality" (23).

The ruins within which we need to survive are those of certainties, those of "substitute theologies"—to use Steiner's terms—that took the place of religion and functioned as mechanisms of human consolation. It is difficult to deny that we live in a time of a generalized perception of crisis. Already in 1972 Maravall had perceived "some similarities that exist between our current situation and that of the seventeenth century, a time full of conflicts" (*Teatro* 93). Fernando R. de la Flor, a contributor to this volume, wrote not long ago that in the 1600s "decadence and disenchantment [. . .] took hold of the stage of representation (the symbolic space of the Counter Reformation), forecasting in three hundred years the same doubts and the same auto-destructive energy that is acting on our own symbolic production nowadays, a time which is thus living its baroque revival, the neobaroque" (*Península* 14).

That self-destructive tension which de la Flor names as characteristic of our culture is the manifestation of the period of uncertainty which we are witnessing at virtually every level. Ours is a time in which the most extreme side of baroque *horror vacui* is completely justified. It might be worth remembering that the Aristotelian theory which denied the possibility of existence of a vacuum was not refuted until the mid-1600s by Galileo's disciple Evangelista Torricelli. From the important discussions generated in the seventeenth century by this topic there remains today an indelible association between *horror vacui* and the arts of the Baroque. There is actually a twofold connection: while some Baroque and Neobaroque cultural products can be perceived as fighting a vacuum-related anxiety through an extreme or excessive formal density, other products point toward that same "nothingness" by showing a resistance to that very same density. Both positions can be understood as an expressive answer to the "fear of vacuum" that characterizes the creative manifestations of the Baroque and Neobaroque (see Castillo in this volume).

In some of the works of the great Spanish baroque poet Luis de Góngora that great density becomes particularly apparent, as Dámaso Alonso notes when he points out that in "the *Solitudes* the introduction of pompous processions, of series of fruits, delicious foods, beasts [. . .] are decorative elements, contributing within the general plot—in the same way as the exact and shining word does—to give Góngora's poetry its pompous, ornamental and loaded flavor" (312). However, the exuberance of a Baroque artifact such as the *Solitudes* can be seen as something with a deeper meaning than the simple display of spectacular and sensual elements with an ornamental purpose: it responds to an urge to fill the void of the semiospheric *tabula rasa* while reminding us at the same time of the futility of earthly things. As empty signifiers at least on one level (since they correspond to ephemeral, vain realities), those shiny words have been brought into existence to deal with the *horror vacui* that haunted seventeenth-century imaginations. Similar comments could be made about the work of contemporary Spanish poet Guillermo Carnero. In his book *Dibujo de la Muerte*, one of the most celebrated poems, "Capricho en Aranjuez," starts with a remarkable enumeration of luxurious items, namely colorful and delicate fabrics, precious minerals and crafted woodwork. (Aranjuez is the site of one of the Royal Palaces of the Spanish Crown). The lush listing is suddenly interrupted by a somber memento of life's brevity, something to which the poem already points to in its first line. Carnero's piece is therefore a *vanitas* through which we learn about the futility of accumulating material goods and, in a broader sense, about the insignificance of our earthly desires and achievements (Martín-Estudillo, "Neobarroquismo"). As Prieto de Paula has put it, the abundant enumerations in Carnero's compositions are "a true *lesson of nothingness* [*lección de la nada*] of baroque origin. The most important mission of this objectual exuberance is pointing to an inner vacuum: things are not there for what they denote by themselves, but as the answer to some kind of *horror vacui*" (72).

At the beginning of the eighteenth century, Leibniz (see Tymieniecka) wondered why it is that there is Being rather than Nothingness. Today we live on a latent absolute nothingness, and any work of art is a reminder of it. As George Steiner notes, "there is in the most confident metaphysical construct, in the most affirmative work of art a *memento mori*, a labour, implicit or explicit, to hold at bay the seepage of fatal time, of entropy into each and every living form" (*Grammars* 2). We live with the possibility of *overkill*, the total and repeated destruction of the human species and the planet where we dwell. Under these circumstances, our existence must be seen from the point of view of its unavoidable relationship with inexistence. It is, for Heidegger, *Sein zum Tode*, a possibility of Being intrinsically referred to the possibility of not Being. Today more than ever, our existence is a being "for/toward" death, a thought which is as characteristic of Heidegger as it is of Quevedo, one of the great baroque poets of the Spanish 1600s (Martín-Estudillo, "Metapoesía").

It is clear that baroque texts are not defined simply through morphosyntactic concentration. What awes is their extremeness, either through accumulative excess or minimalist representation: in this sense, painters as different as Rubens and Sánchez Cotán may be said to be baroque in their craft. The baroque hyperbolic morphologies of nothingness and excess are two extremes that converge in the common anxiety caused by the perceived closeness of non-existence and of an epistemic and moral vacuum (see also Castillo in this volume). Some of the major figures of the Spanish Baroque dramatize these very tensions in their writings. Thus one might point to Gracián's poetics of silence (Egido), Quevedo's nihilistic accumulation, and Góngora's exuberant verbosity.

Although it was in Latin America rather than Spain where the term "Neobaroque" emerged with more conviction, one should not forget that a major impetus for the revalorization of the Baroque was the commemoration, in 1927, of the third centennial of Luis de Góngora's death. The now illustrious group of poets who celebrated the occasion—ignoring the dominant academic disdain—were to find renewal in their craft not in the staid atmosphere of Spanish Romanticism but from the experimentation with language that had marked the work of the most adventurous Spanish baroque poets, especially Góngora, whose impact on some of them was such that it gave rise to the concept of "neogongorism." One thinks of Rafael Alberti's *Cal y canto* (from 1929), Gerardo Diego's *Fábula de Equis y Zeda* (1926–1929; first published in 1932), and Miguel Hernández's *Perito en lunas* (1932). The last two works are the most manifest cases of homage to Góngora. Hernández's imitation of the baroque poet was so good that sometimes it is difficult, even for informed readers, to distinguish Góngora's work from the pastiche that his admirer created, while Diego's poem is a playful Avant-Garde recreation of the rich language of the *Solitudes*.

The recuperation of the defenestrated Andalusian baroque poet did not respond to a mere caprice of the authors of the so-called Generation of 1927. As Octavio Paz noted, it was the lack of a strong Romantic movement in Spain that made the Spanish Avant-Garde look back toward the Baroque to find in it a ground-breaking discourse.[3] If the modernity of the German poetic voice was born with Goethe and Novalis and that of the French lyric had in its origins the trio conformed by Rimbaud, Mallarmé, and Baudelaire, the great poets of the Spanish generation of 1927 found their own roots in baroque poetry, whose leading figure was Góngora. It is well-known that one of the clearest signs of identity of the Avant-Garde was its rejection of Western high-culture tradition. In this case, however, it must be noticed that the "obscure" Góngora and baroque art in general had a very problematic place—if any—in that tradition. The revival of his poetry was just another manifestation of radical innovation and anti-academicism of the young poets of '27, who despised the corrupt culture of their elders.

The new way of understanding Góngora's poetic project enjoyed a less obvious but deeper reception within the poetry of the members of the 1968 generation in Spain, also known as the *Novísimos*. These authors seem to agree with Gracián's dictum from *Agudeza y arte de ingenio*: "la verdad, cuanto más dificultosa, es más agradable, y el conocimiento que cuesta, es más estimado" (85) (the more difficult it is to achieve truth, the more pleasant it is, and the more cherished is the knowledge it requires). When we deal with the poetry that followed Góngora's footsteps, we must be aware that it is an openly elitist one which explicitly asserts its own difficulty and resonates in what José Ortega y Gasset wrote in his *La deshumanización del arte* (The Dehumanization of Art), "el placer estético tiene que ser un placer inteligente" (32) (esthetic pleasure must be an intelligent pleasure).

Conclusion: A Baroque for All Seasons

The reappropriation of the concept Baroque is an ongoing one, and it seems that its rearticulation changes in line with the particular position that one adopts *vis-à-vis* the social and political realities of a particular time, usually one of transition or crisis. In the case of the Ultrabaroque, its characterization has had less to do with formal or thematic similarities with earlier manifestations of the Baroque (especially that of the seventeenth century) than with an "attitude" toward current issues of personal and institutional relations, touching on questions such as *mestizaje*, hybridity, transculturation, and globalization. This new development may be seen in the work of the organizers of, and contributors to, the exhibition *Ultrabaroque: Aspects of Post-Latin American Art* (2000). The event, which originated in the San Diego Museum of Contemporary Art, sought to expose and explain the artistic production stirred by the importation and recycling of the European Baroque in the Americas.[4] The curators stated that they understood the Baroque as "a model by which to understand and analyze the processes of transculturation and hybridity that globalization has highlighted and set into motion" and that it is "pertinent today more as an attitude than a style and is interdisciplinary in nature" (Armstrong 3).

While the discussion surrounding the Ultrabaroque seems to be quite compelling when framed in terms of an "attitude" toward the issues mentioned above, or when it is tied to critical periods of change, it also seems to lack precision when it characterizes its distant model—the Baroque of the seventeenth century—or when it refers to the erosion of borders within our current globalized world:

> Just as the baroque era was a time of choices—people could choose a different faith, a different occupation, even a different part of the world to live in—so today are we barraged with "lifestyle" options. The eroding borders in contemporary life between virtual and reality, global and local, education and entertainment (to name a few), present us with unfathomable possibilities and choices. The artists represented in *Ultrabaroque* embrace such contradictions in their work and their lives. In this era of global villages, cultures, economies, and networks, which is defining our future in ways we don't yet understand, the baroque resurfaces as a model for coming to terms with the challenges presented by this transitional period. (Armstrong 17–18)

The idea of "eroding borders" should be nuanced, for we know that fences are being raised to separate people along economic, ethnic, and religious lines. And, as for "lifestyle" options, or the freedom to choose how one leads one's life, it must be recognized that is an idea which is particularly ingrained in our own context where, in theory, you can aspire, as the saying goes, to "be all that you can be" or to construct multiple and ever-changing identities (see also Vidal in this volume). There is a Baroque for all seasons.

Notes

1. This position is made clear in several of his major books—*La oposición política bajo los Austrias, La literatura picaresca desde la historia social* and even *La cultura del Barroco,* in which he explicitly says that there are "instances, even frequent ones, of repulsion against what is proposed. The background of conflict and of opposition in the seventeenth century is there for all to see, and without taking it into account—one must also insist on this point—nothing can be understood" (198).
2. All translations are our own unless otherwise indicated.

3. One of the examples mentioned to illustrate her point is Francisco de Quevedo's *Gracias y desgracias del ojo del culo* (Fortunes and Misfortunes of the Ass Hole).
4. The rationale behind the exhibition was derived mainly from Alejo Carpentier's idea of America as a continent that had been baroque even before the arrival of the European conquerors:

Nuestro mundo es barroco por la arquitectura—eso no hay que demostrarlo—por el enrevesamiento y la complejidad de su naturaleza y su vegetación, por la policromía de cuanto nos circunda, por la pulsión telúrica de los fenómenos a que estamos todavía sometidos [. . .] Y si nuestro deber es el revelar este mundo, debemos mostrar, interpretar las cosas nuestras. Y esas cosas se presentan como cosas nuevas a nuestros ojos. La descripción es ineludible, y la descripción de un mundo barroco ha de ser necesariamente barroca, es decir, el qué y el cómo en este caso se compaginan ante una realidad barroca. (123-24)

(Our world is baroque because of its architecture—this goes without saying—the unruly complexities of its nature and its vegetation, the many colors that surround us, the telluric pulse of the phenomena that we still feel [. . .] If our duty is to depict this world, we must uncover and interpret it ourselves. Our reality will appear new to our own eyes. Description is inescapable, and the description of a baroque world is necessarily baroque, that is, in this case the *what* and the *how* coincide in a baroque reality.)

Works Cited

Alberti, Rafael. *Obras completas*. Ed. Luis García Montero. Madrid: Aguilar, 1988.

Alonso, Dámaso. *La lengua poética de Góngora. Obras completas (V: Góngora y el gongorismo)*. Madrid: Gredos, 1978.

Armstrong, Elizabeth. "Impure Beauty/Belleza Impura." *Ultrabaroque. Aspects of Post-Latin American Art*. Ed. Elizabeth Armstrong and Victor Zamudio-Taylor. La Jolla: Museum Of Contemporary Art, San Diego, 2000. 1–18.

Barnes-Karol, Gwendolyn. "Religious Oratory in a Culture of Control." *Culture and Control in Counter-Reformation Spain*. Ed. Anne Cruz and Mary E. Perry. Hispanic Issues 7. Minneapolis: University of Minnesota Press, 1992.

Benjamin, Walter. *The Origin of German Tragic Drama*. London and New York: Verso, 1998.

Bourdieu, Pierre. *Ce que parler veut dire*. París: Fayard, 1982.

Buci-Glucksmann, Christine. *La folie du voir. Une esthétique du virtuel*. Paris: Galilée, 2002.

_____. *Orlan: Triomphe du baroque*. Marseille: Images en manoeuvres, 2000.

Calabrese, Omar. *Neo-Baroque. A Sign of the Times*. Princeton, New Jersey: Princeton University Press, 1992.

Calloway, Stephen. *Baroque Baroque. The Culture of Excess*. London: Phaidon, 1994.

Calvo Serraller, Francisco. *Teoría de la pintura del Siglo de Oro*. Madrid: Cátedra, 1991.

Carnero, Guillermo. *Dibujo de la muerte. Obra poética*. Ed. Ignacio J. López. Madrid: Cátedra, 1998.

Carpentier, Alejo. "Lo barroco y lo real maravilloso." *Ensayos*. Havana: Letras Cubanas, 1984. 108–26.

Cervantes, Miguel de. *El rufián dichoso. Pedro de Urdemalas*. Ed. Jenaro Talens and Nicholas Spadaccini. Madrid: Cátedra, 1986.

_____. *Entremeses*. Ed. Nicholas Spadaccini. Madrid: Cátedra, 1989.

_____. *Viage del Parnaso. Poesías varias*. Ed. Elias Rivers. Madrid: Espasa Calpe, 1991.

Cruz, Sor Juana Inés de la. *Obras completas*. México: Porrúa, 1985.

Descartes, René. *Principles of Philosophy*. Dordrecht (Holland) and Boston: Kluwer, 1983.

Diego, Gerardo. *Obras completas. Tomo I: Poesía*. Ed. Francisco Javier Díez de Revenga. Madrid: Aguilar, 1989.

Díez Borque, José María. *Sociología de la comedia española del siglo XVII*. Madrid: Cátedra, 1976.

Egido, Aurora. *La rosa del silencio. Estudios sobre Gracián*. Madrid: Alianza, 1996.

Giddens, Anthony. *Central Problems in Social Theory*. Berkeley and Los Angeles: University of California Press, 1979.

Góngora, Luis de. *Soledades*. Ed. John Beverley. Madrid: Cátedra, 1984.

Gracián, Baltasar. *Oráculo manual y arte de prudencia*. Ed. E. Blanco. Madrid: Cátedra, 1997.

_____. *El héroe. Obras completas*. Ed. Evaristo Correa Calderón. Madrid: Aguilar, 1944.

_____. *Agudeza y arte de ingenio. Obras completas*. Ed. Evaristo Correa Calderón. Madrid: Aguilar, 1944.

Hauser, Arnold. *The Social History of Art. Volume II; Renaissance, Mannerism, Baroque*. London: Routledge, 1999 (1951).

Hernández, Miguel. *Obra poética completa*. Ed. Leopoldo de Luis and Jorge Urrutia. Madrid: Alianza, 1982.

Horkheimer, Max, and Theodor Adorno. *Dialectic of Enlightenment*. New York: Continuum, 1995.

Jara, René, and Nicholas Spadaccini, eds. *1492–1992: Re/discovering Colonial Writing*. Hispanic Issues 4. Minneapolis: Prisma Institute, 1989.

Jay, Martin. "Scopic Regimes of Modernity." *Force Fields: Between Intellectual History and Cultural Critique*. New York: Routledge, 1992. 114–33.

_____. *Downcast Eyes. The Denigration of Vision in Twentieth-Century French Thought*. Berkeley: University of California Press, 1993.

Juana Inés de la Cruz, Sor. *Obras completas*. Mexico City: Porrúa, 1985.

Ledda, Giuseppina. "Forme e modi di teatralità nell'oratoria sacra del seicento." *Studi is-panici* (1982): 87–107.

Lezama Lima, José. *La expresión americana*. Madrid: Alianza, 1969.

Lope de Vega, Félix. *Arte nuevo de hacer comedias en este tiempo*. Madrid: CSIC, 1971.

López de Úbeda, Francisco. *La pícara Justina*. Ed. Bruno M. Damiani. Madrid: Porrúa/ Studia Humanitatis, 1982.

Lucas, Ana. *El trasfondo barroco de lo moderno (Estética y crisis de la Modernidad en la filosofía de Walter Benjamin)*. Madrid: UNED, 1992.

Maravall, José A. "From the Renaissance to the Baroque: the Diphasic Schema of a Social Crisis." *Literature Among Discourses. The Spanish Golden Age*. Ed. Wlad Godzich and Nicholas Spadaccini. Minneapolis: University of Minnesota Press, 1986. 3–40.

_____. *La literatura picaresca desde la historia social (siglos XVI y XVII)*. Madrid: Taurus, 1986.

_____. *Teatro y literatura en la sociedad barroca*. Barcelona: Crítica, 1990.

_____. *La cultura del Barroco: Análisis de una estructura histórica*. Barcelona: Ariel, 2000 (1st. ed. 1975).

Martín-Estudillo, Luis. "Neobarroquismo en la poesía de Guillermo Carnero." *Revista His-pánica Moderna*, forthcoming.

_____. "Hacia una teoría de la metapoesía." *Revista de Estudios Hispánicos*, vol. XXX, 2 (2003): 141-50.

Moraña, Mabel, ed. *Relecturas del Barroco de Indias*. Hanover, NH: Ediciones del Norte, 1994.

Moreiras, Alberto. "Mules and Snakes: On the Neo-Baroque Principle of De-Localiza-tion." *Ideologies of Hispanism*. Ed. Mabel Moraña. Hispanic Issues 30. Nashville: Vanderbilt University Press, 2004. 201–29.

Ortega y Gasset, José. *La deshumanización del arte y otros ensayos de estética*. Madrid: Revista de Occidente en Alianza Editorial, 2002.

Pacheco, Francisco. *Arte de la pintura*. Ed. B. Bassegoda. Madrid: Cátedra, 1990.

Paz, Octavio. *Los hijos del limo: del Romanticismo a la Vanguardia*. Barcelona: Seix Bar-ral, 1974.

Prieto de Paula, Ángel L. *Musa del 68. Claves de una generación poética*. Madrid: Hi-perión, 1996.

Rabinov, Paul, ed. *The Foucault Reader*. New York: Pantheon Books, 1984.

Rodríguez de la Flor, Fernando. *Barroco. Representación e ideología en el mundo his-pánico (1580–1680)*. Madrid: Cátedra, 2002.

_____. *La península metafísica. Arte, literatura y pensamiento en la España de la Contra-rreforma*. Madrid: Biblioteca Nueva, 1999.

Romero Díaz, Nieves. *Nueva nobleza, nueva novela: reescribiendo la cultura urbana del barroco*. Newark, Delaware: Juan de la Cuesta, 2002.

Sánchez, Francisco, and Nicholas Spadaccini. "Baroque Culture and Individual Conscious-ness." *Indiana Journal of Hispanic Literatures*, 1, no. 1 (Fall 1992): 63–81.

Salomon, Noël. *Lo villano en el teatro del Siglo de Oro*. Madrid: Castalia, 1985.

Sarduy, Severo. *Obra completa.* Ed. Gustavo Guerrero and François Wahl. Madrid: ALLCA XX, 1999.

Sigüenza y Góngora, Carlos. *Seis obras.* Ed. W.G. Bryant. Caracas: Ayacucho, 1984.

Spadaccini, Nicholas, and Jenaro Talens. *Through the Shattering Glass. Cervantes and the Self-Made World.* Minneapolis: University of Minnesota Press, 1993.

Spadaccini, Nicholas, and Jenaro Talens, eds. *Rhetoric and Politics: Baltasar Gracián and the New World Order.* Hispanic Issues 14. Minneapolis: University of Minnesota Press, 1997.

Steiner, George. *Nostalgia del absoluto.* Madrid: Siruela, 2001.

_____. *Grammars of Creation.* New Haven and London: Yale University Press, 2001.

Sypher, Wylie. *Four Stages of Renaissance Style. Transformations in Art and Literature 1400–1700.* Gloucester: Peter Smith, 1978.

Tymieniecka, Anna-Theresa. *Why Is There Something Rather than Nothing? Prolegomena to the Phenomenology of Cosmic Creation.* Assen: Van Gorcum, 1966.

Valbuena Prat, Ángel, ed. *La novela picaresca española.* Madrid: Aguilar, 1962.

Verdesio, Gustavo. "Colonialism Now and Then: Colonial Latin American Studies in the Light of the Predicament of Latin Americanism." *Colonialism Past and Present: Reading and Writing About Colonial Latin America Today.* Ed. Alvaro F. Bolaños and Gustavo Verdesio. Albany: State University of New York Press, 2002. 1–17.

Wölfflin, Heinrich. *Renaissance and Baroque.* London: Collins, 1964.

Part I
The Baroque and Its Dark Sides

◆ 1

On the Notion of a Melancholic Baroque

Fernando R. de la Flor

(Translated by Luis Martín-Estudillo and Nicholas Spadaccini)

A Baroque of Hispanic Melancholy

Can an epoch or a certain chronological space (or, a geographical one) be *melancholic*? Would it be possible to speak of the high temporality of history and events as one does about a person and the state of his/her soul? Can one attribute to them what might properly be called a passion that lives as the dark manifestation of a conflicted interiority? Can one ascribe it to the long time of common and general history, or even to what has completely disappeared? These questions are now being brought to life in an imaginary debate expressed through an abusive figure of language to define early Spanish modernity. One wonders whether or not it is possible to say that the classic prestige of the concept (melancholy) covers, in an imperialistic way, the symbolic and material determinations of a "modern" national culture, to the point of becoming its master, defining it as if it were its most precise and exclusive emblem.[1]

Might it be possible to speak about the secular "state of sadness" of a whole nation (of an "illness of Spain," as was put by Juan Caramuel, one of its most important ideologists)? Can we do so in the same terms as when we speak about the disease of melancholy in a man, an occasional lover, a sorrowful clergyman willing to come together with divinity, or even a nobleman attacked by the malady of remembrance in his winter quarters? Is this within our reach today or, to put it differently, do we have an obligation to define a *melancholic ethos* of the Hispanic Baroque?[2]

Certainly, epochs are not melancholic even when they are lived in extreme tension. Thus, one cannot say that the Hispanic Baroque was melancholic despite the fact that neo-stoic ethics had preached abstention from the world and had guaranteed some kind of disinvestment of libidinal energies from it, or if Christian neo-platonism had trusted in the values of contemplative suspension, setting itself free from all that might have appeared as given to the senses. The well-known Spanish hostility toward the criterion of utility and its refusal to develop economic and technical know-how for its own material profit could not disrupt the equilibrium of a society which was, after all, mercantilist and imperial.

It would be somewhat extreme to subject the production of Spain's "classical age" (often referred to as *Golden*), with its formal achievements and the impressive aesthetic display of its representations, to the tyranny of a restrictive metaphor, that of "tenebrous humor." Such metaphor cannot be allowed to stand as a final image of the period, for in the end, Melpomene, the muse of tragedy, does not completely control the space of representation. And neither can a country be melancholic, even if one is talking about imperial Spain, regardless of the dismantling of the libidinal social energies and the decline of its fortune or even if one were to consider the burden placed on it by the "heaviness of its Majesty," as the poet Medrano put it. Spain could not be melancholic, despite the tendency on the part of some of the more notable intellectuals of the time to effectively surround the nation with a fatal aura and a bitter destiny that would eventually bring about a "republic of wind" (Bocángel) or, in contemporary parlance, a "maniacal Spain" (Loureiro) where we could find what W. Frank called "the *spiritual drama* of a great people." Such fatal destiny would operate regardless of a real expansion of material culture which historians nowadays have considered a sign of a certain "Spanish normality," one which must be balanced with the notion of a "común tristeza que atormenta a la España" (Alfonso de Palencia 352) (common sadness which torments Spain), and which was the object of so many representations. Fortune and caducity always seem to be superimposed on the game of politics, which, eventually, had the mission of overpowering them.

It could be argued that the spiritual sadness, the figures of melancholy, and the exacerbated Augustinism (which became so extreme as to be almost anti-humanistic and psychologically pathetic) were to be identified with the Spanish

Golden Age, conforming a "model of intelligibility" which finds its proof in the analysis of contemporary documents (Van Delft 449–59). As Baltasar Gracián wrote (perhaps remembering Francesco Guicciardini, who in his *Relación de España* (Relation of Spain) had already said at the beginning of the sixteenth century that "los hombres de esta nación son sombríos" (the men of this nation [Spain] are somber):

> ¿Quién vio jamás contento a un sabio, cuando fue siempre la melancolía manjar de discretos? Y assí veréis que los españoles, que están en opinión de los más detenidos y cuerdos, son llamados de las otras naciones los tétricos y graves. (Gracián, *Criticón* III, 9)

> (Who ever saw a wise man happy, when melancholy was always the food of the discreet? You will thus see that Spaniards, who are considered to be prudent and sensible people, are called gloomy and grave by other nations.)

The insistence on the notion of "epochal anxiety" to define Spanish national culture has its origin in the nineteenth century (see Sáinz Rodríguez). We can argue that the phantom of negativity and scenescence of an entire country was advanced by means of a strong dialectical authority. So strong was it, that its visions, characterized as metaphorical (or even "metaphysical") have gone unnoticed. They have not been truly contested by modern historiography, but only displaced and undermined in their authority through material, economic, and administrative evidence.

The "normalizing" arguments and the usual de-dramatization that are often exercised in our days when dealing with the problematics of the Spanish empire in the 1600s cannot hide the fact that the perception of decay and of the existence of forces of de-stabilization were already at play during the expansive years of the sixteenth century. Slowly, they became a referential *topos* regarding Spain and things Spanish and a way of penetrating the country's imaginary, thus becoming a specific form of cultural elaboration, one that was then strongly differentiated and, in a sense, nationalized. Behind the negative production and in the unconscious of an art which was often meta-empirical there is the presence of a strong nihilistic *ethos*, which I would like to tentatively explore in this essay.

In Spanish symbolic production, the values that sustain the temporal order are negated, openly contradicted, and de-valorized. Such production is rarely favorable to an understanding of the notion of self-interest (or *amor sui*) and does not support the presumable benefits of material earnings. Finally, it abominates economic and technical activity, distancing itself from the criterion of the useful and rejecting instrumental progress in favor of a voluntary Christian exacerbation of the rejection of the world and worldly things. As early as the fifteenth century the chronicler Alfonso de Palencia was to refer to Spain as "una nación muy oscura e dañosa por una entrañable saña afecionada a pensamientos muy malignos" (352) (a very dark and harmful nation because of its old viciousness, so akin to malignant thoughts).

In approaching representations, we are compelled to believe in texts (or images) even when the material and factual conditions are rhetorically deformed. However, we must acknowledge that something becomes obstinately *melancholic* (perhaps even painful) when the conscience of those of us who have become its (illegitimate) heirs is tensed in the imagination of a past—the *Golden Age*—which has always been prestigious and overvalued even while that very same age presented itself in the terms of a pessimistic anthropology.

The *tristitia* is a dominant feeling which eventually overwhelms the Spanish intellectual elites; it does so in spite of their tendency to manifest the burlesque, the festive, or the ludicrous. In spite of Gracián's warning on the seasons of life, which has moments of pain and tribulation as well as leisure and rest (*Discreto* XXV), the truth is that "Heraclitus's company" grows, and that bitter skeptics end up dominating the cultural field of the moment, imposing their own psychological economy of sadness.

It is even more difficult to interpret the period's masterworks, inserting them back in the normalized frame of economic and social tensions which are characteristic of the old capitalist organization of its geographical area. Within those tensions, the singularity of the monarchical-confessional Spanish configuration would finally dissolve its "difference," which was based precisely on its bitter pessimism. In the end, the great tragic figurations of the period were built by the theo-poets of that time. It was they who placed the empire's material power under the strict vigilance of the Seven Angels of the Apocalypse, as the Jesuit Andrés Serrano defends in his *Los Siete Príncipes de los Ángeles. Validos del rey del Cielo. Misioneros y protectores de la tierra, con la práctica de su devoción*.[3] The productive energies of symbols during that period manifest a serious tension towards the *phantasmagoric*. Anything that may question (or view with suspicion) the order of the real is vehemently welcomed by a society which installs itself in the delirium and in the de-regularization of the literal sense of language. That phantasmagoria has the effect of drawing the individual away from the profane and mechanic dimension of time, allowing him or her to foresee ultra-temporal and meta-empirical flashes that are diverted from the *tempus maior* or the "eternity" of which neo-scholastic metaphysics speaks.

The Hispanic Baroque gives aesthetic reason, above all, to mourning or melancholy, or "sadness of living" (or, as Saint Paul wrote, "sadness of the world" [Cor. 7:10]),[4] building the corpus of its figurations under the indubitable regime of an idea of *mundus senescit*, and already placing itself far away from the concept of Christian joy promoted by Erasmus' *Epicureus* in the first stages of Humanism.

It could be said that in the "metaphysical Peninsula" (Rodríguez de la Flor, *Península*), the complex view of the world which was hidden behind the concept of disillusionment (*desengaño*) induced a particular mode of the tragic consisting in the powerless witnessing of the formations of a past based on values such as religiosity, honor, generosity, disinterest and the neurotic and suicidal blockage of the attitudes and energies needed to conquer the future: profit, interest, and usefulness (Rohou 14 ff.). Thus, that time produces a disturbing document about itself, since "la pérdida, el duelo, la ausencia desencadenan el acto imaginario y lo alimentan, en la misma medida que lo amenazan y lo arruinan" (Kristeva 13) (loss, mourning, and absence trigger the imaginary act and they feed it in the same way that they threaten and ruin it).

It is the ruin of the messianic as promise which gets to the very gates of the Baroque, evidencing a closure of the future and a radical negation of a harmonious and favorable providence, something which will be made more palpable in earthly life. The gaze which moves toward the double dimension of history and nature only manages to construct a nihilist vision of it. For the Spanish moralists of the Baroque, history and nature constitute the formidable universal "factory" which produces ruins (history) and corpses (nature).

The imaginary act—the symbolic production—encloses onto itself by choosing master figurations as its guide. Thus, it tends to either ignore facts or interpret them primarily from a dramatic sense. This allows for an understanding of the world as a place of disaffection, a view upon which a culture can be built, one that is metaphysically determined as a structure of loss, nostalgia and anxiety. At the same time, it is a culture which bonds consciences to knowledge and archaic representations of the world, preventing them from facing desire, i.e., the future.

The Baroque is also a time in which the symbolic production gives itself as an object beyond itself, trying, in an essentially melancholic strategy, to save things in the formal languages of allegory, as if the signifiers entered a "delirious" regime (conceptist/culteranist) in a desperate search for meaning: the meaning of the world and the threat of losing it if it is not continuously reified by the work of art. The "Christian turn" develops its own negative representation in favor of a higher effect which is presided by a total distrust of the world;

by the fear and the weeping within it, since it chooses the shapes of beauty and wit in order to refer to that "new instability" (Sarduy). Christian anthropology is, therefore, related with uncommon strength to the idea of guilt, which cannot be completely redeemed by grace; the heritage of corruption defines the negative fate of man.

Pedro de Acebedo conceptualizes his own literary production only as the reflection of the true anxieties of the world: "El argumento y la materia la daban las tragedias del mundo y los desastrados fines que en él se ven cada día, y el blanco de todas sus composiciones era no engañar el tiempo, sino desengañar las almas; no reír culpas, sino llorarlas y enmendarlas" (cited by Astrain 587) (The plots and subject matter were provided by the tragedies of the world and the disastrous ends which are seen in it every day. The goal of all of his compositions was not to deceive the world, but to reveal the truth to souls; not laughing at guilt, but weeping for it and rectifying it). Therefore, in the symbolism of loss grows the role of the *tristitia* (desolation), in agreement with the structurally important position that Saint Ignatius of Loyola gave to that affection in his *Ejercicios espirituales* (Spiritual Exercises), which would become so influential for everything that was to follow. As a salvation project, in that and other similar documents of the time, there is the fulfillment of Saint Paul's maxim regarding the labor of Christianity as necessarily developed with affliction: "Work for your salvation with fear and tremor" (2 Phil. 12).

Peninsular Christianity develops a special way of living through effective representations as well as a fearsome ability to implicate the totality of the Spanish empire in the drama of last perfection: in agonizing fights where the afterlife has an exorbitant and tragic presence, imposing a sort of "terror of glorification" through deep discourses on the structure of totality, and, finally, flowing into a *furor metaphysicus*. The idea was to drag the whole sphere of the secular world toward its forced integration in the mechanism of divinity—*in unum versum*—in which nothing is really integrated without pain or mourning. Fighting the "reason of State", forcing it to assume a mask of religiosity, the goal of the moralists is to block the harmonic development and the promotions of temporal life. In the Hispanic world the political space "implodes," giving place to the social emergence of the *unpolitical*, which could be defined as the nostalgic search of pre-political values with which to oppose strongly the devaluation of politics (see Cacciari 61–79).

The exigency of perfection brings tension to the national mood, relegating the goals of worldly life to secondary status. To put it in a more exact way, the projection of the ideal enters in open confrontation with daily life, which rips apart the baroque subject, who is forced to maintain a discourse that is denied by material evidence. The result is the opening of a space for a morality in crisis.[5] When this is observed, as we do nowadays, from a historical perspective which responds to an anti-metaphysical turn, our glance as post-contemporary reflexive observers (who live at the end of the process of modernization) must correct itself in every historical moment toward a posture that has become progressively serious and meditative with respect to documents from the past, unless it is directly overwhelmed and interpellated by the dramatic density that the considered fragment evokes. The tragic in postmodern times brings us back to that of our "classical" period (the Golden Age) and binds us to it with unavoidable strength (Benjamin, Maffesoli).

This is therefore the meaning (the "sign") under which our time decides to recognize the past it is constructing. Nowadays, the practices of appropriation of that past culture can only be directed toward a path pointing to the meaning of "ruin" and to a generalized catastrophe of the historical. This is due, perhaps, to what was pointed out by R. Koselleck who said that what we call "experience of the past" is, in reality, the expression of the ways in which a certain historical formation undertakes the task of formalizing its vision of the "ruins" into which the prior formation has been transformed.

That is how the intimate meaning of the baroque age appears in the present: as an ominous time, pregnant with negativities. Such is the way it is if it seems to be so. This kind of conceptualization leads to an enigmatic satisfaction, for every epoch dreams of the demise of past ones, as Benjamin observed. This is, perhaps, the distinct way of feeling superior to them while giving a certain direction to the arrow of time. It also happens that ours is one that has experienced changes and destructions of such magnitude that we see ourselves forever separated from the productions of the past, thus carrying out their reification under a bitter sign and a constellation which is definitely Saturnine. Our century also heads toward a melancholic future like Klee's angel which looks back at the ruins into which the past has been transformed.[6]

Following the laws of the new science, the position of the observer, our own historical perspective modifies and even creates or endows with continuity the object that we call the "Hispanic Baroque." Ours is a vision that, for the moment, culminates and completes those that have preceded it in history. Thus, it is a time such as ours, one that is given to summarization and projection, that produces the "definitive" reflection on the "enigmatic" Baroque (Rousset). Our postmodern sensibilities are directed to the "classic" moment *par excellence,* the so-called Golden Age, and its unique contrivances of representation built in the material orbit of an imperial totality that had a "Hispanic" sign for the first and last time in history. It is necessary to deal with this issue now, however untimely it might seem, as it dissolves in the globalizing "ether."

By carefully analyzing the "concave mirrors of the Empire" that are its paintings, texts, programs and environments, the past is constituted in the present, and even in the future, thus forming a sort of "past future" that allows for the possibility of survival (Koselleck). Without a doubt, the encrypting of the Baroque question is a fact among us. Under the leadership of J.A. Maravall, the Spanish historiography of the period of Spain's transition to democracy in the early 1970s was to stage the hurried funerals of the *Ancien Régime*, burying such undesirable memory near the most significant Philippine monument, the monastery of El Escorial, which is located in the mountainous heart of central Spain.[7] That time and culture were buried with the inscription "Here lies Spain" (*Hic iacet Hispania*), consecrating the impossibility of its phantasmatic projection by relegating it to a forced oblivion under tons of stone, thus eliminating all ties to present-day Spain by covering the conscious paths that could lead to a relapse into the Baroque.

Some thirty years after the appearance of Maravall's masterful *Culture of the Baroque*, the very same "Baroque issue" must be reincorporated into the veins of a particularly anemic and atonal moment, which is so perceptible in the symbolic production. The allegorical features of the Baroque appear on the stage of contemporary art as the founding gesture of the current allegorical production which, surprisingly, now claims a baroque ancestry (see Owens 25–33; Brea).

What now returns from the Baroque are precisely the power and abundance of its images, the gloomy enigma that they contain, and the background of fascination that its maximalist products promote. I believe that, at the core of the realization of the "obscurity and ignorance of the world" (Montaigne), the baroque imaginary constitutes a necessary counterbalance to the final triumph of instrumental reason, and it also deconstructs the legitimating foundations of a "society of spectacle." As that imaginary is vertebrated around the idea of sublimation, its being is resolved in the weaving of a hyper-sign; in a mega-discourse structured around the depressive vacuum in which the discourse of representation is inscribed. Its singularity comes, perhaps, from the refulgence achieved by such obscurity. It is "dark with excessive bright" as has been said about the effects generated by the work of Góngora (Carne-Ross). The "formalist neurosis" which presides over the cultural production of that time persuades us of a paradoxical evidence which H. Ciocchini has verbalized in the case of Góngora: "Las obras de belleza equilibrada y rara perfección son obras de desesperados que hallan su salvación momentánea en un orden expresivo, en una provisoria claridad que mitigue las crecientes olas de sombra de su existencia" (11) (The works of balanced beauty and rare perfection are works made by desperate people who find their momentary salvation in an expressive order, in a provisory clarity which could mitigate the growing waves of shadows of their own existence).

As a culture of the magnificent, the Baroque chooses as its center what has ceased to be (or, perhaps, what has never been), while it constructs around it the living allegory of the splendorous ephemeral. That finally came to be an "Iron Age" of the spirit, "harsh times," a moment when, according to Baltasar Gracián, "las mismas entrañas parece se han vuelto de bronce" (*Criticón* 203) (the very heart seems to have become bronze).

Structural Anxiety

Far from the conceptual architecture that has become canonical, from which the world of the Hispanic Baroque has been explained and which, from my point of view, configures a paradigm to be completed, I seek to discover those paths (and the documents present in them) that seem to reveal the existence of a "structural anxiety." Let us recall briefly the figures that sum up the *pessimistic anthropology* of the Spaniards of the baroque period. I do so by taking into account the recent hermeneutic constructions that arose from a need to channel a sentiment of "discomfort in culture," and the conviction that history—any history—is developed in the *mood of tragedy* when the legitimacy of the master narratives that justified it and declared it endowed with a "finality" has been undermined.

In this respect, the peculiarity of the Hispanic Baroque is that during the first half of the seventeenth century, the new hermeneutic instruments (the logics of reason), which were being created to better govern the world and to dispose in a more effective way to the "reason of the State," were consciously avoided. Meanwhile, in the private sphere, the individual tried to adapt the world to the philosophy of self-interest. This principle of appropriation of reality is vehemently attacked and the effects of happiness associated with it are rejected. It is not a matter of theorizing or legitimizing the material exploitation of the world, but of remaining installed in contemplation, which goes from being "admiring" in the Renaissance to being "disillusioned" in the Baroque. Such disillusionment is manifested through discursive artifices, in non-operative representations of a spectacular and persuasive character.

A "Benjaminian spirit" seems to guide current reinterpretations of the Baroque as the issue reappears in the form of a "spectral" figuration to remind us that the "elaboration of its mourning" has not been carried out. It could be argued that what that time offers us has not been rationalized by the experimental and technical progress that has illuminated our world. This seems to be more apparent than ever as we look at ourselves from the portrait galleries of baroque people, or from the spaces of representation opened by them in the broad field of words, loosening them from stable references, dynamiting the field of signifiers.

In its maniacal thirst for formal beauty, this emphasis on aesthetics reveals a lack of worldly happiness which is at the core of its mechanism. In short, aestheticism is the other side of melancholy (see Hunt Dolan on Góngora's exemplary case). Moreover, the power of illusion that is made so explicit in this effort covers up a painful reality and coincides with the asceticism of some of the great figures of the century.

In order to confront the "cadaverous face" of the Hispanic Baroque, I take into account a vast space of epochal symbolic elaboration, focusing on the interpretative field of discourse or representation as mediator. My conceptualization does not aim to achieve the objectivity of historical processes, for we know that the artistic language cannot take responsibility for that which is compromised in the pathology of a political system, nor of transferring what is implied in its material processes (Kristeva).

It is clear that an epoch can neither reproduce nor transfigure itself in its images and representations with measured precision. Yet, somehow, an epoch *is* also its representations, the symbolic production which explains it and whose only mission is to offer a meaning for it, reintegrating it in a master narrative, in a possible view of the world, and in a coherent and stable discourse of representation (Chartier). This is often all the objectivity that remains from a time that is gone forever. In any case, in the philosophy of appearances and in the ontology of the *imago* produced by the Baroque, what will always stand out is the great interest in giving substance to representation, to language, while the real referents are played down. It is a tense and paradoxical affirmation of the supremacy of the virtual, which Vieira echoed when he wrote that "Mais verdadero e mais propio mundo era este mundo aparente que o mundo verdadeiro; porque o mundo aparente eram aparências verdadeiras, e o mundo verdadeiro sâo as aparências falsas" (IV, 210) (This world of appearances was more real than the true one; because the former was composed of true appearances, and the true world is composed of false appearances).

Here, more than in other analyses which pretend to be objective, the epoch is the effect of a reconstruction, developing itself in the mode of a narrative, a "scene," or, even better, a *scenography*. There is, therefore, a melancholy, and there is also a "theater of melancholy." Only the latter offers itself momentarily and in disguise to the interpretative disposition of the analyst. My inquiries into the baroque field ask about the search for fleeting beauty—how it was carried out—and the creation of a registry of complex signifiers, exploring the enigmatic satisfaction obtained from the construction of a stage or representation that sought to explain an ephemeral world through structures which were paradoxically more durable.

It is not enough to refer exclusively to what could be called "written melancholy," as if only the discursive scene were worthy of our inquiry. Western tradition strives to deal with symbolic strategies that illuminate a "depressive state" of the subject and his/her culture. This is to be taken seriously as symptoms or manifestations of inner conflict in the social space, producing this "Saturnine constellation," which presents itself through fearsome figurations of scarcity and precariousness.

Melancholic humor constantly transfers its negative energy to all of the behaviors and systems of signs, which it deeply contaminates and from which it is, in turn, contaminated. The negative representation is in itself a negative fact, one more feature among those constructed under the "logic of the worst" (Rosset).

Because of that, the analysis must fatally take us to the establishment of a correlation between those pure objects of art working as true epochal emblems and the strategies that discourses follow in their representation. Oftentimes one witnesses the fast evocation of the events of a historical reality which must necessarily structure their base even though one is conscious of the fact that they are not in any way comparable realities. For instance, the debacle of the Invincible Armada, as a historical event, is positioned at the same (tragic) height as the artistic manifestations which locate this fact in an ideologizing process which seeks specific ends and effects. That is what happens in the *Tratado de la tribulación* (Treaty of tribulation) by Ribadeneira, a true legitimizing document in which the material perspectives and the interpretations of the great military and moral disaster of the Spanish Navy are relocated within the perspective of transcendence and a sort of "will of fatality" which dominates the period.

I believe that there is a certain baroque mechanics that operates in an effort to transcend and sublimate the historical processes which are extracted from their frames of insertion in order to be elevated and confronted with a supra-temporal dimension and, eventually, with a providentialist history. Under this history, those processes would seek to become meaningful as brief instants soon lost in the immensity of the spacial-temporal dimension. Then, as the Jesuit Nieremberg proposed, things belonging to the temporal order find themselves compelled to compare their indigence with the regime in which the "eternal" is disposed. In his work *De la diferencia entre lo temporal y lo eterno* (About the Difference between the Temporal and the Eternal) he states that man loses with this confrontation, since "being a small world, we cannot encompass with our lives the biggest world" (cited by Enríquez 192).

In any case, what is deeply at work in the baroque moment is the higher law that embarks the emerging societies on a journey that ends fatally in a relapse into the *shadows* and into the "negative" side of history. In line with this political and moral perception of a development that is unavoidable, its symbolic producers have the epochal certainty of entering an inevitable phase of collective decline. The discovery of the cyclical character of infinite time breaks into sequences the rigid directionality of a universe which is supposedly walking toward its re-absorption by divinity; the lights are then extinguished and the "kingdoms of the shadows" begin. This produces specular inversions of the constructed worlds and makes everything enter a generalized regime of instability (Sarduy). It is the reign of vicissitude, of change and permutation of things, of great transformations and cataclysms, which, according to the thinkers of the time, seem to have shortened its periods. This concentration of rises and falls in a short chronological time frame is typical of the Baroque and follows a model of historical thinking which reflects the classic ideas on the topic.[8] Juan de Borja spoke about this crisis of certainty:

> Si se considera atentamente lo que en el mundo pasa, se verá bien la variedad y mudanza que, en todas las cosas hay en él. Y aunque esto debió ser desta manera en todo tiempo, en éste, en que vivimos, parece que se echa algo esto más de ver que en muchos de los siglos pasados; pues vemos personas haber subido de muy bajo estado a ser coronados por reyes; otros que, poseyendo reinos, han sido echados y despojados dellos; y otros que, del polvo de la tierra, han sido levantados a tan altos lugares, que casi se perdían de vista, de donde han dado también muy grandes caídas. (106)

> (If we closely consider what happens in the world, it will be easy to see the variety and mutability present in all its things. However, although it must have been always like that, nowadays it seems more apparent than during most of the past centuries: we now see people who came originally from a low state crowned by kings; others, who were owners of kingdoms, to be deposed and thrown out; and still others who have been raised from the dust of the earth to places so high that they were practically out of sight, but from where they have also experience great falls.)

Other moralists, theoreticians and observers also point to the chain of causalities that work against the logics of hope and illusion. Thus, "pobreza engendra humildad; humildad, riqueza; riqueza, soberbia, soberbia, guerra, guerra, pobreza, y así anda rodando siempre" (Aguilón 27) (poverty generates humility; humility, richness; richness, pride; pride, war; war, poverty; and so does the world on and on).

Therefore, what happens must be read as if perpetually expecting change, and the longer some good lasts the closer the imminence of its demise. Thus, "Tienen su período los Imperios: el que más duró, más cerca está de su fin" (Saavedra Fajardo 935) (Empires have their moment and the one which lasted the longest is the closest to its end).

Here, one's attention is directed toward the search for a superior evidence of the mutability of things in nature which is the true ideal "theater" where great changes are worked through, and where nothing ever remains as it is for a long time. In the words of a modern poet, nature is the "temple of caducity" (Ponge). The figure of vicissitude appears as the unavoidable and unpredictable causal chain which destroys everything that has once been powerful while it annihilates any ideal of permanence in its own being. In baroque Spain all this was a reminder of forgotten empires, thus establishing an evident parallelism between what happens in nature and what transpires in the political sphere. Cities such as the ancient Itálica are the best examples of what has succumbed to vicissitudes (on the poetic representation of the ruins during the Baroque, see Ferri Coll). "Either you grow or you decline," says Gracián laconically, understanding that future decline is included in growth, adding that one becomes "desvariando siempre con tanto variar" (*Discreto* 298) (always derailed by such changes).

The idea is one of returning destruction; of the impossibility of permanence, of unstoppable growth; and of final abandonment of the hope that something new could interrupt the chain of destruction. Such hope is supported by rebirths which themselves are doomed to extinction. All this endows time with a circular, cyclic structure embodied in the image of a wheel of fortune and its unavoidable end in a fall. These are the premises upon which the Hispanic Baroque's worldview is constructed. It follows discourses such as the one dealing with "the moral theater of human life," and the idea that "nothing under the Sun is eternal" (*Aeternum sub sole nihil*) (Vaennius's "Emblem 89").

If this is the general regime of things, marked by its tendency to fall, this period slowly builds the reality of a divine instance which regulates the "political machine" of the world, demolishing human constructions as a sign of warning or punishment. Such is the understanding of Pedro Portocarrero, a contemporary scholar of the absolutist confessional monarchy, who says in his *Teatro Monarchico*: "No depende de la fortuna la transmigración de los Imperios, sino meramente del Criador universal, que, irritado de los pecados las castiga desolando sus dominios, sin dejar más señas de su poder que la confusa memoria de la posteridad" (13) (The migration of Empires does not depend on fortune, but merely on the Universal Creator, who, annoyed by sins, punishes them by laying waste to their lands, leaving no more signs of His power than the confused memory of the future).

Everything in this epoch is part of a superior "melancholic moment" composed by a real or imaginary loss of meaning which profoundly affects the whole social space. Moreover, there is also a feeling of despair which appears as an internal tension, working with devastating effects within the texts of the time, texts which vertebrate the collective imaginary of such a grave moment.

It happens that the redemptive promise may become something inane and empty; happiness is deferred and blocked by a painful present which "colonizes" the dimensions of both the future and the past:

Sí—dixo Andrenio—pero ¡qué me importa a mí que hayan de suceder después las felicidades, si a mí me cogen de medio a medio todas las calamidades? Esso es dezir que para mí se hizieron las penas, y para otros los contentos.

—Buen remedio, ser prudente, abrir el ojo y dar ya en la cuenta. ¡Ea, alégrate!, que aún volverá la virtud a ser estimada, la sabiduría a estar muy valida, la verdad amada y todo lo bueno en su triunfo.

—Y cuando será eso—suspiró Critilo—ya estaremos nosotros acabados y consumidos. (*Criticón* 756)

("Yes," said Andrenio, "but, what do I care if good things are to come later, if I am caught in the midst of all calamities! This tells me that the sorrows were made for me, and the happy moments for some others."

"It is a good remedy to be prudent, to open your eyes, and to realize it. Come on, cheer up! Some day virtue will be esteemed again, wisdom will be very appreciated, truth will be loved and all things good will triumph."

"And whenever that happens," Critilo sighed, "we will all be dead.")

A deconstructive reading of the order of the real is put to work (in an age supposedly understood as "naturalist" and "realist"), and the effect is that the value of reference is continuously lost in favor of a delirious, symbolic representation of the material meaning of the world which is understood by those who trust it as "following shadows and embracing deceptions" (Góngora 127). What is tragic about this time is not only the sudden free fall of reality, without any discursive shelter, and without any symbolic reference or legitimation, but also the imposition of a negative signification upon this reality. A double crisis is thus installed in modern Spanish subjectivity, which begins to to take shape from the end of the sixteenth century. Such crisis implies a break of the harmony between man and the physical world that will later unfold in the insecure relationship of the self with the metaphysical sphere. It is not only life that has become unstable and unsafe, but also salvation, allowing Vieira to conclude: "temo a imortalidade" (185) (I fear eternity).

Notes

1. Melancholy had a classical prestige and was often attributed to creative minds. Klibansky et al. studied its Renaissance forms.
2. Ricard was to explore this problem in a chapter in which he related Spain with melancholy.
3. The "politic angeology" of the Spanish empire has been analyzed by Mújica Pinilla.
4. However, many historians still have doubts about the characterization of the century. See, for example, Poletto.
5. For an application of these notions to the study of Gracián, see Aubrun.
6. Regarding the imminence of a new "melancholic age" that would connect with the Baroque, see Hagnel et al. and Klerman.
7. For an analysis of this monument as the "cenotaph" of a culture and a closed worldview, see Cacciari, *Drama*. For an interpretation of what the emergent Spanish democracy was to bury in the Valley of the Fallen (*Valle de los Caídos*), in a sort of mimesis of the symbolism of El Escorial, see Medina Domínguez.
8. It follows, among others, Plato's *Republicae* (3696–3740), Lucretius' *De rerum natura* (end of cantos II and V), and Cicero's *De natura deorum* (II, 4, 118).

Works Cited

Aguilón, Pedro de, *Historia del Duque Carlos de Borgoña*. Pamplona: Thomas Porralis, 1586.

Astrain, Antonio. *Historia de la Compañía de Jesús en la asistencia de España*. Madrid: Sucesores de Ribadeneira, 1905.

Aubrun, Charles V. "Crisis de la moral. Baltasar Gracián (1601–1658)." *Cuadernos Hispanoamericanos* 182 (1965): 229–37.

Benjamin, Walter. *El origen del drama barroco alemán*. Madrid: Taurus, 1990.

_____. *La dialéctica en suspenso*. Santiago de Chile: Arcis, 1990.

Borja, Juan de. *Empresas morales*. Ed. Carmen Bravo-Villasante. Madrid: FUE, 1981.

18   FERNANDO R. DE LA FLOR

Brea, José Luis. *Nuevas estrategias alegóricas*. Madrid: Tecnos, 1997.

Cacciari, Máximo. "L'impolitico nietzscheano." *Desde Nietzsche. Tiempo, arte, política.* Buenos Aires: Biblos, 1994.

_____. *Drama y duelo*. Madrid: Taurus, 1989.

Carne-Ross, D.S. "Dark with Excessive Bright: Four Ways of Looking at Góngora." *Instaurations. Essays in and out of Literature. Pindar to Pound.* Berkeley: University of California Press, 1979.

Ciocchini, Héctor. *Góngora y la tradición de los emblemas*. Bahía Blanca: Universidad, 1960.

Chartier, Roger. *Entre poder y placer*. Madrid: Cátedra, 2001.

Delft, Louis Van. "Les caracteres des nations a l'àge classique." *Travaux de Littérature. Mélanges Hepp* (1990): 449–59.

Enríquez, Antonio. *El siglo pitagórico y vida de don Gregorio Guadaña*. Ed. P. Teresa de Santos. Madrid: Cátedra, 1991.

Fernández Albadalejo, Pablo. "El pensamiento político, perfil de una *política* propia." *Calderón de la Barca y la España del Barroco*, I. Ed. J. Alcalá Zamora and E. Belenguer. Madrid: Centro de Estudios Políticos y Constitucionales, 2001.

Ferri Coll, José María. *Las ciudades cantadas. El tema de las ruinas en la poesía española del Siglo de Oro*. Alicante: Universidad, 1995.

Frank, Walter. *España virgen. Escenas del drama espiritual de un gran pueblo*. Buenos Aires: Losada, 1958.

Gracián, Baltasar. *El Criticón*. Ed. S. Alonso. Madrid: Cátedra, 1993.

_____. *El discreto*. Ed. Aurora Egido. Madrid: Alianza, 1997.

Hagnel, O., J. Lanke, B. Rorsman, and L. Ojesjo. "Are we entering an age of Melancholy?" *Psychological Medicine* 12 (1982): 279–29.

Hunt Dolan, Karen. *Cyclopean Song: Melancholy and Aestheticism in Gongora's Fábula de Polifemo y Galatea*. Chapel Hill: University of North Carolina Press, 1990.

Klerman, G. "Is this the Age of Melancholy?" *Psychology Today* 12 (1979): 36–42.

Klibansky, Raymond, Erwin Panofsky and Fritz Saxl. *Saturno y la melancolía*. Madrid: Alianza Editorial, 1991.

Koselleck, Reinhart. *Futuro pasado. Para una semántica de los tiempos históricos*. Barcelona: Paidós, 1993.

Kristeva, Julia. *Sol negro. Depresión y melancolía*. Caracas: Monte Avila, 1991

Loureiro, Alberto G. "España maníaca." *Quimera* 167 (1998): 15–20.

Maffesoli, Máximo. *El instante eterno. El retorno de lo trágico en las sociedades posmodernas*. Barcelona: Paidos, 2001.

Maravall, José Antonio. *La cultura del Barroco*. Madrid: Ariel, 1975.

Medina Domínguez, Alberto. *Exorcismos de la memoria. Políticas y poéticas de la melancolía en la España de la Transición*. Madrid: Ediciones Libertarias, 2001.

Mújica Pinilla, Ramón. *Ángeles apócrifos en la América virreinal*. México: FCE, 1996.

Nieremberg, Juan Eusebio. *De la diferencia entre lo temporal y lo eterno*. Ed. E. Zepeda. Madrid: Atlas, 1957.

Owens, Charles. "El impulso alegórico: hacia una teoría del posmodernismo." *Atlántica* (Las Palmas) 1 (1991): 25–33.

Palencia, Alfonso de. "Tratado de la perfección del triunfo militar." *Prosistas castellanos del siglo XV.* Madrid, Atlas, 1959.

Poletto, Christine. *L'art et pouvoirs a l'age baroque. Crise mystique et crise esthétique aux XVIe et XVIIe siècles.* Paris: L'Harmattan, 1990.

Portocarrero, Pedro. *Theatro Monarchico de España, que contiene las máximas de Estado.* Madrid: Juan García Infançon, 1700.

Ribadeneira, Pedro. *Tratado de la tribulación.* Madrid and Salamanca: FUE/Univ. Pontificia, 1976.

Ricard, Robert. "En Espagne: jalons pour une histoire de l'acedie et de la paresse." *Nouvelles études religieuses.* Paris: Centre de Recherches de L'Institut Hispanique, 1973.

Rodríguez de la Flor, Fernando. *La península metafísica: Arte, literatura y pensamiento en el barroco hispano.* Madrid: Biblioteca Nueva, 1999.

_____. *Barroco. Representación e ideología en el mundo hispánico (1580–1680).* Madrid: Cátedra, 2002.

Rohou, Jean. *Le XVIIe siècle, une révolution de la condition humaine.* Paris: Éditions du Seuil, 2002.

Rosset, Clement. *Lógica de lo peor. Elementos para una filosofía trágica.* Barcelona: Seix Barral, 1976.

Rousset, Jean. *Circe y el pavo real.* Barcelona: Seix Barral, 1972.

_____. *Dernier regard sur le Baroque.* Paris: José Corti, 1998.

Sáinz Rodríguez, Pedro. *Evolución de las ideas sobre la decadencia española.* Madrid: Rialp, 1962.

Sarduy, Severo. "Nueva inestabilidad." *Ensayos generales sobre el Barroco.* Mexico City: FCE, 1987. 9–53.

Serrano, Andrés. *Los siete príncipes de los ángeles. Validos del Rey del Cielo. Misioneros y protectores de la tierra con la práctica de su devoción.* Brussels: Francisco Foppens, 1699.

Vieira, Antonio. *Sermões.* Ed. Gonçalo Alves. Porto: Lello e Irmâo, 1959.

Vaennius, Otto. *Amorum emblemata figuris.* Antuerpiae: Henrici Swingenÿ, 1608.

◆ **2**

Aesthetic Categories as Empire Administration Imperatives: The Case of the Baroque

Hernán Vidal

The attempt here is to identify the term "Baroque" as a category emerging from the bureaucratic imperatives of empire administration. The issue raised is that there is abundant evidence in the historical literature to show the arbitrariness with which labels such as "Mannerism," "Baroque" are affixed to the logic of a certain historical period. For instance, the socio-political trends in Spain and the rest of Western Europe during the last decades of the sixteenth century until the middle to late seventeenth century are associated with the term "Baroque." Yet the factors generating and maintaining these trends are traced back to the fourteenth century in Italy at the dawn of modern capitalism. Descriptions of the material conditions of production and formal features of the art produced in Italy during the fourteenth century coincide in most respects to those of the "Baroque," as much as the description of "Mannerism" associated with the 1530s–1570s coincides with that of the "Baroque." Similar arbitrariness can be found in the way the term "colonial Baroque" has been recycled in Latin America as of the 1950s.

The label "Baroque" is open to the suspicion of being a forced correlation between an aesthetic category elaborated in totally formalistic terms and narratives prepared as reconstruction of the socio-political logic of a historical period. No wonder J.H. Elliott's irony:

For some, baroque has been the art of the Counter-Reformation Church and of an absolute monarchy, an art expressive of power and triumph. For others (a diminishing band in recent years), it has been the art of an expanding and creative seventeenth-century Europe, an art of exuberance. For still others, it has been the art of a society in crisis, an art of anxiety and tension. All of these 'explanations' have had their critics, and none has proved very persuasive. This is scarcely a cause for surprise. It is hard enough to find common denominators in the infinitely complex and varied Europe of the seventeenth century, and harder still to make convincing connections between the aesthetic and literary sensibility of an age and its political and social organization.

The fact is, though, that the Baroque has become an established issue in the academic industry, and students must be introduced and guided into and through a labyrinth of canonized literary texts, scholarly commentaries, and a daunting number of social science studies. We have no other choice but to keep on trying "harder still to make convincing connections between the aesthetic and literary sensibility of an age and its political and social organization." My intention is to attempt such introduction and guidance in the smoothest, simplest manner possible, avoiding an overload of scholarly apparatus. For this purpose I have chosen the entry points into the issue provided by a very small number of historical works summarizing the vast literature related to the "military revolution" initiated in the fifteenth century. The military revolution was the background for the expansion of modern capitalism, the rise of the modern state, and modern empires. I have particularly resorted to works by Torbjørn L. Knutsen and Geoffrey Parker.[1] Their approach has been used to rearticulate the theses on the "Baroque" provided by such "classic" authors as Arnold Hauser and José Antonio Maravall.

Organizing the material according to contemporary notions of empire-building and administration provides an opportunity to use present-day geopolitical concepts such as grand strategy, national objectives, national security, psychological operations, labor force management, population and territorial mass domination, and population control in "strategic villages." This retro-application of military terms is justified by the fact that contemporary notions of empire administration are an abstract refinement of past imperial experiences.

All in all, my approach can be construed only as a pedagogical device to allow students of literature to deal in a quick, orderly manner with the confusing relationship between aesthetic concepts and historical logic. Under no circumstance should this essay be understood as an exhaustive use of the existing scholarly literary and social sciences resources available. Given that I disclaim historical originality I feel justified in quoting extensively to provide pertinent information. Perhaps the saving grace of my arguments is the implied attempt to extirpate Hispanic Baroque studies from a reductive, formalistic approach and situate them in the context of present-day discussions of cultural and economic globalization.

An Archeology of the Term "Baroque"

From a very broad, cursory perspective, through the centuries statements from Diderot, the Schlegel brothers, Burckhardt, García Berrio, Casalduero, Sypher, and Lacan provide a consistent formalist image of the Baroque as the *angst* of the established order before chaotic trends that may bring it to fragmentation and demise: "the ridiculous taken to excess"; "evolution unbridled, without measure, infamous"; gentle sensuality overwhelmed by outright sexuality; the Baroque as an attempt to recoup before the "formal disintegration of Mannerism"; the Baroque as the "discourse of corporeal excess, of *jouissance*" (Spadaccini and Martín-Estudillo).

Wölfflin's conception of the Baroque provides the best schemata for the socio-historical interpretation I have in mind. He situates his description in the micro-dimension of everyday life, which is the site of routine motions, actions, and perceptions. In the automatism of daily routines, sight perceives the shapes of reality fleetingly, dissolving the massive substance of entities into impressions and appearances. This is what he calls "the painterly." What is firm, plastic, and linear becomes moving, hovering, difficult to grasp; boundaries among entities and the environment become blurred. Shapes become "open," unregulated; they seem to point to a realm beyond themselves, in an inarticulate fashion. Human encounters and relationships do not seem to be recorded as lasting projections in time; they are simply overheard or spied out. There is "an attempt to arouse in the beholder the feeling of inexhaustibility, incomprehensibility, and infinity in the representation" (Hauser 177). This feeling of the unrestrained is exacerbated by a simultaneous groping toward unity, synthesis, and orderly arrangement as ultimate principles of artistic composition, yet still keeping that feeling of the unrestrained. This is symptomatic of a greater power hovering above everyday life, seeking to regain strategic focus and subordinate content. Form strives to discipline content.

For Arnold Hauser, the contradiction form/content responded to the propagandistic endeavors of an authoritarian Catholic Church that, after the Council of Trent (1545–63), sought to neutralize the subversive inroads of the Reformation throughout Europe. Following strict theological guidelines, painting, sculpture, architecture, music, theater, and literature became instruments to mount spectacles directed to provide symbologies to control the everyday life experience of the populace. Art, in general, was supposed to either mesmerize the populace and bond their emotions and intellect in loyalty to the establishment or cast anathemas against those marginal creatures who could not be ideologically homogenized. The monumental projection of the Crown and State power onto the populace through ceremonial rituals inevitably translated into overloaded, ornamental sumptuousness as gratuitous exhibition of the Crown's absolute power.

Although the Council of Trent had originally envisaged artistic propaganda according to austere representational guidelines, the sumptuousness of material implementation of monumental spectacle appealed to the nobility who adopted it as a component of their private environment and public, courtly ceremonialism. The Baroque that originated in Italy was transnationalized and syncretized with the local, national ethos and folklore to become the official style of all seats of power in the absolutistic monarchies of France, England, and Spain, as well as in bourgeois households in the Netherlands. In this context the representational spectrum had to run from the ostentatiousness of the court on one end to the absolutistic project of controlling the mass psychology of the subordinate classes on the other. All of this under the umbrella of the massive and pervading violence and fear generated by Charles V's prolonged military campaigns throughout Europe and continued by Philip II's, with constant and simultaneous interventions in the Netherlands, Germany, Italy, Hungary, and the Mediterranean. The objective was to secure dynastic ascendancy, quell the Reformation, neutralize the French-Turkish alliance, and then attempt to crush the Dutch independence movement and the rise of English power.

Pervading violence is the connection between Wölfflin's formalistic description of the Baroque and Hauser's historiography. Violence is the category that connects militarism, the absolutistic monarchy, the modern nation-state, empire, and the Baroque as a category of imperial administration. I will pursue these connections in this sequence.

The Military Revolution

With uneven results, Spanish military interventions throughout Europe entailed attempts at a complex logistical organization to feed, pay, transport, arm, discipline, and train massive armies and navies. As indicated by the famous sack of Rome in 1527 and the frequent revolts of the permanent Spanish army in Flanders, discipline was constantly breaking down, turning masses of soldiers into roving, marauding rabble. Internal security in Spain was also under strain, as shown by the *comunero* and the *germanías* rebellions in Castile and Valencia, and subsequent social unrest as the economic base deteriorated. The Inquisition was in constant alert against heresy and political opponents. Charles V is supposed to have created an excellent police system throughout Spain and the Netherlands.

It has been pointed out that the practical effects of Modernity in Europe were triggered by the need of the main States of the period—Spain, France, England, and Sweden—to accomplish efficient mobilization and deployment of massive armed forces. Indeed, the revolutionary aspects of Modernity are supposed to have been triggered by military imperatives. Geoffrey Parker points out that "by the 1630s, the armed forces maintained by the leading European states totaled perhaps 150,000 each and, by the end of the century, there were almost 400,000 (and almost as many ranged against them)" (*Military Revolution* 24). Naval war preparations were of comparable magnitude. Thus, "the 400 galleys which clashed at Lepanto . . . probably carried, between them, some 160,000 men, making that battle the largest ever fought in sixteenth-century Europe" (89).

Supporting such forces demanded a better trained bureaucratic corps and centralized institutions to secure stable, reasonably efficient recruitment and procurement systems to supply soldiers and sailors, financing, food, clothing, weaponry, transportation, and hospitals. In turn this required alignment of scientific personnel and material resources in chemistry, physics, mathematics, architecture, astronomy, medicine, and pedagogy to provide the cartography and instruments for more reliable navigational systems; the metal alloys needed for better artillery and small fire weapons; good designs for army fortresses; engineering to design faster, more resilient war and merchant shipping; care of the sick and wounded; troop drilling; and strategic and tactical maneuvering of large masses of soldiers.

These imperatives could only be met with higher private capital investment, higher economic productivity and commerce, and higher taxation, all of which Charles V and Philip II successfully organized in the Netherlands, other parts of Europe, and America. In imperial situations, transnational economic transactions led to a *cosmopolitanism* based on the ramification of subsidiaries of the main European banking and lending institutions and the homogeneity of processing transfers of capital through exchange instruments such as letters of credit. Individuals associated with these banking institutions become elites of special political power over the grand nobility.

Balanced coordination of military, scientific, economic, and administrative matters was the functional imperative of the absolutistic monarchies of the period and the State they administrated. In contemporary terms, such balance would be considered as a most fundamental priority of national security.

The modern State became a set of highly coordinated command and control institutions to channel doses of violence in differently modulated ways—in sequence or simultaneously—to guarantee stable economic, social, political, and ideological conditions inside the national territory and outside, in order to project abroad geopolitical interests and objectives. The bureaucratic corps manning these institutions had to be vastly increased, which significantly increased the cost of running the public business.

Procurement and supply for the military masses profoundly altered class relations throughout Europe. Opportunities in war industries and contracting gave rise to bourgeois entrepreneurial and professional middle classes whose capital accumulation, investment, and strategic importance in state planning provided them with advantages in a political field traditionally controlled by the nobility. General prosperity brought about substantial growth of the population, which in Spain was sustained until the 1570s, to decline from that point. Population growth and the wealth coming from America allowed for increased investment in agriculture and increased food productivity. Migration to city factories and abroad for military service and the American colonies altered the wage scales. José Antonio Maravall speaks of three kinds of mobility affecting class relations: *horizontal mobility,* whether territorial or change of position; *professional mobility,* or change of profession; and *ascendant vertical mobility,* or change of rank (Maravall, "From the Renaissance to the Baroque" 16).

Traditional seigniorial power was profoundly altered, introducing a factor of political instability, which brought about an ever-increasing concern among the nobility in matters of national security as time elapsed:

> But professional mobility may present even greater dangers. The aspiration to achieve more-to earn more, to be worth more, to climb the social ladder (the third and final form of mobility)—becomes even more forceful. In terms of the drawbacks it offered, this took on a serious aspect in Spain: the abandonment of tilling the fields . . . If all mobility is socially dangerous, professional mobility, or change of profession, is particularly so: it brings about disorder in the distribution of population or of resources, and the confusion that it introduces threatens to damage the hierarchical power structure. (18–19)

Much earlier, Italy appeared to be the most representative ground of the acute conflicts caused by social mobility throughout Europe. Arnold Hauser provides an extensive narrative of the nobility being dislodged from political, military, and economic power by a capitalistic cluster of *condottieri*, and a bourgeois oligarchy that controlled finances at usury rates, monopolized the industrial base, and manipulated the food supply by hoarding and price gouging. In need of mobile, flexible, cheap, technical support and labor force, the oligarchy also had to undermine the rigid hierarchies and work procedures of the guilds, which brought about generalized strife with the professional middle classes and the proletariat. Parallel strife took place between the professional middle classes who controlled the guilds and the proletariat:

> The wage-earning class was hit the worst of all by the prohibition of any coalition to protect their interests and by the qualification of any kind of strike movement as a revolutionary act. The worker is here the subject of a class State and finds himself completely deprived of all civil rights. In this State, capital rules more ruthlessly and less troubled by moral scruples than ever before or after in the history of Western Europe. The situation was all the more hopeless in that there was no awareness of the fact that a class struggle was in progress, no understanding of the proletariat as a social class, the propertyless wage-earners being described as the 'poor' 'which are always with us in any case.' (Hauser 20)

In this respect Maravall observes the following:

> There occurs a change in the concept of 'worker', who frequently made the decision to abandon family and occupation; from being an element of the family, a worker becomes converted into an outside, foreign element. Remuneration in money, no less than other types of remuneration that are accounted for in monetary terms, leads from the old system of defraying personal expenses (lodging, food, clothing) through incorporation into the family, to a new system fostered by the development of the spirit of calculation, of the frequent use of money, and by an increase in supply: receiving a salary facilitates change of a professional nature for it provides workers with greater flexibility in managing their own pleasures and time. This however, also changes the character of the relation of work: it provokes a loosening of social bonds *(desvinculación)* and brings with it a feeling of opposing interest. But such characteristics appear not only in salaried workers but in all those who are displaced. (17–18)

Gradually there was a rapprochement between the grand nobility and the financial oligarchy in an alliance that became hegemonic. Financiers bought noble titles, bought *latifundia*, and adopted the seigniorial lifestyle. This made all forms of art and luxury artisanship booming commodities-painting, sculpture, frescoes, jewelry, gold and silversmithing, altar vestments, candelabra, tapestry, pottery, exquisite textiles, fine furniture, and musical instruments. Artists and artisans became entrepreneurs running big studios with numbers of apprentices to speed up production. Art pieces became collectible items; purchase of art went well beyond household and church or private chapel needs. Ostentation of art in palaces and villas became political tools for the European Crowns, the wealthy nobility, and the financier oligarchies to magnify their prestige and inspire overwhelming awe through material magnificence in the courts and intellectual salons. The wealthy professional middle classes followed suit.

Together with military and bureaucratic expenditures, luxury consumption became an integral budgetary component in the modern state, officially and privately: "The social function of the court life is to enlist the support and adherence of the public for the ruling house. The Renaissance princes want to delude not only the people, they also want to make an impression on the nobility and bind it to the court. But they are not dependent either on its services or its company; they can use anyone, of whatever descent, provided he is useful" (Hauser 47).

Syncretism was an especially important feature of the symbolic universe created by the art and literature of the period. For various reasons, several levels of ideological fusion took place. First, mass production rapidly exhausted the usual representational assets available, and new form and content had to be rapidly found. Then there was the variety of the clientele to be supplied, church authorities, guilds, nobility, the court, wealthy bourgeois and petty-bourgeois professionals, and the working class. The purpose of their purchases was personal use or household or chapel ornamentation. Thus form and content accumulated throughout the European tradition either coalesced in parallel terms in the market or were fused in individual artistic items: the suprasensorial transcendence of Christianity; the naturalistic vision and strict formalistic organization of space and volume in affinity with the mindset of bourgeois and professional scientific and administrative personnel; the alchemical, astrological residues still associated with the inception of modern science; and the ancient Greco-Roman philosophy, mythology and allegory associated with Renaissance Humanism.

In its history, the Catholic Church, and Christianity in general, have either tolerated or encouraged syncretism in developing theological doctrine. During the Middle Ages, Aristotle was the grounding of Scholasticism; Plato was used to break away from Scholasticism and deal with the empiricist trends of emerging modern science. Two of the missionary orders that went to America after the conquest of Mexico, the Franciscans and the Jesuits, clearly favored syncretism in their evangelical work.

Spanish Imperial Hegemony

This notion of the modern state prevails in the contemporary social sciences regarding the rise, development, and decline of modern empires. Imperial hegemony is understood as constant pressuring maneuvers by a powerful nation-state to preserve security within the national territory and abroad. This maneuvering takes place in a back-and-forth sliding motion within overlapping areas—military, economic, and ideologically normative. These areas are mutually supportive in strategic and tactical decision making.

The rise of modern empires is directly related to waves of great wars in Europe that succeeded each other in cycles of approximately one hundred years. Spanish imperial hegemony emerged from the Italian wars (1494–1529); that of the United Provinces in the Netherlands was originated in the Thirty Years Wars (1618–1648); England became pre-eminent twice with the wars of the French king Louis XIV (1672–1713) and the Napoleonic Wars (1791–1815). The international hegemony of these powers was preceded by internal social upheavals. Control demanded superior military and economic administrative skills from a leading politico-military group to achieve domination of the national territory and population mass. Once achieved, the bureaucratic bodies that managed internal pacification located their institutions in urban centers from which radiated national administrative directives, commands, and orientations—Seville and then Cadiz in the case of Spain.

From these urban centers, the surplus of strategic, tactical, and organizational knowledge and skills accumulated allowed the bureaucracies to project their military, economic, and ideological experience to successfully exploit opportunities abroad. In their forays abroad, emerging imperial powers projected an influence leading to coalitions in which the norms they established in interstate relations go uncontested, until a new wave of great wars gradually undermined or abruptly terminated hegemony. The capacity to impose international norms is the reason why modern empires should be understood as "world orders."

In describing the internal upheaval that gave rise to Spanish imperial power, Torbjørn L. Knutsen points to the cohesion achieved by the Christian nobility in the crusade against Islam in the Peninsula. Throughout centuries of disorder and violence, sustained through the generations, the *Reconquista* became a project and a mindset that molded a particularly intense and belligerent Christianity, as well as governing institutions that tended to centralize military and economic resources, all of which gave a cohesive, coherent existential mission to the lesser and grand nobility. Most of the *Reconquista* had been accomplished toward the end of the thirteenth century, except for the small kingdom of Granada which, after all, was a tributary to Castile until 1492. The enormous territories recovered from Islam in relation to the small size of the Iberian population, and the arid nature of most of the soil, led to the concentration of large property in the hands of small numbers of noblemen who had distinguished themselves for their military exploits. The outcome was the consolidation of a feudal-like political economy based on *latifundia*, led by an aristocratic establishment reinforced by strong military orders and the Church. By 1492 and the initiation of the naval exploration to the west, the Spanish aristocracy had already experienced one hundred years of centralized nation-building.

The preliminary results of Columbus' expedition ignited an industrial boom across Spain in ship building and foundries to produce quality cannons. Fifteen years of exploration of the continental land mass from Caribbean bases eventually led to the invasion of the Aztec and Inca empires. During the reign of Charles V, Spanish expansionism toward America and northern Europe led to the control of the Atlantic market in such a way that it eclipsed in importance that of the Mediterranean and Near Eastern markets. In two decades, during the 1530s and 1540s, the bullion extracted from America and extorted especially from the Netherlands doubled from 670,000 ducats to 1.2 million ducats, to double again in the 1550s to 2 million ducats.

With the Peace of Cambrai of 1529, after the defeat of the France-Papacy alliance in Italy, Spain had the military power and a free hand in Europe to face (as of 1526) the threat of Ottoman expansionism. Suleiman the Magnificent had been pressing with incursions into Hungary, toward Vienna, and in the Mediterranean. There was also the threat to naval routes from North African pirates. This juncture finally secured European hegemony for Spain. Spain showed to be the only nation with the economic and military capabilities, national unity, and ideological resolve to face the Turkish threat in a grand scale, in various and simultaneous war theaters. Less powerful nations could only acquiesce to a coalition for which there were no alternatives. Thus the theological tenets elaborated by Charles V's principal advisors—Mercuriano de Gattinara, Ginés de Sepúlveda, and Francisco Vitoria—became the uncontested guidelines for interstate relations and concerted action. Spain became the hegemone in European geopolitics.

Knutsen provides a succinct, useful description of the various modulations of violence entailed by imperial hegemony:

> Coercion is associated with the material aspects—the punitive and the remunerative—of political power. First of all, the punitive aspect of power concerns a social actor's ability to punish (or to threaten to punish) another. It is the simplest aspect of power; and it is most commonly associated with the use of force. Punitive power represents coercion in its purest form: it is an actor's ability to destroy another's prized possessions. Second, the remunerative aspect of power concerns an actor's ability to reward (or promise to reward) another—the ability to exchange a *quid* for a *quo*. It is associated with an actor's ability to create material wealth and with the economic functions of production and allocation. It is also associated with the denial of rewards, or the withholding of wealth and capital. Consent is associated with a third, more intangible phenomenon: that is, the normative aspect of power. It concerns the power of symbols-words, images, and signs—ideas and knowledge. It is vaguer than the punitive and remunerative dimensions of power; it rests on more abstract and indeterminate concepts and it is the most complex and problematic of the three aspects of political power. Consent describes a particular state of a society's belief system. It can be defined as a shared understanding among the decision-making élite about the ordering rules of society. (61)

National Security in the Spanish Empire

The Baroque as a category of imperial administration is obviously located in the consent area in the application of violence. In contemporary national security terminology this is labeled *psychological operations* (PSYOPs). Before tackling the issue of the Baroque, clarification is needed of PSYOPs as the main instrument of national security maintenance.

The U.S. government's *Joint Publication 3–53 Doctrine for Joint Psychological Operations* provides the following definition: "Psychological operations are operations planned to convey selected information and indicators to [. . .] audiences to influence their emotions, objective reasoning, and ultimately the behavior of [. . .] governments, organizations, groups, and individuals." The goal is social domination, both internal and external, without applying actual violence, yet perhaps also accompanying or complementing the virtual or actual use of force. Above all, PSYOPs should not only be considered as concerted attacks, temporarily implemented by a nation-state against occasional internal and/or external enemies. PSYOPs are a permanent administrative imperative for governments so as to carry out the policies that will further national objectives as defined by hegemonic power.

The pressure points exercised by PSYOPs are the connective flows of cohesiveness elements among the three centers of gravity (COG) of a nation-state: the military, the government, and the population (Bowdish 28–36). In terms of social and political psychology, and the survival capacity of nation-states in a world of intense competition, cohesiveness is understood as the flow among COGs of values: the general, full recognition of the legitimacy of authority; trust and loyalty shared among the governmental leadership and representatives according to traditional and legal protocols; prestige of the national "we" as compared to sundry, rival, foreign "others"; pride in cultural identity and national symbols; visible and actual commitment of the authority to the general welfare and justice according to the prevailing definitions of the "good society" and the "quality of life"; credibility and public transparency of the decision-making process; general adherence to traditional norms; and reasonable communication of the truth in governance. The viability of a nation depends on the relative balance of these COGs which, in turn, depend on the free flow of the values described.

Offensive PSYOPs aim at blocking this flow and destabilizing the COGs; defensive PSYOPs aim at preservation and enhancement of the flow. Blocking or enhancing stimuli may be introduced by agencies that want to remain anonymous (grey propaganda), agencies that may choose to attribute stimuli to opposing agencies (black propaganda), or agencies that acknowledge sponsorship from an accredited friendly agency (white propaganda). These interventions require knowledge of mores, traditions, and communicational venues of the targeted populations. Input from the social sciences linked to the power structures is needed in this respect, such as they may exist in a particular period.

It must be pointed out that PSYOPs which maintain an existing, internal power structure are always successful at absorbing dissent within the ideological thematic bounds set by the hegemonic intellectual establishment. Indeed, dissenting intellectuals must be considered as members of the establishment because their expertise and critical mindset originate in official institutions and respond to the social problematics these institutions elaborate and disseminate. Dissenters themselves will set some kind of limit to their own conflicting ruminations. This is directly related to Knutsen's notion of hegemony as a situation "maintained to the extent that social consent takes precedence over coercion":

Typically, hegemony exists when social order is guaranteed by consent alone; when the key members of society employ the same political discourse; when they possess similar beliefs and regard these as natural and good; when they agree about the allocation of authority, status and privilege; when they entertain a notion of unity with each other and with society as a whole. More abstractly, hegemony can be defined as a temporal universalization in thought of a particular power structure conceived not as domination but as the necessary and natural order of things. (62)

Offensive and defensive PSYOPs are accomplished by *reflexive control* of the everyday life environment. Stimuli at all sensory levels are orchestrated to create a symbolic horizon where human reactions are expected to unconsciously respond to the thematic criteria specifically selected by the intervening authority. This orchestration points to a formalistic menu of effect patterns to be achieved. In a scale of increasing pressure these patterns may run as follows: diffusing of vague suggestions of unease; inducing peaceful and content attitudes causing the loss of vigilance (i.e., pacification); disorienting subjects about the real hierarchy of importance of issues at stake; exhausting by direct provocation or inducing an overload of anguishing information and images; paralyzing by contrived threats that have an overwhelming effect; projecting on subjects an image of overwhelming power from opponents (i.e., deterrence); and dividing friends and allies by delivering contrived information. In defensive PSYOPs, this menu is turned around to neutralize such offensive interventions.

Knutsen's notion of imperial normative hegemony must be connected with the formalist patterns implemented with PSYOPs in order to ascertain the extent of ideological manipulation feasible. Thus it becomes evident that whatever can be done with PSYOPs stays within the symbolic boundaries set by the founding mythologies created during the upheaval period preceding imperial hegemony. Knutsen provides a useful schematic outline of the mythological core igniting Spanish imperialism, which he calls the "Advent of Christian Colonialism" (50–51).

The late medieval *Reconquista* generated a particularly virulent eschatological version of the Christian myth of the Promise of God and the Second Coming of Christ. This version conceived Christ's redemptive sacrifice for humanity as the militant call to defeat and punish recalcitrant evil. Militancy turned military with the experience of the *Reconquista*. Islam and all heathens came to personify recalcitrant evil, the Anti-Christ. They had to be either destroyed or converted. Missionary conquest became the paramount goal of Spanish world expansionism. This can be proven by the fact that the Crown only much later than 1492—once the commitment to missionary expansionism had already been made—came to understand the extraordinary economic potential of America. Isabella, Ferdinand, Charles V, and Philip II saw themselves primarily as "God's standard bearers" who "justified their struggle against all foreign enemies in universal terms like 'holy mission,' 'God's will' and 'natural law'" (50). As much as Hernán Cortés was driven by greed, he "believed 'that God had arranged the discovery of Mexico in order that Queen Juana and Charles V should obtain special merit by the conversion of its pagan inhabitants'" (50). Cortés spent a good part of his loot supporting the work of the missionary orders in Mexico.

For Knutsen this eschatology was profoundly imbued with a theatricality which can be connected with baroque extravaganza:

> Acts of remembrance are often standardized into ritualistic celebrations in which decisive political events are celebrated as birth pangs of nationhood and sovereignty and key participants—generals or delegates—are revered as heroes and founders. Such formal ceremonies of remembrance contribute importantly to a nation's self-definition. They keep a nation's political history alive. And they introduce new generations to the values, norms and rules which its political mythology articulates. (27)

In this respect Knutsen has *El Cid* in mind, an icon that Spanish nationalism has recycled through the centuries.

There was a perfect fit between this religious-militaristic mindset and the rest of Europe's deep concern for the Turkish threat during the sixteenth century. Because of this, "Spain exerted a great influence on the rest of Europe, partly through its formulation of Christian values and partly through its example. Spain articulated—perhaps more insistently than any other early sixteenth-century state—the basic views and values of the age" (51). Obviously, there were modulations of emphasis vis-à-vis governmental policy. Against Protestantism, Charles V tended to be conciliatory and stood for formal mediation within the Church, if possible. He was the principal promoter of the Council of Trent. As the Islamic threat grew, Philip II's attitude became recalcitrant. Vis-à-vis economic factors, Charles V sought better administration to promote more productivity and fiscal revenue to meet military expenditure. Philip II was predominantly ideological and expanded military deficit expenditures even at the cost of committing outright extortion of bankers.

PSYOPs are propelled by the state institution which has the following assets: the best social theory; the most articulated conception of the cultures targeted; panels of experts to set guidelines for content and implementation; continual evaluation of results; flexibility to exploit new junctures; the best venues for planning and dissemination of directives among those who carry on enforcement; the best means to channel the material resources involved; and the coercive measures needed. Given that Spanish imperial action derived from theological and missionary assumptions, the Church was undoubtedly the best available coordinating agency.

Challenge and Decline of the Spanish Empire

The hegemony gained over Europe by Charles V after 1529 was severely shaken when the Turks attacked the Spanish fleet in the Mediterranean in 1559, sank twenty eight galleys and forced the surrender of ten thousand troops. In 1560 a Tripolitanian corsair ambushed and destroyed seven Spanish galleys. In 1562 a storm off Málaga destroyed twenty five galleys and drowned four thousand sailors. "In three years the thin peel of Spain's naval defenses was stripped and the fragility of Spanish sea power in the Mediterranean cruelly exposed" (Knutsen 74).

Philip II countered the challenge with an intense rearmament program. At this point the implications of Charles V's military financial policy became acutely evident. In order to finance the wars in Europe, he borrowed so much money that "at his accession in July 1556, Charles's son, Philip II, discovered that all his Spanish revenues had been pledged to repay loans, or pay interest, up to and including the year 1561" (Parker, "The Making of Strategy" 63).

To finance his rearmament program, Philip II resorted to outright extortion of the banking system, a measure that became a standard operation within the Habsburg monarchy until its demise at the end of the seventeenth century.[2] Forced by total bankruptcy, in 1599 Philip III escalated extortion to a maximum degree, now against the entire Spanish population—the king imposed copper coinage as legal tender at a par with gold and silver.[3]

Philip II's way of dealing with the bankers signaled his unwillingness to keep the balance among the military, economic development, and ideological normative components of modern state and empire maintenance and furtherance. Normative considerations related to Philip II's intransigent ideological zeal of his Counter-Reformation politics and Spain's Christian world mission were pursued out of proportion to the other support areas. War became an insatiable engine of fiscal expenditure, unsupported by scientific and capital investment to enhance Spanish economic productivity. Economic development was stunted by increases in all possible areas of taxation. Enormous, unproductive bureaucratic expenses had to be increased. Prestige and luxury expenditures continued unabated. No policies to increase the growth of the population were undertaken. Migration to America and military service abroad increased. The decline of the Spanish empire was inevitable.

There were political alternatives to war open to Philip II, which he disdained. The geopolitical European power struggles during the king's reign were focused on the northern Atlantic. The Turkish threat in the Mediterranean was really of secondary importance; it could have been neutralized through diplomatic negotiations. Imperial projection toward the Pacific loomed as a future project for all contending nations. Military control of the Spanish Netherlands was imperative to neutralize the challenge from the Dutch Northern United Provinces, England and France. Geoffrey Parker points out that between 1583 and 1587 Spain had recovered much of the Netherlands and peace could have been secured for a long time, "although the Spanish Habsburgs could win battles, they seemed incapable of winning wars" ("The Making of Strategy" 132).

Behind Parker's statement is Philip II's unwillingness to maintain the Spanish hegemony peacefully. He intervened in France in support of the Catholic "League" of Henry Duke of Guise. Guise had been successful in preventing Henry of Bourbon, King of Navarre and leader of the French Protestants, from acceding to the throne of France since Henry III would die childless. Philip II supported the Catholics and prevented a civil war. The treaty of Joinville of December 31, 1584, formally allowed Spanish assistance in case of a civil war. In 1585 the League forced Henry III to participate in the elimination of Protestantism in France. In July, through the treaty of Nemour, Henry III acquiesced.

Thus Spain came to control both France and the Netherlands, indirectly neutralizing England. Queen Elizabeth had incurred high secret expenditures to bolster Dutch resistance against Spain since England could not afford to engage the Spaniards in open warfare. Philip II's victories in the Netherlands and France were overwhelming and left England isolated. The Queen's advisors recommended appeasement of Spain. Long term peace was, therefore, an objective option. The annexation of the whole Portuguese empire in 1580–83 would have allowed Philip II to pursue other adventures in Africa and the Pacific to strengthen the empire. Nevertheless, his Counter-Reformation zeal intruded. Since 1571 Philip II had been planning the invasion of England to crush one more protestant seat of power. He decided to go ahead with this enterprise and used Dutch contraband into Spain as an excuse. In May 1585 the king ordered all merchant ships in Spanish harbors to be confiscated, including England's. England was forced into war. Against the advice of admiral Medina Sedonia, in

June 1588 Philip II sent the Armada to a disaster in midwinter and in unknown, treacherous English waters.

Geoffrey Parker conveys the impression that the enormous expenses for the battle of Lepanto and the invasion of England would not have happened if Philip II had established the modern equivalent of a "general staff" or "combined chiefs of staff" to independently evaluate priorities in the use of military force for furthering the imperial grand strategy. In the intransigent belief that he was the providential tool of God to impose a universal Christian empire—he thought "God is Spanish"—Philip II monopolized national and international policy and personally took all strategic decisions. To avoid the questioning of his decisions he purposefully parceled out the study of military and economic matters among the Council of War (military affairs within Spain), the Council of State (international military, economic, commercial, and diplomatic affairs), the Council of Finance (military budgetary affairs), the Council of the Indies (military, economic, and commercial affairs in America), and a special council for the defense of the Portuguese empire. For special contingent issues such as preparations for the battle of Lepanto, the Armada against England, and the temporary solution of the permanent fiscal deficits he appointed small committees of ministers *(juntas)*. He restricted this bureaucracy to nothing more than collating information and routine reporting.

Philip II severely chastised dissidence among his councilors, and encouraged dissent among councilors and ministers by encouraging them to directly report to him outside regular channels. He had a prodigious influx of confidential information from agents, friends, and spies in all bureaucratic organizations in Spain and abroad. Repression of immediate collaborators was an index of the state terrorism he was prepared to unleash.

In terms of national security, this is the moment of critical and prolonged loss for the Habsburg monarchy of the flows of cohesiveness among the three centers of gravity (COG) of a nation-state-the military, the government, and the population. All of its normal COGs connecting elements came under severe questioning, from all social sectors: full recognition of the legitimacy of authority; trust and loyalty shared among the leadership and representatives according to traditional and legal protocols; prestige of the national "we" as compared to sundry, rival foreign "others"; pride in cultural identity; visible and actual commitment of authority to the general welfare and justice according to the prevailing definitions of the "good society" and the "quality of life"; credible, public transparency of the decision-making process; general adherence to traditional norms; and reasonable communication of the truth in governance. The barest minimum of connectiveness could only be kept by means of systematic repression. Along these lines Maravall quotes a revealing statement from the Conde-Duque de Olivares addressed to Philip III:

> the people, lord, occupy third place, inferior because the individuals of this status are inferior, although one can and must consider the greatest power not only with respect to other strengths *(brazos)* but also comparing it alone to the others together . . . It is infinitely advisable to keep them under the vigilance of justice, teaching with punishment and *terrifying* them so that they stop short of excess, a means that works on them better than any other, and produces effects they so readily heed. ("From the Renaissance to the Baroque" 33)

To stay the course of his policies Philip II institutionalized massive amounts of violence, at various, simultaneous levels: against suspected heretics, in pursuance of Counter-Reformation policies; against the financiers and small and medium investors who protested against extortion and ruin; against municipal bodies protesting high taxation; against anyone protesting the imposition of copper coinage as legal tender; and against actual or potential sedition among the rural or urban populace. Such repression was prolonged by the rest of the Habsburg kings. Maravall sketches the general impact of these actions:

> [intellectuals] who reportedly criticized the powers that be and unleashed the rulers' wrath; persons who were persecuted by powerful ministers of the Inquisition, and as a consequence their works came to be confiscated, censored or prohibited; who were even subjected to incarceration, in some cases for an extended time; who had to escape to foreign countries where neither the civil nor ecclesiastical jurisdiction of the Spanish monarchy could reach; who remained in prison until their death; who lost their lives or disappeared without a trace. (24)

The role of the Inquisition was expanded well beyond the exclusive concern for heretics to include any critic or opponent to established authority: "Whether it be by means of the secular arm or the ecclesiastical arm, the growing necessities of physical repression give rise to a new role for the jail; instead of being merely a place to retain the prisoner temporarily, it is converted into a place of punishment, where the convicted live out their penalty—sometimes a judge never passes sentence and, like a true abduction, imprisonment is suffered clandestinely; other times it is a torture chamber" (Maravall 35).

To coordinate repression special bureaucratic bodies were set up in all towns to collect anonymous information about subversives. Judges were encouraged to rapidly move to punishment without exhausting due process. Summary executions became common. Military barracks were located in strategic positions around towns for fast intervention. Walls around towns were raised or fortified to keep the rural poor out. Notable persons were recommended to organize vigilante groups to protect their property and keep an eye on strangers.

The level of violence that notables were prepared to use can be gauged by the advice given to authorities for social control. For instance, to suppress professional mobility, they would "guide many toward following the occupations of their fathers." To control horizontal mobility,

> the Royal Council to Philip III and the Council and Reformation Board to Philip IV proposed measures that would force the poor to return to their places of origin, they expected that, once back in their places, the workers would return to their former professional occupations; thus these recommendations—brought up first to one and then to the other sovereign—added that not only would the poor see themselves compelled to abandon the court and the big cities, but also the rich and the nobles, because the former depended on the latter if they were to recover their previously abandoned occupations and the means to support themselves. In this way the big urban centers would be emptied of people who are so 'free,' restless, and dangerous. (Maravall 19)

In fact, a policy of massive deportation was being espoused; it was a monstrous contradiction in that, out of sheer establishment fear, violence was to be applied to crush the natural consequences of the very same imperial grand strategy the royal authority was implementing.

An inkling of monstrosity in public policy passing as rational solutions for a deep social crisis reveals a grotesque social sensibility. The grotesque is a perception of reality in the midst of which human beings lose control of the most fundamental routines of everyday life. Overwhelming forces beyond control seem to undermine the values, hierarchies, and disciplines that in the past showed society to be a stable order where life's processes could evolve "normally." Reason and corrective action now seem to be of no avail. Useful tools, objects that used to provide comfort, points of reference that assured good orientation, and human relations that put us at ease in a friendly environment suddenly become menacing, out of place, or distorted. In the midst of total alienation there seems to be no refuge or safety.

Although his language is not clear, Maravall seems to call Baroque this grotesque sensibility: "To confront this threatening situation of upheaval society segregates the culture that gives birth to the Baroque, which comes about through the tensions and conflicting movements of a new epoch in which some are striving to elaborate an ideology to confront the threatening forces, and others are attempting to make use of the possibilities that are offered, taking advantage of them from their nonconformist position" (30). What does *segregate* mean?

Based on Maravall's framework, Spadaccini and Martín-Estudillo worked out a typology of the personae created by Spanish baroque literati to represent performance and survival in a public sphere pervaded by fear, suspicion, and mistrust. A reading of this material is useful at this point.

In their view, the collapse of social cohesion during the period cancels any trusting continuity there might normally be between the intimacy of the "I" and the realms of the private and the public. If society should be understood as a community where values of reciprocity predominate, under the aegis of the baroque state the normal continuity of these spaces was totally fragmented. Traversing them and surviving requires utmost control and discipline, either of the self or the collective. For this reason Spadaccini and Martín-Estudillo characterize the Baroque as a culture where freedom is fundamentally understood as the maneuvers possible within the stark acceptance of repressive limitations.

On one end of the spectrum we find the Jesuit Baltasar Gracián, whose persona moves in the everyday life of a notable person uncoupling the tempo of subjective experience from that of objective, ongoing contacts and relations with people. As in a slow-motion cinematic sequence, subjectivity surveils the faster dynamics of inter-personal situations to detect possible traps and threats, reacting with a careful modulation of language, gestures, and emotions, with no spontaneity, applying at the right moment postures and principles designed well in advance to counter possible risks. Individuals must hide and mask their authentic "I" in order to "negotiate" the world with utmost prudence.

In *La vida del buscón* Francisco de Quevedo assumes the persona common to all picaresque novels of the time—that of the penetrating eye who wants to protect the established order from the transgressions of evil. Evil is incarnated in the uprooted upstarts (the *desvinculados)* who want to infiltrate the nobiliary estate, feigning possession of an "honorable" genealogy. These are creatures whose Machiavellian notion of *virtù* leads them to plan success like in a military campaign where morality and sacred values are an impediment to victory. These are monstrous beings because they are homunculi purposefully created by the author to show how essentially distorted they are—in important segments of their first-person narratives, *pícaros* confess and show total conviction that they are evil. These homunculi must be detected, carefully scrutinized, and unmasked as an exercise in cleansing the social body. Exposure will alert those threatened and serve the criminals notice that punishment will unfailingly come. In reference to another genre—the *comedia*—and in a different context, Spadaccini and Martín-Estudillo highlight in Calderón de la Barca's *La vida es sueño* a concern for the infiltration of monsters in the seat of government as the two main characters expose abnormal antinomies in their personality: Segismundo = man/beast; Rosaura = male/female.

Public spaces were the arena of *dirigismo*, i.e., the PSYOPs mounted and sustained by the absolutistic State to control the everyday life of the unemployed masses through spectacles—carnivals, festivals, theater, and bullfights. Through these spectacles, stimuli at all sensory levels were orchestrated to create a symbolic horizon where human reactions were expected to ignore pressing, immediate concerns of hunger, sickness, unemployment, and high criminality, and make the spectators passive recipients of the themes specifically selected by the intervening authority. In a society rife with all kinds of conflicts, Lope de Vega's *comedia nueva* projected soothing myths of well-integrated peasants in communities that would reestablish social harmony against all odds; love as a universal force of social cohesiveness, and honor (the one distinctive feature of the nobility) demagogically presented as a patrimony shared by all. The *comedia nueva* tried to ideologically homogenize a population going through severe social tensions. (See Maravall's *Culture* and *Teatro y literatura*).

Public spaces pollute the collective psyche with ideological deceptions designed to produce mental sloth and passivity by means of a debased hedonism. For this reason Spadaccini and Martín-Estudillo single out Cervantes' temporary renouncement of public spaces for the theater in the early 1600s and the withdrawal to privacy to perform readings of literature as a cleansing, redemptory ritual. Cervantes' literature implies that traversing the written page becomes an exercise in impugning and disassembling the logic of authoritarian discourses. Invigorated by this demystifying exercise, the awakened critical mind will perceive that the aesthetic problematics presented in the text are directly related to the issues distorting the public sphere. Ultimately, this would create an elite of discerning readers prepared for active, democratic political participation in contrast to the mass-oriented reception of the *vulgo* who frequents the public theaters or *corrales* (Castillo and Spadaccini 153–63).

Within the scenario of a culture of fear provided by Maravall, this typology is a very plausible fusion of the historical logic delivered by a social science narrative and the range and function that the literary scholar may impute to the literary imagination. But why call it "Baroque"? Here we come to the crux of the issue raised in this essay.

In a socio-historical approach to literature it is of paramount importance to situate in credible terms the possible range and function of the literary imagination of a historical period within the categories provided by what the scholar considers to be the most empowering social science available. Therefore, labeling that historical range and function with a formalistic category is a totally arbitrary decision. The student of literature should be fully aware of this arbitrariness so that s/he may choose the best possible option. This is an ideologico-political decision to be conscientiously weighed in its implications. Rather than being overly worried about the formalistic label to be used, the educational purpose of a socio-historical approach to literature is to show how human beings create metaphorical systems to account for their existence within power structures. At the risk of belaboring the point, I will conclude this section insisting on the arbitrariness of the Baroque label.

There is practically no difference between Arnold Hauser's definition of the Baroque and Mannerism, its preceding stage. Mannerism is presented as an intense seigniorial reaction to the destabilizing effects of modern capitalism, in total coincidence with Maravall's description of the Baroque:

> Mannerism is the first modern style, the first which is concerned with a cultural problem and which regards the relationship between tradition and innovation as a problem to be solved by rational means. Tradition is here nothing but a bulwark against the all too violent storms of the unfamiliar, an element which is felt to be a principle of life but also of destruction. It is impossible to understand mannerism if one does not grasp the fact that its imitation of classical models is an escape from the threatening chaos, and that the subjective overstraining of its forms is the expression of the fear that form might fail in the struggle with life and art fade into soulless beauty. (100–101)

Furthermore, if we consider the Baroque to be an ideological tool of the Counter-Reformation, can we accept 1600 to be the year of the inception of the Baroque? Historiography shows that Pope Paul IV began the sustained campaign to implement the Council of Trent policies between 1555 and 1559. El Greco and Cervantes are considered Mannerists, although at the same time they are exhibited as baroque intellectuals. Hauser compounds the confusion by stating that some "scholars interpret mannerism as a reaction following the early baroque, and the later baroque as the counter movement which then supersedes mannerism. The history of sixteenth-century art would then consist in repeated clashes between mannerism and the baroque, with the temporary victory of the mannerist and the ultimate victory of the baroque tendency—but such a theory unjustifiably makes the early baroque begin before mannerism and exaggerates the transitory character of mannerism" (Hauser 104).

Definitions that rely on period concepts reach a chaotic stage when Hauser locates the rise of the Baroque in the 1400s:

> Even the precarious balance which arouse around the turn of the Quattrocento, as the creation of the sated, courtier-aping upper middle class and of the capitalistically strong and politically ambitious curia, was short of duration. After the loss of Italy's economic supremacy, the deep shock sustained by the Church in the Reformation, the invasion of the country by the French and the Spaniards and the sack of Rome, even the fiction of a well-balanced and stable state of affairs can no longer be maintained. The predominant mood in Italy is one of impending doom, and it soon spreads to the whole of Western Europe, though not merely from Italy as its point of origin. (99)

No matter how confusing formalistic labeling can be, it is an irrefutable fact that the art and the literature produced between the 1570s and the 1650s must be related to measures taken by the Crown/State to deal with the severe crisis of the Spanish empire.

But what does *segregate* mean? It also means *to secrete, to excrete*, or discharge of some bodily waste or fluid. The term points to Maravall's arbitrary decision to apply the label "Baroque" to the crisis of empire administration. There must have been an ideological agenda in his choice. Maravall was too fine a social scientist to vaguely suggest that the "Baroque" was a "natural" excrement of repression. Was he trying to discredit the Francoist exaltation of the "Golden Age" as Spain's finest hour? Interestingly, Maravall had been working for a long time with the basic issues and interpretation which were to be synthesized in *La cultura del Barroco*, a book published in 1975, just a few months before Franco's death and Spain's definitive journey toward democracy. Further research is needed on Maravall's ideological agenda.

Recycling the Colonial Baroque in Latin America: The Case of the Neo/Ultra/Baroque

My discussion of the Spanish Baroque turns out to be a methodological proposition which now I intend to apply to the Neo/Ultra/Baroque in circulation in Latin America as of the 1950s. Again I will begin with a composite description of the Neo/Ultra/Baroque as found in extant discussions, and then submit them to a historical scrutiny. In this composite description I have not only relied on material by Alejo Carpentier, José Lezama Lima, and Severo Sarduy. I have also resorted to statements by artists who claim they have absorbed Neo/Ultra/ Baroque notions into their life-styles.

As used in contemporary Latin American/Latin Americanist academic and art circles, the term "Baroque" is an explanatory metaphor derived from a formalistic definition of the term anchored in the sixteenth and seventeenth centuries and projected as a transhistorical notion of Latin American cultural identity. This projection creates a pseudo-historicism in that icons such as Sor Juana Inés de la Cruz are invoked and analyzed in relation to the present. Yet a closer examination reveals the analogy stays strictly within metaphoric bounds. Historical data of the evolution of Latin American societies is in fact absconded. In a leap of faith we are expected to accept that modern Latin America has always been "Baroque."

Those who use the analogy have in mind a Latin American style of expression and representation deemed to be "hypertrophic," "hyperreal," "exuberant," "frantic," "excessive," whose energy borders on an "obscene" spectacularity, as shown by instances such as the Mexican Day of the Dead, the Brazilian carnival, soccer mania, religious festivals like La Tirana in Chile, and the overwhelming, never-ending melodrama of *telenovelas* (soap operas). This energy surplus was generated by the explosive collision of a European culture enclosed within homogeneous, geopolitical points of reference with the "preposterous" racial, ethnic, fauna, flora, and topographic diversity found in the newly discovered continent. To give an account of the New World, European intellectuals were forced to make syncretic/hybrid fusions that polluted the "purity" of their language and symbolic forms.

The antinomy purity/pollution is placed within a dependency theory geopolitical scheme overlaid with a sexual signification. Purity belongs to the center/conqueror, which is translated into form understood as the male, paternal principle; pollution belongs to the periphery/enslaved, which is content of a feminine, maternal nature. As representation of imperialist nations, the purity/ center/conqueror/male/form complex imposes limits and discipline on the pollution/periphery/enslaved/maternal/content complex from a rational, centralized position of domination.

Nevertheless, the confrontational tension implied in syncretism/hybridity is supposed to afford an amount of ambiguity where liberational impulses can be found and spawned. This entails adopting a deliberate game of hypocritical masking of the self to confuse, disorient, escape, weaken, and disperse the rationality of the male, paternal, disciplinary eye. In this sense, syncretic/hybrid metaphorization must be understood as "counter-conquest." If the "pure" symbolic forms of the conqueror are the measure of human perfection, symmetry, reason, and clear, transparent language, the subjugated, polluting creatures should be understood as monsters distorted in shape and mind, driven by unreason, who must take refuge in the obscurity and ambiguity afforded by syncretic/hybrid imagery. Such obscure imagery point to the richness of unspecified magic realms that the rational European mind simply cannot reach.

If hypocritical masking of the self is the strategic defense of the enslaved, "feminized," periphery, then the transvestite is the most emblematic icon. Sor Juana Inés de la Cruz thus becomes a key figure in the contemporary Neo/Ultra/Baroque. At the dawn of an independent *criollo* identity in the seventeenth century, her awareness of the subversiveness of cross-dressing and her sexually immature body within the Catholic Church established a direct genealogy with the contemporary male transvestite, the most representative symbol of the Latin American cultural identity.

In Severo Sarduy these lucubrations take on a psychoanalytical bent that excludes historical evolution. Transvestism is an essentialist archetype that set the Latin American collective psyche forevermore. What change there is has to do with who wants to cross-dress. In the seventeenth-century Baroque it was mainly done by women who wanted to appear as males. In contemporary transvestism, the most culturally significant cross-dressing is attributed to males, either real or fictitious. The male transvestite functions on the assumption that femininity is essentially hysterical and consciously uses hysterics to activate energies leading to compulsive, hyperexcited, theatrical extravaganzas. In changing clothes the male cross-dresser brings about a balance between the masculinity of the conqueror and the femininity of the enslaved.

These changeovers are supposed to be cosmic rituals commemorating and reenacting the liberational androgynous myth of origin implied in the colonial Baroque. Since the real Latin American history was/is the permanent clash between the rationality of the imperialist will against the feminine hysteria of the enslaved, the hermaphroditic ritual contains a higher truth than actual history. Therefore the validity of language as mimetic representation is denied and replaced by the truth contained solely in the ritual and the myth, with no external, objective referent. In replacing actual history, myth and ritual become icons that point to a void, to an origin that cannot be said to exist anymore. In this sense the androgynous myth/ritual should also be understood as a wake for an origin irretrievably erased and lost. The historical vacuum is compensated by the freedom the mind can find in exploring new imaginary dimensions in the literary writing of the hermaphroditic myth/ritual.

Such musings have spawned an interpretive industry within academic circles who want to connect scholarly endeavors to a homosexual and feminist vindication agenda. Research should be done on the possible connection between this kind of discourse and the practical, political activism of homosexual Human Rights organizations.

A socio-historical approach to literature must obviously proceed to restore the historical dimension to this mythography. As in the previous sections of this essay, I will attempt this by resorting to the logic of empire administration. Two particular points in the hermaphroditic myth/ritual should be especially considered—the ambiguity concerning the human body and the liberational value attributed to syncretism/hybridity under colonial rule.

This androgynous/hermaphroditic myth does reflect the ambiguity of the Crown-Spanish State conception of the body of the Amerindian. At the micro-experiential, face-to-face level, Mario Cesáreo has tried to fathom the first impact of the Indian bodily materiality on the main agent of imperial domination, the priest:

> The material, corporal, evidence of these beings seen, touched, smelled and talked to by the missionary in his exploration and evangelization travels turn this transgression of his mental order into an existential mystery. When the first-sight impression of the Indian as a satanic mask gives way to the Indian as an individual face the possibility is opened that the monstrous aspect may be actually related to the I; the option of understanding him as another way of being human. In other words, to try to situate this alterity within some anthropological framework entails a crisis of the necessary and natural character of one's own culture and identity. (128; my translation)

At the macro-administrative level, ambiguity was shown in the bureaucratic concern for the preservation of the body of the Amerindian as labor force (Byrd Simpson). The initial colonizing experience in the Caribbean—Hispaniola, Cuba and Puerto Rico—was crucial in this respect. Between 1492 and 1517 the indigenous population had declined from more than 150,000 to around 4,000. Obviously, no colonial enterprise could prosper with such a catastrophic decline. In solving the problem, the Council of the Indies had to come to a well-defined, stable policy regarding *encomiendas* and *repartimientos*—the allotment of an Indian contingent of workers related to or independent of concessions of land to Spaniards in America. The Council could never come to a clear-cut policy.

The ambiguity of the *encomienda/repartimiento* issue stemmed from the acute political contradictions involved. On the one hand, such concessions were the only incentives to have Spaniards settle in America. But on the other, *encomiendas* and *repartimientos* would probably establish feudal fiefdoms that at some point could be beyond the control of the Crown/Spanish State. The imperial authority always considered abolishing the *encomiendas* and *repartimientos*. Furthermore, without such concessions America would be underpopulated and open to occupation of territories by other European powers. For a long time—until the Crown/Spanish State were able to establish regular armed forces in some areas by the end of the sixteenth century—the only military deterrent to foreign incursions were the *encomenderos*.

Responding to ideological entreatments from the priestly movement represented by Bartolomé de las Casas, the Crown/Spanish State also felt compelled to acknowledge and respect the humanity of the indigenous population as rightful subjects of the kingdom and empire. Here the Crown/Spanish State found the option of balancing these conflicting imperatives. Recognizing them as rightful subjects meant immediate protection and long-range preservation of the labor force, and gradual integration of the Indians into the productive roles they were expected to play in empire maintenance. Needless to say, this solution would take many, many generations. The Crown/Spanish State was forced to respond to immediate events. The catastrophic Caribbean experience showed that *encomenderos,* pressed by debts with the metropolis and uncertain about the future of their *encomiendas,* tended to solve their problems by squeezing from the Indians, as quickly as possible, the longest and most intense working schedules, leading to unnaturally short life spans.

In 1516 Bartolomé de las Casas prevailed upon the Regent Cardinal Ximénez de Cisneros to put the colonies under Church administration, terminate the *encomiendas,* and completely liberate the Indians. No doubt, in this scheme imperial authority had to find some middle course between Las Casas' outlandish ideals, the imperative to provide *encomenderos* with a labor force, and the biological preservation of the Indians. In order to have reliable, objective evaluators of the experiment, Cisneros commissioned three representatives of the Order of St. Jerome, not the Franciscans or the Dominicans who until then had had a monopoly of the mission in the Americas. The Jeronymites were able to keep their distance from all interests involved.

They came to Hispaniola with the guidelines set by the *Leyes de Burgos,* which paid special attention to the bodily welfare of the Indians. The laws established a range of measures to improve working conditions for the Indians: required periods of four months' rest after a schedule of five months work at the gold mines; required the *encomenderos* to provide the Indians with nourishing food such as meat to compensate for heavy bodily attrition; allowed Indians to complement their diet by working their own plots; prohibited the use of Indians as carriers, it being a disabling, degrading kind of work for which animals could be used; prohibited brutal treatment of the Indians; set a yearly salary; and prohibited work by women and children to assure biological reproduction. *Encomenderos* were to have not more than one hundred and fifty Indians and not less than forty.

The most important experiment the Jeronymites were expected to implement and report on was the establishment of separate Indian villages. Spaniards invented the concept of what, in contemporary military terms, are called "strategic villages" as tools for the concentration, control, and pacification of potentially hostile masses. These villages were set up close to main productive areas. *Caciques* were persuaded to move their people into them; *encomenderos* were prohibited from transferring their labor gangs to their property. These concentration camps were good indoctrination machines since they were equipped with churches and schools. Indians were expected to attend mass daily; the children of *caciques* under thirteen had to attend school and be boarded there at least four years before returning to their families. Indians had to dress, nudity was prohibited. They were prohibited to sleep on the ground, and were required to use hammocks or beds. Indians were required to be legally married and monogamous, and to baptize their children within a week of birth. All community ceremonies *(areytes)* that did not contain elements of idolatry were allowed.

By January 1519, the Jeronymites had built thirty strategic villages populated by three hundred Indians each. The expectations of enhancing the quality of life to preserve the Indian labor force were dashed by the outbreak of an epidemic of smallpox that killed one third of the Indian population. A decision was made to begin the immediate importation of African slaves to continue gold mining. The extraordinary potential of these strategic villages as cultural/racial syncretism/hybridity-producing machines came to full fruition during the colonization of Mexico.

After the elimination of the leadership of the Aztec empire and the various demonstrations of military violence by Hernán Cortés and other conquerors, the Franciscans and Dominicans had no problems in concentrating a pacified Indian population in the strategic villages built throughout the Valley of Mexico. Pacification was expedited by a long tradition of disciplined socialization in their native city-state system. The challenge for the Spaniards was to control and indoctrinate a large Indian population and spread throughout a large territory, with a small number of missionary personnel. Among the Indians fear of Spanish violence was strong enough not to expect massive revolts. Secret worship of the old gods was easily detectable and punished. Indian children educated by the friars eventually served as a network of informants. With scant missionary personnel, domination had to proceed by means of a concerted, systematic policy promoting cultural/racial syncretism/hybridity.

Fully understanding the pacification potential of the indigenous city-state tradition, Hernán Cortés decided to rebuild Tenochtitlan and make it the seat of imperial power. Bringing together a Spanish, *mestizo*, and Indian population in an urban grid would naturally encourage miscegenation (Parry). Although marriage with Indian women was not promoted, all Spaniards of a certain standing had several Indian mistresses; good numbers of priests serving the Indian villages were known for a similar practice. A rising *mestizo* population with greater ties to the Spanish culture, despiteful of the Indians, would certainly give population control a vaster range.

In Mexico City and other towns, the urban grid and the building of churches and public offices were intended to create a social horizon with routine circulation patterns and material references exhibiting overwhelming power. Indigenous stone-cutters, carvers, painters, silversmiths, and other artisans were gathered for these projects, working together with Spanish master artisans. Unavoidably, a syncretic fusion of styles and imagery resulted, not necessarily as Indian expression of a will to resist the oppressor but simply as the need to deliver the products contracted and keep a steady job. Understanding the important function religious ceremonies played in the previous, indigenous social organization, Church authorities tried to fill the void either by replacing them with the Catholic ritual performed with greater splendor than in Europe or allowing the continuity of many of the pagan rituals, implanting Christian content in them and purposefully connecting their meaning to some aspect of the Christian mythology. Pagan pilgrimages and processions were intertwined with images of saints, virgins, and Church hymns. As illustrated by the *Virgen de Guadalupe,* the Church took great care in promoting the association of the Virgin Mary with Indian fertility rites and earth-mother and corn-goddess symbology.

These PSYOPs seem close to the *dirigismo* associated with the Spanish Baroque. Then, should we say there was a Latin American Baroque well before the metropolitan Baroque? Or should we say this syncretism/hybridism was simply a policy of empire administration? But the point I originally raised is that the choice of labels to designate particular policies of empire administration is an ideological decision whose meaning should be scrutinized closely. In the description of the Neo/Ultra/Baroque discussed above, four were the salient points: the liberational space found in syncretic fusions, understanding these fusions as hypocritical masks to deceive the oppressor; the designation of the transvestite as the emblematic figure of this liberational masking; the designation of the transvestite as essential icon of the Latin American cultural identity since its inception in the seventeenth-century Baroque; and the transvestite metaphor as the sole container of a history whose origin has been irretrievably lost. The issue behind these four points is the nature of human freedom.

Given that human beings are in essence social entities, freedom can only be understood as the choices individuals may make within the routines of everyday life set by the encompassing economic and political order of society. Human survival is inconceivable outside these routines. Social orders are characterized by the type of routines they establish and the administrative measures they take to create, preserve, or reform them. The mercantilist system generated periodic Indian revolts due to monopolistic practices in food production, commerce, and high taxation; Spaniards frequently engaged in civil wars trying to keep or obtain *encomiendas*. Yet in spite of these commotions, colonial society did maintain a disciplined social order based on stable everyday life routines. The Indian population and the black slaves submitted to these disciplines not only because of impending repression but also because there were no other livelihood sources after their old, indigenous social order was shattered. They could only find their freedom within the colonial limits. No further discussion of this issue is necessary if one considers that Spanish colonial rule in Latin America lasted until the end of the nineteenth century.

Non-routine incidents like Sor Juana's cross-dressing are very short-lived. Once discovered, she had no other option but to return to her gender identity and find some other way to have full access to an intellectual lifestyle, which she did by becoming a nun, living the routines of the convent, within the Church—the most fundamental institution in the Spanish colonial order. Can such an ephemeral, cross-dressing incident be legitimately projected as a macro-metaphor for the entire Latin American cultural identity? Certainly, as an act of poetry, but not as an act of historical identity definition. After all, once the male transvestite finishes his spectacular extravaganza, he will have to undress, remove his make-up, and at some time return to his regular work unless he is a professional entertainer. Identification as a professional entertainer certainly disqualifies him as a macro-cultural metaphor.

Notes

1. I have selected Knutsen's text because in comparison to other well-known studies such as Paul Kennedy's *The Rise and Fall of Great Powers*, he fully integrates the ideological-normative dimension.
2. "So in 1577, Philip II issued a 'decree of bankruptcy' which unilaterally converted all these short-term loans at high interest rates into long-term redeemable annuities *(juros al quitar)* at 5 percent interest. Then in 1560, after borrowing heavily for three more years in order once more to defeat the French, the king repeated the maneuver; and in 1575, 1596, 1607, 1627, 1647 and 1653, he and his successors did so yet again. Naturally the bankers whose capital was thus confiscated bitterly resented the king's breach of faith, and for some time after each decree they refused to lend any further funds; but the crown always won them over again by the simple expedient of refusing to pay any interests at all on existing loans or *juros* until new loans were advanced. This clumsy and brutal system enabled the Spanish government to increase its funded debt from 6 million ducats in 1556 to 180 million" (Parker 63).
3. "Philip II had refused to the repeated suggestions that he should find an easy solution in the debasement of the coinage [. . .] Under his successor debasement became virtually unavoidable. Finding all the ordinary and extraordinary revenues for 1599 and 1600 pledged in advance to money-lenders, Philip III began the process. He issued a *vellón* currency—which had formerly contained about four grains of silver per mark of copper—containing no silver at all. He was thus able to make 140 *maravedís* out of a copper mark worth only 34 *maravedís* and so secure rather more than 100 percent net profit. A further ordinance (June 13, 1602) reduced the weight of the *vellón* currency to half on the pretext that the reduction would make it easier to handle and to carry. Next year (September 18, 1603) the Crown made another profit of nearly 100 percent by causing holders of the old copper *vellón* to have it restamped at double its face value" (Davies 266).

Works Cited

Bowdish, Commander Randall G., United States Navy. "Information Age Psychological Operations." *Military Review.* (December, 1998-February, 1999): 28–36.

Byrd Simpson, *The Encomienda in New Spain. The Beginning of Spanish Mexico*. Berkeley: University of California Press, 1982.

Carpentier, Alejo. *Obras completas*. Mexico City: Siglo XXI, 1983.

Castillo, David, and Nicholas Spadaccini. "Cervantes y la Comedia Nueva: lectura y espectáculo." *Theatralia* 5 (2003): 153–63.

Cesáreo, Mario. *Cruzados, mártires y beatos. Emplazamientos del cuerpo colonial*. West Lafayette, IN: Purdue University Press, 1995.

Davies, R. Trevor. *The Golden Century of Spain*. New York: Harper Torchbooks, 1961.

Elliott, J. H. "Concerto Barocco." *New York Review of Books*. April 9, 1987.

Hauser, Arnold. *The Social History of Art*. Vol. 2, *Renaissance, Mannerism, Baroque*. New York: Vintage Books, 1951.

Kayser, Wolfgang. *The Grotesque in Art and Literature*. Bloomington: Indiana University Press, 1963.

Kennedy, Paul. *The Rise and Fall of Great Powers*. New York: Random House, 1987.

Knutsen, Torbjørn L. *The Rise and Fall of World Orders*. Manchester: Manchester University Press, 1999.

Lezama Lima, José. *La expresión americana*. Santiago de Chile: Editorial Universitaria, 1969.

Maravall, José A. *Culture of the Baroque. Analysis of a Historical Structure*. Minneapolis: University of Minnesota Press, 1986.

_____. "From the Rennaissance to the Baroque: The Diphasic Scheme of a Social Crisis." *Literature Among Discourses: The Spanish Golden Age*. Ed. Wlad Godzich and Nicholas Spadaccini. Minneapolis: University of Minnesota Press, 1986.

_____. *Teatro y literatura en la sociedad barroca*. Madrid: Seminarios y ediciones, 1972.

Parker, Geoffrey. *The Military Revolution*, 2nd ed. Cambridge: Cambridge University Press, 1996.

_____. "The Making of Strategy in Habsburg Spain: Philip II's 'Bid for Mastery,' 1556–1598." *The Making of Strategy: Rulers, States, and War*. Ed. Williamson Murray, MacGregor Knox, and Alvin Bernstein. Cambridge: Cambridge University Press, 1995.

Parry, J. H. *The Age of Reconnaissance. Discovery, Exploration and Settlement 1450 to 1650*. Berkeley: University of California Press, 1963.

Sarduy, Severo. *Barroco*. Buenos Aires: Sudamericana, 1974.

Spadaccini, Nicholas, and Luis Martín-Estudillo. *Libertad y límites. El Barroco hispánico*. Madrid: Ediciones del Orto, 2004.

Part II
Baroque Anxieties and Strategies of Survival

Of Baroque Holes and Baroque Folds

William Egginton

The purpose of this essay is to test a philosophical hypothesis about a historical period against literary evidence. The hypothesis belongs to Gilles Deleuze, and it concerns his implicit description of the Baroque, taken as a cultural and philosophical whole. The literary evidence against which I wish to test this hypothesis comes from the seventeenth-century Spanish author Baltasar Gracián, in particular from several passages of his *Criticón* that deal with artifice and its relation to human being. In the essay's first section I argue for describing the Baroque in philosophical terms as a problem concerning the separation between the space of representation and the space of spectatorship. I then explain this claim historically with reference to changes in the theater and painting from the late Middle Ages to the Baroque, and support the claim by way of a discussion of baroque spatiality in literature and visual arts. In the next section I outline two philosophical strategies—which I call, with Deleuze, *holes* and *folds* respectively—for negotiating the fundamental separation of baroque space, and then indicate where these strategies are at work in a variety of baroque artifacts. In this section I also confront and ultimately reject Deleuze's appropriation of baroque cultural production for a philosophy of folds. Finally, in the essay's last section, I argue that baroque cultural production—and here I work specifically with Gracián's writing—offers clues to another philosophical description, one that undermines the tension between folds and holes that ostensibly characterizes the Baroque.

Two Spaces

José Antonio Maravall famously argued that the Baroque should be considered as a historical structure, rather than more specifically as a stylistic descriptor. Moreover, for Maravall the Baroque had to be understood as an international phenomenon; analysis that remained too focused on a single national context risked missing the forest for the tree (xvii). For the purposes of this discussion, I will assume the basic truth of the these claims, but regarding the former I will expand the discussion and regarding the latter I will remain somewhat more specific. On the one hand, in respecting the notion of the Baroque as structure, I want to move beyond what for Maravall remained a mostly sociological view of the Baroque—and a largely functionalist one at that—and open up a philosophical perspective on the Baroque; on the other hand, although I will draw on some examples of baroque production outside of Spain, for the purposes of this discussion the emphasis will remain on the Spanish context.[1]

Insisting that the Baroque be understood philosophically means that there is at work in everything we recognize as baroque an effort of thought to deal with a common problem. This problem was not such an issue prior to the period of dominance of those artifacts we call baroque, and will have undergone some significant change in order for the dominance of baroque production to have waned. The common problem I want to identify at the heart of baroque phenomena is widely known, has been called by many names, and has been described in bewildering variety. For the moment let me borrow the term used first by T. S. Eliot and more recently by Geoffrey Thurley to describe a problem they associated more with Romanticism than with any earlier period: namely, "the dissociation-of-sensibility" (18).[2] Dissociation-of-sensibility refers principally to the modernist critique of the romantic and realist tendencies of the nineteenth century, and specifically to the subordination of art to something outside of, greater than, or more important than art—such as the absolute, for romantics, or the world as it is in itself, for realists. But as Michel Foucault, in *The Order of Things*, and Martin Heidegger, in his entire oeuvre but specifically in his classic essay "The Age of the World Picture" (115–54), have argued, dissociationism is perhaps the fundamental characteristic of a European modernity dating to more or less the beginning of the seventeenth century—to the period, in other words, known as the Baroque.

As I have argued elsewhere,[3] if modernity can be characterized philosophically by a sort of generalized dissociation of the world of the senses from an interior world of the knowing subject, the model of this essentially spatial organization can be found in the thoroughgoing structural changes undergone by spectacle in the time leading up to the Baroque. This change in the organization of spectacle and its ramifications for conceptions of space are illustrated by the emergence during the sixteenth century of a technique in the staging of spectacle called "the theater in the theater."[4] For a modern theater-going audience, it goes without saying that a theater scene could be part of what is represented on the stage in a theater. The modern audience, for instance, can be expected to negotiate the complexities of a performative action taking place on that stage within a stage—such as a wedding ritual or a religious conversion—without losing track of the several levels of reality being represented. To take an example from Lope de Vega's 1608 play, *Lo fingido verdadero,* Ginés, actor to the Roman emperor Diocletian, performs the conversion of a pagan to Christianity in which he himself, pagan actor, is converted to Christianity. At this point in the play one of the spectators within the play, a member of Diocletian's entourage, exclaims in admiration, "No hay diferencia desto al verdadero caso" (Lope de Vega 275) (There's no difference between this and the real thing). At first glance this might seem unproblematic. Upon closer examination, however, an apparent paradox creeps in. How, to be specific, are we to understand that there is "no difference" between Ginés's performance and a real conversion? On the one hand, if the spectator is speaking truly, and there really is "no difference," how do we as spectators even begin to understand the reference of the sentence, namely Ginés's performance, which we must be able to distinguish from "reality" for the sentence to make any sense at all? On the other hand, if the spectator is lying, and there really is a visible difference between Ginés's acting and his real conversion, then his real conversion could not take place, and the play's plot becomes impossible.

What is happening here is, in fact, neither of the above options. Rather, what occurs is that we spectators in the real world fluently project the very distinction that constitutes us as spectators into the space thereby distinguished from ours: that is to say, we override the paradox with ease because we are accustomed to dividing the world into a world on the stage and a world off the stage without applying the rules of the one to the other. This division of the world, however, is not limited to cases where our skills as spectators are called upon in the theater or, today, in front of televisions or at the cinema. The point to grasp is that once entire populations became fluent in assuming and projecting this division in order to function correctly as theater spectators, that fluency became a generalized spatial structure for conceptualizing the world as a whole.

It is for this reason that the paradigmatic philosophical text of the early modern period, Descartes's *Meditations*, ultimately posits the division of being into two fundamental substances: a *thinking* substance that looks out onto a world of *extended* substances. As Richard Rorty, another contemporary critic of dissocationism, claims that prior to Locke and Descartes there was no "conception of the human mind as an inner space in which both pains and clear and distinct ideas passed in review before a single Inner Eye" (50). But this conception has a clear cultural model: spectators watching actors performing before them as characters. Look at what Descartes says in his *Meditations* on the subject of what can and cannot be false: "Now as to what concerns ideas, if we consider them only in themselves and do not relate them to anything else beyond themselves, they cannot properly speaking be false; for whether I imagine a goat or a chimera, it is not the less true that I imagine the one rather than the other" (quoted in Rorty 56). Descartes's formulation is clearly derived from the model of the stage, for the distinction between ideas that do not relate to anything beyond themselves and ones that do is precisely the distinction between the world of characters and that of the actors that portray them: although I can doubt that what I am seeing on the stage is a true representation of reality, I cannot doubt *that I am seeing something.*

As I said at the outset, if the Baroque can be described in philosophical terms, that is because there is at work in everything we recognize as baroque an effort of thought to deal with a common problem. With reference to the modernist critique of previous artistic attitudes, I have called this common problem dissociationism, and have located its roots in the spatial practices of early modern spectacle. I have furthermore pointed to the origins of Descartes's paradigmatic act of dissociationism—the separation of being into thinking and extended substance—in the theatrical division of space into that of the spectator and that of the representation. In the remainder of this section, I will identify the problem of dissociationism as it emerges in several examples of baroque cultural production.

Heinrich Wölfflin is often credited with having resuscitated the Baroque's almost universally negative perception among art historians, a perception revealed in the fact that (in his time) the term Baroque "in general use [. . .] still carries a suggestion of repugnance and abnormality" (23). Recognizing a series of stylistic innovations common to painting and architecture in the period following the Renaissance, Wölfflin proceeded to provide a theory for a period and style that did not have one of its own. The core of his theory is what he calls "the painterly style" as applied to architecture:

> If the beauty of a building is judged by the enticing effects of moving masses, the restless, jumping forms or violently swaying ones which seem constantly on the point of change, and not by balance and solidity of structure, then the strictly architectonic conception of architecture is depreciated. In short, the severe style of architecture makes its effect by what it *is*, that is, by its corporeal substance, while painterly architecture acts through what it appears to be, that is, an illusion of movement. (Wölfflin 30)

This distinction between what something is—its corporeal substance—and what it seems to be is essential for Wölfflin's theory of the Baroque, and is essential as well, I would argue, for any understanding of the Baroque itself. It is perhaps unneccesary at this point to note that the language Wölfflin uses to characterize baroque architecture is precisely the language of dissociationism, the language that pits appearances against corporeal substance. The point of his description and its generalization to baroque art, however, is that what we identify as stylistically baroque—and what shared a dominance in the historical period known as the Baroque—depends on the play of appearances in relation to a corporeal substance assumed to exist beyond that play of appearances. Furthermore, the play of appearances is very much the effect of the basic spatial configuration I outlined above, because baroque space produces an effect of depth on surfaces, just as theatrical space provokes the possibility of *mise en abîme*, where characters inhabit characters inhabiting characters.

The production of depth on surfaces is most evident in the baroque, painterly technique of *trompe l'oeil*, used to great effect by such architects as Balthasar Neumann in his Würzburg Residenz (1719), where only our knowledge that no real dog could actually stand for so long on the narrow molding bordering the ceiling to the grand staircase can convince us that the dog standing outside the painting ceiling is not real. In its most extreme form, anamorphosis, the painterly manipulation of perspective can make images appear or disappear entirely on the basis of the viewer's position.[5]

The Spanish cultural historian Emilio Orozco Díaz also defines the Baroque generally in terms of the increased fluidity between spatial levels or strata:

> Responde a una concepción y visión de continuidad espacial que considera la obra inmensa en un espacio continuo, como situada en plano o término intermedio en

relación con los otros planos que quedan detrás y los que existen delante, y dentro de los cuales estamos nosotros, los espectadores . . . Esta interpenetración expresiva y espacial es esencial de la concepción artística barroca; lleva a la auténtica incorporación del espectador a la obra de arte. (40)

(It responds to a conception and vision of spatial continuity that views the immense work as occupying a continuous space, as if situated on an intermediate plane in relation to the other planes that exist in front of and behind it, within which we the spectators can be found . . . . This expressive, spatial interpenetration is essential to the artistic conception of the Baroque; it produces the authentic incorporation of the spectator into the work of art.) (My translation)

This last sentence is of great importance, because, as I suggested with the example of Neumann's dog, one of the effects of baroque trickery is to engage or compromise the viewer in the represented space—to try to blend or bleed the distinction between the space of the spectator and that of the representation.[6] The play between the frame or border separating these two spaces and the dissolution of that frame is paramount in baroque artifacts, and in some ways represents what is perhaps most recognizable about baroque style, what Orozco Díaz calls the overflowing of borders. Take what is probably one of the most famous examples of baroque painting, if not of European painting in general: Diego Velázquez's *Las meninas* (1656–57). As Foucault's influential reading has shown (3–16) all the play and paradox of the age of representation are caught up in the intricacies of this painting, which questions the viewer's relation to the viewed space, to the point of view of the painter, and to that of the center of political power itself. In Foucault words, "[a]s soon as they place the spectator in the field of their gaze, the painter's eyes seize hold of him, force him to enter the field of their gaze, assign him a place both privileged and inescapable, levy their luminous and visible tribute from him, and project it upon the inaccessible surface of the canvas within the picture" (5).

Foucault's reference to assigning the viewer a place both privileged and inescapable points to the implication of baroque spatial play in conceptions of power—and perhaps in the very idea of political agency—prevalent in the societies of early modern Europe. Such an idea of political agency is clearly at work in Baltasar Gracián's writings, especially in his manuals of advice for courtly politics.[7] For Gracián, life at court is a relentless battle for influence or power. One's greatest weapon in this battle is knowledge: the knowledge one has of others and the control one wields over what and how much others know about oneself. The powerful man is, for Gracián, one who knows how to manipulate public knowledge of his self. He cultivates an intimate core, which Gracián calls his *caudal*, his capital or resources. And if there were a leitmotif among his strategies for how to get ahead in the dog-eat-dog world of early modern society, it would be best expressed in the motto *incomprensibilidad de caudal*. This has nothing to do with actually having infinite resources at one's command. The point is rather that the depths of one's resources should never be made known to others. What others do not know about your hidden resources they will respect and desire, and the result will be more power for you. The most powerful person in any society is the one who manages to convince all others that his inner resources are the most unfathomable, and hence infinite in terms of social capacity: "[. . .] mayores afectos de veneración causa la opinión y duda de adonde llega el caudal de cada uno que la evidencia de él, por grande que fuera" (*Oráculo manual* maxim 94) (greater affects of veneration are inspired by public opinion and doubt as to how deep one's resources go, than by evidence of them, as great as they may be).

It should be clear that this image is thoroughly theatrical, and hence thoroughly baroque. We only have *caudal* insofar as we present ourselves socially in the person of a character. Or, to put it in another way, a *persona*—which, as is well known, derives from the Greek word for mask—both serves as Gracián's figure for the ultimate goal of personal development[8] and at the same time implicitly imports into that figure all the trappings of the stage. What distinguishes the *persona* is his ability to stay within character, to convince the greatest number of people possible that his character is his character *all the way down*—that there is no other self, or actor, behind it to ground it in the world and limit the eternal sounding of its resources: "Hombre con fondos, tanto tiene de persona" (*Oráculo,* maxim 48, my translation) (As much depth as a man has, so much is he a *persona*). What distinguishes this person, what makes him *persona*, in other words, is his ability to use the spatial play of the baroque to entice the participation of his fellow players as participants in his representation, to capture their commitment, their belief, and ultimately their libidinal investment through the manipulation of strata and appearances that we have identified as baroque.

To conclude this section, what we should retain from these examples of baroque production in written and visual culture is a sense of how, in every case, what we identify as baroque—namely, the play of appearance against the backdrop of an ostensibly inaccessible corporeal substance—can be understood as an effort of thought to deal with a common problem. This problem stems from the dissemination of certain assumptions concerning the nature of the space in which people interact, assumption that themselves support the skills and practices related to a new kind of spectacle in early modern Europe: the theater. The theatricalization of space ultimately means that, in whatever medium is used for expression, a fundamental separation is assumed between the space occupied by the viewer and the space occupied by the represented reality. This separation, later theorized as the dissociation-of-sensibility, is the common problem at the heart of a philosophical understanding of the Baroque.

Two Solutions

Thought's effort, in the theatrical world of the Baroque, is to breach a divide. Such an effort was clearly underway in all of the cases we have considered so far, but there would also seem to be a profound similarity to the strategies adopted. Imagine, for example, the experience of dissociation as inhabiting a house. Everything within the confines of the house pertains to one substance; everything outside its walls pertains to another. The communication between substances in such a scenario must take place through a wall or, more specifically, through some sort of hole in a wall, like a window or door. The soul is a house that looks out on the world through its windows and doors. It is not difficult to see how baroque artifacts can be mapped onto this image of thought. In painting, both exterior and interior frames serve as windows through which spectators look out on or into other worlds;[9] in architecture, real windows and doors are paired with borders that are made to play the role; Gracián's *persona* takes on the model of a house containing a veritable *mise en abîme* of concentrically organized rooms. In all cases, the play of the Baroque involves a bleeding of borders, an invitation to the spectator to step into another reality.

According to this model, the basic problem of the Baroque seems profoundly Cartesian: a world of holes offering us multiple, more-or-less successful means of communicating between substances. But in 1984 (trans. 1993) the philosopher Gilles Deleuze published *The Fold*, in which he argued that this image of thought was seriously flawed.[10] Descartes, he claimed, was not a baroque thinker, but rather a leftover from the Renaissance;[11] the Baroque, rather than being characterized by Cartesian holes, is more properly understood under the figure of the fold. Folds, as Deleuze writes, replace holes:

> The monad is a cell. It resembles a sacristy more than an atom: a room with neither doors nor windows, where all activity takes place on the inside. The monad is the autonomy of the inside, an inside without an outside. It has as its correlative the independence of the façade, an outside without an inside. Now the façade can have

doors and windows—it is riddled with holes—although there may be no void, a fold being only the site of a more rarified matter. (28)

Yes, there are holes, but these holes are not the open passages between substances that a Cartesian world would require. They are rather sites of relative rarification in a façade that emphatically do not lead through to some interior. What appear to be holes are in fact folds, a case of invagination in a plane that for some point of view may appear to be a hole.

The passage from inside to outside is further inhibited by the fact that, for Deleuze (and Leibniz), there is no absolute distinction between interior and exterior space, but only one relative to point of view. What traditional thought interpreted as the play of appearance against immobile, corporeal substance, Deleuze (and Leibniz) understand as the inevitable result of the monad's embedded perspective, its point of view. The separation between thinking and extended substance is translated into one between endogenous folds (organic matter) and exogenous folds (inorganic matter) (7). Because every point of view is a monad, the "external world" is folded into the walls of its cell: "The world is an infinite series of curvatures or inflection, and the entire world is enclosed in the soul from one point of view" (24). This translation of exteriority and interiority into an effect of point of view obviates the language of dualism and leads Deleuze to a reinterpretation of baroque architecture:

> Baroque architecture can be defined by this severing of the façade from the inside, of the interior from the exterior, and the autonomy of the interior from the independence of the exterior [. . .]. A new kind of link, of which pre-Baroque architecture had no inkling, must be made between the inside and the outside, or the spontaneity of the inside and the determination of the outside [. . .]. What makes the new harmony possible is, first, the distinction between two levels or floors, which resolves tension or allots the division. The lower level is assigned to the façade, which is elongated by being punctured and bent back according to the folds determined by a heavy matter, forming an infinite room for reception or receptivity. The upper level is closed, as a pure inside without an outside, a weightless, closed interiority, its walls hung with spontaneous folds that are now only those of a soul or a mind. (29)

This severing of façade from inside, which translates into the division between two floors, serves, according to Deleuze, to resolve a tension, and it is not too difficult to see which tension needs resolution. The common problem at the heart of baroque culture emerges clearly here as well, in the "spontaneity" of the inside and the "determination" of the outside. The difference is that Deleuze's Leibniz has come up with an image of thought that refuses the separation of being into the two worlds "common to the Platonic tradition" (29), an image, moreover, that is echoed in baroque art and architecture, as well as in its mathematics and its music.

If Descartes is, for Deleuze, a Renaissance thinker, this is because Deleuze wants to reconstruct an alternate history of thought, a hidden, minor one suppressed by the philosophical tradition that calls Descartes its father and that reduces the question of knowledge to that of the relation between fundamentally incompatible substances. This history—which Deleuze recounts throughout a series of interventions on philosophers from the medieval Duns Scotus[12] through Spinoza,[13] Nietzsche,[14] and finally Leibniz—attempted to show that beneath or alongside a tradition that had banished the world to some unattainable outside of sensation, there was a tradition of thought at least as rich that had refused such a nihilistic gesture.

Against a Cartesian world characterized by fundamentally incompatible substances, Deleuze argues with Scotus for the univocity of being, and with Spinoza for a notion of a single substance that manifests itself in various attributes (*Expressionism* 42). In light of this trajectory, Deleuze's attraction to the German mathematician and thinker Leibniz is not hard to explain. Inventor of a form of calculus more or less simultaneous with Newton,[15] Leibniz added to the latter's achievements an entire literary, philosophical, and theological dimension in harmony with his mathematical insights. Although Leibniz's thought is too extensive to treat in any detail here, much of the force of Leibniz's vision for Deleuze is contained in this sentence, quoted at the outset of Deleuze's considerations: "The division of the continuous must not be taken as of sand dividing into grains, but resembles a sheet of paper or a tunic in folds, in such a way that an infinite number of folds can be produced, some smaller than others, but without the body ever dissolving into points or minima."[16] An ontological vision more in tune with the insights of differential calculus would be hard to imagine. Refusing the atomistic world view of the Cartesians, in which analysis would indeed eventually resolve around points or minima—and in which objects are conceived of as occupying points in a space measurable and mappable in terms of three-dimensional coordinates—Leibniz's monad does not look out onto an independent world composed of atomistic unities, but engages in a kind of sounding of the infinitesimal, a process in which space opens or unfolds out of ever-receding, ever-diminishing folds within folds.

As we have already seen, Deleuze's interpretation incorporates the basic tenets of baroque architecture: rather than the façade playing appearance off against a hidden corporeal substance, façade and sacristy are now situated as part of the same building. Extension and receptivity are the attributes of an exogenous folding specific to façades; mind and spontaneity become the attributes of endogenous folding, of organicism, and are likened to a room walled with folds but with no windows or doors. In the chiaroscuro of baroque painting, Deleuze sees what he calls the "effacement of contour" (32), a differential undermining of Cartesian linearity and atomism. And certainly we need not go far into the world of baroque sculpture to find excessively eponymous illustrations of Deleuze's theme. If Bernini's *Ecstasy of St. Theresa* (1647–52) is among the most luxuriant examples, it is, for Deleuze, still one among many: "In every instance folds of clothing acquire an autonomy and a *fullness that are not simply decorative effects*. They convey the intensity of a spiritual force exerted on the body, either to turn it upside down or to stand or raise it up over and again, but in every event to turn it inside out and to old its inner surfaces" (122). This molding of inner surfaces into the infinite complexity of the fold lies at the heart of Deleuze's interpretation of all baroque culture. If baroque culture reveals an effort of thought for the philosopher, what it reveals for Deleuze is the force of the fold itself—as the churning difference within the univocity of being—against the gestures of Platonism and the abstractions of epistemology, to impart itself to the world in a material way.

    According to Deleuze, then, it would seem that the alternate history of philosophy he resurrects represents not an effort of thought to deal with the problem of a fundamental separation of space, but rather an image of thought in which the problem is not really a problem. And yet in some of Deleuze's formulation he would seem to acknowledge a kind of pre-existing tension, as if Descartes's Renaissance issues were not merely throwbacks, but were somehow still at work disrupting the univocity of being and provoking the thought of the fold. If the latter scenario has truth to it, however, then we cannot agree that Descartes is to be disregarded in favor of models of baroque thought that are somehow truer or closer to the mark, for Descartes's formulation would have to be seen as responding to the same fundamental problems that provoked the thought of Spinoza and Leibniz, the painting of Velázquez and Caravaggio, or the architecture of Bernini and Neumann. These problems, as I have argued, stem largely from the emergence of basic assumptions necessary for negotiating the complexities of theatrical space. While both holes and folds can be understood as more or less successful, more or less failed efforts of thought to deal with the problem of dissociationism, there are clues, in the writing of Baltasar Gracián, to another way of thinking through the apparent paradoxes of theatrical space. We will turn to this writing in the next section.

Artifice and Theatrical Space

In his *Criticón*, in a chapter titled "Las maravillas de Artemia" (The Marvels of
Artemia), Baltasar Gracián explores what we have identified as the basic problem of the Baroque—that is, dissociationism—but does so as if fully cognizant
of its indebtedness to theatrical structures of spatiality. The episode recounted
in the chapter deals with the attempts of Critilo—one of the heroes of the book
and a clear allegory for man's critical capacity—to rescue his young and naïve
traveling companion, Andrenio, from the snares of illusion and deceit set by
Falibundo, master of lies and de facto ruler of the world. What is fascinating
about the chapter is that this salvation from deceit can only come about through
the intervention—in the form of a good and wise goddess—of artifice. As the
narrator explains: "Es el arte complemento de la naturaleza y un otro segundo
ser [. . .]. Éste fue sin duda el empleo del hombre en el paraíso cuando le re-
vistió el Criador la presidencia de todo el mundo y la assistencia en aquél para
que lo cultivasse; esto es, que con el arte lo aliñasse y puliesse. De suerte que
es el artificio gala de lo natural, realçe de su llaneza; obra siempre Milagros"
(*Criticón* 173) (Art is nature's complement and another second self . . . . This
was doubtlessly man's purpose in paradise when the Creator endowed him with
the presidency of the entire world and his presence there in order to cultivate it;
that is, that with art he should keep it in order and cleanliness. In this way we
say that artifice is nature's regalia, the splendor of its sincerity; it always works
Miracles) (my translation). That is to say, art begins already in a precarious
position. Is it to be distinguished from nature, or is it rather part of nature? It is,
for Gracián, a complement or, we might add, a supplement, very much in the
sense used by Derrida in his reading of Rousseau.

At first glance, it seems that Gracián's description of the relation between
art and nature confirms a hierarchy also at work in Rousseau: art cultivates nature; it dresses it up; it adds splendor to nature's sincerity. According to Derrida,
however, Rousseau's dismissal of writing as merely supplemental to speech—
to something that would be, as regards the supplement of writing, complete in
itself—reveals that speech, like nature, must itself contain some lack that writing in turn comes to fill. The something, in other words, to which a supplement
is added can never be, in fact, complete in itself; for something that is complete
will not bear being added to. Rousseau's natural man, in other words, could not
be complete if culture's supplement of education could later come and add to
him in any way.[17] But we need not subject Gracián to much pressure, or indeed
to any at all, for his text to come to strikingly similar conclusions.

Speaking of the goddess or witch, the narrator goes on to say: "Llamábase

aquélla, que no niega su nombre ni sus hechos, la sabia y discreta Artemia
[. . .]. Muy diferente de la otra Cirçe, pues no convertía los hombres en bestias,
sino al contrario, las fieras en hombres. No encantaba las personas, antes las
desencantaba[. . .]. Y aun dizen que realmente enseñaba a hablar las bestias
(*Criticón* 172). (She was called, who denies neither her name nor her deeds,
the wise and discrete Artemia . . . . So different from the other Circe, because
she did not convert men into beast but on the contrary beast into men. She did
not enchant people, but rather disenchanted them . . . . And they even say that
she truly taught the beasts to speak). Sorceress, witch—her powers however
do not enchant, but rather disenchant, which fact can only lead us to assume
that the enchantment was there to begin with. She does not change men into
beasts, but beasts into men; and she teaches the beasts to speak, which means
that her power must be aligned with the power of language. But again, in adding
language to nature she would appear to be disenchanting, that is, to be taking
something away, not adding something inessential.

The image becomes clearer when Critilo actually witnesses Artemia's creation of a human being: "Pero lo que más admiró a Critilo fue verla coger entre
las manos un palo, un tronco, y irle desbastando hasta hazer dél un hombre
que hablaba de modo que se le podía escuchar; discurría y valía, al fin, lo que
bastaba para ser persona" (178). (But what most astonished Critilo was to see
her take a stick, a trunk in her hands and start chiseling away at it until she
made of it a man, who spoke such that he could be understood; he reasoned
and was worth something, in the end, what was needed for him to become a
persona." As we saw in our earlier discussion of Gracián, *persona* is something
to which one aspires; to be *persona* is itself an art—the art, in fact, of appear-
ing to be natural, through and through, to be real. For Gracián, in other words,
the nature of human being is to be naturally incomplete; there is an *originary
lack*, as Derrida would say, that allows the supplement of artifice to emerge as
a kind of natural corrective force.[18] In the same way that Artemia must remove
material from nature in order to form a human being who reasons and speaks,
the cultivation of *persona* requires the careful removal of something natural to
humankind as Gracián and his society encounter it. But that something, also a
kind of original lack, is primordial deceit.

In order to save mankind—whom Gracián represents by the character Andrenio—Artemia sends an agent to the land of lies where he has been drawn by
his folly: "Y él empeñó su industria: vistióse al uso de aquel país, con la misma
librea que los criados de Falimundo, que era de muchos dobleces, pliegues,
aforros y contraforros, senos, bolsillos, sobrepuestos, alhorzas y capa para todas
las cosas" (177). (And he got on with his work: he dressed himself according to

the manner of that land, in the same livery of Falimundo's servants, which were made of many doublets, folds, linings and counterlinings, breasts, pockets, overlappings, pleats and cloaks for all things). Artifice, in other words, adopts the duplicity and all the trappings of deceit in order to save man from its allures. Indeed, the final instrument needed to break Falimundo's spell is nothing other than a mirror; not because it mirrors nature as it is, but rather because, by forcing us to look at nature awry or in a denatured way, nature is revealed in its primordial deceit: "las cosas del mundo todas se han de mirar al revés, volviendo las espaldas, para verlas al derecho" (182) (the things of the world must be seen backwards, turning one's back, in order to see them straight). And then there is what Andrenio sees in the mirror: "Veo un monstruo, el más horrible que vi en mi vida, porque no tiene pies ni cabeça; que cosa tan desproporcionada, no corresponde parte a parte" (182). (I see a monster, the most horrible I have seen in my life, because it has neither feet nor a head; what a disproportionate thing, its parts do not correspond). The mirror, which allows Andrenio to look at the world backwards—twisted around from his normal, natural perspective—reveals to Andrenio nature as it is in itself: distorted, foul, deceitful.

It is important that we not just write this off as a case of typical baroque morbidity. The comparison with Rousseau, at least as interpreted by Derrida, is insightful: what Derrida's reading shows is that under Rousseau's proto-romantic faith in nature lies a deep-seated suspicion of nature's propriety, its natural and undisturbed self-identity. Gracián shows us the same thing, but with a clarity of insight that requires little commentary. All that is left is to situate Gracián's insight both into our discussion of the Baroque's philosophical description, which also means to link it to the problem posed to modernity by theatrical dissociationism. As far as the latter is concerned, what is privileged in Gracián is quite simply his nearness to the constitutive theatricality of baroque interaction. If deceit is primordial, that is necessary because, in a profound or ontological sense, being is at heart deceptive or, rather, deceit is primordial for the baroque mind because the baroque mind negotiates space according to theatrical assumptions. Everything, people included, are posited as being engaged in a constant and thoroughgoing play of appearances over against some core being of corporeal substance—a model borrowed freely from the stage. If Gracián describes base reality in such terms, that is merely because reality, for the Baroque, was in some sense clearly caught up in this dynamic, a dynamic covered up by the efforts of later cultural production.

As far as the former question is concerned—namely, Gracián's relation to our current discussion of folds and holes—his insight is simultaneously simple and profound: what Gracián shows us, already from his seat in a nascent modernity, is that the choice of the Baroque is perhaps a false one. The claim of holes is that we are separated from truth; the claim of folds is that we have always known, always been our own truth. The marvel of Artemia, of baroque artifice, is the revelation that neither claim stands on its own; rather, the truth hidden by holes and revealed by artifice is that the truth we have always known and been is folded, duplicitous, and artificial all the way down. Better yet, we are connected to our truth by folds; but the truth we are thereby connected to is a fundamental separation from our most intimate and other self that no folding can ever overcome.

Notes

1. While I think there are good reasons to emphasize the overwhelmingly Hispanic nature of the Baroque, this is not the place to make this argument.
2. Thurley goes to list as "dissociation-of-sensibility books" Michel Foucault, *The Order of Things*; Gabriel Josipovichi, *The World and the Book*; Cleanth Brooks, *Modern Poetry and the Tradition*; Erich Heller, *The Disinherited Mind*; and Peter Ackroyd, *Notes for a New Culture*. Aside from Eliot, Thurley credits José Ortega y Gasset with having "most brilliantly" articulated the thesis in his *The Dehumanization of Art*.
3. The following argument is drawn from my book *How the World Became a Stage: Presence, Theatricality, and the Problem of Modernity*.
4. See Georges Forestier, *Le théâtre dans le théâtre sur la scène française du XVIIe siècle*; and Robert J. Nelson, *Play within a Play*.
5. See David Castillo, *(A)wry Views*; Jurgis Baltrusaitis, *Anamorphic Art*; and David Castillo and William Egginton, "The Perspectival Imaginary."
6. See my "Reality is Bleeding: A Brief History of Film from the 16th Century."
7. See my "Gracián and the Emergence of the Modern Subject," as well as the other contributions in that volume, especially David Castillo, "Gracián and the Art of Public Representation."
8. "Todo está ya en su punto y el ser persona en el mayor." (Everything is now at a crest, and being *persona* is the utmost). *Oráculo,* maxim 1, my translation.
9. "A painting always has a model on its outside; it is always a window." Gilles Deleuze, *The Fold: Leibniz and the Baroque.*
10. For an excellent exposition of Deleuze's argument, see Gregg Lambert, *The Non-Philosophy of Gilles Deleuze.*
11. "It is the relativity of clarity (as much as of movement), the inseparability of clarity from obscurity, the effacement of contour—in short, the opposition to Descartes, who remained a man of the Renaissance, from the double point of view of a physics of light and a logic of the idea" (*Fold* 32).
12. See, for example, *Difference and Repetition.*

13. Deleuze, *Expressionism in Philosophy: Spinoza.*
14. *Nietzsche and Philosophy.*
15. There seems to be consensus that Leibniz invented the differential form of notation—whereas Newton was using the fluxion form—in or around 1676, although there is controversy as to whether Leibniz did so under the influence of Newton or independently. See W. W. Rouse Ball, *A Short Account of the History of Mathematics*, excerpted as part of collection of online material relating to the history of mathematics at the School of Mathematics, Trinity College, Dublin: http://www.maths.tcd.ie/pub/HistMath/People/RBallHist.html.
16. *Pacidus Philalethi*, in Louis Couturat, ed., *Opuscules et fragments inédits de Leibniz.* 614–15, quoted in *Fold* 6.
17. "Therefore this property of man is not a property of man: it is the very dislocation of the proper in general: it is the dislocation of the characteristic, of the proper in general, the impossibility—and therefore the desire—of self-proximity; the impossibility and therefore the desire of self-presence" (Jacques Derrida, *Of Grammatology* 244).
18. "Nature: that there is *lack* in Nature and that *because of that very fact* something is *added* to it" (Derrida 149).

Works Cited

Ackroyd, Peter. *Notes for a New Culture: An Essay on Modernism.* New York: Barnes and Noble Books, 1976.

Ball, W. W. Rouse. *A Short Account of the History of Mathematics.* 4th Edition, 1908.

Baltrusaitis, Jurgis. *Anamorphic Art.* Trans. W. J. Strachan. New York: Abrams, 1977.

Brooks, Cleanth. *Modern Poetry and the Tradition.* Chapel Hill: University of North Carolina Press, 1939.

Castillo, David. *(A)wry Views: Anamorphosis, Cervantes, and the Early Picaresque.* West Lafayette, IN: Purdue University Press, 2001.

_____. "Gracián and the Art of Public Representation." *Rhetoric and Politics: Baltasar Gracián and the New World Order.* Ed. Nicholas Spadaccini and Jenaro Talens. Hispanic Issues 14. Minneapolis, University of Minnesota Press, 1997. 191–208.

Castillo, David, and William Egginton. "The Perspectival Imaginary and the Symbolization of Power." *Indiana Journal of Hispanic Literature* 8 (1996): 75–93.

Couturat, Louis, ed. *Opuscules et fragments inédits de Leibniz.* Paris: F. Alcan, 1903.

Deleuze, Gilles. *Difference and Repetition.* Trans. Paul Patton. New York: University of Columbia Press, 1994.

_____. *Expressionism in Philosophy: Spinoza.* Trans. Martin Joughin. New York: Zone, 1990.

_____. *The Fold: Leibniz and the Baroque.* Trans. Tom Conley. Minneapolis: University of Minnesota Press, 1993.

_____. *Nietzsche and Philosophy.* Trans. Hugh Tomlinson. London: Athlone Press, 1983.

Derrida, Jacques. *Of Grammatology*. Trans. Gayatri Chakravorty Spivak. Baltimore: Johns Hopkins University Press, 1997.

Egginton, William. "Gracián and the Emergence of the Modern Subject." *Rhetoric and Politics: Baltasar Gracián and the New World Order*. Ed. Nicholas Spadaccini and Jenaro Talens. Hispanic Issues 14. Minneapolis: University of Minnesota Press, 1997. 151–69.

_____. *How the World Became a Stage: Presence, Theatricality, and the Problem of Modernity*. Albany, NY: State University of New York Press, 2003.

_____. "Reality is Bleeding: A Brief History of Film from the 16th Century." *Configurations* 9.2 (2001): 207–30.

Forestier, Georges. *Le théâtre dans le théâtre sur la scène française du XVIIe siècle*. Genève: Librairie Droz, 1981.

Foucault, Michel. *The Order of Things: An Archaeology of the Human Sciences*. New York: Pantheon Books, 1970.

Gracián, Baltasar. *El criticón*. Madrid: Cátedra, 2000.

_____. *El héroe, el discreto, oráculo manual y arte de prudencia*. Barcelona: Planeta, 1984.

Heidegger, Martin. "The Age of the World Picture." *The Question Concerning Technology and Other Essays*. Trans. William Lovitt. New York: Harper Torchbooks, 1977.

Heller, Erich. *The Disinherited Mind*. Cleveland and New York: World Publishing, 1959.

Josipovichi, Gabriel. *The World and the Book: A Study of Modern Fiction*. London: Macmillan, 1971.

Lambert, Gregg. *The Non-Philosophy of Gilles Deleuze*. New York and London: Continuum, 2002.

Lope de Vega y Carpio, Félix. *Comedias*. Ed. Luis Guarner. 2 vols. Barcelona: Editorial Iberia, 1955.

Maravall, Jose Antonio. *Culture of the Baroque: Analysis of a Historical Structure*. Trans. Terry Cochran. Minneapolis: University of Minnesota Press, 1986.

Nelson, Robert J. *Play within a Play. The Dramatist's Conception of his Art: Shakespeare to Anouilh*. New Haven: Yale University Press, 1958.

Orozco Díaz, Emilio. *El teatro y la teatralidad del barroco*. Barcelona: Planeta. 1969.

Ortega y Gasset, José. *The Dehumanization of Art*. Princeton: Princeton University Press, 1948.

Rorty, Richard. *Philosophy and the Mirror of Nature*. Princeton: Princeton University Press, 1979.

Thurley, Geoffrey. *The Romantic Predicament*. London: Macmillan, 1983.

Wölfflin, Heinrich. *Renaissance and Baroque*. Trans. Kathrin Simon. London: Collins, 1984.

◆ **4**

Models of Subjectivity in the Spanish Baroque: Quevedo and Gracián

Fernando Ordóñez

In this essay I seek to examine various models of subjectivity present in the Spanish baroque period for the purpose of explaining the contradictory functions of certain discourses. In a world touched by disillusion, baroque subjects and their discourses are developed between "freedom and containment," a tension determined by the internal freedom granted by the possibility of doubt and contained within the external limits imposed by an authoritarian social order, which was stressed by the Treaty of Westphalia.[1] Furthermore, we can establish a link among these "models of subjectivity and the gap that opens between society and the self in the mist of an expansive crisis of the estatist system in early modern Spain" (Castillo and Spadaccini198).

My examples will be drawn from some of the writings of Francisco de Quevedo and Baltasar Gracián, and I will undertake this discussion through the work of Enrique Pichon Riviere's,[2] whose psychosocial perspective presents an approach to human subjectivity that helps us to link subjectivity with culture and, analogically, to describe the Baroque in terms of the epistemological shift that characterized this period. This view allows us to reconsider the Spanish Baroque from the point of view of the subjects in order to understand the connections between subject, culture, and society. I envision my reflection as complementary to the analysis of this topic that was undertaken by George Mariscal in *Contradictory Subjects*, because I also "want to show that the idea of the subject in Spain in the 1600s . . . was in no way fixed and was something quite different from those forms that dominate literary criticism and the humanities in the West" (3). In other words, I aim to show how these "contradictory subjects" were produced "through a wide range of discourses and practices" (Mariscal 5) but in the frame of an epistemic crisis that was challenging the common understanding of reality. Certainly, Mariscal presents these contradictions from a metaphysical perspective, focusing on how this subject-in-progress is produced through circumstances like class, blood, family, and so on. In my case the focus will be on the epistemic tools that individuals utilized to perceive and signify their world.

From an institutional perspective, José Antonio Maravall (*Culture*) has characterized the culture of the Baroque as an "urban," "guided," "conservative," and "mass-oriented" culture. This interpretation has been essential for an understanding of the interaction between subjects and baroque institutions. Maravall also describes the Baroque as a "culture of crisis," observing "that the seventeenth century marks the beginning of the consciousness . . . that there are periods in the life of a society in which difficulties emerge in the structure and development of collective life, thereby causing things not to proceed well" (*Culture* 20). This self-consciousness of the crisis was revealing that a new subject was emerging with a better understanding of his/her circumstances; however this subjectivity will state the loneliness and skepticism as a consequence of the loss of a common faith and the dissolution of the humanist idealism. The perplexity expressed by these individuals did not mean the abandonment of the search for a different reality; as Maravall argued, these modern individuals had the capacity to understand that their society was not doing well, and they began to doubt whether things could be improved (*Culture* 20).

The Baroque is a "culture of crisis," but I want to stress the idea of "culture in crisis" in a radical manner, because I conceive the Baroque as a historical structure where one can find a crisis in all social fields. Through this sense of crisis, marked by deep epistemic discontinuity, we can trace the features of baroque subjectivities. In the words of Maravall, "the human being is placed in the midst of this contradictory, uncertain, deceptive, and radically insecure world, and therein lies the drama of his or her story must unfold" (*Culture* 158). These individuals "find themselves in internal combat with their own selves, which gives rise to so many concerns, so much uneasiness and even violence that break out from within and are projected into their relations with the world and others" (*Culture* 159).

An approach that focuses on the subjects would reveal the duality expressed by the plurality of subjectivities of these "divided" persons, for whom the world had turned upside down. Moreover, as was argued by Rosario Villari, "what is unique in Baroque conflictuality lay less in tension between one historical subject and another, than in the presence of apparently incompatible or obviously contradictory attitudes existing within one and the same historical subject" (3). Subsequently traditionalism and renovation, simulation and truth, and sensuality and mysticism could coexist in the baroque world.

In order to understand this gap among the subjects, it is important to explore the connection between subjectivity and common sense. Pichon Riviere's *Social Psychology* is a useful theoretical resource for this type of analysis. According to the Argentinean scholar, human subjectivity is always social, because the person is built in the interaction with other individuals, groups, and social classes. This presence of the other implies a cultural and social field which means that human subjectivity is framed by a symbolic and social dimension (Adamson 4). Therefore, subjectivity is constituted by "structural links" which transcend it and can be conceptualized as different environments, groups, institutions, and communities. These "structural links" are perceived as an open system to the world and, therefore, are in a constant process of restructuring that moves beyond the duality of inwardness/outwardness into a dialectical expression of such tension (Adamson 5).

This structuring process is seen as a learning process because the "scheme of reference" is built by each subject, and it is an instrument used to perceive reality. This "scheme of reference" is defined as the assembly of knowledge and attitudes that each one has in mind and with which the subject interacts in relation to the world and with him/herself. Gladys Adamson comments that "this scheme of reference is what gives account of the reproduction of the conditions of existence that the subject carries out, including the reproduction of its situations of exploitation or subjugation" (5) (my translation). Through this thinking apparatus, we perceive, distinguish, feel, organize, and operate on reality. We can then affirm that the subject thinks, feels, and acts, all along transforming his/her environment. In this way, every "scheme of reference" inexorably belongs to a culture, in a determined social and historical moment (Vezzetti 277).

On the other hand, society is basically a specific culture that generates a network of meanings and establishes what the world, man and God are. But society is not a homogeneous structure; it works in a fragmented way, structuring the different social fields dialectically. That is why we can find narrative discontinuities, which imply institutional, symbolic, and discursive plurality. In conclusion, we can argue that subjectivity emerges from specific institutions, in a specific context. Moreover, society is basically composed of networks of relations structured around linguistic, economic, technological, and power relations. It is for that reason that institutional logic and discursive logic are in confrontation. Therefore we can speak of a plurality of subjectivities in the framework of a culture, where "common sense" is articulated with the logic of the institutional power, which is generated within the culture, structuring the subject in connection with the different institutional frameworks. These ideas provide a characterization of contemporary subjectivity, and at the same time they allow an analogical interpretation of the culture of the baroque. This analogy also works in the other direction, connecting the first modernity that the Baroque constitutes with our own late modernity.

From the perspective of the subjects, the Baroque reveals a series of contradictions. While it is a culture that responded to the actions of the most active dominant groups of the society, which Maravall called the "monarcho-seigniorial complex," we can recognize in it many social discontinuities, despite the relative homogeneity of minds and bodies. At the end of the sixteenth century, Europeans were experiencing many critical situations. Besides the material crisis, there was an epistemic crisis: the ways in which people knew reality and connected with it were distorted. In Pichon Riviere's terms, even though the institutional orthodoxy was at play, baroque subjects were facing the crisis with their own "scheme of references," or, more precisely, they were facing the virtual collapse of their representations of certainty and meaning. At the basis of the crisis was a shift in terms of the designated social places that the individual was experiencing. According to Maravall, "a social crisis is something that affects stratification and is deemed to be a disorder, confusion, inasmuch as it appears as a turbulence that threatens the schema of internal distribution of the society in which ones lives" ("From the Renaissance" 28). The picaresque is a literary expression of this crisis, because the *pícaro* is showing the contradictions of an urban society but within a "feudal" social structure.

Tracking this crisis of common sense, I might mention the skepticism that was generated by the relative failure of the Renaissance with reforms, as highlighted by Maravall:

Many negative events struck the consciousness that the course of the previous epoch had awakened: the economic recession and poverty imposed at the end of the sixteenth century; the disorderliness and unrest created by repeated conflicts between states; the moral confusion deriving from the preceding epoch of expansion; and the unjustifiable conduct of the Church and the critiques it promoted, giving rise either to laxity or to pathological attitudes of exacerbated intolerance. (*Culture* 27)

This skepticism was patent in the destruction of the concept of the Sacred Empire and the universality of Christianity, essential ideas that were developed through a long process which was crucial for the identity of Europe.

At the same time, the "revolution of the heavens" caused by the new astronomy had destroyed the cosmological paradigm that was dominant since ancient times. Moreover, along with the rupture of the geocentric system, the collapse of the circular model was relevant for the ideological implications that this model had. According to Severo Sarduy, "such was the theological connotation, the iconographic authority of the circle, a perfect and natural form, that when Kepler found that Mars does not describe a circle but an ellipse in its orbit around the Sun, he tried to refuse his own observations" (55). In this framework of material and epistemic crisis, the Baroque appears as a time for the search and reconstruction of a unity that was lost in terms of religion and politics, and also in terms of the unity that allows people to understand and signify human experience.

These efforts to find a center that could articulate human experiences emerge in a context of conflict with the previous traditions, especially the Scholastic one. This search for unity intended to go beyond the biases of imagination and senses that had infiltrated philosophy, religion, and politics, especially during the Renaissance. Most baroque philosophers embraced this search for knowledge that allows a perception of the unification of fragmentation, beneath the assumption that this unity could provide harmony. They worked with the tacit hope that this knowledge of reality, based in pure understanding, could reunify the fragmentation because it functioned under the solid foundations of reason. As a consequence, one encounters the paradox of an institutional context where orthodox discourses prevail, but at the same time are challenged by heterodox ideas. This paradox can be traced in different cultural fields that directly affect the manner in which subjects are in the world as individuals and members of a social order. I will focus briefly on some important philosophical ideas which were affected by these tensions.

The Baroque appeared as a moment in which different orders were tested, but in all of them faith was gradually replaced by reason as the central element to explain and unify reality. The medieval ideal of "believe in order to understand" lost its meaning, because the comprehension of reality would now follow the path of reason, with its unique and independent processes. This reason would gradually acquire soteriological functions, in a process fully completed in the Enlightenment. Each of these approaches defined their own salvific process, creating a series of oppositions that implied different levels of meaning: sense-understanding; imagination-reality; chaos-cosmos; dream state-vigil; nature-grace. According to Fuentes Herrero, "these oppositions are an expression of this order or modes of representing and supporting such orders" (4). In that context new narrations about Genesis and the Apocalypse emerged, bringing possible readings about origins and endings, a certain kind of teleological project.

The philosophy of Descartes meant a shift from the epistemological paradigm that was dominant since ancient times. For Scholasticism truth was a form of grace, a revelation from a deity who protected the individual from insecurity and anguish. A hierarchical character of knowledge and the moral organization of reality emerged from this revelation. Descartes found in mathematics a series of rules of universal applicability to any hypothetical-deductive analysis, and from his "cogito" he ordered the first principle of philosophy. Additionally, as has been pointed out by Egginton, "with Descartes, the modern philosophical tradition has described the grammatical, first person subject as the foundation of all possible knowledge, thereby making the world in which the subject and all the other thinking and perceiving beings dwell a secondary object, a 'standing reserve' of resources in which the subject moves about, picking and choosing at will and constructing his or her own surroundings, and a 'world picture'" (*How the World* 125).

The same interest in the reunification of reality can be found in Baruch Spinoza, despite the fact that he had interpreted Cartesian concepts in a different way. In his philosophy there is no exterior revelation of truth from God or as a result of an encyclopedic synthesis of sciences; instead, truth will arise from one's own inquiry. According to the Dutch thinker, the individual must originate his or her understanding of reality in the idea that can express exactly the whole nature, deriving all judgments from this one. This idea operates as a foundation of human knowledge, and is centered in the idea of God, whom he defines as "a substance consisting of infinite attributes, each of which expresses an eternal and infinite essence" (*Ethics* I def. 6). In Spinoza's system God is not the creator or lawgiver through a revelation, "he is the nature and he coincides with the world; he is power, infinite if considered at the level of nature as a whole, finite if seen at the level of finite being" (Ariew 235). This first idea is the beginning of his theory of knowledge and is based on the suggestion that God is the one and only reality, and it is present in our thinking (Jaspers 197).

These philosophic ideas were circulating in the baroque world, challenging the strict limits established by the authorities, who kept a rigid control of the spread of new doctrines, while the official institutions were developing "extensive programs of education or indoctrination (from catechism to sermons, to sacramental plays, and so on)" (Castillo and Spadaccini 195). In that context, orthodoxy and heterodoxy could be found in the same individual. Some subjects were able to support the orthodox discourses institutionally, while in many ways their intellectual products might contradict what was politically correct.

Without denying the conservative and guided character assigned by Maravall to the culture of the Baroque, I believe that Spanish baroque subjects, when expressing themselves, convey the discontinuities of "common sense." As Fernando R. de la Flor has argued, "the particularity of the Hispanic baroque resides in the declared capacity of its expressive system to go against any establishment. During the baroque era, Spanish society had the ability to deconstruct and pervert, in the first place, what can be conceived as interests of class, that actually govern that system and are paradoxically supported by them, proclaiming a dual adhesion" (19) (my translation).

Among the many writers of the Spanish Golden Age who could exemplify this paradoxical tension, I have chosen Baltasar Gracián and Francisco de Quevedo, the first a member of the Jesuit Order and the latter a member of the Order of Santiago, and a gentleman at the royal court. While these writers can be considered to be part of the hegemonic institutions of seventeenth-century Spain, in their writings they simultaneously support and challenge the status quo.

In Quevedo as well as in Gracián one can find characteristic topics of baroque literature: the madness of the world, the world upside down, the confusing labyrinth, the world as a stage, the world as hostelry, and the world as large plaza, all of which represent the mutability of human experience. As Maravall says, "if we regard assertion that everything changes, one judges that everything in the world is found to be distorted, it is because an underlying rational structure exists whose alteration allows for considering the existence of disorder: if one can speak of the world upside down it is because it can be right-side up. Quevedo's satirical *Discursos* (Discourses) and *Sueños* (Dreams) played on the basis of that structure" (*Culture* 152). These discourses are conservative in general, but they allow other readings: if this world ruled by the monarchical-seigniorial complex is upside down, can a different world be considered?

In "The World from Inside," Quevedo presents an interesting example of his skepticism: "Dícelo así el doctísimo Francisco Sánchez, médico y filósofo, en su libro cuyo título es *Nihil Scitur*. No se sabe nada. En el mundo hay algunos que no saben nada y estudian para saber, y éstos tienen buenos deseos y vano ejercicio: porque, al cabo, sólo les sirve el estudio de conocer cómo toda la verdad le quedan ignorando" (181) (That is how the most learned doctor and philosopher Francisco Sánchez puts the argument in his book entitled *Nihil Scitur*, where he comes to the same conclusion: there are some men in this world who know nothing and study in order to learn something. Their aims are laudable, but a waste of time, for in the last analysis their efforts will only reveal how unknown [and unknowable] the truth really is). He then characterizes different approaches to the truth in a satirical and sarcastic way. This extreme skepticism seems to be in conflict with the Scholastic realism dominant in Spanish culture, which reads the truth as *adecuatio rei ad intelectum*, since the Scholastics had confidence that the human intellect could achieve truth with certainty, since, according to St. Thomas Aquinas, "natural reason cannot be contrary to the truth of the faith" (*Contra Gentiles* i.9). Differing with this Scholastic idea, Quevedo offers his skepticism, a perception of reality that can be unorthodox, for the reason that it can deconstruct the order of revealed truths.

Another ambiguous element present in Quevedo's work is his satirical approach to ecclesiastical doctrine, including the eschatological problems present in "The Dream of the Last Judgment." The general milieu of this text presents a carnivalesque and grotesque approach, as was pointed out by Soraya Nogueira: "the last presence of life and death and the inversion of the social roles are presented in the *Sueños* as the model of the upside-down world, a central idea of the carnivalesque vision of the world" (3) (my translation).[3] The narrator witnesses the last Judgment from a distance, similarly to St. John in the Book of Revelation, but he is not part of the scene. The descriptions give the impression of a profanation of one the most sacred moments for the Christian narrative.

On the other hand, in the parade of the penitent, the list of damned citizens related to the administration of power—constable, lawyers, and members of the court is clear. "Don Fulano" is a good example, because even though he is a nobleman and a knight, he was damned like anyone else: "Preguntóle un portero, de parte de Dios, si era hombre; y él respondió con grandes cortesías que sí, y que por más señas se llamaba Don Fulano, a fe de caballero. Rióse un diablo y dijo: De codicia es el mancebo para el infierno. Preguntáronle qué pretendía y respondió: Ser salvado. Y fue remitido a los diablos para que le moliesen. Y él sólo reparó en que le ajarían el cuello" (56) (So straightaway Don Fulano was asked what it was he sought there. 'Why, to be saved,' was his reply. At which time he was immediately handed over to the devils for a good flogging, to which his only objection was that they might spoil his ruff) (57). In a culture where eternal salvation was so important, these satirical discourses can expose the "upside-down" state of the dominant order.

According to Rivers, "Quevedo was acutely aware of what he considered to be the degeneration of Spanish society. He constantly satirized Spaniards of all social ranks, and was deeply preoccupied with what he saw as the moral and political decline of the Spanish monarchy" (17). But in *Sueños,* social differences seem to disappear, and we can find different kinds of individuals (gentlemen, rich Genoese, apothecaries, barbers, lawyers, and even pious ladies of the court), dealing with the same problems, in the same ways. The dissolution of social boundaries in the text has moral connotations and argues for a change in social behaviors. Yet, this vision could imply a more egalitarian vision of society, because class differences are all dissolved when faced with God's justice. Under these circumstances it is possible to conclude that eternal salvation is a personal problem and, as a result, class and salvation are not associated.

Providencia de Dios (Providence of God) is another good example of these discontinuities in Quevedo's writings. In this didactic text, with a connection to his stoicism, Quevedo is arguing with an atheist, "one of those men without God," and he is trying to demonstrate the existence of God, the immortality of the human soul, and that the Holy Providence is in control of the world. As Maricarmen Martínez has shown, Quevedo begins his argument with the demonstration of the immortality of the human soul based on its rationality: "Empezaré con la inmortalidad del alma para que enterado el hombre de sí mismo en la mejor parte, sea capaz de esotras verdades" (1389) (I will start with the immortality of the human soul, because when man recognizes this reality in his interiority, he will be able to understand the other truths) (my translation). The first step in the demonstration is the affirmation of human rationality as a self-evident fact. But Quevedo is reformulating the Cartesian *cogito* within a Christian perspective, and his narrative is presented in connection with the dogma. Despite the fact that Quevedo's argument differs from the *cogito*, and his goals are in concordance with the status quo, he establishes the rational essence of the human soul as the first step of his reasoning, recognizing that human subjectivity is the first and most immediate experience for each single human being, a premise accepted by rationalist thinkers.

In Quevedo's text we can also trace the cosmological problems present in his time. In this case, Quevedo presents the same ambiguity that, in many ways, characterizes baroque subjectivity. According to J.J. Tato Puigcerver, Quevedo's writings incorporate the discussion of the respective theories of Copernicus and Galileo, which is an example of the reception of these disputes in the Spanish context. When facing this question, Quevedo seems to embrace an orthodox perspective, but we will see that his position is problematic. In *La Fortuna con Seso y La Hora de Todos* (The Fortune with Brains and Everybody's Hours) we read: "El sol se ha parado, la rueda de la fortuna, nunca" (quoted in Puigcerver

2-3) (The sun has stopped, while the Wheel of Fortune never has). This text is connected with the story narrated in the book of Joshua, from which one of the main arguments used by the enemies of the heliocentric theory was drawn. In *Virtud Militante* (Militant Virtue), Quevedo presents a similar perspective: "La obediencia del ímpetu del mar a la ley que se le escribió en la arena, y el peso de la tierra, que suspendida, se afirma inmoble" (1249) (The obedience that the strength of the sea passes to the law which was written for it on the sand; and the weight of the Earth, which, although suspended, affirms itself to be immobile) (my translation). Moreover, Tato Puigcerver comments that in *Virtud Militante* Quevedo refers to the condemnation of Galileo:

La misma naturaleza en el grande cuerpo de todo este mundo reconoce por movibles sus mayores partes y sus mejores miembros. ¿En qué seguridad permanente podrán estos bienes que se llaman raíces, afirmarse en quietud, si la tierra y el mar de que se rodean son movibles? Antes el propio movimiento es, y un continuo contraste. No digo que se mueva la tierra; sino que toda ella padece mudanzas. (1232)

(In all of the great body of this world, Nature recognizes itself as mobile in its greater parts and best members. In which permanent security could these goods that we call roots be calmly settled, if the land and the sea which surround them are mobile? Movement itself is a continuous contrast. I am not saying that Earth moves, but that all of it suffers changes.)

With the sentence "I am not saying that Earth moves," Quevedo seems to be expressing an orthodox perspective. But in *Gracias y desgracias del ojo del culo* (Adventures and Misadventures of the Anus), referring to the form of the anus, he says: "Pues en su forma circular como la esfera, y dividido en un diámetro o zodiaco como ella. Su sitio es en medio como el del sol" (95) (In its circular shape like the sphere, and it is divided in a diameter or zodiac like the sphere, the anus has its place in the middle like the sun). In this statement we can see a different perspective that shows the oscillation that Quevedo had at this point, affirming that the sun is in the "middle" as described by heliocentric theory. Despite the prevailing conception of Quevedo as a conservative example of the Spanish Baroque, we can conclude with Francisco Ayala that, while Quevedo embraced the orthodox doctrines of the Counter Reformation, his vision of the world revealed a radical nihilism, which expressed a chasm between his expressed convictions and his essential perception of the world (210).

Similarly, Gracián presents a deep concern with the madness of the world, and his criticism surpasses the conservative framework of his culture, to propose an accommodative and discrepant morality. In aphorism 14 of his *Oráculo manual y arte de prudencia*, he says: "La realidad y el modo. No basta la substancia, requiérese también la circunstancia. Todo lo gasta el modo, hasta la justicia y razón" (Both reality and manner. Substance is not "stance" enough. The wrong manner turns everything sour, even justice and reason). However, in Scholasticism, the circumstance is an accident of time, place or mode; the historicity of the substance is introduced by this idea that everything is being spent. The Scholastics did not ignore change, but they preferred fulfilled results, like a perfect ethics or a "sacred" society.

But, according to Gracián, the external code of ethics is not enough to sustain a good and clever behavior in society, and if it is the case, a general moral code, applicable to every situation and circumstance as was proposed by the Church, is almost impossible. In ecclesiastic doctrine, ethics is a consequence of the freedom that God granted to human beings. As a result of sin, people need grace to clarify the options in their intellect that are related to the God's plan, because they are disposed to good and evil. In this ethical system, the option is external and—preexisting the human being—universal, which are characteristics contrary to Gracián's ethics. William Egginton sees other important differences between those ethics. Gracián's moral principles did not recognize the structure of a concentric world, where truth is guaranteed by a center that reveals this truth. Moreover, "what is most important to remember is that the center is not determined by any metaphysical presence; for Gracián, God does not enter the picture" (Egginton, "Gracián" 161). Gracián presents a secular morality and, as Maravall points out, "what is certain is that Gracián is the first writer to consider life as a radical and inexorable reality on which everything else depends" (quoted by Egginton, "Gracián" 161). In his *Oráculo manual*, Gracián insists on the mutability of reality. This is why his moral advice can change depending on the circumstances. Here ontology is not the basis for ethics.

In the first aphorism, Gracián affirms that "Todo está en su punto, y el ser persona es el mayor. Más se requiere hoy para un sabio, que antiguamente para siete; y más es menester para tratar con un solo hombre en estos tiempos que con todo un pueblo en los passados" (All has reached perfection and becoming a true person is the greatest of all. It takes more to make one sage today than it did to make the seven of Greece. And you need more resources to deal with a single person these days than with an entire nation in times past.) In this text, Gracián is sketching an autonomous ethics, developed in the dialectic of daily life and a moral theory that depends on circumstances and on other individuals.

This is also expressed in aphorism 112:

> Ganar la pía afición, que aun la primera y suma Causa en sus mayores assuntos la previene y la dispone. Éntrese por el afecto al concepto. Algunos se fían tanto del valor, que desestiman la diligencia; pero la atención sabe bien que es grande el rodeo de solos los méritos, si no se ayudan de favor. Todo lo facilita y suple la benevolencia; no siempre supone las prendas, sino que las pone, como el valor, la entereza, la sabiduría, hasta la discreción. Nunca ve las fealdades, porque no las querría ver. Nace de ordinario de la correspondencia material en genio, nación, parentesco, patria y empleo. La formal es más sublime en prendas, obligaciones, reputación, meritos. Toda la dificultad es ganarla, que con facilidad se conserva. Puédese diligenciar, y saberse valer della.

> (Even the first and highest Cause, in the important matters, does things this way. Reputation is purchased with affection. Some trust so much in their own worth that they make light of diligence. But the prudent person knows very well that merit can take a shortcut if helped by favor. Benevolence makes everything easier and compensates for whatever is lacking: courage, integrity, wisdom, and even discretion. It never sees ugliness, for it doesn't want to. It is usually born from similarity of temperament, race, family, country, or occupation. In the spiritual realm, benevolence bestows talent, favor, reputation, and merit. Once one wins it—and this is difficult—it is easily kept. You can make an effort to win it, but you must also know how to use it.)

In addition, the concept of *virtù* is transformed in Gracián's ethics; the individual is the producer of his/her genealogy, and "that production now depends upon the use of practical knowledge framed by prudence; by the ability to exercise a discursive constraint and, if need be, to effect the silencing of one's voice" (Spadaccini and Talens xi), as is expressed in the aphorism 181: "Sin mentir, no decir todas las verdades" (Don't lie, but don't tell the whole truth).

However, what is most relevant is Gracián's distinction between reality and appearances, which again contrasts with Scholasticism. In aphorism 99 we can trace his theory of knowledge: "Realidad y apariencia. Las cosas no passan por lo que son, sino por lo que parecen. Son raros los que moran por dentro, y muchos los que se pagan de lo aparente. No basta tener razón con cara de malicia" (Reality and appearance. Things pass for what they seem, not for what they are. Only rarely do people look into them, and many are satisfied with appearances. It isn't enough to be right if your face looks malicious and wrong). As I have already said, this confusion is unorthodox; it is a "disorder" that is altering the order created by tradition. More "dangerous" still is the delegation of "discernment" to the individual.

In this essay, I have tried to establish the contradictory functions of certain discourses, which I conceive as a result of the models of subjectivity present in the Spanish Baroque. Through an examination of Gracián's and Quevedo's texts I have sought to trace the ambiguity of their discourses, which reveals their contradictory understanding of the world. We can argue that their perceptions of the world were in crisis with the discourses portrayed by the monarcho-seigniorial segments of society, even though they were members of the monarcho-seigniorial complex. In fact, Quevedo represented "both traditional and emerging forms of the subject and resultant contradictions, continues to attract the attention of contemporary criticism because it represents one limited textual space in which an early form of modern subjectivity was tentatively worked out" (Mariscal 100). We can conclude that through this effort Quevedo was creating dissonant voices within his institutional context. In Gracián these discontinuities are more evident since he had the explicit goal to rewrite his world practically, emending the monstrosity of the "century" that had perverted the divine order (Checa 208).

On the one hand, during this perplex time that we call the Baroque, the individual had to deal with a cultural complex, specifically with institutions supported by active groups (traditional elite) that were responding against the growth of social and geographical mobility. The political rationale for such behavior was the evidence that this mobility was challenging their privileges (Egginton, *How the World* 154). On the other hand, the disappointment of the systems of representation and signification was creating a dual response in the subjects, because they felt the need to reevaluate their "schemes of reference," the common sense of their time, in order to achieve a better understanding of their world. In summary, they were in many ways loyal to their institutions, but as subjects they revealed the split of their schemes of reference, allowing a heterodox reception of their texts. One might say, with Quevedo, that they show the confusion of individuals framed by a world that seems to be furious.

Notes

1.   Although the Treaty granted religious tolerance for the different Christian groups, the possession of spiritual territories was settled by a compromise, and 1624 was the standard year in order to decide if a land was going to be Catholic or Protestant; enforcing

that meant the people who did not have the possibility to emigrate could not follow personal beliefs.

2. Enrique Pichon Riviere (1907–77) was a Swiss-Argentine psychiatrist and psycho-analyst. He founded the School of Social Psychology in Argentina, which has had a large influence in different academic fields in several Latin American countries.

3. "La presencia última de la vida y de la muerte y la inversión de papeles sociales son presentados en los *Sueños* como el modelo fundador del mundo al revés, idea donde se basa la visión del mundo carnavalesco."

Works Cited

Adamson, Gladis. "Concepción de Subjetividad en E. P. Riviere." *Textos*. Buenos Aires, Escuela de Psicología Social del Sur: 2002. <http://www.psicosocialdelsur.com.ar/textos/concepcion.html>.

Aquinas, St. Thomas. "Of God and His Creatures, an Annotated Translation of the Summa Contra Gentiles." Ed. Joseph Rickaby. London: Burns and Oates, 1905.

Ariew, Roger, et al. *Historical Dictionary of Descartes and Cartesian Philosophy*. Lanham: The Scarecrow Press, 2003.

Ayala, Francisco. *Cervantes y Quevedo*. Barcelona: Seix Barral, 1974.

Castillo, David, and Nicholas Spadaccini. "Models of Subjectivity in Early Modern Spain." *Subjectivity in Early Modern Spain*. Ed. Óscar Pereira Zazo. *Journal of Interdisciplinary Literary Studies*. Vol. 6.2. (1994): 185-204.

Checha, Jorge. "Figuraciones de lo monstruoso: Quevedo y Gracián." *La Perinola: Revista de Investigación Quevediana*. Vol. 2: 195-211.

Egginton, William. *How the World Became a Stage: Presence, Theatricality, and the Question of Modernity*. Albany: State University of New York Press, 2003.

_____. "Gracián and the Emergence of the Modern Subject." *Rhetoric and Politics: Baltasar Gracián and the New World Order*. Ed. Nicholas Spadaccini and Jenaro Talens. Hispanic Isues 14. Minneapolis: University of of Minnesota Press, 1997. 151-69.

Fuentes Herrero, José Luis. "Spinoza: Una filosofía barroca." *Logos*: Universidad de La-Salle N 69 Mexico Sep-Dic 1995. <http://www.hemerodigital.unam.mx/ANUIES/lasalle/logos/69/sec_5.htm>.

Gracián, Baltasar. *The Art of Wordly Wisdom. A Pocket Oracle*. Trans. Christopher Maurer. New York: Doubleday Dell, 1991.

_____. *Oráculo manual y arte de prudencia*. Ed. Emilio Blanco. Madrid: Cátedra, 2000.

Jaspers, Karl. *Spinoza*. Ed. Annah Arendt. New York: Harvest/HBJ Book, 1974.

Maravall, José Antonio. *La cultura del barroco: Análisis de una estructura histórica*. Barcelona: Ariel, 1975.

_____. "From the Renaissance to the Baroque: The Diphasic Schema of a Social Crisis." *Literature Among Discourses. The Spanish Golden Age*. Ed. Wlad Godzich and Nicholas Spadaccini. Minneapolis: University of Minnesota Press, 1986. 3-40.

Mariscal, George. *Contradictory Subjects: Quevedo, Cervantes, and Seventeenth-Century Spanish Culture*. Ithaca, N.Y.: Cornell University Press, 1991.

Martinez, Mariacarmen. "Dualismo metafísico e inmortalidad del alma en *Providencia de Dios* de Quevedo." *Espéculo: Revista de Estudios Literarios*. Universidad Complutense de Madrid. Madrid, 2000. <http://members.fortunecity.com/mundopoesia2/articulos/dualismometafisicoe inmortalidaddelalma.htm>.

Nogueira, Soraya "Audición, visión y carnavalización en los Sueños de Quevedo." *Ciber-Letras: Journal of Literary Criticism and Culture* 8. Lehman College, CUNY New York, December 2002. <http://www.lehman.cuny.edu/faculty/guinazu/ciberletras/index_files/v08.html>.

Rivas, Elias. "Language and Reality in Quevedo's Sonnets." *Quevedo in Perspective: Eleven Essays for the Quadracentennial*. Ed. James Iffland. Newark: Juan de La Cuesta, 1982. 17-32.

Rodríguez de la Flor, Fernando. *Barroco. Representación e ideología en el mundo hispánico (1580-1680)*. Madrid: Cátedra, 2002.

Quevedo, Francisco de. *Obras Completas 1: Obra en prosa*. Ed. Felicidad Buendía. Madrid: Aguilar, 1969.

_____. *Dreams and Discourses*. Ed. and trans. R. K. Britton. Warminster: Aris & Phillips Ltd., 1989.

Sarduy, Severo. *Barroco*. Buenos Aires: Editorial Sudamericana, 1974.

Spinoza, Benedictus de. *Ethics*. Ed. G.H.R. Parkinson. London: J.M. Dent & Son Ltd., 1989.

Spadaccini, Nicholas and Jenaro Talens. "Introduction: The Practice of Worldly Wisdom: Rereading Gracián from the New World Order." *Rethoric and Politics: Baltasar Gracián and the New World Order*. Ed. Nicholas Spadaccini and Jenaro Talens. Hispanic Isues 14. Minneapolis: University of Minnesota Press, 1997. ix-xxxii.

Tato Puigcerver, J.J. "Una nota sobre Quevedo, Copérnico y Galileo." *Espéculo: Revista de Estudios Literarios*. Madrid, Universidad Complutense de Madrid: 2000. <http://www.ucm.es/info/especulo/numero16/galileo.html>.

Vezzetti, Hugo. *Aventuras de Freud en el país de los argentinos: De José Ingenieros a Enrique Pichon-Riviére*. Buenos Aires: Paidós, 1996.

Villari, Rosario Ed. *Baroque Personae*. Trans. Lydia G. Cochrane. Chicago: University of Chicago Press, 1995.

Horror (Vacui): The Baroque Condition

David R. Castillo

The term *horror vacui* evokes images of crowded walls and convoluted mold-ings, the face of the Baroque in its exquisite integration of all artistic crafts. Decorative excess is perhaps the most common—and certainly the most cited— manifestation of baroque expressionism, but one should not lose sight of the fact that baroque architects, artists and authors could also cultivate extreme simplic-ity. In fact, severe simplicity could be just as effective in making the baroque statement. According to José Antonio Maravall, the defining aesthetic impulse of the Baroque is not superabundance, but the pursuit of the *extreme*. Whether the writer or artist cultivates exuberance or holds to a severe simplicity of form, the key is to pursue either route to the extreme. Thus, an empty wall would be as emblematically baroque as an excessively decorated one, as long as it is per-ceived to be empty *in the extreme*, and therefore, to convey the shock of extreme emptiness. On the other hand, a wall that has been completely covered over might call attention to what is hidden. We could think of the excess material in psychoanalytic terms as the mark of compulsive or idiosyncratic behavior, the "cover-up." In this sense, *horror vacui* may be taken to mean something other than a mere cult of exuberance and decorative excess, a more fundamental feel-ing of attraction/revulsion concerning the idea of absence. This notion makes it possible to think of the Baroque as a period concept (à la Maravall), and also as an ongoing "condition" of modernity triggered by a pervasive sense of loss of meaning and a paradoxical longing for the Absolute.

The conviction that the baroque sense of loss is central to the aesthetics of modernity is at the core of Walter Benjamin's seminal work *The Origin of German Tragic Drama.* As Bryan Turner has pointed out, the centerpiece of Benjamin's argument is that "allegory, especially allegories about fate, death and melancholy, is the principle element in the aesthetic of modernity and has its archeological origins in the forgotten and obscured past of modernity—the baroque" (7). In her remarkable book *Baroque Reason: The Aesthetics of Modernity* (1994), Christine Buci-Glucksmann elaborates on Benjamin's notions in arguing that baroque aesthetics "testified to the preeminence of the fragment over the whole, of a destructive principle over a constructive principle, of feeling, as an *excavation of an absence,* over reason as domination" (71, my emphasis). She noted that baroque melancholy is exemplified in the recurrent images of the "world upside down" that permeate the work of seventeenth-century authors and in their fascination with death and decay.[1]

In Spain, baroque writers and artists, from Francisco de Quevedo and Calderón de la Barca to María de Zayas and Valdés Leal, seem eager to capitalize on the shock value of all manner of oddities: mutilated and deformed bodies, spectral visions, miraculous apparitions, and so on. They may have found inspiration for their creative endeavors in the local news. The first European "newspapers," including the Spanish *Avisos* and *Anales de Madrid,* were tabloid-like publications that featured stories of miracles, martyrdoms, gruesome crimes, and monstrosities. Maravall sees this passion for outlandish novelties as a sign of the times or, more precisely, as a mark of "a mental atmosphere" all throughout seventeenth-century Europe (*Culture* 229). He often focuses on the propagandistic possibilities of visual rarities.

On the other hand, in the specific case of optical experiments, Jacques Lacan (1981) and Slavoj Zizek (1989; 2000) have pointed out the destabilizing potential of the visual puzzles associated with the curious perspective, also known in the second half of the seventeenth century as anamorphoses. According to Lacan, the anamorphic form, so dear to baroque painters and authors, is fundamentally unsettling insofar as it reveals the interdependence of gaze and meaning. As Zizek writes: "A part of the perceived scene is distorted in such a way that it acquires its proper contours only from the specific viewpoint from which the remaining reality is blurred [. . .] We thus become aware that reality already involves our gaze, that this gaze is *included* in the scene we are observing" (*The Ticklish Subject* 78). In calling attention to the mechanism that makes the picture work, anamorphic puzzles remind us that *meaning* contains a kernel of arbitrariness and that *reality* is always tainted by the "polluting" presence of our own gaze.[2] The philosophical implications of anamorphosis concerning the unstable and artificial nature of reality are echoed in those literary and philosophical devices that best express what Turner calls the destitute or ruined nature of the modern world: montage, pastiche, allegory and parody, and metaphors such as the ruin, the library, the labyrinth and the artifice. These observations allow Turner to conclude that the baroque period was acutely aware of "the artificial, socially constructed nature of reality (its hyperreality) and the precarious, catastrophic, uncertain and hazardous nature of all human existence" (8).

The idea that material reality is an illusion or "colorful deception" (Sor Juana) that hides the face of death is characteristic of the anamorphic literature of disillusionment or *desengaño* and resonates well with the modern aesthetics of the sublime. Significantly, Maravall resorts to Schiller's conceptualization of the sublime to explain the baroque sense of doom and its obsessive attention to the darkest and most extreme aspects of reality (*Culture* 212–13). According to James Mirollo, the aesthetic of the sublime at work in gothic fiction finds its roots in the "age of the marvelous" (39). In fact, baroque *desengaño*, romantic horror and broadly speaking the *modern fantastic* produce similar shifts in perspective. As Eric Rabkin writes in *The Fantastic in Literature* (1976): "The truly fantastic occurs when the ground rules of a narrative are forced to make a 180 degree reversal, when prevailing perspectives are directly contradicted" (12). This premise is also central to Rosemary Jackson's approach to horror and the fantastic in *Fantasy: The Literature of Subversion* (1981). As a subspecies of the fantastic mode, horror fiction foregrounds "problems of apprehension (in the double sense of perceiving and of fearing) [. . .], everything becomes equivocal, blurred, 'double,' out of focus" (49). Jackson goes on to argue that while traditional fantasies (romances for example) express a longing for a meaningful world, the modern fantastic foregrounds meaninglessness, revealing a dark void inside the apparent fullness of reality (158).[3]

The paradoxical drive of modern fantasies is ultimately the result of the severance of *words* from the world of *things*, as Foucault would have it (see *The Order of Things*). Once the "magical thread" that connected words with things has been cut, the *real* is literally unnamable, and therefore, may only be encountered traumatically outside of the symbolic order. Nature will now be perceived, not as a living organism, but as "dead matter" (Merchant). Hence, the *marvelous* return of the Numinous (Manuel Aguirre) in horror fiction engenders what Lovecraft calls "cosmic fear," a mixture of awe, wonder and revulsion. To be sure, Lovecraft thinks of "cosmic fear" as a reaction against the scientific positivism of the late 1800s and early 1900s and its "callous rationalism" (the expression is from "The Call of Cthulhu"); yet, the notion seems to capture the essence of the baroque response to the objectification of the world, the increased monetarization of the economy, and its accompanying mechanization of human relations. While the modern world is increasingly objectified and *voided of transcendence* (*desdivinizado*, as Maravall aptly puts it in *El mundo social de La Celestina*), the "cosmic fear" invoked in dark fantasies—from baroque and romantic literature to present-day blockbuster movies and paperbacks—expresses a deep-felt desire to reclaim the Numinous, to make it *present*, and an equally strong impulse to negate it, to exclude it from our fortified field of rational certainties (see Manuel Aguirre).

I intend to build on these notions here in arguing that baroque expressionism and the aesthetics of *the modern fantastic* (Jackson) tell the tale of modernity from the symptomatic perspective of the most fundamental of all modern fears: horror vacui. I will first discuss the construction of Self as "character" and the manipulative possibilities of this form of social identification as exemplified in baroque theater and Baltasar Gracián's writings. I will then try to show how the shock of horror (specifically Zayas' brand of horror) uncovers the dark side of conventional (patriarchal) forms of Self-containment. Finally, I will argue that Cervantes' exemplary novel *El coloquio de los perros* may be seen as a *fantastic tale* (Todorov, Jackson) that challenges readers to rethink the nature of the text, the world and their respective limits and limitations.

William Egginton has recently argued that the defining feature of modernity is a fundamental shift in our mode of being-in-the-world (Heidegger), a shift that may be understood as a progressive privileging of *theatricality* over *presence*.[4] According to Egginton, the seed of theatricality is planted with the invention of *character*, which he attributes to Spanish dramatist Juan de la Encina. The term character "designates an entity for which there was, literally, no space in medieval spectacle. This is so because a character inhabits not a full, impressionable space, but an abstract, empty space" (61). Character-play is not something that happens just on stage; rather, character-play will progressively become—and this is the core of Egginton's argument—our primary mode of experiencing ourselves and others, i.e., our individual and collective mode of being in the modern world. We *identify as characters* with institutions and their constituents. We don't have to see the king, for example, in order to think of ourselves as his subjects, i.e., in order *to act as if* we are his subjects. Significantly, by the time of Philip II, the royal seal had replaced the crown as the primary signifier of royalty (see Schramm 76–77). Of course the crown can only work in the presence of the monarch, in a relation of visual continuity with him. The trick now is to identify with the monarch, not in his presence, but in his absence. The mark of the royal seal allows for this type of *identification in absentia* to take place. It is precisely in this *acting out* our characters, our social roles, that we effectively become subjects.[5]

The ideological significance of this shift is perhaps best illustrated in plays such as Calderón's *El alcalde de Zalamea*. As archetypal representations of the social character of the wealthy peasant, Pedro Crespo and his peers are given the directive to be honorable—that is, to act as if they have an "honor" to live by and protect. But for them to invest in/identify with their new role as honorable subjects of the Spanish Crown, they have to (mis)perceive this directive as a matter of personal choice. This is, of course, the ideological fantasy that is being projected in *El alcalde de Zalamea*, as well as in Lope's *Peribáñez y el comendador de Ocaña*, *El mejor alcalde, el rey*, and *El villano en su rincón*, among others. What we (post)modern citizens of the nation-state share with Pedro Crespo and the commoners that he *characterizes* as honorable subjects of the king is the experience of theatricality. In essence, our reality is equally *theatrical*.

Baltasar Gracián gets to the heart of the question in his defense of art over nature: "Es el arte complemento de la naturaleza y un otro segundo ser que por extremo la hermosea y aún pretende excederla en sus obras. Préciase de haber añadido *un otro mundo artificial* al primero. Suple de ordinario los descuidos de la naturaleza, perfeccionándola en todo, que sin este socorro del artificio, quedará inculta y grosera" (*El criticón* I, 8, my emphasis) (Art is the complement of nature, a second being that embellishes it *in the extreme*, and it even aims to surpass it in its works. It has proudly added another *artificial world* to the first one. It ordinarily covers the mistakes of nature, perfecting it in such a way that without this aid of the artifice, it [nature] would remain unrefined and vulgar). Gracián takes his reader on an allegorical pilgrimage of self-discovery or self-realization (literally a journey of self-construction), from the cavernous pits of unrefined nature to the luminous heights of courtly wisdom. According to Gracián, we are not born 'fully made' or complete; rather, we become *personas* (refined subjects, courtly characters) as we master elaborate techniques of self-representation.[6] As the Jesuit explains in *El discreto*, a wise self-representation in the courtly theaters of heroism ("teatros de la heroicidad") engenders a second (brighter) being: "Hay sujetos bizarros en quienes lo poco luce mucho, hasta admirar [. . .]; al contrario, hombres vimos eminentes que, por faltarles realce no parecieron la mitad [. . .] De suerte que la ostentación da el verdadero lucimiento a las heroicas prendas y como un segundo ser" (13) (There are gallant subjects who make their precarious qualities visible and admirable [. . .]; on the contrary, we saw eminent men who, lacking representational skills, shone very little [. . .] Thus, ostentation endows heroic qualities with true brightness, something like a second being).

In the introduction to their edited volume on Gracián (1997), Nicholas Spadaccini and Jenaro Talens reflect on the possible reasons behind the appearance of *The Art of Worldly Wisdom: A Pocket Oracle* (1992) on the *New York Times* best-sellers list. The basic question is: "What does a seventeenth-century Jesuit thinker mean to a postmodern reader here and now, at the end of the millennium?" (xii). Their essay helps explain the functional effectiveness of Gracián's "moral maxims" in the theaters of Silicon Valley and Wall Street. These maxims include the need to identify and follow one's self interest, to manipulate appearances and accommodate them to current circumstances, and to carefully study other subjects in order to figure out how to subjugate their will. As Gracián writes in *El héroe*: "Poco es conquistar el entendimiento si no se gana la voluntad, y mucho rendir con la admiración la afición juntamente" (12) (Conquering minds has little value if wills are not subjugated. Much has been accomplished, however, when the will has been rendered along with admiration). The moralist insists on this all-important aspect of public life in *Oráculo manual*, when he says that the greatest achievement of a man of reputation is his victory over hearts: "Es gran victoria coger los corazones" (122) (It is a great victory to capture hearts).

This conception of the self underscores the fundamental plasticity of the modern subject, as well as the manipulative possibilities that come with it. As Maravall says, "by encountering himself or herself always in a process of realization the individual can act on the self, and others can act formatively on this individual" (*Culture* 169). The notion that top executives and power brokers may still read Gracián's *Oraculo manual y arte de prudencia* as a pocket oracle of practical wisdom suggests that there is a basic continuity between the present world of simulacra and the baroque "theaters of heroism." As Slavoj Zizek has recently noted, the (post)modern pressure to assert our uniqueness and be "all we can be," shifting between increasingly idiosyncratic modes of behavior, hobbies and dress codes, is clearly theatrical in nature. The injunction to be our true Self is paradoxically a call to wear the "proper mask." In this sense, the (post)modern cult of "extreme individualization" may be seen as a paradigmatic form of horror vacui, since "what is behind the mask is ultimately nothing, a horrifying void they [postmodern subjects] are frantically trying to fill in with their compulsive activity" (*The Ticklish Subject* 373).

While much of modern literature has served to sustain and *fetishize* "character" as the unique expression of our essential being, our true Self (see Cixous), dark fantasies tend to question this ideological projection by revealing the void behind the mask. As Jackson writes: "It is the power of the fantastic to interrogate the category of character [. . .], this subversion of unities of 'self,' which constitutes the most radical transgressive function of the fantastic" (82–83). Our assumed character is our means of interaction with others in the modern world, and our "fortification" against the disintegrating forces of chaos and contingency. In their drive to reveal the arbitrariness of the conventions that define our individual and collective character, dark fantasies open up critical perspectives, even if they often hold to the belief that such "fortifications of man" (the expression is from Oliver Onion's "The Beckoning Fair One") are necessary defenses against the powers of darkness.[7]

Admittedly, a "topographical survey" of horror literature and film would show that in most cases the monstrous Thing that disturbs "our character" comes from the uncharted no-man's land that extends beyond the city walls or from the "parasitical" edges of the urban centers, outside the boundaries and controls of reason (see Monleón). While Jackson confirms the conservative slant of early gothic fantasies, she also notes a progressive internalization of the demonic, which would roughly correspond to the modern fantastic privileging of the *uncanny* over the *marvelous*.[8] Thus, by the turn of the nineteenth century, the works of Mary Shelley, R.L. Stevenson, H. G. Wells, and Edgar Allan Poe, among others, would stage far more complex explorations of the increasingly murky frontiers of reason. Something has gone terribly wrong when scientific reason (the ultimate fortification against the powers of darkness) engenders monsters such as Frankenstein, Mr. Hyde and the creatures of Dr. Moreau's island. It is not that "the monster comes when reason sleeps," but that "the dream of reason engenders monsters," as in Goya's *Capricho 43*: "El sueño de la razón produce monstrous" (The dream of reason produces monsters).

Jackson's notion that the demonic is progressively internalized in horror fiction seems to hold true, generally speaking, for the gothic period, but one has to be careful not to overstate this progressivist model beyond its precise social, historical, and cultural boundaries. We should keep in mind, for example, that many of today's literary and cinematic fantasies still mobilize the powers of the marvelous, perhaps as much as those of the uncanny. We must also resist the temptation to think of the marvelous as an inherently conservative or reactionary aesthetic choice, even if it is true that the cultivation of the marvelous in early gothic fiction generally served to reconfirm the dominant value system of Enlightened and post-Enlightened societies. In the twentieth century, some of the more celebrated Latin American storytellers, including Alejo Carpentier,

Gabriel García Márquez, and Julio Cortázar often mobilize the aesthetics of the marvelous against the myths of modernity. The cultivation of the marvelous is just as essential to recent neobaroque poetics and to the neobaroque narrative project of Italian novelist and theorist Umberto Eco.

In baroque Spain, best-selling novelist María de Zayas y Sotomayor consistently staged supernatural prodigies and preternatural marvels, including an array of incorruptible bodies, to interrogate, even to denounce, the code of honor, which is one of the fundamental pillars of the social system. While Zayas' graphic displays of female victimization are reminiscent of gothic literature and painting, her cultivation of the macabre responds to a different aesthetic logic. As Margaret Greer convincingly argues, the *feminine death* that Zayas displays in her second volume of novellas, *Desengaños amorosos* (1647), is tied to the doctrinal concern with "the good death." Greer distinguishes Zayas' quasi-ceremonial displays of female corpses from the iconography of the *memento mori* motif à la Valdés Leal.[9] Her basic argument is that the novelist's spectacular presentation of *corporeal feminine death* is not meant as a philosophical reflection of the spiritual truth of the world, but simply as a reminder of the physical and emotional death threat of amorous relationships (268).

We could say that if the Zayas spectacle of death is the final act in which "ultimate truth is written in the body" (Greer 268), this truth has to do with the inescapable violence of the symbolic law. As women are violated, battered, stabbed, poisoned, strangled, immured, beheaded, and bled to death in order to satisfy honor's unquenchable thirst for blood, the code (the law of the land in the somber world of the 1647 collection) is unmasked as a death trap. For Greer the female victims in Zayas' *Desengaños* are "feminine martyrs to love" (270). I see them primarily as "feminine martyrs to the *fortifications of man*"—if I may borrow Onion's expression. *La inocencia castigada* (II, 5) presents an emblematic illustration of this notion. Doña Inés, a married and virtuous lady, falls prey to don Diego's vile amorous scheme. Unable to sway the will of doña Inés, don Diego resorts to the aid of a Moorish necromancer to satisfy his lust. Armed with the powers of darkness, don Diego calls on doña Inés by night. The helpless lady sleepwalks to don Diego's bed in a trance-like state. The nightly walk-in rapes go on for over a month. As don Diego is finally exposed and prosecuted for his crimes, doña Inés is legally cleared of any wrongdoing. Yet, her husband, brother and sister-in-law refuse to accept the outcome of the legal case. They devise an elaborate plan to punish doña Ines for her desecration of the family honor. They seal her into a wall, where she is kept alive in horrifying confinement for the span of six years. The effect that such extreme confinement has on her body is presented in nauseating detail:

En primer lugar, aunque tenía los ojos claros, estaba ciega [. . .] Sus hermosos cabe-
llos que cuando entró allí eran como hebras de oro, blancos como la misma nieve,
enredados y llenos de animalejos, que de no peinarlos se crían en tanta cantidad,
que por encima hervoreaban; el color, de la color de la muerte; tan flaca y consu-
mida, que se le señalaban los huesos, como si el pellejo que estaba encima fuera un
delgado cendal; desde los ojos hasta la barba, dos surcos cavados de las lágrimas,
que se le escondía en ellos un bramante grueso; los vestidos hechos ceniza, que se
le veían las más partes de su cuerpo; descalza de pie y pierna, que de los excremen-
tos de su cuerpo, como no tenía dónde echarlos, no sólo se habían consumido, mas
la propia carne comida hasta los muslos de llagas y gusanos, de que estaba lleno el
hediondo lugar. (Zayas 287)

(In the first place, although her eyes were clear, she was blind [. . .] Her lovely
tresses, which when she entered were strands of gold, white as the very snow, tan-
gled and full of little animals that breed in such quantity when hair is not combed,
that teemed on top of it; her color, the color of death, so thin and emaciated that her
bones showed as if the skin on top of them were but a thin veil; from her eyes to her
chin, two furrows dug by her tears, as if a thick cord lay hidden in them; her clothes
turned to ashes so that most parts of her body were visible; her feet and legs bare,
because the excrement from her body, since she had nowhere to dispose of it, had
not only eaten into them, but her very flesh was eaten up to the thighs with wounds
and worms, which filled the stinking place.)

Graphic images of "death in life" abound in baroque art and literature, but
this vision of decomposing worm eaten flesh has nothing to do with the *vanitas*
and *memento mori* motifs. This is quite simply a representation of unspeakable
violence and cruelty. Who is to blame for the torture of this innocent woman?
The fact that blameless women ("martyrs," "innocent lambs," as they are presented throughout the novellas) are systematically tortured and murdered by
their own husbands, fathers, and siblings in response to the pressures of honor
suggests that the symbolic law cannot be easily exonerated. It is not just an
isolated incident that we could dismiss as a tragic mistake, an aberration, a mis-
reading or mishandling of the demands of the honor code. Rather, in the very
repetition of the honor crime, the paternal law, the *name-of-the-father* (Lacan)
takes on the appearance of a death trap that condemns the (feminine) subject to
extreme forms of material confinement and repression.

Marcia Welles, Elizabeth Ordóñez, and Amy Williamsen have all noted
a connection between Zayas' oppressive and virtually claustrophobic view of
the house as an instrument of confinement and what Sandra Gilbert called the
architecture of patriarchy in reference to the gothic obsession with enclosures.

Williamsen argues that in the *Desengaños*, "the house serves as an instrument of torture employed against women" (144). Her study of the narrative frames of *La más infame venganza* (II, 2) and *El verdugo de su esposa* (II, 3) confirms that the "gender-inflected response of the narratees further heightens the criticism of the unjust [honor] code" (147). The image of an innocent woman literally buried alive in a wall in the name of honor is an extreme dramatization of the confining aspects of the architecture of patriarchy. If these walls could bleed!

In *El traidor contra su sangre* (II, 8), the walls of the house magically open up to show don Enrique the bleeding corpse of his beloved doña Mencía, murdered by her brother don Alonso with their father's blessings. Bathed in supernatural light, the uncorrupted body of doña Mencía bleeds for the span of a year. After the murder, don Alonso flees to Naples, where he will fall in love and marry doña Ana, a noble but poor young woman. Furious that his son has stained the family honor by marrying into poverty, don Pedro disinherits him. As the money runs out, don Álvaro is again driven to murder. With the help of a friend, don Álvaro decapitates his wife at the dinner table, stuffs her headless body down a well and buries the head in a cave. While doña Ana's body resurfaces in the morning, the head remains missing for over six months. When the severed head is finally found, everyone is shocked to see that doña Ana's features have been miraculously preserved in all their prodigious beauty.

As Greer observes, doña Mencía and doña Ana "die in streams of blood, leaving bodies whose miraculously incorruptible beauty testify (*sic*) to their innocence and sanctified status as martyrs to masculine cruelty" (282). Moreover, the incorruptible bodies of doña Mencía and doña Ana are material testimonies of the dark side of the Law. After all, in his murderous rage, don Álvaro is simply a diligent agent of his father's will, a faithful enforcer of the honor code. Don Pedro's reaction to the news that his son has been executed for the murder of doña Ana is the perfect illustration of the heartless indifference of the paternal law. The father barely interrupts his card game to calmly proclaim: "Más quiero tener un hijo degollado que mal casado" (398) (I would much rather have a son beheaded than one ill-wedded). Marina Brownlee sees this situation as a dramatization of the cruel effects of the honor code "taken to its *extreme*" (152, my emphasis). As a literal embodiment of the paternal law, don Pedro is a representation of the enemy within, the horror that comes with the house.

The obsessive preoccupation of Spanish baroque culture with matters of honor, legitimacy, and purity of blood (*limpieza de sangre*), is rooted in deep-seated institutional fears: fear of change, fear of social mobility, fear of new political ideas—as Maravall suggests—and, most of all, fear of chaos and meaninglessness. Thus, if the code of honor is a "fortification" in service of the social dream of meaningful self-containment, the *Desengaños* nightmarish parade of bleeding corpses is a shocking reminder of its arbitrariness and violence. The dream of honor engenders monsters! At the same time, we should note that Zayas' interrogation of the honor code does not result, as one might expect, in an explicit questioning of the monarchical-seigniorial system, or a problematization of the notions of cultural centrality shared by the moral majority. After all, the cancer of misogyny is said to spring from the ignorance and malice of the common people (*el vulgo*), while the Moorish Other is often endowed with demonic powers. Yet, these apparent contradictions and ideological inconsistencies should not hide the fact that mutilated bodies and beautified corpses are presented in the *Desengaños* as evidence of the precarious situation of women in seventeenth-century Spain. To be sure, the marvelous and the horrific are here invoked strategically in the midst of a discourse that constructs a new viewpoint for the reader. From this *extreme* (feminine) perspective, the Zayas reader may be able to catch a glimpse of the terrifying void at the center of the social order.

María de Zayas exploits the shock value of both the supernatural and the preternatural. Aquinas' distinction between natural events, supernatural prodigies (unmediated divine acts), and preternatural marvels is still functional in the mid-1600s. As Lorraine Daston writes: "Although preternatural phenomena were in theory difficult to distinguish from natural events (since they belonged to the same, lower order of causation), and in practice difficult to distinguish from supernatural events (since they evoked the same astonishment and wonder), they nonetheless constituted a third ontological domain until the late Seventeenth century" (81). While supernatural portents had the status of signifying facts that would announce catastrophic or triumphant things to come, preternatural wonders did not always qualify as signs. In theological terms, demons were denied the power of working true miracles. Hence, when the narrator of Zayas' *El jardín engañoso* refers to the marvelous garden created by the devil as a deception or lie (*engaño, mentira*), she is simply reminding us of Saint Paul's warning against the "lying wonders of Satan" (quoted by Daston 84).

On the other hand, spectral apparitions are often presented, in the literature of the period, as warnings against a life of sinful pursuits and disorderly freedom. The frightful visitations of count don Julián narrated in the anonymous *Libro de cosas notables que han sucedido en la ciudad de Córdoba* (1618) must be understood in this light. As a traitor to don Rodrigo, his natural king, don Julian had been instrumental in the defeat of Visigothic Spain at the hands of the Moorish invaders. While don Julián is said to be burning in Hell for his treacherous act against his king, his country, and the Christian faith, the count is periodically allowed to reappear in this world in the form of a specter to re-mind the living of the horrifying consequences of sin (reproduced in *Cuentos del siglo de oro* 111–16).

According to Daston, in the 1500s and 1600s preternatural phenomena pro-gressively swung from the quasi-supernatural extreme of portents to the quasi-natural extreme of what she calls "Baconian facts": "They began as signs par excellence and ended as stubbornly insignificant. The crucial step in this aston-ishing transformation was the naturalization of preternatural phenomena" (88–89). These observations are very useful to understand some seventeenth-cen-tury texts dealing with outlandish and grotesque material. In Cristóbal Lozano's "La cueva de Hércules" (1667), for example, we are left with a preternatural version of the events surrounding don Rodrigo's exploration of the seemingly bewitched cave of Hercules. Yet, perfectly natural explanations are provided for the death of the members of successive expeditions, from the extreme coldness and dampness of the cavern, to irrational fears inspired by preexisting legends and the natural gloom of the cave. In the case of Rutilio's bizarre tale of sexual predation and witchcraft in Cervantes' *Persiles* (1617), several explanations of the grotesque events are also provided. Thus, while Rutilio holds to the belief that he has rustled and ultimately killed a witch-wolf, Mauricio assures every-one that those men and women who appear to turn into fierce animals are sim-ply suffering from a medical condition known as "mania lupina." Finally, the much-celebrated Cervantine novella *El coloquio de los perros* (1613) traps the reader in an inescapable textual labyrinth. Multiple explanations of a series of "marvels" ("maravillas" in the text), including the famous talking dogs, coexist in this bizarre exemplary novel. Symptomatically, even the witch at the center of the story is really not sure whether her encounters with the devil actually happen "in reality," or whether they are fanciful creations of her own mind.

By providing both a natural explanation and a preternatural version of the same events, these dark fantasies of the baroque period come very close to Todorov's definition of the fantastic as the moment of oscillation between the marvelous and the uncanny. Franklin García Sánchez has explored the appli-cability of the concept of the fantastic to the literature of the Spanish Golden Age: "Resulta evidente que el Siglo de Oro y particularmente su segmento bar-roco ofrecen una dinámica favorable al brote de lo fantástico" ("Orígenes" 89) (It is evident that the Golden Age, and in particular its baroque phase, offers a favorable dynamic for the emergence of the fantastic).[10] He maintains that the problematic coexistence of modern rationalism with preexisting forms of knowledge is a crucial feature of the modern fantastic and the aesthetics of nineteenth-century romanticism, and also, generally speaking, of the baroque mentality. Romantic and baroque aesthetics would thus converge in their exploration of the frontiers of knowledge and reality, and in their cultivation of *admiratio* (99).

In the case of *El coloquio de los perros* and its frame tale *El casamiento engañoso*, the narrative calls attention to its own hybrid structure and the problematic nature of the coexistence of different discursive modes and their corresponding worldviews: the pastoral romance, the picaresque, the sentimental novella, the humanistic dialogue, etc. The result is a self-reflective text that leaves the reader hanging, suspended in doubt. Whatever solution of the epistemological puzzle we happen to endorse, this solution or resolution is always already tainted by the presence of our own constructive gaze, unmasked by the narrative structure as an arbitrary choice on our part. Since we don't seem to be able to account for the "whole" from the safety of a single viewpoint, we are left with the unsettling feeling that there are multiple and equally valid solutions to the puzzle. We are therefore reminded that, as the duchess tells Sancho in *Don Quixote* II, 41, "por un ladito no se vee el todo de lo que se mira" (336) (from a single side we cannot see the whole of what we look at). Sancho's response to the duchess underscores the "illusory" nature of our certainties: "pues volábamos por encantamento, por encantamento podía yo ver toda la tierra y todos los hombres por doquiera que los mirara" (336) (since we were flying by way of enchantment, by way of enchantment I could see the whole of the Earth and every man from wherever I looked). Only by way of enchantment or illusion may we see "the whole" from the comforting certainty of a bird's view.

The emphasis on questions of point of view finds its roots in the developments of the fields of optics and geometry, and the artistic and literary experiments of the Renaissance. In Spain, perspectivistic works such as *Lazarillo de Tormes* coexist in the 1500s with the closed literary worlds of chivalric, Byzantine, and pastoral romances. Baroque authors such as Cervantes would bring these different narrative genres, and their corresponding worldviews, into (problematic) contact with each other in the form of parodies and allegories. While Zayas' cultivation of the supernatural and the marvelous is not devoid of perspectivism and irony (see Brownlee and Williamsen), the *Desengaños'* bloody parade of mutilated corpses functions as a deadly serious reminder of the horrific aspects of reality (women's reality). On the other hand, the preternatural events narrated in Lozano's "La cueva de Hércules," and the earlier folk tales dealing with the problematic historical figure of count don Julian, appear to be meant as graphic illustrations of the terrifying consequences of sin. Finally, the grotesque tale of Rutilio in Cervantes' *Persiles*, and the exemplary novel *El coloquio de los perros* stage ironic encounters between the emerging rationalistic mentality and the marvelous, magical-religious world of were-wolves, witches, demonic apparitions and talking dogs.

In their exploration of the limits and/or limitations of preexisting modes of representation, and their taste for the macabre, the grotesque, and, generally speaking, extreme expressionism, these baroque tales of fantasy and horror may move, shock and manipulate the emerging consumer of print-culture (as Maravall would have it), but they may also challenge this brave new reader to reflect on the arbitrariness of inherited forms of knowledge, social values, and structures. Taken together these "literary novelties" may be said to simultaneously hide and reveal the fragility of the beliefs that sustain our "reality," i.e., the "fortifications," that protect our individual and collective character against the destabilizing forces of contingency, chaos, and meaninglessness (the powers of darkness).

The unsettling feelings of alienation, self-estrangement, and lack of authenticity that we associate with our digital age are not easily distinguishable from the early modern experience of loss of meaning and the baroque fascination with the theatricality of life and the deceptive nature of appearances. After all, questions of perception, perspective, disillusionment (*desengaño*), presence and absence, and reason and unreason are just as prevalent in (post)modern aesthetics and philosophy as they were in the baroque period. Moreover, we still dream early modern dreams of self-containment (the Subject, the Nation, Reason, the Modern World . . .), and we are still haunted by the void at the center of it all. This is the "baroque condition."

Notes

1. For more on this melancholic drive of the baroque and the fascination of Spanish art and literature with absence and death, see the recent book by Fernando R. de la Flor *Barroco. Representación e ideología en el mundo hispánico* (2002).

2. I have touched on some of these issues elsewhere. In *(A)wry Views: Anamorphosis, Cervantes and the Early Picaresque* (2001), I elaborate on the use of anamorphic techniques in literature, painting and the graphic arts in early modernity. I pay especial attention to canonical works of the Spanish Golden Age such as the anonymous *Lazarillo de Tormes*, Mateo Alemán's *Guzmán de Alfarache*, López de Ubeda's *La pícara Justina*, *Don Quixote*, *Persiles*, and "El retablo de las maravillas."

3. Jackson illustrates this idea with a quote from Poe's *The Pit and the Pendulum*: "It was not that I feared to look upon things horrible, but that I grew aghast lest there should be *nothing* to see" (quoted by Jackson, 109).

4. Egginton is very clear about this: "What I am describing, then, is best termed a shift

in dominance between the two modes of spatiality, such that, from the turn of the sixteenth century, theatricality begins to play an ever larger role in the mediation of experience while presence is confined into ever more specific and limited arenas of everyday life" (60).

5.   For more on this aspect of social identification, see Zizek's "How Did Marx Invent the Symptom?" The central notion here is that social reality is essentially an "ethical construction" supported by our willingness to act as if we believe in its premises and institutional projections. Zizek reflects on the implications of this idea in connection with our 'belief in the Nation' in *Tarrying With the Negative* (1993). The following passage captures the essence of his argument: "It would, however, be erroneous simply to reduce the national Thing to the features composing a specific 'way of life'. The Thing is not directly a collection of these features; there is 'something more' in it, something that *is present* in these features, that *appears* through them. Members of the community who partake in a given 'way of life' *believe in their Thing*, where this belief has a reflexive structure proper to the intersubjective space: 'I believe in the (national) Thing' equals 'I believe that others (members of my community) believe in the Thing' [...] The national Thing exists as long as members of the community believe in it; it is literally an effect of this belief " (201–202).

6.   For an elaboration on the moral and political implications of the baroque *theatricalization* of public life, see my article "Gracián and the Art of Public Representation." The immediate context of Gracián's thought is the changing landscape of the baroque court inhabited by professional bureaucrats and administrators. The changes in the court are tied to the evolution of the Spanish state and its institutions, and the appearance a new power elite (see Maravall, *Poder, honor y élites en el siglo XVII*).

7.   Onion's ghost story foregrounds some of the obstacles the critic is bound to encounter in dealing with the politics of horror fiction. The narrative reveals the arbitrariness of our 'usages,' 'modes' and 'conventions' which are nonetheless seen as man's necessary defenses against the 'altering' forces of terror and darkness: "To the man who pays heed to that voice within him which warns him that twilight and danger are settling over his soul, terror is apt to appear an absolute thing, against which his heart must be safe-guarded [. . .] unless there is to take place an alteration in the whole range and scale of his nature. Mercifully, he has never far to look for safeguards. Of the immediate and small and common and momentary things of life, of usages and observances and modes and conventions, he builds up fortifications against the powers of darkness" (ed. Pockell 312).

8.   In her conceptualization of the *marvelous* and the *uncanny*, Jackson draws directly from Tzvetan Todorov's classic study *The Fantastic. A Structural Approach to a Literary Genre*.

9.   Greer suggests that, in Counter Reformation Spain, death is "a spectacle in which a tranquil expiration and a beautiful corpse were testimony of salvation, even of sainthood if the corpse displayed particular beauty, whiteness, fragrance, light, and most particularly, incorruptibility" (268). In support of her argument, she quotes an eloquent

description of the death of Teresa de Avila by P. de Ribadeneira. This is her translation of the passage: "Her death completed, her face stayed most beautiful, white as alabaster without a single wrinkle, although she had had abundant ones because she was old, her hands and feet of the same whiteness, all transparent, . . . and as soft to the touch as if she were alive. All her members became beautified with clear signs of the innocence and sanctity that she had conserved in them. The fragrance that emerged from her saintly body when they dressed her and prepared her for burial was so great that it spread throughout the whole house" (268–69).

10. His account of the origins of the fantastic in Spanish literature incorporates selected passages from *La vida del escudero Marcos de Obregón* (1618) by Vicente Espinel, *Varia Fortuna del soldado Píndaro* (1626) by Céspedes y Meneses, and *La Garduña de Sevilla* (1642) by Alonso de Castillo Solórzano, as well as Cervantes' *Persiles* and his *Exemplary Novels*, and Zayas' collections of novellas. For a full list of the texts that Franklin García Sánchez incorporates in his survey, see "Orígenes de lo fantástico en la literatura hispánica" (89–90). See also "Génesis de lo fantástico en la literatura hispánica." García Sánchez concurs with Antonio Risco (1987) in pointing out that the Cervantine novella "El coloquio de los perros" ought to be regarded as a manifestation of *the pure fantastic* ("lo fantastico puro"). They both see "El coloquio" as a paradigmatic product of what García Sánchez calls "the dualism of the baroque mentality" ("el dualismo de la mentalidad barroca" [95]). This "dualism" would result from the conflictive encounter of "an emerging rationalistic spirit and an irrational, phantasmagoric space, which feeds from a deep magical-religious stratum" ("un espíritu racionalista en ascenso y un espacio irracional, fantasmagórico, alimentado por un profundo estrato mágico-religioso" [95]).

Works Cited

Aguirre, Manuel. *The Closed Space. Horror Literature and Western Symbolism.* Manchester: Manchester University Press, 1990.

Benjamin, Walter. *The Origin of German Tragic Drama.* London: New Left Books, 1977.

Braunstein, Philippe. "Toward Intimacy: The Fourteenth and Fifteenth Centuries." *A History of Private Life.* Vol. 2. Ed. Georges Duby. Trans. Arthur Goldhammer. Cambridge: Belknap-Harvard University Press, 1988. 535–630.

Brownlee, Marina. *The Cultural Labyrinth of María de Zayas.* Philadelphia: University of Pennsylvania Press, 2000.

Buci-Glucksmann, Christine. *Baroque Reason. The Aesthetics of Modernity.* Trans. Patrick Camiller. London: University of Teesside, 1994.

Castillo, David. *(A)wry Views: Anamorphosis, Cervantes, and the Early Picaresque.* West Lafayette, IN: Purdue University Press, 2001.

_____. "Gracián and the Art of Public Representation." *Rhetoric and Politics: Baltasar*

Gracián and the New World Order. Ed. Nicholas Spadaccini and Jenaro Talens. Hispanic Issues 14. Minneapolis: University of Minnesota Press, 1997.

Cervantes, Miguel de. *El ingenioso hidalgo don Quixote de la Mancha*. 2 vols. Ed. John Jay Allen. Madrid: Cátedra, 1998.

_____. *Los trabajos de Persiles y Sigismunda*. Ed. Carlos Romero Muñoz. Madrid: Cátedra, 1997.

_____. *Novelas ejemplares*. 2 vols. Ed. Harry Sieber. Madrid: Cátedra, 1990.

Cixous, Hélène. "The Character of 'Character'." *New Literary History* 5, 2 (Winter 1974): 383–402.

Daston, Lorraine. "Marvelous Facts and Miraculous Evidence in Early Modern Europe." *Wonders, Marvels, and Monsters in Early Modern Culture*. Ed. Peter Platt. Newark: University of Delaware Press, 1999. 76–104.

Egginton, William. *How the World Became a Stage: Presence, Theatricality and the Question of Modernity*. Albany: State University of New York Press, 2003.

Foucault, Michel. *The Order of Things. An Archeology of the Human Sciences*. New York: Vintage Books, 1973.

García Sánchez, Franklin. "Génesis de lo fantástico en la literatura hispánica." *Teoría semiótica. Lenguajes y textos hispánicos*. Ed. Miguel Angel Garrido Gallardo. Madrid: Consejo Superior de Investigaciones Científicas, 1984.

_____. "Orígenes de lo fantástico en la literatura hispánica." *El relato fantástico. Historia y sistema*. Ed. Antón Risco, Ignacio Soldevila, and Arcadio López. Salamanca: Ediciones Colegio de España, 1998.

Gracián, Baltasar. *Obras Completas*. Madrid: Aguilar, 1944.

_____. *The Art of Worldly Wisdom. A Pocket Oracle*. Trans. Christopher Maurer. New York: Doubleday, 1992.

Greer, Margaret. *María de Zayas Tells Baroque Tales of Love and the Cruelty of Men*. University Park: Pennsylvania State University Press, 2000.

Jackson, Rosemary. *Fantasy: The Literature of Subversion*. London: Methuen, 1981.

Lacan, Jacques. *The Four Fundamental Concepts of Psychoanalysis*. Ed. Jacques Alain Miller. Trans. Alan Sheridan. New York: Norton, 1981.

Libro de cosas notables que han sucedido en la ciudad de Cordoba (1618). Cuentos del Siglo de Oro. Ed. Félix Navas López and Eduardo Soriano Palomo. Madrid: Castalia, 2001.

Lovecraft, H. P. "The Call of Cthulhu." *The 13 Best Horror Stories of All Time*. Ed. Leslie Pockell. New York: Warner Books, 2002. 346–78.

Lozano, Cristóbal. "La cueva de Hércules." *Historias y leyendas*. Ed. Joaquín de Entrambasaguas. Madrid: Espasa-Calpe, 1943.

Maravall, José Antonio. *Culture of the Baroque: Analysis of a Historical Structure*. Trans. Terry Cochran. Minneapolis: University of Minnesota Press, 1986.

_____. *El mundo social de La Celestina*. Madrid: Gredos, 1986.

_____. *Poder, honor y élites en el siglo XVII*. Madrid: Siglo XXI, 1979.

Merchant, Carolyn. *The Death of Nature: Women, Ecology, and the Scientific Revolution.* San Francisco: Harper and Row, 1980.

Mirollo, James. "The Aesthetics of the Marvelous: The Wondrous Work of Art in a Wondrous World." *Wonders, Marvels, and Monsters in Early Modern Culture.* Ed. Peter Platt. Newark: University of Delaware Press, 1999. 24–44.

Monleón, José. *A Specter is Haunting Europe. A Sociohistorical Approach to the Fantastic.* Princeton: Princeton University Press, 1990.

Onions, Oliver. "The Beckoning Fair One." *The 13 Best Horror Stories of All Time.* Ed. Leslie Pockell. New York: Warner Books, 2002. 275–345.

Ordóñez, Elizabeth. "Woman and Her Text in the Works of María de Zayas and Ana Caro." *Revista de Estudios Hispánicos* 19 (1985): 3–15.

Rabkin, Eric. *The Fantastic in Literature.* Princeton, NJ: Princeton University Press, 1976.

Risco, Antonio. *Literatura fantástica de lengua española.* Madrid: Taurus, 1987.

Rodríguez de la Flor, Fernando. *Barroco. Representación e ideología en el mundo hispánico (1580–1680).* Madrid: Cátedra, 2002.

Schramm, Percy. *Las insignias de la realeza en la Edad Media española.* Madrid: Instituto de Estudios Políticos, 1960.

Spadaccini, Nicholas, and Jenaro Talens. "Introduction." *Rhetoric and Politics. Baltasar Gracián and the New World Order.* Ed. Nicholas Spadaccini and Jenaro Talens. Minneapolis: University of Minnesota Press, 1997.

Todorov, Tzvetan. *The Fantastic. A Structural Approach to a Literary Genre.* Trans. Richard Howard. Cleveland: The Press of Case Western Reserve Library, 1973.

Turner, Bryan. "Introduction." *Baroque Reason. The Aesthetics of Modernity.* By Christine Buci-Glucksmann. London: University of Teesside, 1994.

Williamsen, Amy. "Challenging the Code: Honor in María de Zayas." *María de Zayas: The Dynamics of Discourse.* Ed. Amy Williamsen and Judith Whitenack. Madison: Fairleigh Dickinson University Press, 1995. 133–51.

Welles, Marcia. "María de Zayas y Sotomayor and Her Novela Cortesana: A Reevaluation." *Bulletin of Hispanic Studies* 55 (1978): 301–10.

Zayas, María de. *Desengaños amorosos.* Ed. Alicia Yllera. Madrid: Cátedra, 1983.

_____. *Novelas amorosas y ejemplares.* Ed. Agustín González de Amezúa. Madrid: Aldus, 1948.

Zizek, Slavoj. "How Did Marx Invent the Symptom." *Mapping Ideology.* Ed. Slavoj Zizek. London: Verso, 1994. 296–331.

_____. *The Sublime Object of Ideology.* London: Verso, 1989.

_____. *Tarrying with the Negative. Kant, Hegel, and the Critique of Ideology.* Durham: Duke University Press, 1993.

_____. *The Ticklish Subject: The Absent Centre of Political Ontology.* London: Verso, 2000.

Part III
Institutions and Subjectivities
in Baroque Spain

◆ 6

From Hieroglyphic Presence
to Representational Sign:
An Other Point of View
in the *Auto Sacramental*

Bradley J. Nelson

A working hypothesis of much current criticism of Spanish Golden Age literature is that the Baroque is a modern or even post-modern cultural phenomenon.[1]
Recently, religious and political festivals and celebrations have come to occupy
a rather privileged place within such studies due in part to the tension that arises
when these massive and guided politico-religious spectacles (Maravall) encounter a heterogeneous public whose diverse energies are thought to challenge
the conservative message ostensibly conveyed by participatory rituals such as
the annual Corpus Christi celebrations (Moraña; Schumm). There are two main
currents of criticism in this inquiry into festive culture: on the one hand, critics
such as Antonio Bonet Correa and José María Díez Borque, following the work
of José Antonio Maravall, study what Díez Borque has termed "la alteración
dramática de la calle" ("Relaciones" 21) (the dramatic alteration of the street);
on the other hand, much work in the area of Colonial Studies focuses on the
conflict between this centripetal drive for political and cultural hegemony and
the resistance to or appropriation of festive cultural practices by marginal or
subaltern subjects and groups. In neither case, however, has a serious attempt
been made to consider the modern or postmodern persistence of what we might

call "the theatrical fabrication of presence" as manifested in public celebrations such as the *auto sacramental*.[2]

Since most critics agree that the main theme, or *asunto*, of the *auto* is the dramatic embodiment of religious signs with a transcendental or hypostatic substance, it stands to reason that a focused consideration of the status of such signs in Counter Reformation Spain would be useful in understanding the particular modernity of the *auto* and, conversely, the persistence of presence in modernity. The emerging field of emblematics provides a useful framework for such a study.[3] Emblematics involves the study of what Peter Daly has termed the "emblematic mode of representation," which is to say, the multifarious symbolic practices that combine visual symbols with verbal commentary in by and large morally based and exemplary games of wit. Both in theory and practice, the emblem configures a series of hybrid discourses. This hybridity is found in the aforementioned visually and verbally constructed form; the use of multiple languages; the ingenious combination of classical, religious, and popular motifs, *sentencias*, proverbs, symbols, and so on; its multiplicity of concrete forms—hieroglyphics, enigmas, devices, *imprese*, etc.—and, finally, its central rhetorical role in virtually every literary and artistic genre of the Renaissance and Baroque. More to the point, the emblem occupies a transitional place in historical and paradigmatic terms, with one face turned toward the Middle Ages and the profound iconicity that characterizes the symbolic and "artistic" practices of medieval religious rituals,[4] while the agile and changeable allegorization employed by its renaissance and baroque practitioners anticipates and extends the fragmentation and ambiguity that characterize modern modes of symbolic expression (Russell). It is this "marginal" status that most concerns this emblematic study of the *auto*, as my hypothesis is that the emblem appears in theatrical representation in moments of heightened dramatic tension in order to evoke the impression that one is witnessing a transcendent event, i.e., the transubstantiated sacramental body.

Both canonical as well as more recent studies of Golden Age theater have recognized the importance of the emblematic modes of representation for understanding the aesthetic conventions as well as the ideological embeddedness of allegorical and mythological tropes and motifs in early modern festive culture. Walter Benjamin, Mario Praz, Fernando R. de la Flor, Peter Daly, and Maravall have all noted the formal and thematic homologies between the construction and reception of emblems and the way in which theater involves the spectator in the staging of imaginary actions. According to John T. Cull, the theatrical use of emblems would include the following:

the invention of original word emblems, the emblematic argument in dialogue, the epigrammatic maxim, the emblematic character, the emblematic backcloth, the inclusion of actual emblems in the dramatic action, the use of emblematic stage properties, the use of chorus to provide emblematic commentary, and the extended emblematic portrayal conveyed by such dramatic forms as the dumb-show, the masque, pageants and processions. ("Emblematics" 115)

Further use of emblems include the combination of easily recognizable figures and symbols, formulaic plots that employ strategies of misdirection and discovery to create suspense, curiously framed and therefore compelling objects, such as letters, daggers, devices, etc., and witty and portentous dialogue. In the words of Maravall, "basta[n] para hacernos sospechar que entre el teatro barroco y emblema hay un estrecho parentesco" ("La literatura" 149) (it should be enough for us to suspect that between baroque theater and the emblem there is a close relationship). In the case of the *auto sacramental*, the spectator is offered nothing less than a public performance of the emblematic modes of representation. Aurora Egido offers this:

El auto calderoniano operaba como los emblemas. El título proponía la *inscriptio* que la puesta en escena visualizaba en el cuadro o *pictura* y que la *subscriptio* o texto poético glosaba por extenso, aunque aquí dramatizándolo. (70)[5]

(The Calderonian *auto* operated like emblems. The title proposed the *inscription* which the staging of the play visualized in the scene or *picture* and which the *subscription* or poetic text extensively glossed, although dramatizing it in this case.)[6]

Building on this already significant body of work, the object of this study is to explore the theatrical encounter between metaphysical presence, political ideology, and the creation of emblems through an analysis of Calderón's 1635 *auto, El gran mercado del mundo*. My argument is that the fabrication of the theatrical effect of presence is dependent on the presentation of two competing points of view that are not so much synthesized as situated and maintained in an unequal tension in a manner quite typical of the Baroque and of modernity in general. These competing yet interdependent points of view, furthermore, can be better understood as conflicting symbolic practices central to the evolution of the emblem.

One of the factors that make the emblem pertinent to a study of the phenomenon presence is its simultaneous resistance to and dissemination of the fragmented, symbolic world of modernity. As Daniel Russell observes, "the

emblematic form should be seen primarily as a symptom of a transitional mentality that defines the period between the Middle Ages and the coming Romanticism in the middle eighteenth century" (*Emblematic Structures* 8). Looking
back toward the Middle Ages, the emblem partakes of the mystical status of
the hieroglyphic, or religious icon, which "ensures 'presence' of the idea in a
way that a text alone could not do" (*Emblematic Structures* 29). Looking toward modernity, "the emblem is in many respects an increasingly fragmented,
secularized and decadent form of late medieval allegory" (*Emblematic Structures* 40). This Janus-faced character of the emblem is synthesized in Walter
Benjamin's reading of the emblematic nature of baroque allegory, in particular
his observation that the preferred image of the emblem and of baroque art in
general is the corpse, which evokes a curiously negative experience of disem-
bodied presence:

> Whereas in the symbol destruction is idealized and the transfigured face of nature is
> fleetingly revealed in the light of redemption, in allegory the observer is confronted
> with the *facies hippocratica* of history as a petrified, primordial landscape. Every-
> thing about history that, from the very beginning, has been untimely, sorrowful,
> unsuccessful, is expressed in a face—or rather in a death's head. (166)

In light of these definitions of the emblem, it would not be farfetched to
characterize Maravall's reading of the baroque, and modernity, as emblematic.
The first chapter of his landmark work *Culture of the Baroque* convincingly establishes that the baroque mentality is conditioned by a perceived loss of social,
economic, and political stability and a steady movement toward a fragmentary,
individualistic, and crisis-ridden consciousness of history. It is in the context of
this instability and fragmentation that the monarchy and the Church are latched
onto by the ruling elite not as a de facto presence, in the iconic sense of the
term, but rather as an *empresa*, in the emblematic sense of the term. Which is to
say, they become dominant figures in the representation of an intention or desire
for hegemony, constituted through the assemblage of cultural symbols, such as
the globe, the cross, the ship of state, and the scepter, and held together by a
constantly evolving and contradictory assemblage of texts. Like the emblem,
absolutist ideology simultaneously looks at the past as an era of plenitude lost
and to the future as the time to fill or remedy this loss.

   This melancholic view of history also informs the cosmological landscapes
of the *auto sacramental*, where the stated goal is the ritualistic making present
of the indivisible body of Christ in the divisible substance of the bread and
wine, or transubstantiation. Transubstantiation, much like monarchical embodi-

ment, is a complex enterprise in early modernity, as Russell's observations concerning the iconic degradation of the emblem demonstrate. All the same, with its historically ambivalent role, part iconographical symbol and part representational sign, the emblem becomes a very important structure in this process, as noted by Cull, Egido, and others. In the words of Pablo Restrepo-Gautier, "la enseñanza del sacramento de la Eucaristía por medio de figuras alegóricas es emblemática por naturaleza" (34–35) (the teaching [or display] of the sacrament of the Eucharist by means of allegorical figures is emblematic by nature). This rather uncomplicated view of Calderón's achievement of spiritual, or transcendental, synthesis of image (body) and substance (soul) is exemplified by Antonio Regalado, who writes:

> El diálogo supraterrestre en el teatro de Calderón entre los poderes divinos sobre la creación y redención del mundo o entre modos de presencia divina, son manifestaciones de la presencia del Dios personal y no meras personificaciones o *abstracta* subsumidas en las imágenes poéticas, interpretación fijada al imponer sobre los textos la definición racionalista de la personificación. (28)

> (The supraterrestrial dialogue in the theater of Calderón between the divine powers about the creation and redemption of the world or between modes of divine presence, are manifestations of the presence of the personal God and not mere personifications or *abstracta* subsumed in the poetic images, an interpretation secured by imposing the rationalist definition of personification on the texts.)

Such views, although infectious in their enthusiasm, fail to take into account the modernity of the emblematic mode of representation and, by extension, of Calderón's theater. This "achievement" of Eucharistic presence is complicated even more by the Catholic Church's systematic attempts to empty religious icons of their "magical" properties in their push for institutional control over religious imagery. According to the policy of the Council of Trent, "due honour and reverence is owed to [religious images], not because some divinity or power is believed to lie in them [. . .] but because the honour showed to them is referred to the original which they *represent*" (cited by Belting 554, my emphasis). One result of this differentiation between representational signs and iconic embodiment is that the doctrine of transubstantiation—in which the ritual combination of words and gestures performed both by and under the authority of a priestly "emblemist" brings the communicant toward the perception and ingestion of the real presence and body of Christ—becomes the only acceptable form of symbolic embodiment in early modernity, or an exception to the rule. In order to understand the profound nature of the distinction that is being made between representational and iconic signs, a short digression on similar changes in theater will be instructive.

In *How the World Became a Stage*, William Egginton characterizes the constitutive nature of medieval dramatic space in the following way: "the Middle Ages experienced space in a fundamentally different way: as full, impressionable and substantial, whose dimensions existed relative to observers and, more specifically, participants, as opposed to being empty and independent of them" (37). Egginton reminds us, moreover, that the "actors" in these medieval spectacles are not modern, itinerant professionals but rather ecclesiastical and public officials or, in the case of aristocratic society, monarchs and nobles, whose dramatic roles are not easily separable from their identity in the community. To summarize, "the hyperbolic solidity of the space of medieval drama reflected the instability of the distinction between the reality being represented and the reality of the representation" (55). This space, in other words, is inseparable from the dramatization, or making present, of the divine substance, which depends on the collapsing of the temporal and spatial difference between the archetypal event, say of the Last Supper, and its dramatic performance and recital (Surtz). By contrast, the appearance and eventual predominance of the homogeneous theatrical space of the *comedia nueva*, as well as the self-conscious interval that emerges between the modern professional actor and his or her theatrical role, place the *auto* in a highly contentious and mediated space, one in which the relatively open and homogeneous space of the public plaza and the professional status of the actors function in direct opposition to the conditions of efficacy of medieval rituals of presence (Egginton). In the words of Bolívar Echeverría, "El dramatismo judeo-cristiano de la existencia humana, con su secuencia cíclica de los estados de pecado, culpa y redención, pasó a necesitar del contenido de la experiencia individual para poder realizarse como tal" (*La modernidad* 201) (The Judeo-Christian dramatism of human existence, with its cyclical sequence of states of sin, guilt and redemption, came to depend on the content of individual experience in order to fulfill itself as such).

Such is the case with the emblematic image, which, as Daniel Russell explains, is a stage on which the conflict between medieval and early modern modes of representation is performed: "it is [. . .] interesting to observe the increasing tension between representation and symbolization in the Renaissance as it surfaces in these emblem pictures and emblematic views of nature. The blurring of the two was fought by science and religion, and gradually representation won the day, but in the meantime, the struggle continued throughout the age of the emblematic" ("Perceiving" 80). This tension is most easily recognizable in the effort expended by emblemists such as Juan de Borja and Juan de Horozco y Covarrubias in the articulation of a "correct" emblem theory that would then inform a more correct practice and reception, or interpretation, of emblems (Gombrich; Nelson). In Counter-Reformation Spain, the emblem rapidly becomes an arena where the uneasy compromise between discursive freedom and theological necessity is played out in favor of the latter. As Giuseppina Ledda observes, "Las letras humanas se vuelven otra vez divinas" ("Los jeroglíficos" 597) (human letters once again become divine). This process, however, is not able to entirely erase the scene on which the struggle takes place.

Doctrinal changes seldom reflect the actual state of religious and symbolic cultures in early modernity, or any other historical period, as Sarah Nalle's studies of religious practices in Sixteenth-century rural Castile demonstrate. Religious practices are actually quite diverse, and the use of iconic, or magical, religious images and ceremonies does not disappear when religious authorities decide to reform and reorganize their official definitions and customs. For example, the popular, or immanent, reception of the *auto sacramental* has been noted by virtually all of its critics with tones ranging from mystification to applause, depending on the objectives and sympathies of the critic. For Díez Borque, as for Bruce Wardropper and Marcel Bataillon, the performance and reception of the one-act dramas are inseparable from the festive atmosphere and varied public spectacles of the Corpus Christi celebrations, in which the *auto sacramental* plays but a small part, albeit that of festive and institutional protagonist. The heterogeneous nature of the spectacle, in particular its combination of what Raymond Williams might call *residual* and *emergent* dramatic and theatrical cultures, is neatly summarized by Díez Borque:

> El auto sacramental es el lugar de encuentro de liturgia y teatro, de ceremonia y acción escénica, de sobrenaturalidad y contingencia terrenal mediante los limitados medios humanos de la alegoría, y otros elementos escénicos, para penetrar lo trascendente. ("El auto sacramental" 49)

> (The *auto sacramental* is the meeting place of liturgy and theater, of ceremony and staged action, of the supernatural and earthly contingency by means of the limited human medium of allegory, and other stage elements, in order to penetrate the transcendental.)

In this light, the *auto*, much like the emblem, can be seen as a crossroads between conflicting and in some cases contradictory practices. This appreciation for the complex nature of early modern religious and festive themes and tropes carries serious methodological and philosophical implications for theological, aesthetic, and social models of *auto* criticism.[7] One of the most important questions that arise concerns how the movement from medieval liturgical drama to early modern theatrical representation affects the ritual evocation of hypostatized presence.

The story of Lope de Rueda, a pioneer in both sacred and secular theater, is exemplary of this dramatic ambivalence. Wardropper notes that in 1552 Lope de Rueda became perhaps the first "professional" playwright to practice his craft as a municipal functionary when the city of Valladolid, the Spanish Court at the time, contracted his services as well as his civic presence due to overwhelming enthusiasm for an *auto* he had written and produced: "se le otorga un sueldo de 4.000 maravedís anuales con que viva en esta villa y reside" (*Introducción* 73) (he is granted 4.000 *maravedís* annually with which to live and reside in this city). The *batihoja*'s contractual transition from popular marketplace bard to civic functionary highlights the historical movement from *popular* to *popularizing* art (Molho) with astounding precision, a historical transformation that provides an early indication of the changes that will occur in the form and function of the *auto sacramental*. Wardropper goes on to note that in 1561, "se estableció la costumbre en Toledo de contratar únicamente a compañías profesionales" (*Introducción* 80) (in Toledo the custom was established of contracting only professional companies). In cases such as these it is apparent that the Corpus Christi celebrations very quickly become a municipal, which is to say, commercial and political enterprise in which religious spectacles come to serve many purposes, not the least of which is the desire of *cortes* and *comunidades* and their authorities to display and legitimate their terrestrial power and wealth.[8] Bataillon is even more succinct, writing "[a]quí interviene la simbiosis del teatro sagrado y del teatro profano, pues encargo y remuneración recaen, en ambos casos, en los mismos autores y en los mismos actores. Literalmente el auto sacramental tuvo idéntico destino que la comedia. [. . .] Tal es el camino que se abre desde el momento que el teatro edificante pasa a manos de profesionales en lugar de seguir en las de aficionados piadosos" (here is where the symbiosis of sacred and profane theater intervenes, as commission and remuneration fall back, in both cases, onto the same directors and the same actors. Literally the *auto sacramental* had an identical destiny as the *comedia*. [. . .] Such is the path that is opened from the moment that edifying theater passes into the hands of professionals instead of remaining in those of pious aficionados) ("Explicación" 197).[9]

These "pious aficionados," of course, are the very problem the Council of

Trent has in mind when it attempts to appropriate all religious imagery in its defensive war against the Reformation (Belting). Although the baroque rationalization of festive culture is still a ways off, Maravall's observation that the "institutionalization of the fiesta reveals its linkages with the social system and with the means of integration on which the baroque monarchy was based" is still valid (*Culture* 244). In this transitional and contradictory space the emblem becomes very useful in evoking the effect of divine presence, and it is my view that Calderón uses emblematics to construct a type of symbolic anamorphosis in which two perspectives, one legitimate and one illegitimate, vie for symbolic supremacy in and through a dramatic conflict that is itself a struggle between differing regimes of interpretation and subjectivity.[10] In the end, the divine presence is not so much enacted as negatively suggested by dialectically privileging a vacant point of view consistent with the philosophy of *desengaño* (disillusionment) at the expense of a point of view that is framed as more materialistic and rebellious in nature.

In order to focus on this rhetorical framework, my method here will not begin with the assumption that Calderón's dramatic theory and practice ingeniously reveal and disseminate a pre-existing, consistent, and integral pearl of cosmological or theological divine wisdom, as in the studies of critics such as Alexander A. Parker, Barbara Kurtz, and, more recently, Antonio Regalado and Vincent Martin. Quite the contrary, I will concentrate on what Bourdieu calls the *modus operandi* as opposed to the *opus operatum* of Calderón's *auto*. In the words of Victor Turner, "My method is perforce the reverse of that of those numerous scholars who *begin* by eliciting the cosmology, which is often expressed in terms of mythological cycles, and *then* explain specific rituals as exemplifying or expressing the structural models they find in myths. It is therefore *necessary* to begin at the other end, with the basic building blocks, the 'molecules,' of ritual" (14). These "building blocks," as it were, are made up of various emblematic, i.e., allegorical, modes of representation, and by studying these modes and the way they interact *theatrically*, it is my aim to offer a series of hypotheses concerning the relationship between modern theatricality and the performance of divine presence. In short, I will argue: (1) that the *argumento* of *El gran mercado del mundo* structures a contest of interpretation in which the character who interprets the confusing appearances, or merchandise, of the great marketplace of the world more "emblematically" and ultimately wins the day; (2) that what is at stake here is not just a way of reading or interpreting the meaning of material objects, since their meaning is never explicitly stated, but rather a normative way of desiring meaning which pits two semiotic regimes against each other: a discourse of immanence, or earthly love of material existence; and a discourse of deferral in which the relation between the subject and his reality is always mediated by a third, authoritative and transcendental gaze; and (3) that this construction of legitimate and illegitimate methods for seeing and acting in the world is constitutively linked to a perceived political need for identifying an ideological other in the interest of a program of social control. In the end, I will claim that the early modern, or theatrical, representation of Eucharistic presence is dependent on the threat posed by what we might call a diabolical, semiotic regime of fragmentation.

El gran mercado del mundo

We can outline the main contrapuntal *argumentos* of *El gran mercado del mundo* as follows: a chivalric contest and romantic triangle; the biblical parable of the *talents*; and the paradigmatic rivalry between brothers, i.e., Cain and Abel, Jacob and Esau, etc. To summarize, the two sons of the *Padre de familias*, *Buen Genio* and *Mal Genio*, vie for the object of desire, *la Gracia*, who, as the *serrana más serafín*, will accompany the winner across the threshold of life—death—to the *Santa Cena*, but only after the *Padre de familias* has determined which of the two has invested his *caudal* most prudently in the great marketplace of the world.[11] In emblematic terms, each brother can be seen as the dramatic representation of differing emblematic modes: *la empresa* and *el emblema*.

There are few tasks as confusing as attempting to define and differentiate the multitude of symbolic games and contests that make up the emblematic modes of representation, of which the *empresa*, the emblem, the device, and the hieroglyphic are the most recognizable tropes. An important theoretical source of this confusion is the prologue of Juan de Borja's *Empresas morales*. Borja redefines both modes by taking the more cultured term *empresa*—which generally referred to a personal symbolic *enterprise* used by noble and humanist subjects to communicate a military or amorous intention in a highly coded and veiled manner—and confuse it with the emblem, which began to be associated with the cultivation of customs in the collective sense (Nelson). For Daly, "The *impresa* represents the 'principle of individualtion' (Sulzer, p. 35)," while "[t]he emblem, on the other hand, is addressed to a larger audience" (23). It is the emblem, moreover, that becomes a centerpiece in both Jesuit education and religious propaganda in the Baroque (Praz, R. de la Flor)

An excellent example of the liberating potential of the *empresa* is provided by the *invención*, an early mode of courtly emblematics. A poetic precursor to the *empresa*, *invenciones* were a favorite pastime of courtly subjects in fifteenth-century Spain, who participated in the competitive creation and public performance of these contests of wit. Brian Dutton's anthology of *cancionero* poetry contains the following *invención* by "Vicens":

Vicens trujo por cimera un monto de piedres con huna crus y dezia
la letre
Si quien dyo fin a mi vida
con dolor pyedra posyera
perderla no me dolyera (151)

(Vicens brought for a crest a mound of stones with a cross [,] and the words read: If she who brought an end to my life with pain possessed a stone, losing it [my love? my life? the stone?] would not pain me)

In the combination of *cimera* and *letre*, we can see how the desire and wit of the poet uproot and reframe a messianic symbol and metaphor around a personal, amorous, and witty enterprise. The imagined figure on the empty cross is the poet-lover himself, who would not regret losing his life (or his love or the stone) were his beloved to possess a "rock": a jewel or *prenda* of some sort accepted, or not, by the *amada enemiga* as a sign of her corresponding desire. If we take this figure a bit further we can see how the beloved's hypothetical rock metonymically refers to the rocks that anchor and support the crucifix. By linking the difficult meaning of the enigma to the poet's genius and love, the religious connotations of cross, rock, and sacrifice are redirected toward a celebration of the poetic wit and amorous sacrifice of the poet-lover. What is suggested in the end is not the transcendental meaning and power of the religious symbols but the genius and daring of the embodied subject, Vicens, who destabilizes the meaning of seemingly univalent symbols in a search for personal fame. Indeed, the crest is a common symbol of fame, as we will see in Calderón's *auto*. For R. de la Flor, "El emblema personal adoptó siempre un punto de rebeldía, de expresión de una idea de desorden social" (*Emblemas* 91) (the personal emblem always adopted a point of rebellion, of the expression of an idea of social disorder). Borja's solution to the conflict between a courtly practice of wit that stages the superior nature of the genius or amorous desire of the courtly subject and an Ignatian interpretive praxis designed to deflect human aspirations by staging the penitent's meditative *confusión* provides an illuminating frame for analyzing Calderón's *auto*.[12]

To wit, Borja's *Empresas morales* contains a similar *empresa*, but his stated goal could not be more different than that of Vicens. In the *empresa* headed by the motto (*lema*) "Satiabor cum apparverit" (I will be satisfied when it appears), the reader discovers the Egyptian letter TAV engraved on a pyramid, whose meaning is not so much elucidated as absorbed into Borja's enterprise as a pre-figuration of the crucifix.[13] In this way the crucifix is projected into the Egyptian hieroglyphics while the mysterious, arcane symbols and their transcendental aura are used to anchor the symbolic order of Spanish Catholicism outside of the present, embodied moment. Unlike the historical specificity, or individual-ity, suggested by the name of the poet Vicens, the only individual in Borja's emblem is the absent figure of Christ, whose universal status works to collec-tivize the idea of sacrifice, which then becomes part of a program of moral and allegorical guidance. As Karen Pinkus concludes, "The emblem is conceived of, then, as a kind of simple, monolithic gesture, a resolver of contradictions, an embodiment of an essence" (54). Contrary to how the courtly poet directs the gaze of the reader/spectator to an appreciation of his wit, as well as evoking surprised (and guilty?) enjoyment due to the carnivalesque use of religious ima-gery, in the case of the emblem the reader's search for meaning is dehistoricized and absorbed by the absent authorial guarantee of Borja's emblem book, which gazes on its own retroactively constructed narrative of Catholic destiny.

Similarly, *El gran mercado* is a story about how one simultaneously navi-gates the world of signs and converts oneself into an emblem—or sign—of a worthy intention—or inclination—as indicated in the names of the protagonists *Buen Genio* and *Mal Genio*. In other words, we are looking at the theatrical per-formance of opposing *empresas*, constructed and performed for the alternately loving and castigating gaze of *Gracia* and the *Padre de familias*. The correct employment of *ingenio* and *agudeza* in the interpretation of signs and appear-ances, and the subsequent invention of a legitimate and legitimizing enterprise are, in essence, the *modus operandi* of the contest.

The play opens with a problematic, and emblematic, invocation of Fame:

Sale la FAMA, *cantando por lo alto del tablado en una apariencia que pasa de un lado a otro*
FAMA   ¡Oíd, mortales, oíd,
y al pregón de la Fama
todos acudid! (1–3)

(*FAME enters, singing from high upon the stage in an appearance that passes from one side to the other.*
FAME: Hear, mortals, hear / and to the call of Fame / present yourselves!*)

What follows this opening call to action is an anamorphic portrait of Fame, as the main characters—*Buen Genio* and *Malicia, Mal Genio* and *Gracia, el Padre* and *Inocencia*—all provide different descriptions of Fame according to their inclinations. It is as if the mere entrance of Fame onto the stage produces the type of anamorphic fragmentation and instability that characterize the *invención*. In the pairing of opposing descriptions, Calderón presents what are in effect emblematic inscriptions designed to simultaneously obscure and illuminate the "real" meaning of the *carro* of Fame: a rhetorical strategy common not only to Calderonian drama but to *conceptista* and *gongorista* poetry as well (Egido).[14] There are many ways in which one might envision Fame. Here the various descriptions that evoke the burnt feathers of Icarus or the desolation and destruction of Phaeton are contrasted to the untainted plumage of a magnificent bird that competes with the sun in power and beauty.[15] We might also note how Fame's wears a *penacho*, whose synonyms include Vicens's *cimera* as well as "vanity." As will be the case throughout the *auto*, the momentary confusion caused by the entrance of Fame is partially resolved by the explanation of the *Padre* in answer to a challenge by *Mal Genio*, who doesn't understand the pessimistic attitude of the patriarch toward what seems to him to be a sublimely beautiful ideal: [16]

> PADRE   Porque también de la Fama
> en ese pregón oí
> que vende el Mundo de todo,
> y sólo será feliz
> quien su talento empleare
> bien o mal; se ha de advertir
> que dijo que el bien o el mal
> no se conoce hasta el fin. (72–79)

(FATHER: Because I also heard in the call of Fame that the World sells all kinds of things, and only he who employs his talent well or poorly will be happy; but it must be noted that she said that good and evil will not be known until the end.)

It is important to note that the Father does not give the "correct" meaning of the visual figure; indeed, the meaning of *Fama* is immaterial or even counterproductive to Calderón's purpose. The verbal definitions are strategically allusive and elusive, shifting our gaze as spectators toward the way in which each character approaches the figure. In Catherine Bell's words, "some type of ambiguity or blindness in ritualization is linked to its distinctive efficacy" (109). *Buen Genio* observes what Fame does without either desiring or abhorring what he sees; *Mal Genio* is awestruck, lost in ambivalent desire but obviously enraptured by what he sees; while *Gracia* is likewise amazed by the monstrosity. Once presented with the hierarchical oppositions through which the contest is framed, the reader/spectator is led to contemplate what it might mean to employ one's *caudal* well so s/he can subsequently "fill in" the concept accordingly.[17]

Like the *comedia*, the main argument of this *auto* revolves around the topics of love and marriage and their relationship to differing paths to knowledge of self and the world. The amorous contest begins when *Buen Genio* offers to give up his birthright, held by the *Padre de familias*, in order to prove his worthiness for the hand of *Gracia*. His brother immediately declares his own competing interest, but the comments of *Buen Genio* make it apparent that their desires are not equal: "No lo hace por amar, / sino por contradecir" (164–65) (he is not doing it for love but rather to contradict). Where *Buen Genio* approaches his desire for *Gracia* through the mediation of the gaze of the Father, *Mal Genio* gauges his own desire by comparing it with his brother's and thus marks off a path that goes directly to the goal without considering paternal authority. This is Calderón's way of providing an interpretive rubric for all subsequent actions and judgments, as he frames *Mal Genio* for the crime of contradictory or market-based desire, even though *Buen Genio*'s preemptive desire for sole possession of *Gracia* could also be identified as sparking the conflict. Moreover, at no time is the possibility that both brothers might achieve grace suggested.

When the brothers depart on their journeys, the movement of their bodies begins to take on significance both within the plot and according to the theological apparatus of the play. *Buen Genio* undertakes an arduous pilgrimage through the mountains while his malevolent double initiates a rather quixotic romp on the plains. The first stop for both is an inn, where Calderón introduces the figure of *Culpa*, who will translate the meaning of these movements in her role as a self-proclaimed "afterthought." She appears in the guise of a woman scorned with designs on revenge, reflecting the dark side of the *enemiga amada*. We learn from *Culpa*, for instance, that *Buen Genio* and *Mal Genio* represent the two inclinations that struggle against each other in man's conscience; that if either fails to serve *Gracia* with perfect works they will never receive eternal grace; and that *Culpa*'s role is to make sure they both fail by confusing them with her changing appearances: "pues nació / la culpa de la mentira; / en varias formas mudada / en varios trajes vestida, / veré si de sus empleos / las elecciones peligran, / de suerte que nunca puedan / ser de la Gracia bien vistas" (492–99) (as guilt was born from a lie; mutated in various forms, dressed in various costumes, I will see if their elections endanger their tasks, so that they will never be approved of by Grace).

As in the plays analyzed by Viviana Díaz Balsera, *Culpa* acts as a deceptive impresario in this play within the play, and in this way she configures a competing point of view to that of the Father. Her cynical use of poetic imagery corresponds to what David Hildner, Malcolm Read, and John Beverley have all termed the illegitimate or diabolical status of sensual poetry.[18] Díaz Balsera writes, "Lo ambiguo del auto es entonces que al hacer de la representación del mal del pecado algo deleitoso, irónicamente repite lo que hacen la Culpa y Lucifer al tentar al Hombre" (92) (The ambiguity of the *auto* then is that by making the representation of the evil of sin pleasing, it ironically repeats that which Guilt and Lucifer do when they tempt Man). However, in addition to reading this nuance as a theological "contradiction" or, in Vincent Martin's view, as another example of Thomist dialectics, I think it is useful to consider how *Culpa* underlines the (diabolical) genius of the *autor* in artfully assembling the allegorical artifice of the play, while distancing her illegitimate and dishonorable art from Calderón's more legitimate deployment of theatrical wit.[19] What is more, *Culpa* is a vital source of theological information, as she often explains the allegorical meaning of the signs and actions on the stage. Thus, this *other* point of view, diabolical in nature, becomes a constitutive mechanism in bringing the Eucharistic structure and its theological meaning to life. To reduce the role of *Culpa* to that of an illegitimate mediator between the brothers' desire and the immanent worlds of the inn and the market obscures important aspects of her activity. An equally important part of her function, as she herself states, is to dramatically represent the afterthought, or the effect that each brother's choice has on his pursuit of *Gracia*. Finally, in *Culpa* Calderón creates an *empresa* of heresy that is reminiscent of the *invención* analyzed earlier in this paper, when she declares "seré la piedra / del escándalo y la ruina" (508–09) (I will be the rock of scandal and ruin). If the rock that the *cancionero* poet gives to his beloved symbolizes the foundation of his absolute love for her, *Culpa*'s rock is the foundation on which the crumbling edifice of immanent and transgressive desire is erected.

Mal Genio occupies this terrain very early in the play when he falls for the charms of *Lascivia* at an inn, which was recently abandoned by *Buen Genio*. It is at this point where the former loses his *rose*, allegorically misplacing the grace deposited in him by God. This is an important moment, for it defines the difference between the brothers according to their powers of sight and inter-pretation. *Mal Genio* literally does not recognize *Culpa*, who is at *Lascivia*'s side disguised as a servant. As *Culpa* states, "Este no me ha conocido. / pues a pensar no ha llegado / que hay culpa en haber deseado; / con que el favor ha per-dido" (766–69) (This one has not recognized me. Since he has not considered that there is guilt in having desired, he has lost favor). As Martin observes with respect to the role of Apostasía in *El nuevo palacio del Retiro*, *Mal Genio*'s reading of *el mundo* is "ciego a su sentido místico y actual de la historia de la salvación que también incluye a él" (168) (blind to the mystical and actual meaning of the history of salvation which also includes him). *Culpa*'s observa-tion, however, underlines a problem that goes beyond the search for meaning.

Mal Genio's shortcomings precede his failure to recognize a mystical and "true" meaning, as desire moves into the sphere of action, or *obras*, which in turn introduces a problem relative to the relationship between desire and sig-nification. One cannot act or read correctly unless one first desires correctly. By the same token, one's desire, or intent, is not directly observed but is rather one step removed from itself and can only be recognized through one's actions. However, since external signs or choices may be deceptive—their interpretation being contingent on the desire of the reading subject—the correct identification of the character's desire is not as straightforward as Calderón would have it. There is no absolute solution to this endless circular movement of desire, mean-ing, and action, and therein lies the importance of establishing a dualistic matrix of interpretation that sidesteps the contradictions and circularity upon which the matrix is mounted.

To continue, the argument of the play rests on a progression of emblematic, or decisive, moments leading up to the final duel between the brothers, which will measure each one's ability to purchase merchandise based on its spiritual, as opposed to material, value. When they arrive at the "Marketplace of the World," *Mundo* introduces the various vendors and their merchandise as each contradic-tory pair parades before the audience: *Soberbia* and *Humildad*; *Lascivia*, dis-guised as *Hermosura* and *Desengaño*; *Gula*, disguised as blind *Apetito*—who is accompanied by an image-hawking *Culpa*—precedes *Penitencia*; finally, *Here-jía*, loaded down with books of diverse sciences, appears beside blind *Fe*, who is selling flesh and blood, or bread and wine. There is no need to go into the merchandise that each brother purchases and its implications, but I would like to look more closely at two of the figures and their relation to the plot.

Apetito and *Fe* are both blind, but each one's blindness symbolizes in turn the gaze that each projects onto the stage of the world. Appetite, or gluttony, is a desire that can only see material objects in the here and now, in the historical time of the subject, and judge them for what we might call their immediate use value on the plane of immanence. As Martin observes, this desire to read the world more "literally" appears whenever Calderón brings his heretical characters onto the stage, thus legitimizing the play's allegorical gyrations while branding all material knowledge or interpretation of the world, or marketplace, as Protestant, Jewish, Moorish, and *other* (29). Curiously, however, this perspective, which collapses the nullified meaning of the object into the equally nullified *thingness* of the object itself, is structurally similar to the phenomenon of embodiment, or presence, albeit in an absolutely negative manner. As such, the diabolical meaning of science, for example, inhabits the books themselves, just as the sacred host embodies the divine essence of Christian sacrifice. Faith, in the meanwhile, is blind to all but the extensive, or hypostatic, meaning of material reality on the plane of transcendence. This perspective, emblematic in nature, reads reality as a representational sign that refers, negatively, to something else. What these two characters demonstrate then is that the performance of a point of view is constitutive of one's relationship to sin or salvation. Much more problematic is the relationship of their limited perspectives to the ontological status of the sacramental body.

When *Fe* and *Herejía* debate the merits of their merchandise, the dogma of the Counter-Reformation meets the aesthetics of the emblematic mode of representation, and participation in the perspectivalism of emblematic aesthetics becomes acutely constitutive of ideology. One need not have *scientific* knowledge to function in this mode; indeed, Calderón denigrates erudition and science by equating a lack of education with the very cultural competence required to understand the doctrine of the *auto*: "Darnos la herejía todas las ciencias" (1351–52) (we give all the sciences to heresy).[20] The books that *Herejía* is carrying are those of Calvin and Luther, and the debate that follows is nothing less than the crux of the theological (and aesthetic) conflict between the Protestant Reformation and Catholic Counter Reformation as seen, of course, from Calderón's point of view:

HEREJÍA   Este
afirma que todo cuerpo
ocupar debe lugar,
y que no es posible aquello
de que esté el Cuerpo de Dios
en el blanco Pan, supuesto
que en él no ocupa lugar.

FE   El cuerpo extenso, concedo;
          el Cuerpo que está con modo
          indivisible, eso niego;
          y así está el Cuerpo de Cristo
          en el Pan del Sacramento,
          con el modo indivisible,
          y declárame un ejemplo:
          el alma de un hombre, ocupa
          todo un hombre, sin que demos
          lugar dónde esté, pues queda
          tan cabal, después de muerto,
          la cantidad, como estaba
          antes que muriese; luego,
          sin ocupar lugar, puede
          Dios estar en ese velo,
          y estar o no estar le hace
          ser Pan vivo o ser Pan muerto. (1271–93)

(HERESY: This book affirms that every body should occupy a place, and that this is not possible, whereby the body of God is in the white Bread, since it occupies no space therein.
FAITH: The extensive body, I concede; but the body that is there in its indivisible form, I deny; and thusly is the body of Christ in the Bread of the Sacrament, with indivisible form, and it shows me an example: the soul of a man, occupies the whole man without our being able to find where this place is, since it fits so perfectly, after death, the quantity remains as it was before he died; therefore, without occupying a place, God can be in that shroud, and his being or not being makes live Bread or dead Bread.)

Taking over the pedagogical role of *Culpa*, *Fe* goes to great lengths to explain how Christ's body, understood in its universal, or indivisible, status, inhabits the extensive body of the bread. To demonstrate, she explains how the indivisible presence of the soul temporarily inhabits the body of man. But we should take note of how both proofs are constructed through a type of postmortem that shows how incarnation is represented, or made present, precisely by referring to the exiting of the indivisible soul from the extensive body, which becomes an emblem in the modern sense of the word: a hieroglyphic that stands in for that which has gone. In the same way that the *talento* is to be interpreted allegorically as representative of the human soul, the bread acts as simultaneous placeholder and medium for the indivisible body of Christ. In the end, the bread becomes more substantial than the human body that ingests it, as "lo indivisible ya no es ni figurativo ni simbólico, sino presencia, misterio de los misterios que violenta los límites de la representación humana" (Regalado 80) (the indivisible is no longer figurative nor symbolic, but rather presence, mystery of mysteries that shatters the limits of human representation).

According to Catherine Bell's study of ritual, it would probably be more correct to say that the incarnation effect actually *depends* on the limits of human representation: "[t]his process yields the sense of a loosely knit and loosely coherent totality [. . .]. One is always led into a redundant, circular, and rhetorical universe of values and terms whose significance keeps flowing into other values and terms" (106). The indivisible essence always seems to be moving, exiting from the body, moving into the bread, then into the communicant, whose bodily excrescence seems a poor host, since desire usually sends the essence fleeing. In the end, the polyvalent emblem, or symbol, cannot overcome its semiotic instability anymore than the flesh and blood actors, as Regalado calls them, can overcome the actor/role opposition. As Julián Gállego notes, one cannot, for example, simply erase the popular and secular use of eucharistic metaphors: "Lejos de mí la intención de hacer chistes baratos; lo que pretendo es mostrar que no hay dos lenguajes pictóricos, el sacro y el profano, sino uno solo, que se adapta a las circunstancias" (41) (Far be it from me to make cheap jokes; what I intend to do is show that there are not two pictorial languages, the sacred and the profane, but only one, which is adapted to its circumstances). One can, however, frame such irony in a diabolical position on a dualistic hierarchy of moral values.

In the last scene, the two brothers approach the elevated gaze of the Father, who judges their approach as if he were interpreting the meaning of two emblems. In fact, what we as spectators see are two *empresas*, but *empresas* whose interpretation points not toward symbolic meaning but toward the desire of their creators. As they approach with their retinues of followers—Innocence, Faith, and the Virtues with *Buen Genio*; Greed, Malice, and Guilt with *Mal Genio*—the Father waits to make his judgment until he sees and understands how it is that each brother has come into possession of their goods: "Ni a uno ni a otro, hasta ver / a quién se la debo dar" (1508–09) (neither one nor the other, until I see to whom I should grant it). In emblematic terms, the meaning of each *empresa* needs to be elucidated not by the material words of its inventor but rather by his occult intention, so that the reader/Father, as final judge, can place him on one or the other side of his axiological vision of the world. With a single act of insight-obedience *Mal Genio* could, in theory, redeem all of the blind judgments he has made and make good on the symbolic debt he incurred when he asked for the favor of *Gracia*. If he were to do so, however, Calderón's insistent infusion of evil and blindness (not to mention Lutheran heresy, gypsy-like behavior, theological sophistication, etc.) into the ostensibly equal brother would come unraveled. When it is clear that *Mal Genio* takes full and deliberate ownership over his deceptively beautiful merchandise and the earth-bound ethos it represents, the Father damns his profligate son, permanently expelling him from the heavenly realm. Likewise, when it is clear that *Buen Genio* has purchased goods that reflect his ability to read their value from the Father's point of view—an act of judgment that exactly mirrors the absolute obedience the Father seeks—the Father embraces him, and the Holy Trinity is reunited. All the same, the allegorical interpretation performed by the Father has produced little concrete knowledge, which is characteristic of ritual practice. Moreover, the absolute condemnation of the errant son significantly translates, or suppresses, important aspects of the biblical references Calderón selects in order to add allegorical depth to his drama. Neither Cain nor Jacob, for example, was summarily sent to the infernal regions of the cosmos for their violation of patriarchal authority. As in the case of the letter TAV, meaning has little or no relation to the emblematic image, which can only be evaluated when it is employed; and in the *auto sacramental* this semiotic performance generally results in the unilateral placement of the subject on an absolute axis of judgment. As I have maintained, however, the staging of ritual oppositions cannot entirely resolve the contradictions brought about by the marriage of the doctrine of transubstantiation to the insistent relativity of modern theatricality.

Gerhard Poppenberg notes that the "diferencia entre 'imagen' y 'él mismo,' entre presencia teatral y presencia real eucarística, entre signo literario y signo sacramental permanece problemática" (116) (This difference between "image" and "he himself," between theatrical presence and real Eucharistic presence, between literary sign and sacramental sign remains problematical). The solution to this problem in the *auto*, as in the case of the *comedia*, appears to be the construction of a negative emblem, or ruin, which projects and contains a diabolical presence: a presence that both initiates the movement of theatrical signs and, once identified and chastised, acts as a stopgap to this incessant movement. Egginton's term for this "full space" within the homogeneous and empty space of the stage is the *crypt*, and its function "within the economy of theatricality[,] is to respond to this desire for substance, for presence, for the real" (111). In *El gran mercado del mundo*, the signs cease their movement when the crypt is filled with the demonic abomination associated with the desire of *Mal Genio*. Thus, the answer to Viviana Díaz Balsera's question regarding the impression that the *auto* simultaneously incites the spectator to sin while punishing sinful desire is located not in medieval theological dialectics but in the modernity of the *auto sacramental*. The *auto*, the sacred play, does not "make present" the body of Christ and the ecclesiastical and social body in the liturgical and medieval sense of the rite; such presence can only come about through an act of faith on the part of the participant. It evokes, rather, the modern, theatrical representation of a death-driven specter that threatens an imagined Spanish hegemony, thus bringing the desire for the presence of this identity into the psyche of the spectator. In other words, the modern (split) subject identifies with (is attracted to) both the transgressive desire and its repression.

Conclusion: Presence and Modernity

Donald T. Dietz makes an important observation about the theatrical performance of sacred rituals when he observes "it is impossible to conceive of theater without the presence of a protagonist-antagonist situation" (176). One can make the same statement concerning the relation between antagonistic social relations and the ideology of the modern nation state and its crisis-ridden identities. Recent historiographical work on the Spanish Inquisition strongly suggests that the relationship between the *auto sacramental* and the historical reality of early modern Spain is much more complex than most criticism of the *auto* acknowledges. Jaime Contreras, for example, warns us that any historical documentation of *conversos* and Judaizers has to be read with extreme care, since the primary sources of information, largely transcriptions of Inquisition trials, relate a very biased view of the actual social reality, or even the historical existence, of Spanish Jews and converts: "The conversos who judaized did not bequeath to posterity their own testimony; on the contrary, they were obliged to accept the fact that this task would be undertaken by others: at times, by their bitterest enemies, the inquisitors, and at others, by the Jews of the Diaspora, who frequently demonstrated a manifest unwillingness to integrate them into their communities" (129). Joseph Silverman adds, "By the time that Lope was writing for the theater the Jew was only a phantasmagorical presence in his land, an imaginary threat to the Catholic unity of the Spanish faith" (164). Sarah Nalle informs us that the spectacular trials and executions of Lutherans in Valladolid in 1559 are more the exception than the rule, as for all intents and purposes there were no Lutherans in Spain. In matters of heresy, Richard Kagan's studies of *profetas de la plaza* conclude that the juridical persecution and castigation of so-called false prophets was motivated far more by concrete political factors than by matters of doctrine: "the criteria for distinguishing true prophets from false remained somewhat vague, and this perhaps explains why inquisitorial persecution of would-be prophets was haphazard and generally limited to those whose prognostications constituted a direct political threat to the monarchy" (110).

All of these observations beg the question: if the dramatic representation of heretics is completely out of proportion to their historical existence, why do they play such a prominent role in Calderón's sacred dramaturgy? The answer is provided in part by ritual scholars such as Bell, Bourdieu, and Turner and their studies of the importance in ritual practice of the "motivation of bias." As Victor Turner notes, "Members of despised or outlawed ethnic minorities play major roles in myths and popular tales as representatives or expressions of universal human values" (110). According to the historians cited above, however, Turner's positive identification of these "members" does not describe the de facto social situation of Golden Age Spain. This does not mean, of course, that one cannot make the other present through the creation of images, or emblems, of otherness. Like hieroglyphic symbols, entire social, ethnic, or religious groups are uprooted from their specific historical fields of social and cultural activity and arranged according to the binary oppositions of ritual discourse. The following statement by Bell, moreover, casts a curious light on the various purges of Jews, *conversos*, and *moriscos* that echo in the *autos* whenever the figure of the heretic is introduced:

> The historical record suggests that dramatic purges occur in inverse ratio to the presence of real enemies or policy failures. When analyzed more symbolically, these political performances appear to divide up the world into two absolute camps, the good and innocent on the one hand and the deviant and the reprehensible on the other. (*Perspectives* 163)

As Poppenberg concludes in his study of the dramatic development of Calderón's *auto*, "El hereje aparece en efecto con mucha más frecuencia en las piezas, pertenece formalmente a su dotación básica y es, a su vez, ejemplo del enemigo que también puede ser el paganismo, el judaísmo o el islamismo. [. . .] [A]l fin de cuentas [. . .] la eucaristía [funciona como una] forma de la relación con el enemigo" (90) (The heretic appears in effect with much more frequency in the pieces, formally belongs to its basic makeup and is, at the same time, an example of the enemy who can also be paganism, judaism, or islam. [. . .] In the end [. . .] the eucharist [becomes a] form of relation with the other).[21] In other words, a dominant political order configures both a series of transgressive symbolic practices that threaten their hegemony and an antagonistic figure, such as the Jew or the Protestant, who by threatening to deploy said practices becomes the avatar of historical change. As a result, any attempt to question the monarchical or ecclesiastical right to rule based on their political failures or excesses is characterized as demonic, perverse, unpatriotic, and *other*. The imagined presence of the indivisible, political, and social body of militant Catholic Spain cannot be separated from the theatrical performance of a demonic *presence* that both threatens and necessitates adherence to the national body.

Notes

1. José Antonio Maravall's concept of "baroque guided culture" is, of course, a main point of reference in these studies, but the recent proliferation of studies that move freely between the social tensions and cultural practices of the Latin American Colonial "Baroque" and discussions of the baroque or "neo-baroque" nature of capitalist and post-capitalist Latin American identities has enriched and problematized research throughout Hispanic Studies (Sarduy, Chiampi, Moraña, Schumm).

2. William Egginton's recent book *How the World Became a Stage* is an excellent study of this phenomenon of *presence* from a philosophical point of view; it does not, unfortunately, discuss the *auto sacramental*.

3. For another emblematic analysis of a Calderonian *auto*, see Danker.

4. I have placed the term *artistic* in parentheses due in part to Arnold Hauser's study of the profound cultural, economic, and aesthetic changes that helped bring about the appearance of the individual and philosophically inclined Renaissance artist as opposed to what he considers to be the artisan status of medieval craftsmen in the creation of medieval, iconic art. See Belting for a convincing response to Hauser's historicist reading of iconographical art.

5. Cull also writes, "Emblematic staging is clearly the most important manifestation of emblematics in the Corpus plays" ("Emblematic Representation" 118); and Restrepo-Gautier connects the aesthetics of the emblem with the staging of eucharistic presence itself: "Quizás el final del auto sacramental, cuando se exponen a manera de *pictura* la hostia y el cáliz, sea la parte más obviamente emblemática del género: unas imágenes acompañadas de parlamentos e xplicativos enseñan a la audiencia la doctrina cristiana" (35) (Perhaps the end of the sacramental play, when the host and chalice are displayed in the manner of a *picture*, is the most obviously emblematic aspect of the genre: images accompanied by explicative speeches teach christian doctrine to the audience). See also Danker and Mariscal.

6. *Pictura, inscription*, and *picture* are the terms used by emblemists and critics alike to refer to the visual image, enigmatic motto (often in Latin), and interpretive commentary (in verse or prose) that characterize much but not all emblematic literature (see Praz). Lately, the ever-widening definition of what is considered an emblem, typified

by Daly's inclusive definition, has made the original "tripartite" definition a problematic if still universally employed touchstone of emblematics.

7. Díez Borque answers this critical fragmentation of the *auto* which seems to correspond to its textual and spectacular reality by stating "La necesaria fragmentación, para su estudio, de los elementos que integran fiesta y teatro puede producir una falsa idea de independencia y desconexión, cuando la realidad—puesta de relieve por los especialistas del tema—es la unidad orgánica de todos ellos, en un proceso de integración de distintas artes y técnicas. [. . .] La espectacularidad, con las funciones que ya veíamos, es la idea unificadora que articula, con una intencionalidad calculada, los distintos componentes de la fiesta sacramental en una perfecta simbiosis de lo visual y lo sonoro, de la estructura de ideas y la estructura escénica" (*Una fiesta* 70–71) (The necessary fragmentation, for their study, of the elements that make up festival and theater may produce a false idea of independence and disconnection, when the reality—placed in relief by specialists on the topic—is the organic unity of all of them, through a process of integration of different arts and techniques. [. . .] The 'spectacularity,' with the functions that we have already seen, is the unifying idea that articulates, with a calculated intentionality, the different components of the sacramental festival in a perfect symbiosis of the visual and the aural, of the structure of ideas and the stage techniques).

8. Wardropper's study points out that this tendency toward municipal regulation goes as far back as 1372, when Don Jaime de Aragón, bishop of Valencia, "se da cuenta que el Corpus Christi no podrá ser una fiesta verdaderamente popular sin la colaboración de las autoridades seglares. [. . .] De esta manera, la procesión de Valencia, a los dieciséis años de su inauguración, cesa de funcionar bajo la supervisión directa de la Iglesia" (*Introducción* 71).

9. "La temporada teatral comenzaba en Pascua, y, para que fuera posible prepararla, los compromisos anuales de los actores tomaban como punto de partida el Carnaval. Estos compromisos señalaban claramente que el Corpus era el momento culminante del año, estipulando una gratificación considerable 'por la fiesta del Corpus'" (199) (The theater season began at Easter, and, so that it would be possible to be ready for it, the annual contracts of the actors also used Carnival as a point of departure. These compromises clearly indicated that the Corpus was the culminating moment of the year, stipulating a considerable gratification 'for the Corpus festival').

10. See Maravall (*Culture* 207–24) and David R. Castillo for illuminating studies on the relation between theatrical and literary anamorphosis and ideological interpellation.

11. Many of the Father's verbal contributions to the play occur in the form of a soliloquy, which, as Hesse points out, acts as an anchor for meaning in many of Calderón's plays and, furthermore, reinforces our thesis concerning the importance of the spoken and heard word in the interpretation of the visual spectacle: "En muchos casos, el soliloquio sirve para transmitir una explicación plausible de una acción o actitud de la cual el motivo verdadero, aunque a menudo inconsciente, es tal, que uno lo repudiaría.

Algunas veces Calderón emplea argumentación en forma de soliloquio como sustituto a la acción. Es decir, el soliloquio puede revelar tanto el carácter como la acción." (580) (In many cases, the soliloquy serves to transmit a plausible explanation for an action or attitude for which the true motive, although often unconscious, is such, that one would repudiate it. Sometimes Calderón employed argumentation in the form of a soliloquy as a substitute for action. Which is to say, the soliloquy can reveal as much about the character as about the action).

12. See R. de la Flor's "La sombra de *Eclesiastés.*"

13. The relevant part of the commentary reads, "como lo significaban los Egipcios en sus Letras Hieroglyphicas por la Cruz, como se ve en los Obeliscos, que hicieron con la letra: TAV" (442) (as the Egyptians signified in their Hieroglyphic Letters for the Cross, as is seen in the Obelisks, which they made with the letter: TAV).

14. Dámaso Alonso and Carlos Bousoño concur, writing: "Así ocurre con mucha frecuencia en los autos, pues casi toda su trama conceptual (sobre la que se moldea simbólicamente la dramática) está basada en la pluralidad diferenciada de seres que tienen un elemento común, es decir, en la agrupación de entidades diferenciadas específicamente, dentro de un género. El pensamiento filosófico y especialmente teológico del auto calderoniano se sitúa, por tanto, fundamentalmente en el terreno donde la reproducción del pensamiento produce la plurimembración (y con ella la tendencia correlativa), que ha sido nuestro punto de partida para todo este estudio: y así las falsas religiones . . . , la Santísima Trinidad . . . , las Virtudes Teologales . . . , las Cardinales . . . , los enemigos del hombre . . . , las potencias . . . , las estaciones . . . , los elementos . . . , los sentidos . . . , los Doctores de la Iglesia . . . etc.," (149) (Thus, it very frequently occurs in the *autos*, as almost the whole conceptual plot (on which the dramatic concept is symbolically molded) is based on the differentiated plurality of beings who have a common element, in other words, in the grouping of specifically differentiated entities, within one genre. The philosophical and especially theological thought of the Calderonian *auto* is fundamentally situated, therefore, in the terrain where the reproduction of thought produces a 'plurimembration' (and along with it a correlating tendency), which has been our point of departure for the entire study: and so the false religions. . . , the Holy Trinity. . . , the Theological Virtues. . . , the Cardinal [Virtues] . . . , man's enemies . . . , the faculties . . . , the seasons . . . , the elements . . . , the senses . . . , the 'Doctors' of the Church . . . , etc.,).

15. Mal Genio: Prodigio de asombro tanto,
    que al cielo el penacho encumbra,
    cuyo bellísimo encanto
    con la vista nos deslumbra,
    nos suspende con el canto.

Gracia: Monstruo, que con las supremas
    regiones las plumas bates,
    sin que aire y fuego temas,

las hielas si las abates,
y si las alzas, las quemas. (16–25)
(Mal Genio: Marvel of such wonder, that its plume of feathers exalts the heavens, whose beautiful charm dazzles us with its sight, astonishes with its song. Gracia: Monster (freak), who beats down on the supreme regions with its wings, without fearing air nor fire, you freeze them if you humble them, and if you raise them, you burn them.)

16. Eugenio Frutos explains the function of doubt in relation to *Entendimiento* in the following manner: "La relación del Entendimiento y la Fe en Calderón es siempre la misma. El Entendimiento duda primero, pero acaba por dar crédito al Oído, por el que es 'cautivo de la Fe'" (494) (The relation between Understanding and Faith in Calderón is always the same. At first, understanding doubts, but [it] ends up lending credence to the Ear, through which it is 'captivated by Faith'"). Although later he is more specific, showing how the doubting tendencies of *Entendimiento* actually belong more properly to the inventive faculty of *Ingenio*: "Esta opinión se refuerza si tenemos en cuenta que Calderón considera como propia del Ingenio 'la razón de dudar', según se dice en la loa de *El jardín de Falerina*" (509) (This opinion is reinforced if we keep in mind that Calderón considers the 'reason [or right] to doubt' as belonging to the inventive faculty, as expressed in the *loa* for *El jardín de Falerina*).

17. See Maravall (*Culture* 207–24) on the "technique of incompleteness."

18. See also Wardopper, who writes, "la imaginación es al mismo tiempo la facultad *creadora* de los poetas y la facultad *traidora* de los personajes imaginados por ellos" ("La imaginación" 925) (the imagination is the creative faculty of the poets and the *treasonous* faculty of the personages imagined by them).

19. See Greer for a discussion of a self-parodying example of Calderón's self-representation in the context of the *comedia nueva*.

20. Parker locates the originality and genius of Calderonian theater in his inclusion of the spectator in the 'completion' of the dramatic artifice: "[Calderón] allows his audience to follow each step in the train of thought as it emerges from the mind of a character on the stage actually conceiving the action before their eyes. The importance of this strikingly original device lies in the remarkable clarity it can give to an abstract theme, since it enables the action to be cut short at any moment for the character who is imagining it to retrace the steps in his train of thought, to comment on particular points, and to sum up the preliminary conclusions he has arrived at before proceeding further" (82–83).

21. Poppenberg backs up his assertions with careful analyses that locate examples in which, for example, the rebels of Cataluña are represented as Judaizers, or Lucifer is linked to the *comuneros* (95).

Works Cited

Alonso, Dámaso. "La correlación en la estructura del teatro calderoniano." *Seis calas en la expresión literaria española*. Ed. Dámaso Alonso and Carlos Bousoño. Madrid: Gredos, 1951.

Bataillon, Marcel. "Ensayo de explicación del 'auto sacramental.'" *Varia lección de clásicos españoles*. Madrid: Gredos, 1964. 183–205.

Bell, Catherine. *Ritual Theory, Ritual Practice*. New York, Oxford: Oxford University Press, 1992.

Belting, Hans. *Likeness and Presence: A History of the Image Before the Era of Art*. Trans. Edmund Jephcott. Chicago: University of Chicago Press, 1994.

Benjamin, Walter. *The Origins of German Tragic Drama*. Trans. John Osborne. London: NCB, 1977.

Beverley, John. *Del Lazarillo al Sandinismo: Estudios sobre la función ideológica de la literatura española e hispanoamericana*. Minneapolis: Prisma Institute, 1987.

Borja, Juan de. *Empresas morales*. Brussels: F. Foppens, 1680.

Bonet Correa, Antonio. *Fiesta, poder y arquitectura. Aproximaciones al barroco español*. Madrid: AKAL, 1990.

Bourdieu, Pierre. *Outline of a Theory of Practice*. Trans. Richard Nice. Cambridge: Cambridge University Press, 1977.

Calderón de la Barca, Pedro. *El gran teatro del mundo. El gran mercado del mundo*. Ed. Domingo Yndurain. Madrid: Istmo, 1974.

Castillo, David R. *(A)wry Views: Anamorphosis, Cervantes and the Early Picaresque*. West Lafayette, IN: Purdue University Press, 2001.

Chiampi, Irlemar. *Barroco y modernidad*. Mexico, D.F: Fondo de Cultura Económica, 2000.

Contreras, Jaime. "Family and Patronage: The Judeo-Converso Minority in Spain." *Cultural Encounters: The Impact of the Inquisition in Spain and the New World*. Ed. Ann Cruz and Elizabeth Perry. Berkeley: University of California Press, 1991. 127–45.

Cruz, Anne J., and Mary Elizabeth Perry. *Cultural Encounters: The Impact of the Inquisition in Spain and the New World*. Berkeley; Los Angeles; Oxford: University of California Press, 1991.

Cull, John T. "Emblematics in Calderón's *El médico de su honra*." *Bulletin of the Comediantes* 44 (1992): 113–30.

———. "Emblematic Representation in the *autos sacramentales* in Calderón." In *The Calderonian Stage: Body and Soul*. Ed. Manuel Delgado. Lewisburg, PA: Bucknell University Press, 1996. 107–32.

———. " 'Hablan poco y dicen mucho': The Function of Discovery Scenes in the Drama of Tirso de Molina." *The Modern Language Review* 91 (1996): 619–34.

Daly, Peter M. *Literature in Light of the Emblem. Structural Parallels between the Emblem and Literature in the Sixteenth and Seventeenth Centuries*. Toronto: Toronto University Press, 1979.

Danker, Frederick E. "Emblematic Technique in the *Auto Sacramental*: Calderón's *No hay más fortuna que Dios.*" *Comparative Drama* 6 (1972): 40–50.

Díaz Balsera, Viviana. *Calderón y las quimeras de la culpa. Alegoría, seducción y resistencia en cinco autos sacramentales.* West Lafayette, IN: Purdue University Press, 1997.

Dietz, Donald T. *The Auto Sacramental and the Parable in Spanish Golden Age Literature.* Chapel Hill: North Carolina University Press, 1973.

Díez Borque, José María. "El auto sacramental calderoniano y su público: funciones del texto cantado." *Calderón and the Baroque Tradition.* Ed. Kurt Levy, Jesús Ara, and Gethin Hughes. Waterloo, Ont.: Wilfrid Laurier University Press, 1985. 49–67.

_____. *Una fiesta sacramental barroca.* Madrid: Taurus, 1984.

_____. "Relaciones de teatro y fiesta en el Barroco español." *Teatro y fiesta en el Barroco: España e Iberoamérica: seminario de la Universidad Internacional Menéndez Pelayo (Sevilla, octubre de 1985).* Ed. José María Díez Borque and José Alcina Franch. Barcelona: Ediciones del Serbal, 1986. 11–31.

Dutton, Brian, ed. *El Cancionero del siglo XV, c. 1360–1520.* Salamanca: Universidad de Salamanca, 1990–1991.

Echeverría, Bolívar. "La Compañía de Jesús y la primera modernidad en América Latina." *Barrocos y modernos: Nuevos caminos en la investigación del Barroco iberoamericano.* Ed. Petra Schumm. Frankfurt/Madrid: Vervuert Ibero-Americana, 1998. 49–65.

_____. *La modernidad de lo barroco.* Mexico City: Ediciones Era, 2000.

Egginton, William. *How the World Became a Stage: Presence, Theatricality, and the Question of Modernity.* Albany: State University of New York Press, 2003.

Egido, Aurora. *La fábrica de un auto sacramental. Los encantos de la culpa.* Salamanca: Universidad de Salamanca, 1982.

Frutos, Eugenio. "La filosofía del Barroco y el pensamiento de Calderón." *RUB* 9 (1951): 173–230.

Gállego, Julián. *Visión y símbolos en la pintura española del Siglo de Oro.* Madrid: Cátedra, 1987.

Gombrich, E. H. *Symbolic Images: Studies in the Art of the Renaissance.* Chicago: University of Chicago Press, 1972.

Greer, Margaret R. "'La vida es sueño ¿o risa?' Calderón Parodies the *auto.*" *Bulletin of Hispanic Studies* 72 (1995): 313–25.

Hauser, Arnold. *The Social History of Art.* Vol. 2. New York: Vintage Books, 1961.

Hildner, David Jonathan. *Reason and the Passions in the Comedias of Calderón.* Purdue University Monographs in Romance Languages. Amsterdam, Philadelphia: John Benjamins, 1982.

Horozco y Covarrubias, Juan de. *Emblemas morales.* Zaragoza: Alonso Rodrigues y Juan de Bonilla, 1603.

Kagan, Richard. "Politics, Prophecy, and the Inquisition in Late Sixteenth-Century Spain." *Cultural Encounters: The Impact of the Inquisition in Spain and the New World.* Ed.

Ann Cruz and Elizabeth Perry. Berkeley; Los Angeles; Oxford: University of California Press, 1991. 105–26.

Kurtz, Barbara E. *The Play of Allegory in the* Autos Sacramentales *of Pedro Calderón de la Barca.* Washington, DC: The Catholic University of America Press, 1991.

Ledda, Giuseppina. *Contributo allo studio della letteratura emblematica in Spagna (1559–1613).* Pisa: Pisa University Press, 1970.

_____. "Los jeroglíficos en el contexto de la fiesta religiosa barroca." *Literatura emblemática hispánica. Actas del I Simposio Internacional (La Coruña, 14–17 de septiembre, 1994).* Ed. Sagrario López Poza. La Coruña: Universidad da Coruña, 1996. 111–28.

Maravall, José Antonio. *Culture of the Baroque: Analysis of a Historical Structure.* Trans. Terry Cochran. Minneapolis: University of Minnesota Press, 1986.

_____. "La literatura de emblemas en el contexto de la sociedad barroca." *Teatro y literatura en la sociedad barroca.* Madrid: Seminarios y ediciones, 1972. 149–88.

Martin, Vincent. *El concepto de "representación" en los autos sacramentales de Calderón.* Prologue by Fernando R. de la Flor. Kassel/Pamplona: Edition Reichenberger/Universidad de Pamplona, 2002.

Menéndez y Pelayo, Marcelino. *Calderón y su teatro.* Madrid: Murillo, 1881. Rpt. in *Estudios y discursos de crítica histórica y literaria, III.* Santander, 1941.

Molho, Maurice. *Cervantes: raíces folklóricas.* Madrid: Gredos, 1976.

Moraña, Mabel, ed. *Relecturas del Barroco de Indias.* Hanover, N.H: Ediciones del Norte, 1994.

_____. "Barroco y conciencia criolla en hispanoamérica." *Revista de Crítica Literaria Latinoamericana.* XIV (1988): 229–51.

Nalle, Sara Tilghman. *Mad for God: Bartolomé Sánchez, The Secret Messiah of Cardenete.* Charlottesville, London: University of Virginia Press, 2001.

Nelson, Bradley J. "Emblematic Representation and Guided Culture in Baroque Spain: Juan de Horozco y Covarrubias." *Culture and the State in Spain: 1550–1850.* Ed. Tom Lewis and Francisco Sánchez. Hispanic Issues 20. Minneapolis: University of Minnesota Press, 1999. 157–95.

Parker, Alexander A. *The Allegorical Drama of Calderón.* London and Oxford: Dolphin Book Shop, 1943.

Paz, Octavio. *Sor Juana or, The Traps of Faith.* Trans. Margaret Sayers Peden. Cambridge, MA: Harvard University Press, 1988.

Pinkus, Karen. *Picturing Silence: Emblem, Language, Counter-Reformation Materiality.* Ann Arbor: University of Michigan Press, 1996.

Poppenberg, Gerhard. "Religión y política en algunos autos sacramentales de Calderón." *Calderón: protagonista eminente del barroco europeo.* Ed. Kurt and Theo Reichenberger. Vol 1. Kassel: Edition Reichenberger, 2000. 87–116.

Praz, Mario. *Studies in Seventeenth-Century Imagery.* 2nd ed. Roma: Edizioni di Storia e Letteratura, 1975.

Read, Malcolm. *Language, Text, Subject. A Critique of Hispanism.* West Lafayette, IN: Purdue University Press, 1992.

Regalado, Antonio. *Calderón: Los orígenes de la modernidad en la España del Siglo de Oro. Vol. II.* Barcelona: Destino, 1995.

Restrepo-Gautier, Pablo. *La imaginación emblemática en Tirso de Molina.* Newark, DE: Juan de la Cuesta, 2001.

Rodríguez de la Flor, Fernando. *Emblemas: Lecturas de la imagen simbólica.* Madrid: Alianza Editorial, 1995.

_____. "La sombra del *Eclesiastés* es alargada. 'Vanitas' y deconstrucción de la idea de mundo en la emblemática española hacia 1580." *Emblemata aurea. La emblemática en el arte y la literatura del siglo de oro.* Ed. Rafael Zafra and José Javier Azanza. Madrid: Ediciones Akal, 2000. 337–52.

_____. "Prólogo." *El concepto de "representación" en los autos sacramentales de Calderón.* By Vincent Martin. Kassel/Pamplona: Edition Reichenberger/Universidad de Pamplona, 2002. 9–16.

Russell, Daniel. *Emblematic Stuctures in Renaissance French Culture.* Toronto: University of Toronto Press: 1995.

_____. "Perceiving, Seeing and Meaning: Emblems and Some Approaches to Reading Early Modern Culture." *Aspects of Renaissance and Baroque Symbol Theory.* Ed. Peter M. Daly and John Manning. New York: AMS, 1999. 77–91.

Schumm, Petra, ed. *Barrocos y modernos: Nuevos caminos en la investigación del Barroco iberoamericano.* Frankfurt/Madrid: Vervuert, Ibero-Americana, 1998.

_____. "El concepto 'barroco' en la época de la desaparición de las fronteras." *Barrocos y modernos: Nuevos caminos en la investigación del Barroco iberoamericano.* Ed. Petra Schumm. Frankfurt/Madrid: Vervuert, Ibero-Americana, 1998. 13–30.

Silverman, Joseph H. "On Knowing Other People's Lives, Inquisitorially and Artisitcally." *Cultural Encounters: The Impact of the Inquisition in Spain and the New World.* Ed. Ann Cruz and Elizabeth Perry. Berkeley; Los Angeles; Oxford: University of California Press, 1991. 157–75.

Surtz, Ronald. *The Birth of a Theater: Dramatic Convention in the Spanish Theater from Juan del Encina to Lope de Vega.* Princeton, N.J.: Princeton University Press; Madrid: Editorial Castalia, 1979.

Turner, Victor. *The Ritual Process: Structure and Anti-Structure.* Foreword by Roger D. Abrahams. New York: Aldine de Gruyter, 1969.

Wardropper, Bruce W. *Introducción al teatro religioso del Siglo de Oro. La evolución del auto sacramental 1500–1648.* Madrid: Revista de Occidente, 1953.

_____. "The Search for a Dramatic Formula for the 'auto sacramental.'" *PMLA* 54 (1950): 1196–1211.

_____. "La imaginación en el metateatro calderoniano." *Actas del Tercer Congreso Internacional de Hispanistas.* Ed. Carlos H. Magis. México: Colegio de México, 1970. 923–30.

Williams, Raymond. *Marxism and Literature.* Oxford: Oxford University Press: 1977.

◆ 7

The Challenges of Freedom:
Social Reflexivity in the Seventeenth-Century
Spanish Literary Field[1]

Carlos M. Gutiérrez

A tantalizing embryo of authorial freedom haunted Spanish baroque literature. In the following pages I will attempt to illustrate what challenges and opportunities accompanied the social emergence of the literary author in seventeenth-century Spain. I am specifically thinking of the interaction between literature and court society and the built-in dialectics between literary freedom and social containment that such interaction presented. The main topics that I will be discussing henceforth deal with several forms of social reflexivity related to seventeenth-century Spanish writers. More particularly, I will discuss how and when they started to perceive themselves as a group; how they perceived their relationship with aristocrats and with court society at large; and what kind of effects arose from that relationship. For those purposes, I will draw on my previous research, which focused on the emergence of the first Spanish literary field[2] circa 1600, as well as on a variety of sociological (Bourdieu, Castro, Elias, and Viala) and historical sources (Maravall, Elliott, and Feros).

Issues such as freedom and containment in early modern Spain cannot be properly discussed without mentioning José Antonio Maravall's interpretation of the Spanish Baroque in *La cultura del Barroco* (1975) (*Culture of the Baroque*, 1986) and other works. Maravall contemplated the Baroque not so much

as an artistic style (as Wölfflin and others did) but, rather, as a historical structure characterized by a culture that was "urban," "mass-oriented," "guided,"
and "conservative." In what pertains to literature, Maravall saw three different
attitudes toward the model propitiated by the monarcho-seigniorial segments
of society: whereas the picaresque novel represents a certain discrepancy and
the essay opted for a tactical accommodation, the theater oriented itself toward
socio-political propaganda (*Teatro* 15–16). At the risk of oversimplifying the
issue, it could be argued that Maravall's model explains the social insertion
of literary genres and of specific works better than the literary trajectories and
the social intricacies associated with the early modern author. As Lollini notes,
some of the issues not studied by Maravall include subjectivity and identity,
which are certainly important when considering authorial agency and, therefore, freedom. It is equally problematic to leave poetry out of a cultural analysis of the Baroque, for poetry was, by all accounts, *the* genre of the time. Its
ambivalent nature (mass-oriented *and* elitist, courtly but popular at the same
time, panegyric *or* satiric toward the field of power) certainly makes poetry a
more difficult fit as a guided form of baroque culture. Finally, we could also
argue that it is problematic to analyze an historical structure using literary texts
(or genres) without taking into account the inner logic and functioning of the
literary field that produced those texts, or the agency of the authors in opting
for certain genres, styles or practices. For that reason, it is the interaction of writers, both among themselves and with the monarcho-seigniorial complex that
I would like to discuss here, pointing to some of the tensions between social
containment and literary freedom that arose in seventeenth-century Spain. This
double interaction can encourage us to rethink the extent to which literature
was a guided form of culture in the Spanish Baroque. Also, this interaction will
frame and reflect the dialectics between freedom and dependency that some
early modern Spanish writers saw themselves immersed in.

In spite of Foucault's effort,[3] the fact that the literary author is a socio-
historical construct is frequently overlooked. After a couple of centuries of
ceaseless romantization of its figure, we often forget that the birth of the modern writer (and, by extension, of the author) was made possible by a slow
process that lasted several centuries and was enabled by significant leaps such
as the emergence of printing, the popularization of narrative fiction in urban settings, and the emergence of gradual forms of intellectual property. At the same
time, it is tempting—and we frequently oblige—to contemplate Literature as
a mere sequence of authors bound by literary history, tradition, or different
forms of intertextuality. The fact that Literature—the texts of whatever past that
we might consider "literary"—can appeal to us through timeless echoes and

reminiscences, should not make us forget that the actual writers who produced those texts—some of them not even true "authors"—might have had little, if anything, in common with what we deem today to be a literary author. By the same token, the social circumstances in which those texts were written differ much from today's.[4] One of the circumstances that must be dealt with when considering early modern literary praxis is the insertion of writers and their texts in the broad context of court culture.

Generally speaking, there were two types of cultural relationships between aristocrats and writers: clientelism[5] and patronage. Although very common in the seventeenth century, clientelism has certain medieval residues and a logic of service that sometimes implied an occupation, gains, or religious benefices (Viala 52–3). Patronage, however, does not entail usually anything more than the material support given by a patron to an artist or writer so he or she can develop some artistic activity. In clientelism, the fact that the writer is serving the aristocrat either precedes or mediates whatever cultural products might be related to this relationship, whereas in patronage the literary works are not necessarily a direct filiation of such relationship. It is truly rare, though, as Viala warns, to find art for art's sake, for the implicit logic of seventeenth-century patronage is founded upon the public, express recognition of the authors as either potential or effective patrons and benefactors (54).

At this point, we have to ponder what kinds of relationships between writers and aristocrats or members of the power field are more frequent. Do they resemble clientelism or patronage? In my opinion we could find traces of both, depending on specific cases. On the one hand we have literary or even metaliterary works that are, by their own nature, by their *inventio*, "autonomous," but they are nonetheless dedicated to a member of the power field. Such is the case, for example, with *Don Quijote* and Góngora's *Soledades*. On the other hand, we have texts that present clear clientelistic features. One thinks of works either commissioned by some person belonging to the power field (as it happens with Quevedo's *Chitón de las tarabillas*) or written by the author with a clientelistic horizon of expectations, as it happens with Góngora's *Panegírico al duque de Lerma*. This poem is clearly a position-taking addressed to a specific reader and potential patron from whom support is sought. In the *Panegírico*, Góngora used, as the abbot of Rute noted, an adulation "descubierta y falsa . . . condenando los tiempos y ministros del rey pasado, por subir de punto el gobierno del duque de Lerma" (Alonso 52) (bareheaded and false . . . discrediting the times and ministers of the former king, in order to praise the Duke of Lerma's government). The truth is that Góngora's poem, starting with the title, left no doubt about its pretensions and goals.

Thus, clientelism and patronage present nuances. Literary patronage co-exists with the printing market, and it is a partial consequence of the existence of a literary field, whereas clientelism is a by-product of the intersection at the Court between politics and culture. Another difference worth mentioning between both is their impact in the choosing of genre, style, or literary subject. As Viala pointed out, patronage dynamics encouraged *encomia* and panegyric poetry, together with entertaining fictions capable of prestige-gain, among mid-seventeenth-century French writers (79). On the other hand, it seems that clientelism did not have a big poetic influence among them.

Another aspect to consider is the genre distribution between clientelism and patronage. Clientelism tends toward heroic or panegyric poetry, a certain kind of theater, the historic chronicle and, exceptionally, the libel. Patronage, on the other hand, is usually connected with either erudite or fictional prose or lyric poetry. Theater is a case in itself because of its dual nature, both textual and spectacular. Aristocrats or even the royal family could become occasional Maecenas by commissioning works for court entertainment or other particular purposes (Viala 79). Published plays, on the other hand, ended up in a no-man's-land between editorial supply and demand with the playwright alluding in the dedications to his relationship with either effective or potential patrons. I shall illustrate with a detailed example the nuances and complexities found in the relationship between aristocrats and writers.

Lope de Vega saw himself immersed in a social oxymoron that originated in what he perceived as his space of possibilities. He was making money selling his *comedias* to the public theaters and accepting commissions to write genealogical and religious plays for members of the power field.[6] At the same time, without perceiving any kind of contradiction, Lope aspired to obtain a prestigious and symbolic court appointment as royal chronicler (Wright 20). While it is true that Lope's case is special, writers still had before them a wide array of possibilities: choosing genre, style, and topic for their works; printing them or leaving them in manuscript form; choosing when to release it; and deciding who should be the addressee, if any. It is certainly not by chance that *Don Quijote* (1605), Pedro Espinosa's *Flores de poetas ilustres* (1605) and Góngora's *Soledades* (*circa* 1612), were addressed to the Duke of Béjar. Cervantes writes in his dedication that the Duke received and honored "all sort of books" as a "príncipe tan inclinado a favorecer las buenas artes, mayormente las que por su nobleza no se abaten al servicio y granjerías del vulgo" (prince so inclined to favor good arts, chiefly those who, by their nobleness, do not submit to the service and bribery of the vulgar). Lope, in turn, opted for approaching the

Fernández de Córdoba clan, dedicating *El peregrino en su patria* (1604) to the Marquis of Priego. A year later, Lope started a complex relationship with Luis Fernández de Córdoba, the sixth Duke of Sessa, which lasted many years and took many forms. I am not convinced that we are facing here a residual dependency of a feudal patronage system, as Malcolm K. Read suggested to describe the relationship between Gracián and Lastanosa (93).[7] The agency exercised by members of the literary field, together with the free will of the very act of writing, should prevent that from happening. An indirect example of the potential exercise of agency, as well as of the complex interaction between writers and aristocrats appears in May 1620, when Lope de Vega writes to the eighth Count of Lemos: "Yo he estado un año sin ser poeta *de pane lucrando*: milagro del señor Duque de Osuna, que me envió quinientos escudos desde Nápoles, que, ayudados de mi beneficio, pusieron olla a estos muchachos" (*Cartas* II, 83) (For an entire year I have not been a *de pane lucrando* poet, a miracle made possible by the lord Duke of Osuna who sent me five hundred escudos from Naples that, together with my own benefice, put food on the table for these children). This quotation contains some of the clues pertaining to the relationship between aristocrats and writers. The letter to Lemos is a subtle way for Lope to entice Lemos to go beyond the pure clientelistic commission of a pious *comedia* in favor of a more sustained patronage which would enable him to write more freely. The bait used here by Lope is, of course, the mention of the "disinterested" generosity of the Duke of Osuna, another powerful aristocrat. This generosity perhaps was conveyed to Lope by Quevedo, who had recently returned from Naples, where he had served as right-hand man for the Duke in his viceroyalty.[8] This mention of Osuna by Lope is not at all naive. Lemos held at the time the other Spanish viceroyalty in Italy, in Sicily, and the (apparent) fact that the Count had not contacted Lope for that past year directly opposes, in the context of the letter, those 500 escudos provided by the Duke. Lope's tone across the letter sounds halfhearted and full of excuses, as if trying to deflect Lemos's commission[9] (finally completed, later, as *La devoción del Rosario*). Ultimately, we find between the lines subtle traces of irony and disappointment toward the Count of Lemos.

Seventeenth-century Spanish literature must be contemplated in the broad context of a highly developed court society and of the culture inherent to such social figuration. In order to contextualize and *re*-historicize this relationship between literature and courtly culture we have to ponder that all of this took place, to a great extent, because of the existence of a centralized, fixed court that, by its own nature, provoked a massive centripetal movement which was social, cultural, economic, and political, toward Madrid. That movement had a clear impact on artists and writers, as Jonathan Brown and John H. Elliott have pointed out:

> The concentration in Madrid of a leisured elite with money to spend had opened up brilliant opportunities for aspiring artists and men of letters in search of what they needed most—patrons and a public. Nobles and courtiers, eager for acclaim, would vie with each other to secure the services of the most glittering talents. (42)

Of course, the question is which came first: the abundant supply of writers or the increasing demands for writers by courtly culture. In my view, it is the "horizon of expectations" created by the cultural logic of court society that primarily fuels this literary "surplus," this historical concentration of writers. At the same time, I firmly believe that this is a defining moment for the "birth" of Spanish Literature which, in the 1600s, is still one among many other discourses (Godzich and Spadaccini xiii). At the same time, the 1600s are also the historical moment in which writers (and literature) start reflecting on themselves, which might have constituted the first historical step toward the institutionalization of literature in Spain.

The accumulation of writers-suitors renders problematic the intrinsic "scientific" isolation in which those writers or their works are often studied. At the same time, the historical situation propitiated by court culture raises three different issues: first of all, the characteristics that this interaction between writers and court society presented; secondly, when and how writers started perceiving themselves as a distinctive, specific social group; finally, what sort of effects this disproportionate accumulation of cultural capital had. I would like to begin by addressing the context (a court society) and the effect of the interaction between writers and members of the power field. Later, I will focus on the specific effects pertaining to the relationships among writers.

The court was not just a palace but also, and by extension, the city that harbored it. The city-court became the urban reference *par excellence* and, more significantly, it became a literary character[10] often portrayed as a magnet for all sorts of aspirants and human pursuits, including the ones found on the margins of society (as it happens in *El Buscón*). The appeal of such a sophisticated urban dwelling, enhanced by the court, especially in the beginning of every new reign,[11] had two effects that I would like to bring up here. First, Madrid attracted many wishful *letrados* (lettered or learned ones) who hoped to join the increasingly cumbersome bureaucracy of the Spanish monarchy. At the same time, the kind of cultural demand created by the city-court (both high and popular culture) made possible a change in what we could term as "behavioral mentality" of the men of letters that were serving or hoping to serve in the court. This mutation had two main effects related to our subject. From a general point of view, it transformed what was known in the sixteenth century as *cortesano* (courtier) into the *discreto* (discreet).[12] In other words: the courtier was *attached*—the word refers back to the court, to the physical realm of the palace—whereas the word *discreto* suggests the idea of someone who has to carefully exercise his agency, navigating the challenging and competitive waters of court society—the wittier, the better. The other effect of this mutation is that this accumulation of men of letters (lawyers, historians, theologians, clergymen), who, perhaps, just happened to write as a fashionable pastime, led, after a relatively quick process of specialization, to the birth of the literary author.

The historical process that mediates between the writing of texts that we consider today as literary, and the birth of a socially defined literary field, is directly related to the progressive autonomy of its authors and, therefore, to the autonomy of the professional field that contains both the texts and its authors. All writers pursuing social legitimacy in early modern Spain had first to fortify their social network, both in and out of the literary field. Consequently, those writers practiced forms of competition founded upon a given cultural capital: wit, knowledge of the classics, literary excellence, or some other property or quality potentially perceived as distinctive. If such cultural capital was recognized by the members of the power field, that could mean, perhaps, an indefinite patronage, an appointment at Court or some other symbolic recognition.

As Domínguez Ortiz noted, the abundance of lettered men required by civil and religious institutions became one of the most active enhancers of upward social mobility (*La sociedad* 46–47). Many of those *letrados* belonged to a middle class of sorts whose education could situate them above their social origin. Writers were no exception within this general perception of educated men.[13] Some of the most famous seventeenth-century European writers (Cervantes, Lope, Greene, Shakespeare, Jonson, Racine, Corneille, Molière) belonged to what we would deem today the middle class. All of them had access to a considerable level of education. Ultimately, this education allowed them to distinguish themselves within literary practice and even to obtain some type of social recognition. Of course not all of them were equally fortunate, but the "professional" or almost professional[14] status of some of these writers clearly tells us about the opportunities that literature had to offer, in terms of social promotion and recognition, during the first half of the seventeenth century. As examples we could cite the particular cases of Shakespeare, Góngora, and Corneille, who were indirectly ennobled as a result of their literary accomplishments by Court society or, to use a term closer to Golden Age studies, by the monarcho-seigniorial complex (Maravall).

Elizabethan literature reflects the reactions of other writers when a *"grant of arms"* was bestowed upon Shakespeare's father, in 1599, together with the acquisition by the writer of 107 acres of land: "With mouthing word that better wits had framed, / They purchase lands, and now esquires are made"[15] (Wyndham lv). Corneille was, in turn, also indirectly ennobled through his father in 1637 (Viala 222). As Góngora writes to the *licenciado* Heredia, on January 4th, 1622:

> He llegado a mejor estado: a ser oído de mi rey y de sus ministros superiores, y de alguno de ellos a ser bien visto (. . .) déjanme abierta la puerta a las esperanzas, dándome intención que la merced hecha es sola remuneración de mis padres, que mis servicios tendrán premio después; que me entretenga ahora con la merced de este hábito . . . y que luego pida para mí. (*Epistolario* 139)

> (I have reached a better state: to be heard by my king and his higher ministers, and to be well liked by some of them (. . .) they leave the door of my hope open, showing me intent that the granted mercy [a military order robe] is just a reward on behalf of my parents; that my own services will be rewarded later; that I should enjoy now the mercy of this robe . . . and then ask for myself.)[16]

We have only to consider the full extent of Góngora's "services" to realize how much cultural capital had been achieved by his literary practice. Otherwise, one would be hard-pressed to fathom what services, other than poetry and a theater play, were rendered to the King by the exquisite Cordovan poet.

These three examples serve to illustrate the recognition that literary practice could acquire in the early modern European courts. Although blood (especially blood purity) continued to be an important factor, there was a certain margin for maneuver within the aristocratic patronage system. Every writer played with the cards dealt to him (blood, class, education, religion, and wit), trying to distinguish himself before the power field. In order to do so, writers could exercise their agency with dedications, when choosing subjects or genres or by entering literary competitions where some sort of hierarchy could be established and capitalized upon. This process is closely bound to an urban environment. To a huge extent, the literary author and the literary field were urban phenomena. So were literary academies.

Academies originated in mid-fifteenth-century Italy. The most famous was founded by Marsilio Ficino, who gave such a name to his own house, in

Platonic remembrance. In the beginning, they were conceived as philological meetings devoted to the translation and interpretation of classical texts. Over time, these reunions took a literary turn and developed internal rules (King 12–13). By the sixteenth century they were already present in Spain, where they enjoyed a huge success during the next century.[17] The main conclusion that can be drawn from all these works is the capital importance that these institutions had in seventeenth-century Spanish culture. That much is by now clear—although not necessarily always taken into account—together with some of the motives for this academic blossoming. The main factor for this abundance of academies is the existence of a court culture, geographically reproduced. We may also consider as a factor the privileged status reached by certain literature within that culture, and the significant number of its practitioners, be they writers or "wanna-bes." The cultural demand posed by court culture, which started recognizing certain forms of symbolic capital, such as wit or poetic artistry, helped to consolidate a literary field founded upon distinction.

On the one hand, academies were *sociotopoi* (or even *socio-chronoto-poi*),[18] socially interactive *loci* for the literary field where social and symbolic exchanges took place. The social exchanges are obvious: academies were, in fact, literary gatherings for writers and some kind of public (mostly aristocrats). Concerning the symbolic exchanges that could take place in academies, we could mention intertextualities, and "influences," a trading of social or literary legitimacy, as well as literary quarrels.

It is reasonable to assume that some friendships and networking of some sort (social or literary) would often develop. We could probably trace many dedications, panegyrics, quotations, intertextualities and all sorts of literary references to the academies. We can also presume that *vejámenes* (institutionalized burlesque compositions) by many academies could grow into disputes or professional jealousies. The same result probably arose from within the literary field, in struggles to occupy the same position. An example of this can be found in the *Rimas* by Cristóbal de Mesa (1611):

Si algunos dellos [los Príncipes] hace una academia
Hay setas, competencias y porfías,
Más que en Inglaterra y en Bohemia,
Algunas hemos visto en nuestros días
Que mandado les han poner silencio,
Como si escuelas fueran de herejías.
(fol. 218 r./v; quoted by King 45)

(If some of them [the aristocrats] start an academy, there are more sects, competitions and disputes, than in England and Bohemia. In nowadays we have seen some [academies] ordered into silence, as if they were schools for heresies.)

Nineteenth-century French salons were centers not just of social but also of symbolic interaction between the literary field and the power field (Bourdieu, *Rules* 51). So were the literary academies in seventeenth-century Spain. Members of the nobility attending academies or presiding over them became a common fixture. Many were even poets themselves, such as the counts of Villamediana and Salinas or the Prince of Esquilache. There were times in which an academy was created by a nobleman, although it was often the dynamic of the emerging literary field, with its hierarchies, competitions, and exercise of symbolic violence, represented by the *vejámenes*. It is, then, after this internal associationist impulse of the literary field, with the goal of attaining social recognition and legitimacy (Viala 42–43), that aristocrats enter the picture. Accordingly, Lope writes, in February 1612: "Hoy ha comenzado una famosa academia, que se llama El Parnaso, en la sala de don Francisco de Silva: no hubo señores, que aún no deben de saberlo; durará hasta que lo sepan" (quoted by Romera Navarro 498) (Today started a famous academy, called "The Parnassus," at Sir Francisco de Silva's salon: there were no lords [in attendance], because they probably do not know about it yet; it will last until they do). As time went by, however, and as academies became fashionable,[19] it seems that they were, more often than not, presided over by aristocrats. That is what can be guessed from the words of the Andalucian poet Álvaro Cubillo de Aragón (1596–1661):

Si en Academia alguna te hallares,
donde, ya por costumbre recibida,
algún señor presida,
obedece el asunto, y no repares
en que sátira sea. (Monreal, chapter x)

(If you happen to find yourself in an Academy, where, by received custom, some lord is presiding over, just follow the subject, and don't mind if it is a satire.)

Academies turned sometimes into truly public spectacles where, besides writers, aristocrats of both sexes were often in attendance.[20] It is not unthinkable to assume that many writers could harbor second thoughts when confronted with the fact that aristocrats were officiating as symbolic judges of an

increasingly competitive practice, while lacking the minimum literary creden-
tials. We certainly know about Lope's discomfort with their presence and some
of its consequences (Rozas 207–11), but it seems to have been a widespread
feeling across the literary field. One example of those complaints appears in
La peregrinación sabia (1635), by Alonso Jerónimo de Salas Barbadillo. This
curious text uses the technique of fables to describe an academy of animals,
comprised of "four avians" (thrush, eagle, mockingbird and turtledove) and
"four terrestrials" (horse, dog, monkey and cat) (Salas 44). Of those, the horse
represents nobility. It is a character "muy presumido de su grandeza y genero-
sidad [que] querría que el saber consistiese no en haber estudiado más ni en
tener más ingenio que los otros, sino en haber nacido mejor que ellos; hablaba
con grande presunción, escuchábase él mismo y compraba su aplauso con
dádivas y caricias" (44) (vainly convinced of his greatness and generosity who
believes that knowledge is not a matter of studying or being wittier than others
but, rather, of being born better than they; when he speaks, he does so with
vanity, buying applause with gifts and endearments). The satirical bitterness
of Salas Barbadillo is clear: some aristocrats, not endowed with either wit or
knowledge who have done nothing to change it, buy their seat on Parnassus
offering indulgences and gifts.

The *Peregrinación* was published posthumously and appeared in *Coronas
del Parnaso* (1635). There, Salas Barbadillo let us know about the discomfort
that writers felt having to "forcibly" share part of the literary field with members of the power field. Also, this text shows that, despite its social dependency
on the power field, there existed sufficient cracks for a certain subjectivistic
agency to slip through. That agency presents clear reflexive tones, since Salas
Barbadillo already writes and feels as a writer, and this feeling of "belonging"
could be traced only to the social realm, to the space where writers and aristocrats interact. It is in this shared space, be it material (academies) or symbolic
(dedications, quest for patronage), where the social self-awareness of writers
arises. It is, therefore, the space in which the literary field is born.

The main conclusion that we could extract from all this interactivity
between writers and aristocratic patrons is the disproportion that existed between several indicators of literary modernity (such as certain literary genres
and practices, literary reflexivity, the existence of a publishing market) and a
few others that had more to do with a patronage culture. Literature was almost
ready to achieve its full autonomy and shift into modernity, but the societal
structures, still anchored in the *Ancien régime,* were not quite there yet. Indeed, it took almost two hundred more years for European societies to get

rid of aristocratic patronage as a literary factor altogether. This situation was an obstacle for the real professionalization of seventeenth-century Spanish writers. The sophistication of the hierarchical structures of the literary field did not exactly correspond with a clear-cut distributional opposition between pure production and massive production, as happens in modern times. Literary practice was still influenced by its direct interaction with the power field, which often meant that literary capital had to be recognized by the latter. At the same time, there was a clear conflict between means and goals. On the one hand, a reflexive literary field and a germinal publishing market coincided with patronage and clientelism. As for the goals, writers were seeking social legitimacy[21] *and* economic autonomy. These conflicts rendered the relationship between writers and aristocrats increasingly problematic.

Let us turn now to the interaction between writers, for human relationships generate meaning. This postulate of symbolic interactionism (a sociological approach that focuses on how individuals and groups interact with each other) should not be forgotten when dealing with historical times and places in which cultural capital accumulated in an uncommon fashion (such as say, seventeenth-century Madrid or Vienna at the beginning of the twentieth century). Let us pause for a moment, and think how precious and rare a moment in cultural history it was when Vienna coffeehouses could claim as patrons the likes of Arnold Schoenberg, Gustav Mahler, Adolf Loos, Egon Schiele, Sigmund Freud, Ludwig Wittgenstein, Gustav Klimt, Oskar Kokoschka, Hugo von Hofmannsthal, or Arthur Schnitzler, to name just some of the most prominent names in several disciplines. Equally intriguing is imagining what it was it like to live in Madrid at the beginning of the seventeenth century, where an unusual accumulation of cultural agents (writers, painters, musicians, architects, and comedians) gathered. Let us focus on literature. The first third of the century saw the concurrence of Cervantes, Góngora, Lope de Vega, Quevedo, Calderón and Tirso de Molina, not to mention dozens of other less well-known writers. They shared urban spaces (streets, theaters, printing houses and places of gossip or *mentideros*), as well as social practices (academies, churches, brotherhoods, aristocratic affiliations, and literary contests). This unusual concentration of writers and activities represented the peak of a literary praxis and a courtly fashion, but it also paved the way for writers to take a reflexive look at themselves and perceive themselves as a group with a common denominator.

Using a combination of theoretical approaches (urban space studies, cultural field theories) García Santo-Tomás has studied the juxtaposition of a shared urban space (Madrid) and of an intellectual space (the literary field) during the 1621–1626 period. According to García ("Espacio" 32), the result of that juxtaposition is a third space characterized by all sorts of socio-literary confrontations, alliances, triumphs, and failures. The examples of such features are portrayed in a realistic fashion in Lope's letters to the Duke of Sessa, allegorically in Tirso de Molina's *autos sacramentales*; and in mythical representations, exemplified by the countless "Parnasos," "Coronas," "Jardines," and "Laureles," so frequent in the published literature of the epoch (32). At the same time, this space is both circular and centripetal in what concerns its material and symbolic aspects and simultaneously provokes attraction and rejection (33). It is my contention, as we will see later, that many of the textual manifestations of that rejection had to do with a growing frustration in many writers over the influence that patronage and clientelism were still exerting on literary practice.

The spatial-temporal proliferation of writers represents an intense interaction (social, spatial, intra-historical,[22] and literary). This interaction develops while sharing the same public spaces and institutions, but also when visiting the same literary genres, and when competing for the same prizes and honors or, more prosaically, for the same share of the readership. Elsewhere,[23] I have suggested the coinage of a concept, "inter-authoriality," in order to assess the potential effects and consequences that the spatial and temporal coincidence of a given group of writers opens up. By inter-authoriality, I understand the social, intra-historical, and textual contemporary interaction of a group of writers or authors. This interaction takes place around social practices and institutions, as well as in the literary practices themselves. Different sources and approaches, including Pierre Bourdieu's theory of professional fields and concepts such as Julia Kristeva's "intertextuality," Unamuno's "intra-history," and Américo Castro's *intercasticidad* ("inter-casteism").[24]

The fact that social differences related to caste, faith, or social status are often neglected in literary history should not cloud our judgement. Two intra-historical forces crossed early modern Spanish literature. On the one hand, we have a powerful social drive for upward mobility, which was favored by an increasingly urban society and by the influence of the Court. On the other hand, we have the social and legal situations derived from the emphasis on lineage and blood purity. It is in this intersection, for instance, where we could better understand Lope's "pilgrimage" (Wright) and his self-ennoblement attempt (he included a spurious coat of arms in *Arcadia* and *El peregrino en su patria*). We could also contextualize better Quevedo's anti-Semitism or fathom the courtly disdain of Cervantes' biographical heroics (his military deeds or his captivity). As I have already mentioned, Castro (70–74) wrote about the presence of inter-casteism in *Don Quijote*. He also believed that caste heterogeneity led to two different kinds of literature: the one conceived according to the system of beliefs of the majority (the *Romancero*, chivalric novels, or the *comedia*) and the other inspired by a perspective more of the minority, as represented by *Celestina* or *Don Quijote* (267, note 67). We could either agree or disagree with Castro on the specifics of his claims, but it sounds definitely appropriate *not* to approach all Spanish writers of the time in an amorphous way, making *tabula rasa* of their diverse social backgrounds. I think that this is especially pertinent for a time and place such as Madrid in the 1600s. What we perceive, from the distance, as similar literary careers had clearly different starting points, strategies, and handicaps. We could ask ourselves, for instance, whether it is entirely appropriate to undertake *readings* of Cervantes, Lope, Góngora or Gracián with the same reading logic. We could also ponder, in other respects, if it is right not to make distinctions between works that were published and others that remained unpublished or circulated only in handwritten copies. Furthermore, for those works that remained unpublished, we could consider if it was because of a choice, a restraint, or a social habit. Also along social parameters, Bourdieu criticizes what he calls "analysis of essence," which is based on the idea of a pure aesthetic (*Rules* 286). For Bourdieu, those analyses create the illusion of universality from a particular, subjective example, and do not account for the socio-historical conditions of possibility of that aesthetic experience or for the conditions under which aesthetic appreciation (*phylogenesis*) and reproduction over time (*ontogenesis*) operate (286). The applications of this social "materialization" of artistic "essence" present interesting outcomes. Thus, intertextuality is not understood anymore by Bourdieu as a purely textual phenomenon but, rather, as a relationship between texts, the structure of the literary field and the specific writers (*Field* 17). It is precisely to give account of this "social intertextuality," as well as to address the issue of the social interaction among writers, that I propose the concept of inter-authoriality.

Inter-authoriality was as much a condition[25] as a generator of social practices in seventeenth-century Spain. Many writers physically coincided[26] in a reduced space that was both material and symbolic but also, and this is even more important, those writers were well aware of their condition. Therefore, that self-awareness created position-takings (*prises de position*) and helped to orient the *habitus*[27] and the trajectory of many of them.

Inter-authoriality fills the conceptual gap between an implicit intratextual dialogism (allusions in letters, quotations, mentions of literary characters, and book dedications) and an implicit or explicit *extratextual* dialectic (adherence to different groups, castes, ideologies, or even regions and, in what concerns specifically the literary practice, the competition for certain positions, either symbolic or professional). Thus, inter-authoriality can appear in two forms: socially and textually. The former presents spatial and socio-professional characteristics and includes the physical coincidence of writers in academies, brotherhoods, and corteges and, by extension, whatever shape their coincidence in Madrid may show. The latter would be comprised of, besides intertextuality itself, the personal allusions found in collections of letters and the paratexts (approvals, forewords, and eulogies) that usually serve as preliminary headings for published works. Sometimes, as it happens with literature produced for literary academies (burlesque reprehensions, proceedings, and common subjects to write or discuss) and with works written on purpose for literary competitions, social and literary realms became virtually indistinguishable.

One clear example of inter-authoriality is found in the nucleus of reformist *letrados* comprised by Cristóbal Pérez de Herrera, Mateo Alemán, Alonso de Barros, and Hernando de Soto, among others. All of them wrote, at some point, about poverty and mendicancy. As Dadson noted, they mutually supported each other in their literary pursuits, publicly praising their works (178–81). Thus, the *Discursos* by Pérez de Herrera and the famous *Guzmán de Alfarache* by Mateo Alemán, include, respectively, an epilogue and a foreword written by Barros. Hernando de Soto praised the *Guzmán*, and his own *Emblemas moralizadas* (1599) were praised, in turn, by Barros. Lastly, Alemán, wrote a foreword to Barros's *Proverbios morales*. Beyond their implications of literary strategy, the frequent presence of crossed paratexts[28] such as forewords, poems, or eulogies, speak volumes to us about certain intra-historical rhythms of early modern Spanish literature.

Another interesting example of inter-authoriality rooted in the sixteenth century, but whose implications and ramifications carried on through the seventeenth century, is found in the academic circle run in Seville by Juan de Mal Lara (1524–1571). Academies were, by functioning nature, interactive places, but what makes Mal Lara's academy unique is how varied its interests were (archeology, philology, painting, literature) and its own continuity. Once Mal Lara died, the leadership was assumed by Fernando de Herrera, the canon Francisco Pacheco (uncle of the painter of the same name) and by Francisco de Medina (Brown 22–25). As Brown (25) noted, Hererra's *Anotaciones* (1580) to Garcilaso suggest a clear collaboration between members of the academy.

Already in the seventeenth century, it is worth briefly mentioning the textual relationship between Lope de Vega and Quevedo. The latter, who belonged to a younger generation of aspiring talents, had Lope's sympathy early on—perhaps because they were aiming at radically different "professional" careers and, therefore, not competing with each other. Unlike Cervantes,[29] Quevedo aspired to a position that Lope was not occupying. Lope and Quevedo handed each other many *encomia* in the form of quotations, panegyric poems, or bureaucratic pre-publishing approvals. Thus, we have, for example, *El peregrino en su patria* (1604), for which Lope required a sonnet from Quevedo ("Las fuerzas, peregrino celebrado"), and the approvals that Quevedo wrote for Lopean works, some thirty years later.[30] These textual references crossed between them must be contemplated within a context of shared social practices and perhaps, as hints of certain ideological coincidences. I am thinking here about their shared *casticismo* and about their ideological and linguistic "Castilianism" (*castellanismo*), as shown in the polemic against the *culteranos* (carried by both of them) or against Herrera (by Quevedo only).

Lastly, I would like to mention an example of what we might call "inter-authorial sociotextuality." In Cristóbal Súarez Figueroa's *El pasajero* (1617), we read criticisms—it is not by chance Súarez's nickname was "Fisgarroa"[31]— aimed at Cervantes, Ruiz de Alarcón, and Lope. The example I want to recall here, though, concerns the friendship that Suárez Figueroa had developed with Luis Carrillo y Sotomayor. Carrillo was a very prestigious Andalusian poet-soldier and nobleman whom he had met during his exile from the Court. They shared a trip to Madrid in late 1606 or early 1607. Consequently, Suárez interspersed several sonnets by Carrillo in his novel *La constante Amarilis* and included him, as a literary character, in *El pasajero*.

I hope that the few examples cited here can convey the idea of how complex, fruitful, and varied was the relationship between coincidental writers in an early modern context. Social and textual relations between seventeenth-century Spanish writers generated a chain of meanings that we cannot afford to ignore. Many works of the time (*Don Quijote, El arte nuevo, El viaje del Parnaso, La perinola,* or *El pasajero*, to name a few) will forcibly resist all attempts to confine them to creative isolation, formalism, or a single hermeneutic principle. In other words, many literary works of that time seem to owe less to literary tradition than to their intra-historical context. In turn the literature that gave birth to those works originated within a competitive court culture and, therefore, it was fundamentally interactive and inter-authorial.

Another facet that owes a great deal to the distinctional, competitive inter-authoriality that comes along with the very existence of a literary field is the frequency with which autobiographical elements and self-fashioning[32] appeared in literary texts. Lope's literary trajectory, recently studied by Elizabeth

Wright, help us to understand why some writers (such as Lope himself and Cervantes) published streams of works in brief periods, why self-references abounded, and why so many writers felt compelled to fashion a public image. When turning into self-representation, authors try to establish a public, literary image and, at the same time or, perhaps, because of that, to compete with other writers for a position within the space of possibles. That space is no longer the one available to sixteenth-century humanists and men of letters but, rather, a "pre-professional" space entirely devoted to literature, a space otherwise called a literary field. This drive for social distinction took shape in the abundance of self-portraits (either drawn or written) and references to the *ethos* of a given writer[33]; as well as in literary effervescences of writers such as the following: Lope in 1598–1604 (*Dragontea, Arcadia, Isidro, Peregrino*); Quevedo circa 1604–1609 (*Buscón, Sueños, Discurso de las privanzas, La España defendida, Discurso de la vida y tiempo de Phocílides*, translation of *Anacreón castellano*); or Cervantes in 1612–1616 (*Comedias, Novelas ejemplares, ¿Topografía e historia general de Argel?*[34] *Viaje del Parnaso*, second part of *Don Quijote, Persiles*).

In a 1620 letter, Lope let his feelings be known about the dependency that he and, presumably, other writers had on aristocrats: "No puedo más: que como la naturaleza hizo un cojo, un tuerto y un corcovado, hizo un pobre, un desdichado y un poeta, que en España son como las rameras, que todos querrían echarse con ellas, pero por poco precio, y en saliendo de su casa llamarlas putas" (*Cartas* 45) (I cannot take it anymore: the same way Nature created lame, one-eyed or hunchbacked men, it also created poor men, unfortunate men and poets, that in Spain are like prostitutes: everybody would lie down with them for a cheap price but, after leaving the brothel, they call them whores). The quote vents, no doubt, part of his frustration with the Court, once he realized that the prestigious office of royal chronicler would not be awarded to him. It also tells us about the small chain of venalities and attached strings that this moment in literary history created, in terms of the interaction between writers and court culture. Lope's outburst is also an example of an ongoing tension between patronage and literature and its reflection. As compared with previous centuries, seventeenth-century Spanish literature is characterized by a reflexive drive. This drive is both social and textual. Literature turns to itself not just for the sake of it but, rather, because it is, in many ways, a historical novelty for its practitioners and it is perceived as such by them. In the 1600s, literature becomes in Spain something of a "historically attested phenomenon" (Godzich and Spadaccini xi). In a way, this reflexivity was forced upon writers when they had to dialectically confront an inherited cultural system, rooted in court society and based on patronage and clientelism, with the possibilities arisen from a widespread urban readership. It is in this dialectic of writing for one vs. writing for many[35] where modern literature, the literary field, and the author himself started to think about their social debut. Nowhere, perhaps, is this tension more obvious than in the preliminary paratexts of *Don Quijote* (1605). While the dedication (the portion written just for One, for the Duke of Béjar) is customary, predictable and even partly taken from elsewhere,[36] the "Prólogo" that follows, addressed to the general readership, is a richly creative text, full of socio-literary and metaliterary allusions. It is, therefore, a precious account of the reflexivity with which seventeenth-century Spanish writers approached their practices, their peers, and the historically inherited containment that aristocratic patronage and clientelism represented for literature. When historically considered, this literary reflexivity is nothing but an ontological discourse of social affirmation. It also announces the birth of the modern author and a certain *esprit de corps* among writers.

Facing the constraints posed by court culture, but paradoxically enjoying its collateral benefits at the same time (mainly, literary concentration), writers turned inward in seventeenth-century Spain. That reflexivity was, I would argue, a modest but clear call for artistic freedom and an attempt to dodge the containment structure built by the monarcho-seigniorial cultural complex.

Notes

1.   I would like to thank Karen Gutiérrez and Lowanne Jones for helping me as generous proofreaders. All the English propriety that this essay might have is theirs; the errors are only mine.

2.   As I defend in the first chapter of *La espada, el rayo y la pluma*—where I adopt and adapt Bourdieu's social approach to literary production and give a more detailed discussion about its adequacy to seventeenth-century Spanish literature—the early 1600s saw the birth of the first Spanish literary field. We could identify four reasons for that: 1) there was an accumulation of writers and works within an urban environment; 2) writers established symbiotic relationships with members of the power field; 3) the power field was eager to use writers as social or political propagandists; 4) writers interacted socially and literarily and started to develop a social identity. The literary field was, then, socially self-conscious and structured around a double hierarchy (works oriented to either popular success or the approval of the learned). The writers that symbolically crowned that double hierarchy were Lope de Vega and Luis de Góngora. The propeller of these field dynamics was distinction, and poetry (in its several manifestations) became the main grantor of literary capital. For a more specific treat-

ment of this approach, see my article on Góngora's *Soledades*. In this essay I will use profusely Bourdieu's terminology: literary field, cultural capital, habitus, space of possibles, position and position takings, etc.

3. "Qu'est-ce qu'un auteur?" *Bulletin de la Societé Française de Philosophie* 22 (1969): 73–104 (Trans. "What's an Author"? In *Textual Strategies: Perspectives in Post-Structural Criticism*. Ed. Josué V. Harari [Ithaca: Cornell UP, 1979. 141–60]).

4. As Chartier notes, the early modern writer, often thought of as a demiurge, usually created in a state of dependency (clientelism, patronage, subsidies, publishing market) and, to a certain extent it is precisely that dependency that renders a literary work conceivable, decipherable and communicable (x).

5. I use "clientelism" and not "clientism," in spite of its propriety, because the former has become the *de facto* term in current scholarship.

6. Teresa Ferrer has studied the genealogical plays that Lope wrote by commission (39–93). Thus, we know that the play *La historial Alfonsina* was commissioned to Lope sometime between 1617 and 1622 by the dukedom of Villahermosa. The goal was to exhibit the heroic feats of one of its ancestors, Alonso de Aragón, who was an illegitimate son sired by Juan II and a brother of Ferdinand the Catholic. Lope had to convey the message "how useful to the Crown are the illegitimate sons of the kings" (53). Ferrer (48–51) also mentions other Lopean plays, also commissioned by aristocrats, including *La buena guarda,* a *La limpieza no manchada, La vida de Pedro Nolasco* (a commission by the Order of Mercy), *Adonis y Venus, El premio de la hermosura, La selva sin amor, El Perseo,* and *La noche de san Juan.* Ferrer also mentions Tirso's trilogy on the Pizarros (*Todo es dar en una cosa, Las amazonas en las Indias* and *La lealtad contra la envidia*), written between 1626 and 1629, "tightly connected with the legal campaign that a descendant of Francisco Pizarro was carrying on, in order to claim the aristocratic title and economic compensations offered to his famous ancestor by Charles V" (50). All of this leads us to believe that these propagandistic practices were fairly common and were perceived as effective.

7. Lastanosa was more of a rich, intellectually curious soulmate than a "patron" to Gracián; on the other hand, Gracián was a somewhat rebellious man of letters who happened to belong to a religious order—the Jesuits—known for its internal discipline and rigor. In that sense, it was not Gracián who *personally* needed Lastanosa's support but his publicly intellectual pursuits that did. This condition is what, in my opinion, dilutes the conditions for the existence of feudal bonds. Gracián did not write for a living; he freely chose to do so when, paradoxically enough, he had chosen previously not to be intellectually free, once he joined the Society of Jesus.

8. It is not surprising that once Osuna returned to Spain and was later imprisoned, Lope would write to Diego Félix de Quijada: "Sir, you should not believe anything about [the trial of] Osuna; he is in prison, only God knows why. He is a great lord, a great gentleman, a great soldier; he cannot be a traitor, since the enemies of Spain feared him" (*Cartas* 245).

9. Lope writes to Lemos that, perhaps, either Mira de Amescua or Guillén de Castro

"pudiera servir mejor a vuestra excelencia en esta ocasión" (*Cartas completas* II, 83) ("might better serve your excellency for the occasion"). Sometimes, those mentions of Lope's malaise toward a member of the aristocracy were used to entice or flatter another aristocrat. Thus, in 1611, Lope (I, 115) writes to the duke of Sessa lamenting the efforts and the cultural capital he had devoted to the duke of Alba, whom he had previously served.

10. Such is the topic of García Santo-Tomás's article, "Artes de la ciudad, ciudad de las artes." Using "humanistic geography" approaches (Soja, Harvey, Yi-Fu Tuan), García studies Madrid's impact as an urban experience and also as a motivating writing force in *El diablo cojuelo* (1641), a novel by Luis Vélez de Guevara.

11. Every dynastic succession provoked a turmoil in which many offices, memberships in councils and prestigious courtly appointments related to court etiquette were renewed by the new king. This was especially noticeable at the beginning of the reigns of Philip III and Philip IV. Often, writers and the at-large members of the cultural field (historians, painters) had to "bet," as part of what Bourdieu calls the "space of possibles," in court power struggles (*Rules* 256–57). That was the case in the first decades of the seventeenth century with an ongoing fight for political prominence between two powerful aristocratic clans, the Sandovals and the Zúñigas (Elliott, *Count-Duke 38–45*; Feros, *Kingship* 101–107).

12. I borrow here from a work by Blanco González whose title, *Del cortesano al discreto*, combines the titles of two famous books by Castiglione and Gracián and conveys the idea of such an evolution.

13. Adrian Marino (186) sees a transition in seventeenth-century Spanish and French writers: instead of aspiring to glory—as the Classics did—they started pursuing literary reputation.

14. Unfortunately, we do not have a comprehensive study addressing in detail the sources of income for seventeenth-century Spanish writers. Viala (see especially pages 107–14) does a great job, tracking sources of income and establishing categories for French writers, according to their social origin and income. Thus, we know that a combination of literary royalties and royal patronage helped Corneille, Scarron, Racine, or Molière to obtain between 3000 and 4000 pounds, allowing them to live "sur un pied d'honnête bourgeois ou de noble modeste" (114).

15. The quotation belongs to *The Return from Parnassus*, by Robert Greene. Previously, and addressing the rest of the "university wits" in *Groat's Worth of Wit Bought with a Million of Repentance* (1592), Greene alluded to Shakespeare's job as an actor and described him as "an upstart crow, beautified in our feathers" (Wyndham liv).

16. Unless otherwise noted, this and the rest of the translations are my own.

17. For a more detailed account of this phenomenon, I refer to the classical works by José Sánchez (*Las academias literarias del Siglo de Oro español*) and Willard F. King (*Prosa novelística y academias literarias en el siglo XVII*), as well as to more recent contributions by Jonathan Brown (*Images*), Aurora Egido, Jeremy Robbins, Clara Giménez and Anne Cruz. All of them can be found in the list of works cited.

18. I am exercising here an "academic license" of sorts with Bakhtin's concept of chronotope ("time space"), as it is formulated in *The Dialogic Imagination* (University of Texas Press, 1981). There, Bakhtin defines literary chronotope as a site where "time, as it were, thickens, takes on flesh, becomes artistically visible; likewise, space becomes charged and responsive to the movements of time, plot, and history" (84).

19. The peak of this increasing "courtlyzation" of the academies is, perhaps, the so-called "Academia burlesca del Retiro," held in 1637 at the palace of the same name. Although the nature of this academy it is unclear (King [93] thinks that this was just a meeting of an ongoing academy in Madrid), it is very significant that the practice reached the royal palace.

20. In this regard see J. Robbins (15–17), where he refers to the social and performative aspects of Spanish academies.

21. It could be argued that social legitimacy is always problematic for the literary field since it requires, somehow, the existence of external legitimazing forces and institutions.

22. *Intrahistoria* or "intra-history" is a concept coined by the Spanish philosopher and writer Miguel de Unamuno in his book of essays *En torno al casticismo* (1895). The term, opposed to traditional history, portrays the importance of the group of facts, rituals and social habits and customs that constitute daily life but do not appear in history books. This intra-historic life, "silent and continuous," is described by Unamuno as "the substance of progress, the true . . . eternal tradition" as opposed to the "tradition of lies . . . buried in books . . . and in monuments" (26–28).

23. "Hacia un concepto de interautorialidad en el Siglo de Oro," Paper read at the Congreso Internacional de la AISO (International Association of Golden Age Scholars), Burgos, Spain, July 2002.

24. By "intercasteism" or *intercasticidad*, Castro meant the social and cultural effects that appear when different castes coincide in the same society. Castro's case study was medieval and early modern Spain where so-called *cristianos viejos* or "old Christians" had certain privileges over recent converts (*cristianos nuevos*) or members from other religious groups (Muslims and Jews). In what specifically concerns early modern Spanish literature, Castro's contention was that works such as Fernando de Rojas's *Celestina* and Cervantes's *Don Quijote* were directly influenced by the social situation and status of their authors (11). Castro suggested a *converso* ancestry for both writers and described literature produced under such circumstances as a "managed form of literature" in which its handler or manager, usually located from birth in the margins of a society perceived, thus, as alien, "makes himself or herself, somehow, visible" (13).

25. I use "condition" with the meaning that Lyotard (5) assigns to it in *La condition postmoderne*—that is, as a description of a sociocultural state of affairs at a given time.

26. See, for instance, José del Corral's article "Las calles de Madrid en 1624," *Anales del Instituto de estudios madrileños* 9 (1973): 643–96.

27. I use the concept "habitus" with the meaning that Bourdieu assigns to it as a "generat-

ing and unifying principle that translates the intrinsical and relational characteristics of a position into a unitary lifestyle; that is, into a unitary ensemble of choices of people, goods, and practices" (*Razones* 19).

28. I use the concept "paratext" as coined by Gérard Genette in *Seuils* (Paris: Seuil, 1987): "tout ce par quoi un texte se fait livre et se propose comme tel à ses lecteurs, et plus généralement au public" (7) (everything that turns a text into a book that proposes itself as such to its readers, and more generally to the public).

29. Montero Reguera has studied the relationship between Lope and Cervantes. According to him, the original friendship turned into "malquerencia, rencor y envidia" in the last years (333).

30. On August 27, 1634, Quevedo approved the *Rimas del licenciado Tomé de Burguillos,* and in May 19, 1635, he did the same for the *Veinte y una parte verdadera de las comedias del Fénix de España fray Lope Félix de Vega Carpio.*

31. In *La peregrinación sabia* (published in 1635 but written *circa* 1621–22), Salas Barbadillo, while describing a literary academy run by animals and full of socio-literary allusions, mentions a dog who bears the name "Fisgarroa." This dog is always *fisgando* (peeking) into other people's writings and, as if they were bones, he cuts them into pieces and gnaws them (*roer*) (King 169).

32. Greenblatt studied the subject focusing on six authors of Renaissance England: More, Tyndale, Wyatt, Spenser, Marlowe, and Shakespeare. One of his main contentions is that self-fashioning appears in connection with something perceived as alien and threatening that, therefore, must be destroyed (9).

33. I am thinking here of Cervantes's self-portraits and autobiographical references, studied by Canavaggio, Gaylord, and Close. As Gaylord noted, "When Cervantes calls our attention to his authorial self, he asks us in effect to see the writer in the shape of human anatomy, of human life history, of human desire" ("Cervantes, Portrait of the Artist," 93). Lope, on the other hand, presents a self-portrait in virtually every work, as if it were his trademark (Profeti 428). Carreira has studied, in turn, the frequency in Góngora's poetry of a self-parodying, burlesque "I" (*Gongoremas* 141).

34. Eisenberg proposes that Cervantes wrote the *Topografía* (1612). Be it Cervantine or not, the truth is that the book is a "hagiography" of sorts for the writer, and its publication coincides with a determined attempt by Cervantes to establish a literary image, capitalizing on the success of the first *Quijote* (1605).

35. Francisco Vivar has recently studied how some early modern Spanish writers tried to balance literary quality with the demands of the reading public. The solution that writers such as Cervantes and others found was to write "para todos, para algunos y para sí" (Vivar 11) (for everybody, for some, and for oneself). This smart adaptation to the changing conditions of literary consumption is yet another example of the social reflexivity that arose within literary practice in seventeenth-century Spain.

36. As the editor, Luis A. Murillo, notes (49, note 1), Cervantes partly plagiarized the de—dication to the Marquis of Ayamonte that Fernando de Hererra wrote for his *Las obras de Garcilaso de la Vega con anotaciones* (Sevilla: Alonso de la Barrera, 1580).

Works Cited

Alemán, Mateo. *Guzmán de Alfarache,* Madrid: 1599, 1604.

Alonso, Dámaso. "Góngora en las cartas del abad de Rute." *Homenaje a la memoria de don Antonio Rodríguez Moñino.* Madrid: Castalia, 1975. 27-58.

Barros, Alonso de. *Proverbios morales.* Madrid: Luis Sánchez, 1598.

Blanco González, Bernardo. *Del cortesano al discreto. Examen de una "decadencia."* Vol. I. Madrid: Gredos, 1962.

Bourdieu, Pierre. *La distinction. Critique social du jugement.* Paris: Minuit, 1979.

———. *The Field of Cultural Production. Essays on Art and Literature.* Ed. Randal Johnson. New York: Columbia University Press, 1993.

———. *Razones prácticas. Sobre la teoría de la acción.* Trans. Julio Vivas. Barcelona: Anagrama, 1997.

———. *The Rules of Art. Genesis and Structure of the Literary Field.* Trans. Susan Emanuel. Cambridge: Polity, 1996.

Brown, Jonathan. *Images and Ideas in Seventeenth-Century Spanish Painting.* Princeton: Princeton University Press, 1978.

Brown, Jonathan, and John H. Elliott. *A Palace for a King. The Buen Retiro and the Court of Philip IV.* New Haven: Yale University Press, 1980.

Canavaggio, Jean. "Cervantes en primera persona." *Journal of Hispanic Philology* 2 (1977): 35–44.

———. "La dimensión autobiográfica del *Viaje del Parnaso.*" *Cervantes: Bulletin of the Cervantes Society of America* 1.1.2 (1981): 29–41.

Carreira, Antonio. *Gongoremas.* Barcelona: Península, 1998.

Castro, Américo. *Cervantes y los casticismos españoles.* 2nd ed. Madrid: Alianza, 1974.

Cervantes, Miguel de. *El ingenioso hidalgo don Quijote de la Mancha.* Ed. Luis A. Murillo. Madrid: Castalia, 1982.

Chartier, Roger. *The Order of Books: Readers, Authors, and Libraries in Europe between the Fourteenth and Eighteenth Centuries.* Trans. Lydia G. Cochrane. Stanford: Stanford University Press, 1994.

Close, Anthony. "A Poet's Vanity: Thoughts on the Friendly Ethos of Cervantine Satire." *Cervantes* 13 (1993): 31–63.

Cruz, Anne J. "Art of the State: The *Academias Literarias* as Sites of Symbolic Economies in Golden Age Spain." *Calíope* 1.2 (1995): 72–95.

Dadson, Trevor J. *Libros, lectores y lecturas: estudios sobre bibliotecas particulares del Siglo de Oro.* Madrid: Arco Libros, 1998.

Domínguez Ortiz, Antonio. *La sociedad española en el siglo XVII.* Madrid: CSIC, 1963.

Egido, Aurora. "Las academias literarias de Zaragoza en el siglo XVII." *La literatura en Aragón.* Ed. Manuel Alvar. Zaragoza: Caja de Ahorros y Monte de Piedad de Zaragoza, Aragón y Rioja, 1984. 101–28.

———. "Una introducción a la poesía y a las academias literarias del XVII." *Estudios Humanísticos* 6 (1984): 9–25.

Eisenberg, Daniel. "Cervantes, autor de la *Topografía e historia general de Argel* publicada por Diego de Haedo." *Cervantes* 16.1 (1996): 32–53.

Elias, Norbert. *The Court Society*. Trans. Edmund Jephcott. Oxford: Blackwell, 1983.

Elliott, John H. *The Count-Duke of Olivares. The Statesman in an Age of Decline*. New Haven: Yale University Press, 1986.

Feros, Antonio. *Kingship and Favoritism in the Spain of Philip III, 1598-1621*. Cambridge: Cambridge University Press, 2000.

Ferrer, Teresa. *Nobleza y espectáculo teatral (1533–1622)*. Valencia: UNED, 1993.

García Santo-Tomás, Enrique. "Artes de la ciudad, ciudad de las artes: la invención de Madrid en *El diablo cojuelo*." *Revista Canadiense de Estudios Hispánicos* 35.1 (2000): 117–35.

_____. "El espacio simbólico de la pugna literaria." *El teatro del Siglo de Oro ante los espacios de la crítica*. Ed. Enrique García Santo-Tomás. Madrid: Iberoamericana, 2002. 31–58.

Gaylord Randel, Mary. "Cervantes, Portrait of the Artist." *Cervantes* 3 (1983): 83–102.

_____. "Cervantes' Portraits and Literary Theory." *Cervantes* 6 (1986): 57–80.

Genette, Gérard. *Introduction à l'architexte*. Paris: Seuil, 1979.

Giménez Fernández, Clara. "Poesía de academias." *Manuscrit. Cao* 2 (1989): 47–55.

Godzich, Wlad, and Nicholas Spadaccini. "Introduction." *Literature Among Discourses. The Spanish Golden Age*. Ed. Wlad Godzich and Nicholas Spadaccini. Minneapolis: University of Minnesota Press, 1986.

Góngora, Luis de. *Epistolario completo*. Ed. Antonio Carreira and Antonio Lara. Zaragoza: Pórtico, 2000.

Greenblatt, Stephen. *Renaissance Self-Fashioning: From More to Shakespeare*. Chicago: University of Chicago Press, 1980.

Gutiérrez, Carlos M. *La espada, el rayo y la pluma: Quevedo y los campos literario y de poder*. West Lafayette, IN: Purdue University Press, 2005.

_____. "Las *Soledades* y el *Polifemo* de Góngora: distinción, capitalización simbólica y tomas de posición en el campo literario español de la primera mitad del siglo XVII." *Romance Languages Annual* 10 (1999): 621–25.

King, Willard F. *Prosa novelística y academias literarias en el siglo XVII*. Madrid: Anejos del Boletín de la Real Academia Española, 1963.

Kristeva, Julia. *Sèméiôtikè. Recherches pour une sémanalyse*. Paris: Seuil, 1969.

Lyotard, Jean-François, *La condition postmoderne,* Paris: Minuit, 1979.

Lollini, Massimo. "Maravall's Culture of the Baroque between Wölfflin, Gramsci and Benjamin." *Yearbook of Comparative and General Literature* 45–46 (1997–1998):187–196.
http://www.uoregon.edu/~maxiloll/pages/MARAVALL.html (accessed February 2, 2004)

Maravall, José Antonio. *La cultura del Barroco*. 5th ed. Barcelona: Ariel, 1990.

_____. *Teatro y literatura en la sociedad barroca*. Madrid: Seminarios y Ediciones, 1972.

Monreal, Julio. *Cuadros viejos*. Madrid: Oficina de la Ilustración Española y Americana, 1878.

Montero Reguera, José. "Una amistad truncada: sobre Lope de Vega y Cervantes (esbozo de una compleja relación)." *Anales del Instituto de Estudios Madrileños* XXXIX (1999): 313–36.

Pérez de Herrera, Cristóbal. *Discursos del amparo de los legítimos pobres . . .* Madrid: 1598.

Profeti, Maria Grazia. "Cervantes enjuicia su obra: desviaciones lúdico-críticas." *Desviaciones lúdicas en la crítica cervantina*. Ed. Antonio Bernat and José María Casasayas. Salamanca: Ediciones Universidad de Salamanca, 2000. 423–42.

Read, Malcolm K. "Saving Appearences: Language and Commodification." *Rethoric and Politics: Baltasar Gracián and the New World Order*. Ed. Nicholas Spadaccini and Jenaro Talens. Hispanic Issues 14. Minneapolis: University of Minnesota Press, 1997. 91–124.

Robbins, Jeremy. *Love Poetry of the Literary Academies in the Reigns of Philip IV and Charles II*. London: Tamesis, 1997.

Romera Navarro, Miguel. "Querellas y rivalidades en las academias del siglo XVII." *Hispanic Review* 9.4 (1941): 494–99.

Rozas, Juan Manuel. *Estudios sobre Lope de Vega*. Ed. Jesús Cañas Murillo. Madrid: Cátedra, 1990.

Salas Barbadillo, Alonso Jerónimo de. *La peregrinación sabia y El sagaz Estacio, marido examinado*. Ed. Francisco A. Icaza. Madrid: Espasa-Calpe, 1941.

Sánchez, José. *Academias literarias en el Siglo de Oro español*. Madrid: Gredos, 1961.

Soto, Hernando de. *Emblemas moralizadas*. Madrid: 1599

Unamuno, Miguel de. *En torno al casticismo*. 7th ed. Madrid: Espasa-Calpe, 1968.

Vega, Lope de. *Cartas*. Ed. Nicolás Marín. Madrid: Castalia, 1985.

———. *Cartas completas*. Ed. Ángel Rosenblat. 2 vols. Buenos Aires: Emecé, 1948.

Viala, Alain. *Naissance de l'écrivain. Sociologie de la littérature à l'âge classique*. París: Minuit, 1985.

Vivar, Francisco. "El uso del público en la creación literaria: *Para todos, Para algunos y Para sí.*" *Hispanófila* 138 (2003): 1–13.

Wright, Elizabeth R. *Pilgrimage to Patronage. Lope de Vega and the Court of Philip III, 1598–1621*. Lewisburg, PA: Bucknell University Press, 2001.

Wyndham, George. "Introduction." *The Poems of Shakespeare*. Londres: Senate, 1994 [original ed. 1898].

8

Revisiting the Culture of the Baroque: Nobility, City, and Post-Cervantine Novella

Nieves Romero-Díaz

The variety of approaches that has characterized the study of the Spanish Baroque throughout history reveals the complexity of the period and its attraction for critics. The homogeneity apparently imposed by a dominant authority falsifies the conflictive reality of a culture that otherwise has been continually adapting before forces of control and resistance. Indeed, the so-called "crisis" of the Baroque arises from the negotiation between power relations of containment and freedom and is represented in the cultural products of the time. The post-Cervantine novella (*novela corta*) is one cultural practice in which this crisis is debated.[1] The novella, then, will be characterized not by its discursive unity (an expression of a dominant ideology) but by dominant and subversive discourses that converge and contradict each other. As we will see in this article, the novels become fundamental in the understanding of the culture of the Baroque.

Despite the oblivion into which the short story has been cast in the last two centuries, recently there has been an incipient interest in its study. The number of reeditions and of monographs dedicated to specific authors have dramatically increased, particularly those involving Lope de Vega and María de Zayas, two of the most well-known masters of the genre.[2] In the last three years no fewer than four monographs have been published on the genre itself:

Rogelio Miñana's *La verosimilitud en el Siglo de Oro: Cervantes y la novela corta* (2002), Carmen Rabell's *Rewriting the Italian Novella in Counter-Reformation Spain* (2003), Isabel Colón's *La novela corta en el siglo* XVII (2001), and my own, *Nueva nobleza, nueva novela: Reescribiendo la cultura urbana del Barroco* (2002).[3] In this essay, I wish to insist on a sociological approach to the study of the post-Cervantine novella.[4] In my view, the proliferation of this genre canonized by Cervantes can only be understood in connection with its historical context.[5] Hence it is necessary to study the novella as an essential component of the culture of the Baroque. My main contention is that the short novel constitutes the cultural space in which one of the most important ideological debates of the time is negotiated and discussed: the redefinition of a new urban nobility. The conflicts that arise from the relations between the young ladies and gentlemen who wander through the pages of the novels translate symbolically into the conflicts of a social group trying desperately to redefine itself. In order to do so, principles and categories that had traditionally determined status are questioned.

On the one hand, I will discuss the way this genre is determined by contextual factors, specifically, the ideological discourses at play in the novels. On the other, I will argue that the short novel can also actively shape the reality in which it takes part. As Raymond Williams explains it, it is not that the relation between literature and society is an abstraction but, rather, that "the literature is there from the beginning as a practice *in* the society" ("Base and Superstructure" 27; my emphasis). Literature and society establish an inseparable relationship, impossible to extract from the cultural process in which they both participate.[6]

As a first step toward comprehending the importance of the post-Cervantine novella, we have to be clear about our understanding of the culture of the Baroque. My approach engages in dialogue recent historical and literary works that reject the idea of the Baroque as a "guided culture" (*cultura dirigida*), the nomenclature dominant since José Antonio Maravall's *Culture of the Baroque*, first published in Spanish in 1975.[7] I am referring to literary studies by Marina Brownlee and Hans Gumbrecht, Anne Cruz and Mary Elizabeth Perry, George Mariscal and Paul Julian Smith among others, and works by Ignacio Atienza, Mauro Hernández, Henry Kamen, I.A.A Thompson, and Bartolomé Yun Casalilla, for example, all of which draw upon history and sociopolitics.

Cultural materialists, building upon the work of Raymond Williams, have questioned the traditional concept of culture. First in his *Culture and Society: 1780–1950* and then in *Marxism and Literature*, Williams breaks with the idea of culture as a monolithic and static unity and defines it instead as "a constitutive social process, creating specific and different 'ways of life'" (*Marxism* 19).[8] Culture is not only a reflection of the world but a structural force that can constitute and transform that world. It is a dynamic process in which contradictory, subversive and challenging discourses intermingle with (official) dominant discourses. From the moment we consider culture in its processual sense, dominant, residual and emergent elements of culture, as defined by Williams, relate to each other. That is, at any given time, culture is comprised not only of practices and discourses of the dominant groups but also of residual ones "formed in the past but . . . still alive in the cultural process, not only and often not at all as an element of the past, but as an effective element of the present" (122). Both dominant and residual cultural elements are also confronted by emergent ones: "new meanings and values, new practices, new relationships and kinds of relationships are continually being created" (123). Dominant culture, then, to the extent that it depends on a real social process, has to be in a constant state of flux and adjustment because, at any given historical moment, Williams adds, "no mode of production and therefore no dominant social order and therefore no dominant culture ever in reality includes or exhausts all human practice, human energy, and human intention" (125).[9]

This dynamic vision of culture relates intrinsically to another concept that Williams also redefines, that of hegemony. After rejecting the traditional definition of "political rule or domination, especially in relations between estates . . . between social classes" (107), Williams concludes that hegemony is "not only the articulate upper level of 'ideology', nor are its forms of control ordinarily seen as 'manipulation' or 'indoctrination'. . . . It is, in the strongest sense a 'culture', but a culture which has also to be seen as the lived dominance and subordination of particular classes" (110).[10] In a hegemonic process, then, the concept of ideology as a conscious rigid set of ideas, values and beliefs imposed by dominant groups proves reductionist (Weiss 184). Ideologies, and not ideology, are also "usually internally complex," as Terry Eagleton points out. They are "differentiated formations, with conflicts between their various elements which need to be continually negotiated and resolved, . . . A dominant ideology has continually to negotiate with ideologies of its subordinate. . . . Indeed what makes a dominant ideology powerful . . . is also what tends to make it internally heterogeneous and inconsistent" (*Ideology* 45). In order to analyze a dominant culture, or more accurately, any hegemonic culture, one has to take into account those discourses that legitimize and at the same time challenge it. With this conceptual frame in mind, when exploring and analyzing the culture of the Baroque, we cannot accept that cultural authority exercises its power without any kind of resistance. It is worth revising Maravall's contribution regarding the culture of the Baroque in the book of the same title, probably the most influential sociological study of seventeenth-century Spain within the last 30 years.

According to Maravall, in baroque Spain, dominant groups acted and controlled unidirectionally, "guiding" (by fear or persuasion) all levels of life. Indeed, for Maravall, seventeenth-century Spanish culture is characterized as conservative, as a reaction to the critical (political, socioecomic, and ideological) changes that had been occurring in Spain since the end of the fifteenth century. Such conservatism attempts to "close off" any type of novelties that might alter the traditional *status quo* (*Culture*, 131). In other words, it works "[to] contain the possible breakdown of the social order on which the monarchy must base itself" (133). Specifically, this emphasis on sustaining and re-strengthening the dominant cultural power—sublimated with political absolutism—becomes, in the work of Maravall, the strict "guiding" authority that defines the Spanish culture of the Baroque (58). Power, authority and control, according to Maravall, are the three axes that provide structure to a culture which, in the end, attempts to present itself as totally homogeneous. In doing so, the Church and the Monarchy mean to exercise absolute control over society and thereby make any capacity for free agency (apparently) impossible.

As Williams has stated, though, for any given culture to be effective, the group in power must redefine its positions continuously so the traditional order remains unthreatened. This pressing need for containment uncovers the existence of emergent responses (some conscious, others unwitting) that challenge and threaten the *status quo*. For Williams in the end, the existence of limits does not eliminate the possibility of active and oppositional responses that may resist and dismantle the position of dominant groups (*Marxism* 114). In fact, and despite his vision of the culture of the Baroque as one of containment, Maravall himself acknowledges challenging and subversive responses within that same culture. In *Contradictory Subjects*, George Mariscal draws our attention to the fact that "Maravall sensed the impossibility of any 'total system'" (21). More recently, in a forum on Maravall's notion of the Baroque, David Castillo pointed out how in his *Culture of the Baroque* as well as in many other works (i.e., *Estado moderno y mentalidad social* [*Modern State and Social Mentalities*] [1972], *La oposición bajo los Austrias* [*Opposition Under the Hapsburgs*] [1972], and *Poder, honor y élites en el siglo XVII* [*Power, Honor, and the Elite in the Seventeenth Century*] [1979], and also in his socio-literary incursions into *Celestina* [1964], *Don Quijote* [1976], and the picaresque [1986]) Maravall speaks of oppositional responses (180). Maravall does not accept, for example, that "rejections of what was proposed did not frequently occur: one must keep in mind the conflictive nature of the seventeenth century" (*Culture* 89). Unfortunately, the translation of this paragraph by Terry Cochran does not completely grasp the strong emphasis Maravall places on the conflict of the time. It is worth examining Maravall's words in Spanish: "esto no quiere decir que no se produzcan casos, y aun muy frecuentes, de repulsa de lo que se propone. Y ahí está todo ese fondo conflictivo y de oposición en el siglo XVII, sin tener presente el cual—también en esto hay que insistir—no se puede comprender nada" (*La cultura* 198) (this does not mean that there do not exist cases, even very frequent ones, of rejection of what it is proposed. Right there you have that whole conflictive and oppositional nature of the seventeenth century, without which—and I also want to insist on this—one can understand nothing) (my translation).[11] For the Spanish Baroque hegemonic authority to be effective, then, the groups in power could not simply guide and manipulate their subordinates. They also had to take into account practices and manifestations of (social, sexual, and racial) marginal groups that problematized cultural authority and provoked conflicts and contradictions. The resulting dialectic between control and opposition, containment and freedom, gave rise to the so-called "crisis" of the Baroque. For instance, in the collection of articles entitled *Culture and Control in Counter-Reformation Spain*, editors Anne Cruz and Mary Elizabeth Perry, clearly influenced by Raymond Williams's understanding of the concept of culture, insist on revising seventeenth-century Spain through the historization of its cultural production. Their research focuses on the ecclesiastic institution as an organism that, through a variety of forces (from the Inquisition to practices such as sermons or religious theater), tried to establish and buttress a certain cultural homogeneity. Nevertheless, as their edition shows, such homogenization was never complete since there existed conflicting responses from racial, sexual and social minorities who attempted to destabilize the traditional order. Therefore, for a cultural analysis of the Baroque, one cannot ignore the existence of oppositional responses that in one way or another are affecting the hegemonic process. By containing them, assimilating them, transforming them or simply accepting them, the monarchical-seigniorial power of the Baroque is continuously negotiating and adapting itself. The result is a contradictory and conflictive culture in crisis and, consequently, in constant flux.

Novellas, as cultural practices, must be understood in materialist terms—that is, as objects and events in the world, as part of human life and of society, as forms of cultural power, and then, as historical artifacts of control and resistance. The post-Cervantine short novel, like the reality in which it participates, is not characterized by its unity but its contradiction. When studying the short novel, the reader needs to look for the way the text represents and deals with the conflicts between discourses of cultural containment and responses of cultural freedom. One cannot "lament those contradictions nor erase them," Paul Julian Smith says, "but [should] place them within the episteme or discursive configuration of Cervantes' time" (189). Therefore, it is not my intention to conclude whether the post-cervantine short novel is responding to official discourse by legitimizing or threatening it (something which has happened, for example, with Lope's plays, which for some critics are *propagandistas*, and, for others, are subversive; or with María de Zayas's novels, whether seen from a conservative perspective or a subversive-feminist one). Rather, we must regard the short novel as what Martínez Camino has called a "place of conflict and negotiation of a variety of different discourses" ("lugar de conflicto y negociación de discursos variados diferentes") (33) and examine how it legitimizes or subverts official discourse, while understanding the conflicts and, more importantly, uncovering the political and ideological implications those conflicts have in the cultural process.[12]

As indicated at the beginning of this study, these popular collections of novellas address one of the most important debates of Spanish Baroque culture: the attempt by the urban nobility to adapt and redefine itself in the face of political, social, and economic crisis.[13] It is well known, as Maravall and other historians have demonstrated (Antonio Domínguez Ortiz, Henry Kamen, I.A.A. Thompson, and Bartolomé Yun Casalilla among many), that the seventeenth-century nobility in general undergoes a crisis of definition. Never a closed social group, it faces a "war of ideas" (Kamen 53) amongst different cultures and different ideological models. Most notably, I am going to refer to a very conflictive sector of this group that corresponds to a middle nobility (*nobleza media o caballeresca*) and that settles primarily in the cities. This urban nobility has broken from both the titled nobility as well as the lower one, and has accepted into its ranks new elements mainly from an incipient bourgeoisie that is altering its traditional way of life.[14] The post-Cervantine novellas, by waging this struggle of the urban nobility on an ideological level, are characterized by a recurring set of conflicting dominant and marginal discourses: on the one hand, the dominant ideology of the time that supports the continuity of the nobility group in cultural power (i.e. blood purity, genealogy, the *mayorazgo*, the principle of honor, the exclusivity of arms, etc.); on the other, "emergent" discourses that from the sixteenth century are obliging this same group to change and adapt in order to maintain its hegemonic position (i.e. importance of virtue, the power of money, access to education, etc.).[15] Since this struggle is in the process of occurring, the new urban nobility lacks a clear and structured set of ideological principles and categories to define itself. Rather, it confronts different—and usually contradictory—models of representation.

To illustrate this struggle, a brief reference to one of the discussions that appear in these novels can be helpful: the role and meaning of the institution of *mayorazgo* (primogeniture). Said discussion is generally presented through the confrontations between two brothers. For instance, in "El Desdén de la Alameda" ("La Alameda's Disdain") (*Historias peregrinas y ejemplares* [*Strange and Exemplary Histories*]) by Gonzalo de Céspedes y Meneses (1623) and in "El envidioso engañado" ("The Envious Fool") (*Sucesos y prodigios de amor* [*Incidents and Wonders of Love*]) by Juan Pérez de Montalbán (1624), the legal practice of *mayorazgo* reaches a crisis when it comes in conflict with the increasing importance of new forms of economic power (particularly, money) not acquired through traditional means. In these novels the urban noble of seventeenth-century Spain seeks to negotiate two fundamental economic forces: one traditional, the inherited *mayorazgo*; and the other, new forms of wealth. Both authors, Céspedes and Montalbán, debate in their novels the incorporation of those emergent forms of wealth into dominant ideology (along with honor, purity of blood, and, of course, the *mayorazgo*) in order to find a new model of the urban noble who is also valued for his virtuous and civic (urban) actions. Significantly, this new model is embodied in the figure of the *segundón*, the second son of noble families who has to overcome a variety of conflicts to redefine himself politically, socio-economically, and, more importantly, ideologically. The confrontation between the two brothers is presented in gender terms: both attempt to possess the same woman who, in both novels, has dazzling beauty and opulent wealth, and who, therefore, embodies a threat. She is the "object" that every man wants to obtain, particularly traditional noblemen (represented by the older brother) who do not want to see their *mayorazgos* in jeopardy but rather wish to ensure and legitimize their dominant power. In any case, the legal value of *mayorazgo* is never eliminated; it is adapted. After inheriting the *mayorazgo* because of the older brother's death, the *segundón*, thanks to his virtuous actions and, more importantly, the support of inhabitants of the city, possesses the woman and what she represents. At the end, in the attempt for a new social group to redefine itself, dominant and emergent discourses transform and come together.[16]

It is no accident that the city in which this conflict takes place is Seville and that the wealth represented by women comes from New Spain. The urban space, conceived in its cultural sense, becomes an essential coordinate in the debate. It is a place of change, "the locus of new social groups and new forms of social relations" (Zimmerman and Weissman 9); the city can be seen not only as a future cultural product but also as a cultural producer (Agnew et al. 8).[17]

The presence of cities in the post-Cervantine novellas attracts the attention of any more or less diligent reader. Cities protagonize the novels at the same level as the noble men and women who populate them. The need for a spatial context for each novel becomes an intrinsic characteristic of the genre. One must highlight the descriptions of, for example, "monstrous" Madrid, "noble" Córdoba, and, as in the previous example, "wealthy" Seville. These cities not only open the stories and function as a stage for their amorous adventures but also participate in the ideological debate of the novels.

These descriptions follow a similar structure, and most authors repeat it almost automatically. In fact, some critics of the genre limit the function of such descriptions to that of a simple spatial frame for the stories.[18] Indeed, for some, they are no more than homogeneous descriptions, with "a same ideological structure" ("un mismo ensamblaje ideológico") (Làsperas 443). The specificity of each space, however, adds an ideological meaning to the plot. As cultural producers, cities have a signifying function that changes depending on the historical moment. As Sybil Moholy-Nagy states in her influential study on urbanism: "[c]ity personality does not rest on material progress but on *historical options* faced by a specific town and no other" (11; my emphasis). The cities chosen for each novel, with their historical and ideological meanings, are woven directly into the cultural discourses of the novel.

In the introduction to *Undoing Place?* Linda McDowell states that the organization and construction of a space are related insofar as they lay the foundations for the identity formation of the inhabitants (2). For McDowell, the peculiarities of every place mean something that goes beyond that of its physicality. That is, each place establishes an ideological relationship with the people that inhabit it and with whom it is identified. Therefore, exclusivity characterizes each space which "define[s] [itself] and [its] inhabitants as 'different from'" (2). The connection between people and a particular space (in its physical and ideological reality) changes historically (11). As Moholy-Nagy summarizes it: "cities, like mankind, renew themselves unit by unit in a slow, time-bound *metabolic process*. . . . The constancy of urban change derives its dynamism from an eternally evolving imagination kindled by the coexistence of past and present" (11; my emphasis). This emphasis on change does not mean breaking with the past. Moholy-Nagy herself emphasizes that "[a]lthough towns are inanimate, they assure the characteristics of their creator. Men create and destroy values with equal intensity. As the only creature with a historical memory, man reveres the past, yet he ignores or denies it in the name of an utterly unknowable future" (11). It has to be noted that seventeenth-century Spain witnesses the proliferation of another genre—the local histories—which, despite being a common medieval genre, reaches its peak during the culture of the Baroque.[19] The popularity of post-cervantine short novels not only is closely related to the equal popularity of this genre, but depends on it for its own generic definition. In fact, as Wlad Godzich and Nicholas Spadaccini explain in their introduction to *Literature among Discourses. The Spanish Golden Age*, in order to demystify Golden Age literature as a superior conceptual entity, there have been two strategies: one, "to fill out . . . the scope of our knowledge of literature in that period"; and two, "[to] recogniz[e] that there is an interaction between the works that we have come to call literature and others" (xii). In a time when the institutionalization of literature as a differentiated discipline was not yet fully carried out and the separation between what was literature and what was not was still blurred, the increasing publication and consumption of these two cultural practices (novellas and local histories) should not be a surprise; however we must also identify the connections between them—connections that any reader of the time would be aware of.

Regarding the cities' need "[de] mostrar al mundo sus grandezas, su nobleza e incluso su santidad" (Marcos Martín 28) (to show to the world its grandeurs, its nobility and even, its sanctity), their seventeenth-century descriptions in the local histories represented an idealized noble imaginary that cities tried to emulate. Indeed, organized in specific sections (name of the city, its origin, settlement and climate, the fame of its buildings, its provisions, wealth and the fame of its inhabitants [Piñero 17]), these eulogies to each city were founded on a traditional nobility model that did not correspond to their present. Paradoxically, along with an ideal image that was recreated for each city, there existed a real one, a living one, in the process of change and transformation.

Valladolid provides a valuable example of this paradox, as it underwent incessant changes provoked by the presence of the court, particularly that of Phillip III from 1601 to 1606. From the fifteenth century, Valladolid had lodged the court almost twenty-five times, and thus had to adapt and renew itself continuously.[20] With the last arrival of the court in 1601, from an architectural point of view, the city had to confront an almost total reconstruction because of the bad conditions in which Valladolid found itself after the fire of 1561. Jean Canavaggio refers to this last reconstruction in her book about Cervantes's life, in particular to the "reconstruction" that "renewed the city's appearance: the Plaza Mayor . . . ; Silver-smiths' street . . . ; her palaces and churches . . . ; shady promenades . . ." (198–99).

The grandeur of the city corresponds to that of the court. After its departure in 1606, however, the city became "un cascarón demasiado grande y medio vacío; [donde] centenares de casas abandonadas se van deteriorando lentamente" (Bennassar 134) (an overly large and half-empty eggshell; [where] hundreds of abandoned houses lie slowly deteriorating). In order to survive the effects of this departure, Valladolid had to modify its urban plan. One goal, for instance, was to reconstruct the wall that had enclosed the city since medieval times. The wall was neglected from the moment the court arrived and was destroyed at one point. This growing courtly city coming out of the wall gave a sense of 'openness' (Gutiérrez 39) and, symbolically, of disorder and chaos. With the abandon of the court in 1606, the city of Valladolid embarked on the construction of a new wall, a task that lasted from 1620 to the end of the century (39–40). The return to civic order and stability was carried out architecturally by the construction of a wall that would help redefine the city as such. The chaotic and dynamic change that the court brings to Valladolid is paradoxically controlled by a wall that "closes off" the city from returning to any other courtly state.

This transformation was limited not only to its architecture, however. Every time the city became the court, and especially from 1601 to 1606, it became the "sede de embajadores . . . , miembros de los consejos . . . , residencia de la alta nobleza . . . , una sociedad rica, abocada hacia el consumo y el lujo" (Ribot 38–39) (headquarters for ambassadors . . . , council members . . . , a residence for the high nobility . . . , a wealthy society inclined toward consumption and luxury). The local (middle) nobility, among other groups, also had to adapt to the changes implied by the presence of the court and its departure. The court, with its new social groups and their ways of life, obliges the local ones to adapt continuously. In the years after 1606, this local nobility would try to define itself finally as "urban" and independent of the changes that the court conveyed; for example, by reaccessing the city government (Gutiérrez 61). The construction of the wall in the non-courtly Valladolid becomes the symbol of the return to a civic control, in the hands of and for an urban nobility that has to rebuild itself socio-ideologically after the court has settled for good in Madrid.

Unlike this conflictive but dynamic reality of Valladolid in the seventeenth century, two local histories of the city portrayed an idealized model of representation. *Historia ilustrada de la muy noble y muy leal ciudad de Valladolid* (Illustrated History of the Very Noble and Very Loyal City of Valladolid) (1625 [?]; also reedited in 1644 with some additions by D. Gaspar Uriarte) by Juan Antolinez de Burgos, and *Excelencias de la ciudad de Valladolid, con la vida y milagros del santo Fr. Pedro Regalado* (Distinctions of the City of Valladolid, with the Life and Miracles of the Holy Father Pedro Regalado) (1627) by Fr.

Antonio Daça, both written during the kingdom of Phillip IV (to whom they are addressed) and following the same aforementioned structure (name, origin, history, etc.), praise a courtly Valladolid. A city that, according to these local histories, had remained relatively untouched by the Moors, Valladolid was exalted for and honored by the royal presence throughout the ages. Instead of highlighting the change that the arrival, stay, and departure of a court bring within (and those almost unnoticed elements that proved to be important for the ongoing redefinition of Valladolid such as the variety of occupations [Antolinez 9], the commerce and contracts [Daça fol. 20r], and the University, with all its professorships [Daça fols. 21r and 25r]), these stories exalted elements that idealized a noble grandeur of a courtly city. The magnificence of a city that had to confront an important transformation during the seventeenth century that takes it to a new civic order, a new urban reality, was recreated through an idealized unchanging model of representation.[21]

Reduced to the limits that the genre imposed, the representations of cities that appear in the post-cervantine short novels try to mystify the same values that most of them, through their local histories, aimed to highlight. In the search of coordinates that help to understand the presence of a new urban nobility and to redefine itself socially and ideologically, there is a need to construct a memory, a past. With this model the nobility negotiates its cultural position in a time of crisis. As Louis Marin states, the representation of a city "is and is not the city: it is a particular representation of the city which reveals the ideology sustaining it, and it does so by what it shows as much as by what it hides" (212). One could read the presence of the dominant noble values in the descriptions of the local histories and in the short novels as the need for an anchored tradition with which to negotiate during a time of urban transformation.[22] The choice of a particular city for each novel is, of course, not arbitrary. Although they follow a similar structure, each description seems to be full of ideological meanings and, depending on the conflict portrayed in each novel, the city changes along with the selection of features and values to be emphasized from each one. Therefore, the descriptions of the cities that contextualized the short novels work not only as a simple frame/stage for the stories but are engaging the social and ideological discourses being discussed with regard to a new urban nobility of the Baroque.

One outstanding example of the intrinsic relationship between the novel, the nobility, and the city is the collection *Historias peregrinas y ejemplares* (1623) by Gonzalo de Céspedes y Meneses.[23] Published in Zaragoza three times (1623, 1630, 1647) in addition to being partially translated into French (1628, 1641 and 1663) during the seventeenth century alone, this popular collection is virtually unknown among contemporary readers. The importance of this collection hinges upon the narrow dialogue between fiction and historiography. The framework for the collection is, in fact, an account of "excelencias y antigüedad de España, teatro digno de estas peregrinas historias" (12–28) (Spain's excellencies and antiquity, a theater worthy of these strange histories).[24] Céspedes is participating in the construction of an idea of Spain through his novels. The Spain he is presenting is a diverse land with many *cabezas* (heads)—its cities—without which the political growth of the State cannot take place. Spain's unity comes, paradoxically, from its very multiplicity. The description of Spain does not escape, however, the noble image represented in the local histories of the time: after explaining its name and fame, the author begins to praise Spain's "origen antiguo, [a] su defensa, riqueza y cristiandad; [a] su inviolable fe, valor y santidad, sabiduría, valentía, dominio, imperio y consejo" (17) (ancient origin, its defense, wealth and Christianity, its inviolable faith, valor and sanctity, wisdom, courage, power, empire and advice). All these are characteristics that led to an exemplary government of order and control.

Each novel opens with a description of a city (Zaragoza, Seville, Córdoba, Toledo, Lisbon, and Madrid) that, like in the description of a diverse Spain, repeats the same structure. However, every chosen city and its description correspond to a particular conflict among the nobility. For that reason, certain characteristics of each city are highlighted for discussion. So, for instance, the institution of *mayorazgo* is questioned in the wealthy city of Seville (wealthy in the sense of commodities and money that came from New Spain) in "El desdén de la Alameda" ("The Disdain from the Alameda"); lineage and arms as an exclusive exercise of the nobility are brought into play in Córdoba, which was famous for having the best nobility of all the cities, in "La constante cordobesa" ("The Constant Woman from Córdoba"); the question of pure blood lines is discussed in the once "contaminated" Toledo, in "Pachecos y Palomeques" ("Pachecos and Palomeques"); and, finally, in "Los dos Mendozas" ("The two Medoza brothers"), the urbanization (civilization) of military deeds is debated in Madrid, which had undergone changes as the court was established permanently there in 1606. Dominant and residual discourses (such as lineage and the institution of *mayorazgo*) are confronted by emergent ones (as the civic [urban] concept of virtue), and their cultural values are being negotiated in order to find an ideological definition for a new urban nobility.

I cannot close this essay, though, without making a brief reference to the female writers of the genre. María de Zayas, Mariana de Carvajal, Ana de Abarca Bolea, and Leonor de Meneses must deal with the social issue of the urban nobility that they belong to, but from the condition of being part of a dominated group, that of being women. María de Zayas is probably the best known of these writers, not only by us today but also during her time.[25] Actively immersed in the culture of her time and praised by her contemporaries, Zayas was always reminded of being a woman, "a wonder of her time" (as one of her translators called her).[26] In this sense, Zayas embodied the paradox of being both in the center and at the margins of baroque culture, being limited but still having a story to tell. As Elizabeth Ordóñez explains, along with the control that the social and cultural context imposed on her, it is evident that Zayas had the need to fight and the "anxiety" to find a voice of her own (15). Her ideological position, however, is not clear. Given that the process of consciousness about her limited freedom is precisely (forgive the repetition) in a process, her position is characterized by contradictions—contradictions that Zayas explores in her novels.[27] As a member of a society in which the model of representation for the urban nobility is in crisis and in the process of redefinition, she discusses the place of an urban noble that is also a woman. María de Zayas, therefore, is also debating her own place as an individual in society.

In contrast with Céspedes y Meneses, in most of the short novels of her two collections, *Novelas amorosas y ejemplares* (*The Enchantments of Love*) (1637) and *Desengaños amorosos* (*The Disenchantments of Love*) (1647), the model of representation Zayas is looking for is recreated by multiple spaces and, in some cases, presented through traveling (*peregrinatio*). This movement from place to place provides a very complex and many times conflictive ideological elasticity that never determines her completely. From the Catalonian Montserrat of the first story to the Portuguese Lisbon of the last one, the characters of Zayas's novels move around the geography of the Spanish Empire and negotiate different models that respond to the contradictory situation of the urban noblewoman of the Baroque. It is not without significance that these two spaces that open and close the stories of her collections are charged with important historical meanings: both are spaces that are fighting for their independence from the central government during that time, bringing to the table a critical contextual frame for her stories.[28]

In general terms, throughout the frame tale and the twenty short stories, Zayas challenges the politics of feminine passivity and proposes models for the urban noblewoman that question those established by the hegemonic (masculine) groups (whether it be the State or the Church). Her arms are the same ones that those groups impose, but during the process of appropriating them, they have been transformed into mechanisms of individual authorization (i.e. the final silence as a way of resistance, the personal choice of entering a convent, the strengthening of a female community/friendship, etc.). Also, ideological principles and categories that are put into question in the process of redefinition of a new urban nobility are presented from a gender perspective. This is the case, for example, with the principle of honor and, more specifically, with the choice for women to seek vengeance when the honor code has been transgressed. In "La burlada Aminta y venganza de honor" ("Aminta Deceived and Honor's Revenge") and "Al fin se paga todo" ("Just Desserts") (both from her first collection of stories), the main protagonists, Aminta and Hipólita, become avengers of their own dishonor. Cross-dressed as man in the first case and protected by the mantle of night and sleep in the second, the avengers assume the agency in defending their honor. Although this action brings finally to the re-establishment of a social principle and, at the end, the acceptance of the honor code (Smith 33), the active role these women have enacted, taken to the ultimate extreme (the death of the deceivers), becomes a threat to the legal and religious authority of the time (Luna 44–45).[29] In fact, these characters neither marry their deceivers, look for a man for help, nor follow the example of those deceived classical women who killed themselves after being dishonored (i.e. Lucretia).[30] As another woman, a political writer of the second half of the seventeenth century, María de Guevara, says: "la reina Dido se mató porque la burló un príncipe troyano, lo mismo hizo Lucrecia, ellas fueron grandísimas majaderas, que mejor fuera matarlos a ellos que no matarse ellas" (18) ([q]ueen Dido killed herself because a Troyan Prince deceived her, Lucretia did the same; they were enormously stupid, better to kill the men than themselves"). María de Zayas and María de Guevara years later propose a model of action for women that breaks with the literary tradition as well as with the moral tradition, present in the books of illustrious women of the period.

After killing the *burladores* (deceivers), though, the order has been definitely altered. Zayas, then, negotiates with that same order to reestablish it. Aminta and Hipólita remarry noblemen and end residing in the court, one in Madrid and the other in Valladolid—while the court was there until 1606.[31] One could say that these endings simply follow the dominant genre structure of the novels and *comedias* of the time: that of a happy marriage. However, in these cases, both women literally choose marriage instead of the convent, as many of the characters in her novels do. Zayas uses this choice of marriage as a tool to reincorporate women into society under their own conditions and start a new life, with a new name and with the protection of the king, respectively. The city, the courtly city, as Castillo y Solórzano says, is "el lugar de los milagros y el centro de las transformaciones" (48) (the place of miracles and the center of transformations).[32] María de Zayas does not reject the code of honor as a defining principle for the nobility, but rather rereads it and adapts it according to the new circumstances and from a gender perspective.

In conclusion, in the culture of the Spanish Baroque, if the urban nobility wishes to ensure its hegemonic position, it must adapt to the needs and changes provoked by an urban culture along political, social, and economic lines. This nobility, settled in the city, is forced to negotiate new ideological models of representation that challenge traditional defining principles and categories. The symbolism of the dynamic cities of the Baroque and the imaginary models recreated in the local histories of the time are important for the formation of this emergent social group. The post-Cervantine novella becomes the cultural space for the ideological debate surrounding the definition of the urban nobility, a debate in which dominant discourses that reinforce authority enter into a dialogue with discourses that subvert it. In this sense, the complexity of such dialogue represented in the short novel is articulated as a process and characterized by contradictions. The study of *novela corta* is essential not only because it sheds light on a new social process of seventeenth-century Spain. It also provides a more comprehensive understanding of a culture that unfolds in a dialectic of containment and freedom: that is, the culture of the Baroque.

Notes

1. The post-Cervantine novella (*novela corta*) is better known by the nomenclature given by Agustín González de Amezúa: "*novela cortesana.*"
2. For instance, the Fundación de Castro and the publisher Montesinos, as well as Cátedra which recently edited María de Zayas's first collection of short stories, *Novelas amorosas y ejemplares* (2000). Interest in Lope de Vega's *Novelas a Marcia Leonarda* (1624) (see monographs by Marina Brownlee [1981], Ivonne Yarbro-Bejarano [1991] and Carmen Rabell [1992] as well as numerous articles) has been replaced by that in María de Zayas's two collections. In fact, Zayas has become the most studied of all writers of the genre in the last five years. Since 2000 alone, three monographs have been published (by Marina Brownlee, Margaret Greer, and Lisa Vollendorf) along with almost one hundred articles, chapters, and dissertations (not to mention conference papers).
3. The first two books focus on the use of rhetoric in the formation of the short novel as a genre (in Miñana's study of *verosimilitud*) and in rewriting the Italian *novelle* during the Spanish Counter Reformation (in Rabell's case). Colón's work, however, presents a general account of the genre, with special attention to the role of women, whether as printers, writers, or readers of the novels. Previous to these works, there have been

four basic studies for the genre: Evangelina Rodríguez Cuadros (1979 and 1986), Jean-Michel Làsperas (1987) and Anne Cayuela (1996).

4.   For a complete revision of the culture of the Baroque and the importance of the post-Cervantine novella, see my book, of which this essay is a brief updated version.

5.   Only in the seventeenth century, Juan Pérez de Montalbán's collection of novellas, *Sucesos y prodigios de amor* (first published in 1624), was reedited at least fifteen times. The success of this book illustrates the good fortune of the more than fifty-eight original collections of novellas published after the very popular Miguel de Cervantes's *Novelas ejemplares* in 1613 and up to 1700. See Arsenio Pacheco-Rasanz's article about the popularity of this genre where he presents statistics of the editions, re-editions, publishers, and booksellers of short novels during the seventeenth century. The bibliographical study by Begoña Ripoll on the baroque novel is also worth mentioning. A section of my book (*Nueva nobleza*) entitled "Nuevos espacios, nuevos lectores: La novela corta como fenómeno social" (41–45) offers a summary.

6.   In this sense, we are breaking the traditional vision of the literary text as an isolated non-historical entity, seen only as a verbal icon (Eagleton *Literary Theory* 47). The formalist J. Hillis Miller—like many critics from different theoretical perspectives—has argued that "[w]orks of literature do not simply reflect or are not simply caused by their contexts. They have a productive effect in history" (152).

7.   I will use Terry Cochran's translation of Maravall's *Cultura del Barroco*. For the rest of the Spanish texts in this article, all translations are my own.

8.   In *The Idea of Culture* (2000), Terry Eagleton has discussed the complexity of the word "culture" from its origin and its etymological meaning, to its contemporary and contradictory meanings. Eagleton contextualizes Williams's contribution to the meaning of culture in the 1960s and 1970s with other important discussions of the term (i.e., by T.S. Eliot, Geoffrey Hartman, etc.) and problematizes it from a contemporary perspective, "[i]n the face of [new] cultural efflorescence . . . in the new millennium" (130). As Eagleton demonstrates, Williams's works are nevertheless fundamental for any discussion of the issue.

9.   Cultural materialist studies regarding the English Renaissance—in particular, those by Jonathan Dollimore and Alan Sinfield—have informed this study. These authors have recognized Williams's contribution to the study of culture. In Sinfield's words, the centrality of Williams "derives from the fact that at a time when Althusser and Foucault were being read in some quarters as establishing ideology and/or power in a necessarily unbreakable continuum, Williams argued the co-occurrence of subordinate, residual, emergent, alternative, and oppositional cultural forces alongside the dominant, in varying relations of incorporation, negotiation, and resistance" (9).

10. "Hegemony d[id] not just passively exist as a form of dominance. It ha[d] continually to be renewed, recreated, defended, and modified. It [was] also continually resisted, limited, altered, challenged by pressures not at all its own" (Williams *Marxism* 112).

11. More examples in Maravall's *Culture of the Baroque* are: "[w]ith this culture, those who propagate it hope to dominate better the tensions threatening society from within,

although they may never come to be eliminated" (80). Or, "[o]f course, there was no absolutely closed and stationary society where some changes did not have to be taken into account" (138).

12. This is how my approach differs from the only other study of post-Cervantine novellas, which also understands them from a sociological point of view. I am referring to the work of Evangelina Rodríguez Cuadros who, despite criticizing the contrary nature of a uniform vision of the Baroque, insists on the forces that a dominant ideology imposes and concludes that the novella is simply an alternative to the theater of the time, and that both theater and novellas are expressions of such a dominant ideology.

13. Paradoxically, despite the conservative character of the principles and categories that the noble group tries to endure, its existence is always in constant change: "el estamento nobiliario es algo que, bajo la apariencia de una continuidad, está encerrando una movilidad continua") (Domínguez Ortiz "Aspectos económicos" 26) (the noble order is something that, under the appearance of continuity, is enclosing a continuous mobility).

14. As Maravall explains: "van a ser las modernas ciudades administrativas del Estado absoluto—y muy particularmente—esas ciudades capitales de las nuevas Monarquías, el espacio sociopolítico en que las élites se definirán y tomarán largo vuelo. Si en el XVI y XVII se hace tan perceptible el nuevo fenómeno es, precisamente, por las experiencias acumuladas por los nobles que han trasladado a aquéllas su vivienda y por la acción homogeneizadora y aglutinante de las monarquías absolutas") (*Poder* 188–89) (the modern administrative cities of the Absolute State—and very specifically—those capital cities of the new Monarchies are going to be the socio-political space in which the elite will be defined and will take flight. If in the sixteenth and seventeenth centuries this new phenomenon becomes so perceptible it is, precisely, because of the experiences accumulated by those nobles who have moved their residences to the cities and because of the homogenizing and unifying force of the Absolute Monarchies).

15. This middle urban nobility is referred to by different names by different historians. Some examples are: *élite de poder* (Maravall, *Poder*), *burguesía feudal* (Hernández), *oligarquías urbanas* (Atienza), or *patriciado urbano* (Molas).

16. For an extensive analysis of "El Desdén de la Alameda," see the section in my book "El caso singular de la 'preciosa y rica Sevilla': La cuestión del mayorazgo" (64–75).

17. "To put the city in cultural context is to view it as the product of both hegemonic and subordinate cultures and at the same time, as the site for their production. Placing cities in the context of their societies, we are able to see how the cultural motifs of a society are embedded in the form of its cities and in the lives of its urban population. . . . To study the city on cultural context therefore requires us to acknowledge that cities are cultural creations and that they are best understood as such" (Agnew et al. 7–8).

18. This limitation was pointed out by González de Amezúa in 1929 and since then it has been repeated by other critics. A recent example is that of Rodríguez Cuadros and

Haro Cortés in their introduction to an anthology of short stories published in 1999 (168).

19. Although of ancient origins, the fashion of this genre has increased since the beginning of the sixteenth century and it is in the seventeenth century when "pocas fueron las [ciudades] que no contaron con reseñas, impresas o inéditas, de sus antigüedades" (Sánchez Alonso 375) (few were the cities that had no descriptions, published or not, of their antiquities).

20. See Bartolomé Bennassar's work on Valladolid (1989).

21. For a detailed analysis of Valladolid in the context of the *novela corta*, see my article "Sobre la política espacial del Barroco: El caso de Valladolid y la novela corta (de Cervantes a Prado)" (forthcoming).

22. Nor is it fortuitous that during the seventeenth century another popular genre was the genealogical treatise. See Domínguez Ortiz (*Sociedad* 161–67) and Carrasco Martínez (74–77).

23. I follow Emilio Cotarelo y Mori's edition (1906) which is older than that of Yves R. Fonquerne in Castalia (1970), because it is complete: it includes the *aprobaciones*, *advertencias*, *privilegios*, the framework about the excellencies of Spain, and all the introductory chapters (the city descriptions) in every story.

24. It is unfortunate that Cotarelo's edition is not annotated and that Fonquerne simply eliminates all descriptions (about Spain and each city) due to editorial restrictions and also because, in his view, those descriptions do not influence the stories whatsoever (40).

25. Zayas was one of the most famous writers of the seventeenth century. During her own time, Zayas's work was edited and reedited, and translated into French, English, or German, (Yllera 82–93). Nowadays the critical bibliography on her is immense and growing. See the updated bibliography by Greer (39–60 and 449–62).

26. Antoine de Méthel Escuier sieur Douville, French translator of Zayas's work in 1656–57, calls her "cette merveille de son sexe" (quoted by Yllera 84).

27. In the chapter dedicated to María de Zayas in my book, I develop on her contradictory ideological positions and conclude that her feminist consciousness results from the tensions between, on the one hand, the limitations imposed by the dominant patriarchal society, accepted by the author as a noble and, on the other hand, the realization of her own inferiority as a woman, which determines her to break with those same limitations (98–115).

28. About the symbolic meaning of Montserrat in Zayas, see Greer (96–101).

29. In fact, Smith affirms that at the end, Zayas "cannot transgress the law of the dagger and the phallus" (33). On the contrary, although Greer accepts that "Zayas gives us no diegetic vision of women definitively *overturning* that law," she also sees "her [Zayas's] interrogation of its legitimacy . . . in subtle modifications in traditional narrative paradigms, including her use of the motif of the cross-dressing" (203).

30. The tradition of the catalogue of illustrious women has its source in the classic antiq-

uity (i.e. Hesiod's *Catalogue of Women*). For the sixteenth and seventeenth centuries, Álvaro de Luna's *Libro de las claras e virtuosas mugeres* (1446) is an important reference, along with Boccacio and Pisan's catalogues. Chastity and integrity are the two main characteristics given to women such as Lucretia. In Zayas's time, catalogues were still popular (i.e. Juan Pérez de Moya, *Varia historia de sanctas e ilustres mujeres en todo género de virtudes* [1583]), not to mention the quantity of manuals, guides, and "mirrors" about the perfect state for women (i.e. from Juan Luis Vives, *Instrucción de la mujer cristiana* [1528, Spanish translation] to Fray Juan de la Cerda, *Vida política de todos los estados de mugeres: en el qual se dan muy provechosos y christianos documentos y avisos, para criarse y conservarse debidamente las mujeres en sus estados* [1599]). For a detailed study of these texts, see Correia Fernandes.

31.   In the section of her book entitled "Crossing Over: Women Who Kill," Vollendorf analyzes these two novels and explores the difference between men who exercise violence against women and women who do the same against men. Vollendorf affirms that women, "[c]laiming the right to defend their bodies" and "[u]nlike Zayas's male characters—many of whom beat and kill women out of jealousy, fear, misogyny, and proprietariness—Aminta and Hipólita exact revenge based on direct evidence of their victimizers' guilt . . . based on evidence of personal injury" (186–96).

32.   For a complete analysis of "La burlada Aminta" from the perspective of the redefining urban nobility, see my study (*Nueva nobleza* 116–25).

Works Cited

Agnew, John et al. "Introduction." *The City in Cultural Context*. Boston: Allen and Unwin, 1984. 1–30.

Antolinez de Burgos, Juan. *Historia ilustrada de la muy noble y muy leal ciudad de Valladolid*. Ed. Juan Ortega y Rubio. Valladolid: Hijos de Rodríguez, 1887.

Atienza, Ignacio. *Aristocracia, poder y riqueza en la España Moderna. La casa de Osuna, siglos XV–XIX*. Madrid: Siglo XXI, 1987.

Bennassar, Bartolomé. *Valladolid en el Siglo de Oro*. Trans. Francisca Arambur Riera et al. Valladolid: Ayuntamiento de Valladolid, 1989.

Brownlee, Marina. *The Cultural Labyrinth of María de Zayas*. Philadelphia: University of Pennsylvania Press, 2000.

_____. *The Poetics of Literary Theory: Lope de Vega's* Novelas a Marcia Leonarda *and Their Cervantine Context*. Madrid: Porrúa, 1981.

Brownlee, Marina, and Hans Gumbrecht, eds. *Cultural Authority in Golden Age Spain*. Baltimore: Johns Hopkins University Press, 1995.

Canavaggio, Jean. *Cervantes*. Trans. J.R. Jones. New York: W.W. Norton, 1990.

Carrasco Martínez, Adolfo. *Sangre, honor y privilegio: La nobleza española bajo los Austrias*. Barcelona: Ariel, 2000.

Castillo, David. "Maravall on Culture and Historical Discourse: A Question of Metho-
dology." *Yearbook of Comparative and General Literature.* 45–46 (1997–98): 177–
81.

Castillo y Solórzano, Alonso. *Las harpías en Madrid.* Ed. Pablo Jauralde. Madrid: Castalia, 1985.

Cayuela, Anne. *Le paratexte au Siècle d'Or. Prose romanesque, livres at lecteurs en Espagne au XVIIe siècle.* Geneva: Droz, 1996.

Céspedes y Meneses, Gonzalo. *Historias peregrinas y ejemplares.* Ed. Emilio Cotarelo y
Mori. Madrid: Librería de la Viuda de Rico, 1906.

Colón, Isabel. *La novela corta en el siglo XVII.* Madrid: Laberinto, 2001.

Correia Fernandes, Maria de Lurdes. *Espelhos, cartas e guias e espiritualidades na Peninsula Ibérica, 1450–1700.* Porto: Instituto de Cultura Portuguesa, 1995.

Cruz, Anne, and Mary Elizabeth Perry, eds. *Culture and Control in Counter-Reformation
Spain.* Hispanic Issues 7. Minneapolis: University of Minnesota Press, 1992.

Daça, Fray Antonio. *Excelencias de la ciudad de Valladolid, con la vida y milagros del
santo Fr. Pedro Regalado.* Valladolid: Juan Laso de las Peñas, 1627.

Dollimore, Johnathan. "Shakespeare, Cultural Materialism and the New Historicism."
Political Shakespeare: Essays in Cultural Materialism. Ed. Jonathan Dollimore and
Alan Sinfield. Ithaca: Cornell University Press, 1995. 2–18.

Domínguez Ortiz, Antonio. "Aspectos económicos de la nobleza española en la Edad Moderna." *Torre de Lujanes* 28 (1994): 23–34.

_____. *La sociedad española del siglo XVII. El estamento nobiliario.* Granada: Universi-
dad de Sevilla, 1984.

Eagleton, Terry. *The Idea of Culture.* Oxford: Blackwell, 2000.

_____. *Ideology: An Introduction.* London: Verso, 1996.

_____. *Literary Theory: An Introduction.* Minneapolis: University of Minnesota Press,
1983.

Fonquerne, Yves R. "Introducción." In *Historias peregrinas y ejemplares,* by Gonzalo de
Céspedes y Meneses. Madrid: Castalia, 1970. 7–48.

Godzich, Wlad, and Nicholas Spadaccini. "Introduction: Towards a History of 'Literature'." *Literature among Discourses. The Spanish Golden Age.* Ed. Wlad Godzich and
Nicholas Spadaccini. Minneapolis: University of Minnesota Press, 1986.

González de Amezúa, Agustín. "Formación y elementos de la novela cortesana." *Opúscu-
los histórico-literarios.* Vol. 1. Madrid: CSIC, 1951. 194–279.

Greer, Margaret. *María de Zayas Tells Baroque Tales of Love and the Cruelty of Men.* University Park, PA: The Pennsylvania State University Press, 2000.

Guevara, María de. *Desengaños de la Corte y mujeres valerosas.* N.p., 1664.

Gutiérrez, Adriano. "Valladolid en el siglo XVII." *Valladolid en el siglo XVII.* Valladolid:
Ateneo de Valladolid, 1982. 13–108.

Hernández, Mauro. *A la sombra de la Corona. Poder local y oligarquía urbana (Madrid,
1606–1808).* Madrid: Siglo XXI, 1995.

Kamen, Henry. *Golden Age Spain.* London: Macmillan, 1988.

Làsperas, Jean-Michel. *La nouvelle en Espagne au Siècle d'Or*. Montpellier: Catillet, 1987.

Luna, Lola. "Introducción." In *Valor, agravio y mujer*, by Ana Caro. Madrid: Castalia, 1993. 9–46.

Maravall, José Antonio. *La cultura del Barroco*. 5th ed. Barcelona: Ariel, 1990.

_____. *The Culture of the Baroque*. Trans. Terry Cochran. Minneapolis: University of Minnesota Press, 1986.

_____. *Poder, honor y élites en el siglo XVII*. Madrid: Siglo XXI, 1979.

Marcos Martín, Alberto. "Percepciones materiales e imaginario urbano en la España moderna." *Imágenes de la diversidad. El mundo urbano en la Corona de Castilla (sig. XVI–XVIII)*. Ed. José Ignacio Fortea Pérez. Cantabria: Universidad de Cantabria, 1997. 15–30.

Marin, Louis. *Utopics: Spatial Play*. Trans. Robert A.Vollrath. New Jersey: Macmillan, 1984.

Mariscal, George. *Contradictory Subjects: Quevedo, Cervantes and the Seventeenth-Century Spanish Culture*. Ithaca: Cornell University Press, 1991.

Martínez Camino, Gonzalo. "La novela corta del Barroco español y la formación de una subjetividad señorial." *Bulletin of Hispanic Studies* (Glasgow). 73 (1996): 33–47.

McDowell, Linda. "Introduction." *Undoing Place?: A Geographical Reader*. London: Arnold, 1997. 1–12.

Miller, J. Hillis. *Hawthorne and History: Defacing It*. Oxford: Blackwell, 1991.

Miñana, Rogelio. *La verosimilitud en el Siglo de Oro: Cervantes y la novela corta*. Newark: Juan de la Cuesta, 2002.

Moholy-Nagy, Sibyl. *Matrix of Man: An Illustrated History of Urban Environment*. New York: Praeger, 1968.

Molas, Peré. *La burguesía mercantil en la España del Antiguo Régimen*. Madrid: Cátedra, 1985.

Ordóñez, Elizabeth. "Woman and Her Text in the Works of María de Zayas and Ana Caro." *Revista de Estudios Hispánicos* 19.1 (1985): 3–15.

Pacheco-Rasanz, Arsenio. "Varia fortuna de la novela corta en el siglo XVII." *Revista Canadiense de Estudios Hispánicos* 10 (1985–86): 407–21.

Pérez de Montalbán, Juan. "El envidioso engañado." *Sucesos y prodigios de amor*. Ed. Luigi Giuliani. Barcelona: Montesinos, 1992. 95–130.

Rabell, Carmen. *Lope de Vega: El arte nuevo de hacer "novellas."* London: Tamesis, 1992.

_____. *Rewriting the Italian Novella in Counter-Reformation Spain*. London: Tamesis, 2003.

Ribot, Luis Antonio. "Valladolid durante el reinado de Carlos I." In *Valladolid. Corazón del mundo hispánico. Siglo XVI*. Valladolid: Ateneo de Valladolid, 1981. 13–69.

Ripoll, Begoña. *La novela barroca: Catálogo bio-bibliográfico (1620–1700)*. Salamanca: Universidad de Salamanca, 1991.

Rodríguez Cuadros, Evangelina. "Introducción." *Novelas amorosas de diversos ingenios del siglo de XVII.* Ed. Evangelina Rodríguez Cuadros. Madrid: Castalia, 1986. 9–81.

_____. *Novela corta marginada del siglo XVII español: Formulación y sociología en José Camerino y Andrés de Prado.* Valencia: Universidad de Valencia, 1979.

Rodríguez Cuadros, Evangelina and Marta Haro Cortés. "Introducción." *Novela de mujeres en el Barroco: Entre la rueca y la pluma.* Ed. Evangelina Rodíguez Cuadros and Marta Haro Cortés. Madrid: Biblioteca Nueva, 1999. 18–118.

Romero-Díaz, Nieves. *Nueva nobleza, nueva novela: Reescribiendo la cultura urbana del Barroco.* Newark: Juan de la Cuesta, 2002.

_____. "Sobre la política espacial del Barroco: El caso de Valladolid y la novela corta (de Cervantes a Prado)." *Voz y Letra.* (Forthcoming).

Sánchez Alonso, B. *Historia de la historiografía española.* Vol. 2. Madrid: CSIC, 1944.

Sinfield, Alan. *Faultlines: Cultural Materialism and the Politics of Dissident Reading.* Oxford: Clarendon Press, 1992.

Smith, Paul Julian. *Writing in the Margin: Spanish Literature of the Golden Age.* Oxford: Clarendon Press, 1988.

Thompson, I. A. A., and Bartolomé Yun Casalilla, eds. *The Castilian Crisis of the Seventeenth Century: New Perspectives on the Economic and Social History of Seventeenth-century Spain.* Cambridge: Cambridge University Press, 1994.

Vega, Lope de. *Novelas a Marcia Leonarda.* Ed. Julia Barella. Madrid: Júcar, 1988.

Vollendorf, Lisa. *Reclaiming the Body. María de Zayas's Early Modern Feminism.* Chapel Hill: University of North Carolina Press, 2001.

Weiss, Julian. "Maravall's Materialism." *Yearbook of Comparative and General Literature* 45–46 (1997–98): 181–87.

Williams, Raymond. "Base and Superstructure in Marxist Cultural Theory." *New Historicism and Cultural Materialism: A Reader.* Ed. Kiernan Ryan. London: Arnold, 1996. 22–28.

_____. *Culture and Society, 1780–1950.* London: Chatto & Windus, 1958.

_____. *Marxism and Literature.* Oxford: Oxord University Press, 1977.

Yarbro Bejarano, Yvonne. *The Tradition of the "novela" in Spain, from Pedro Mexía (1540) to Lope de Vega's* Novelas a Marcia Leonarda *(1621, 1624).* New York: Garland, 1991.

Yllera, Alicia. "Introducción." In *Desengaños amorosos*, by María de Zayas. Madrid: Cátedra, 1984. 11–105.

Zayas, María. *The Disenchantments of Love.* Trans. H. Patsy Boyer. Albany: State University of New York Press, 1997.

_____. *The Enchantments of Love: Amorous and Exemplary Novels.* Trans. H. Patsy Boyer. Berkeley: University of California Press, 1990.

Zimmerman, Susan, and Ronald Weissman, eds. "Introduction." *Urban Life in the Renaissance.* Newark: University of Delaware Press, 1989. 9–15.

Part IV
Strategies of Identity in the Colonial Context

9

Perspectives on *Mestizaje* in the Early Baroque: Inca Garcilaso and Cervantes

Silvia B. Suárez

In Peruvian society today, colonial *mestizaje* constitutes the foundation of the debate about nation and culture among scholars. As in the sixteenth and seventeenth centuries, the nation's racial hierarchy produces an ideology that divides this country into a *mestizo* mass and a white elite to the extent that native Andean values are denied even by the *mestizo* majority of the population. It is noteworthy that a recent study on terrorism in Peru has revealed the underlying presence of this social differentiation in the vicious cycle of violence created by rebel groups and repressive official forces for more than two decades.[2] Ninety percent of the victims of this traumatic process have been *mestizos* with clear ties to Andean traditions. Thus, a revision of colonial discourse from its origins is necessary in order to contribute new insights to the debate on the reconstruction of Peruvian cultural identity. As a starting point in this process, I propose a reinterpretation of the connection between el Inca Garcilaso's *Comentarios reales* (1609) and Miguel de Cervantes Saavedra's last novel, *Los trabajos de Persiles y Sigismunda* (1617) and their authorial critique of dominant cultural values. A reading of the texts from the perspective of the colonized subject illustrates that both authors believe that the Amerindian does retain a certain amount of agency within the restrictive colonial environment and engages in a process of cultural negotiation as a means to preserve his/her own values.

A sociopolitical interpretation of the circumstances that influenced the production of the *Comentarios reales* and *Los trabajos de Persiles y Sigismunda* combined with literary analysis suggests that both texts are engaged in critical dialogue with the sixteenth- and seventeenth-century Spanish literary tradition and the hegemonic discourse of Hispanic societies. Both texts depict the colonized as one who challenges the boundaries of the hierarchical society by forging what I will call an "intermediate identity."[3] As in a diglossic situation where two different languages co-exist and are felt to be alternatives by native speakers, the colonized subject does not renounce his native traditions. Instead, s/he develops a strategy to overcome cultural imposition by making a conscious decision to move from the dominant culture of the colonizer to the inferior culture of the colonized according to the particular type of social interaction in which s/he is engaged (Crystal 138). For instance, a Peruvian Andean man would adopt the values of Spanish culture in Hispanic contexts, while maintaining his native customs within his own community.

In the *Comentarios reales*, Inca Garcilaso "comments" on the official history of the conquest and colonization of Peru and, in so doing, alters certain aspects of the history that are conflictive from the point of view of the colonized. Motivated by his own marginality in Hispanic society, Inca Garcilaso designs a narrative in which he not only expresses sympathy for his Spanish heritage, but more importantly, admiration for his Inca ancestors. The narrator's mobility between different cultures can be understood as a representation of the difficulties that many Andean groups experienced while being forced to assimilate Spanish culture. Given the preeminence of caste values in colonial society, the ability to select among dominant and subordinate cultural practices allowed the colonized subject to develop an "intermediate identity." As a result, the literary discourse in this chronicle illustrates a tension between two socially unequal groups, the superior white man/woman and the inferior Andean, which enables the colonized to modify his social identity.

Similarly, in *Los trabajos de Persiles y Sigismunda*, Cervantes tests the limits of cultural canons by inserting elements from another tradition into them. The geographical description of the "barbarous" setting in which the narrative begins to unfold, reminds the reader of certain passages from Inca Garcilaso's chronicle. Also, the use of native *Taíno* words and the inclusion of famous conquistadors as characters are ways of connecting the work to the colonization of America. Moreover, the portrayal of the "barbarous" characters implies the remolding of the barbaric subject not only within literature but also within prevalent modes of thought. Antonio, the *mestizo* son of a Spanish man (also named Antonio) and an Amerindian woman (Ricla), is one of the "barbarous" characters that are the basis of the Cervantine reply to colonizing discourse. By consciously fluctuating between the monarchical-seigniorial values and those of his native heritage, Antonio refuses to be marginalized by the dominant culture. His refusal to accept an inferior position in the social hierarchy coupled with his refusal to sacrifice aspects of his own culture in return for acceptance by the majority lead to the development of his new identity: that of the "intermediary."

In this essay, I will explore the way in which the "intermediary" is represented in *Los trabajos de Persiles y Sigismunda* and the *Comentarios reales* and the extent to which this figure draws a parallel between both texts. With this objective in mind, first, I will explain why the development of the "intermediary" is a useful category in a colonial/postcolonial world, and, second, I will outline the essential characteristics of sixteenth- and seventeenth-century Spanish society in which both works were written. Finally, I intend to demonstrate that both authors present a vision of the colonization of America that diverges from the norm.

A reading of the *Comentarios reales* that focuses on the process of cultural *mestizaje* highlights the flexibility inherent in the narrator's identity and reconsiders his position as a marginalized *mestizo* intellectual. Such emphasis leads to an interpretation of the text in terms of a hegemonic cultural process. Similarly, for the Latin American reader who is familiar with the chronicles of the Indies, *Los trabajos de Persiles y Sigismunda* establishes an unmistakable link with the colonizing endeavor. Moreover, the contradictory portrayal of the "barbarous" characters favors a reading of the novel from a colonial perspective which is why the concept of "intermediate identity" facilitates the study of these two texts as counter-hegemonic discourses. As diglossia, this "intermediate identity" arises from the marginalized subject's conscious movement between two different cultures. He refuses to be assimilated and, thus, places himself in a new cultural space where the dominant values coexist with the traditions of his so-called "inferior" culture. Thus, it is his ability to play an active role in the redefinition of his identity in colonial society that makes the colonized subject an "intermediary." As a result, the sociological emphasis of this notion facilitates the study of cultural interactions within the context of colonization.[4]

The socio-historic panorama of the sixteenth and seventeenth centuries in Spain and its American colonies demonstrates the strong influence of the principle of a social hierarchy based on race. The pure-blood statutes instituted by the Catholic Kings against Jewish converts in 1449 were a way to guarantee the social and cultural preeminence of "old Christians" who were free from the "bad" influence of Jewish, Moorish, convert, and mulatto blood (Twinam 373). Although these statutes did not address Amerindians specifically, the discriminatory practices on which they were based were transplanted to the colonies where a class society was established despite the lack of systematic and coherent legislation.

The juridical division of the viceroyalties into the *República de españoles* and the *República de Indios* reflected this ethnocentric perception of the Amerindians as people "without reason" or religion that needed to be "Christianized." Thus, the Crown and Spanish society did not approve of the intensification of the interethnic mix beginning in the middle of the sixteenth century because they thought the union to be "impure" and, therefore, "illegitimate." Despite the fact that the Indian legislation was uncertain as to the union between Spaniards and Indians,[5] it did not tolerate unions between Spaniards and black women. Therefore, in response to the high number of mixed unions, a series of legal restrictions was established that affected *mestizos*, the product of these unions. They were denied access to *repartimientos*, careers as scribes or notary publics, and, in the religious realm, they were not allowed to be ordained priests (Mörner, *La corona española* 177).

The rise of documents to legitimize an individual's heritage confirms the presence of the pure-blood ideal in the colonial imagination. For example, for a short period of time in 1591 the viceroys of New Spain and Peru were able to extend the royal decree of legitimation to the *mestizos* in an attempt to promote their assimilation into Spanish culture. In the eighteenth century, the document known as a *gracias al sacar* was frequently purchased by racially mixed people seeking to "erase" their "impure" and, thus, "illegitimate" ethnic origin. Nonetheless, there were repeated cases of individuals who continued to be seen as inferior despite having been "legitimated" by an official document.[6] That is to say, the color of one's skin was not, in and of itself, the cause for social discrimination. "Inferior" ethnic origin also played an important role.

Convinced of the importance of the humanities and a university education, the monarchical-seigniorial Spanish society entrusted the administration of the government to intellectuals and, among them, found great collaborators for the propagation of their aristocratic principles (Maravall 292). Therefore, while certain writers might have been dedicated to defending the *status quo* by modeling the emotions and attitudes of an ideal public complicit with the wishes of the upper class in their own works, there were others, such as Cervantes, who took a different position on their role in society. Instead of viewing the act of creative writing as a way to transmit a set system of knowledge to the reader, many writers believed it should be a shared experience in which the *lec-*

tor avisado would have an active role in the completion of the textual message. As with any other cultural practice, writing was considered a social experience whose meaning was found in the reader's response.[7] In colonial Peruvian society, writers tended to use peninsular literary models as a way to transgress. In the middle of the seventeenth century, the rhetoric of the "relation" and the "appeal" was converted into a discourse that served to vindicate the colonial intellectual. Juan de Espinosa Medrano, one of the most pronounced defenders of Gongora's aesthetic, altered his representation of hegemonic power by granting a leading role to elements of the subordinated culture (Chang-Rodríguez 92).[8] Like Espinosa Medrano, Inca Garcilaso and many other colonial writers used the literary form to defend the unique identity of the colonized subject and to construct a discourse that ran counter to the hegemonic discourse of monarchical-seigniorial power.

I propose a reading of the *Comentarios reales* and *Los trabajos de Persiles y Sigismunda* that focuses on the "hybrid" characteristic of the narrative structure of both works. Cervantes and Inca Garcilaso adopted the canons of the literary genres of their time in order to subvert them from within and, therefore, create a space for the proliferation of thought that would be able to transgress the boundaries of cultural hegemony. Although this tendency varied from case to case due to the presence of a variety of different factors, there is a point of convergence in the writers' attempts to give voice to the marginalized subjects of society which is why their narrative transgressions are able to challenge the dominant discourse of the time.

Inca Garcilaso's *Comentarios reales* complies with the rhetorical and ideological requirements of the monarchical-seigniorial culture in order to contradict the dominant power from within the system. Although many studies on this text have stressed the author's skillful management of Renaissance rhetoric as an identifying characteristic of Inca Garcilaso's writing, I adhere to another body of studies that emphasize the author's ability to incorporate elements external to the lettered culture in his text. By keeping in mind Inca Garcilaso's position as a marginalized intellectual, I maintain that his chronicle was not only a message addressed to Spanish authorities, but was also an attempt to challenge the marginalized position of the Amerindian within colonial society.

Inca Garcilaso is conscious of the underlying theoretical foundations of knowledge and adapts them to his narrative interests. He knows that "truth" resides in the hermeneutic rather than empirical aspects of the work and, therefore, converts the oral nature of Andean culture into the source of narrative authority (Zamora 8). However, the insertion of the *Quechua* language and oral narratives within the written text do not presuppose cultural fusion or the harmonization of opposites. As José Antonio Mazzotti explains in *Coros mesti-zos del Inca Garcilaso*, the discursive ambiguity in the *Comentarios reales* is owed to the author's interest in the simultaneous supervision of two types of recipients: a European and an Andean. Thus, from a strictly narrative perspective, Inca Garcilaso's chronicle is a non-canonical, "hybrid" text that joins two different literary traditions.

In contrast to Cervantes, the development of Inca Garcilaso's intellectual activity was driven by his awareness of being an "Other" within colonial society. The transformational power that rational thought acquired in the seventeenth century was reflected in the Amerindians' insistence on challenging European hegemony. According to Mabel Moraña in *Relecturas del Barroco de Indias*, the educated portion of the *criollo* population set a political agenda with the purpose of overcoming the social and cultural barriers imposed by the monarchical-seigniorial power. So, while the first outbreaks of a new Amerindian identity are emerging, Inca Garcilaso becomes aware of his difference and his capacity for negotiating a more privileged position in society.

In the middle of the sixteenth century, while still in Peru, Inca Garcilaso had recognized his own inadequacies in a culture governed by caste values in which *mestizo* was synonymous with inferiority. However, as many members of the displaced Andean elite, he nurtured the possibility of a new community molded by Andean tradition. As is made known many times in the *Comentarios reales*, Inca Garcilaso maintains an open line of communication with his relatives and friends who are unhappy with their inferior position in the social hierarchy. Although they are dealing with a strongly Hispanized community, this Andean elite sustains a discourse that sees the colonizing process as unjust and searches for a way to reverse the Andean situation by reclaiming the Inca past (García-Bedoya 163). Thus, Inca Garcilaso was part of this ideology based on the Andean past that led him to take a position that opposed the prevailing caste values. That is why he presents the colonial subject as an agent of an ambiguous and indefinite identity who, because of his/her very nature, is able to conserve certain values from his/her native culture and integrate them with certain values from the dominant culture. From this point of view, this chronicle is an example of how cultural *mestizaje* transcends its utopian nature and becomes an ideological counter-discourse.

His awareness of the problems associated with cultural *mestizaje* led Inca Garcilaso to develop a discourse that, in and of itself, is a strategy for giving the marginal subject a voice and, naturally, defending it with the authority of his own knowledge. This is why the narrator of the *Comentarios reales* identifies himself as Indian, Inca, *mestizo*, and Spaniard, depending on the material being presented at the time. By doing so, the narrator assumes the position of the colonized because, as suggested in the second part of the chronicle, the implied reader is not only the European public, but also "los indios, mestizos y criollos de los reinos y provincias del grande y riquísimo imperio del Perú . . ." (*Comentarios* 2:9 [my translation]) (the Indians, mestizos and criollos of the towns and provinces of the great and rich empire of Peru [to whom the work is dedicated]). Thus, the narrator presents himself as an "intermediary" who is able to move freely between different social spaces.

However, throughout the first part of the *Comentarios reales*, the narrator introduces himself as an Indian more frequently than as a *mestizo*. Moreover, he hesitates to refer to his mixed ethnic origin and waits until the last chapters of that part of the chronicle to begin identifying himself as a member of that group. At the beginning of the first part of the chronicle, he presents himself as an Indian in order to reaffirm his authority. To this end, he insists on recalling his kinship with the Inca dynasties, which allows him to convince the reader of the veracity of his account by emphasizing that he is merely writing about his relatives' oral testimonies. On the other hand, it is interesting to note how he employs the affirmation "Soy indio" (I am Indian) to convey his false sense of modesty and to demonstrate that he himself questions erudite knowledge (*Comentarios* 1:50). The narrator apologizes for his possible mistakes in retelling the history, despite having initiated his narration by highlighting the high level of sophistication in Inca culture by comparing it with Roman culture.

The narrator's approach to a *mestizo* identity is progressive and less evident than when he identifies himself as an Indian. In the first half of the chronicle he begins to recognize himself as part of the *mestizo* sector when he retells the story of eight of his fellow *mestizos*. Only later does he include himself in that group of friends, "hijos de españoles y de indias" (sons of Spaniards and Indian women) with whom he used to play as a child (*Comentarios* 1:229–65). As these timid declarations are repeated sporadically in the successive chapters, they are also being transformed into a clear testimony of the narrator's position on the process of cultural *mestizaje*. This is demonstrated by the progressive sequence of the chapters concerning the abundance of European products transplanted to Peruvian soil—"De las frutas de España y cañas de açúcar," "De la hortaliza y yervas, y de la grandeza dellas" and "Del lino, espárragos, visnagas y anís" (On fruits from Spain and sugar cane, On vegetables and herbs, and their greatness, On flax, asparagus, bishop's weed, and anise), that ends in the chapter titled "Nombres nuevos para nombrar diversas generaciones" (New names to refer to various generations).

In the first three chapters of the series, the narrator is dedicated to praising the quality of the fruits and vegetables brought from Spain and transplanted in Peru. He employs the adjective "monstrous" in a positive way to describe the fertility of the Peruvian soil in the production of larger and higher-quality fruits and vegetables than those produced in Spain. However, when the narrator considers the reaction that his European readers could have to such success, he becomes nervous and begins to doubt the existence of radishes and melons of incredible sizes. And so he explains: "[. . .] temía poner el grandor de las cosas nuevas de mieses y legumbres que se daban en mi tierra, porque eran increíbles para los que no havían salido de las suyas [. . .]" (*Comentarios* 9:603) (I was afraid to mention the size of the new crops and vegetables that were produced in Peru, because anyone who had never left his own country would not believe it). He suspects that those who are unfamiliar with the Peruvian territory would not admit the higher quality of the new produce and, therefore, would not appreciate its value.

The meaning of the adjective "monstrous" changes when the narrator emphasizes the abundance of *enxertos* or hybrid products. Their uncontrollable growth could cause, on the one hand, the depletion of the native soil and, on the other hand, the devaluation of the produce originating from it. In the chapter "De la hortaliza y yerbas, de la grandeza de ellas" (On vegetables and herbs, and their greatness), the narrator explains that: "De todas estas flores y yervas que hemos nombrado . . . hay ahora tanta abundancia que muchas de ellas son ya muy dañosas . . . han vencido las fuerzas y la diligencia humana toda cuanta se ha hecho para arrancarlas" (*Comentarios* 9:601) (All the flowers and herbs we have mentioned [. . .] now exist in such abundance that many of them are regarded as weeds [. . .] which have thrived to such an extent in some valleys that they have defeated human effort and ingenuity in every attempt to extirpate them). Thus, from his point of view, the influence of the Spanish element in the production of such products could be dangerous and, therefore, classified as "horrifying."

This insistence on describing agricultural production on Peruvian soil acquires a sociopolitical character when read in conjunction with the following chapter, "Nombres nuevos para nombrar diversas generaciones" (New names for various racial groups). In this case, the narrator inventories the new "racial" species that have been produced in Peru as a result of "cross-breeding" and says:

A los hijos de español e india o de indio y española, nos llaman mestizos, por dezir que somos mezclados de ambas nasciones; fue impuesto por los primeros españoles que tuvieron hijos en indias, y por ser nombre impuesto por nuestros padres y por su significación, me lo llamo yo a boca llena, y me honro con él. Aunque en Indias, si a uno dellos le dizen "sois mestizo" o "es un mestizo," lo toman por menosprecio. (*Comentarios* 9:607)

(The children of Spaniards by Indians are called mestizos, meaning that we are a mixture of the two races. The word was applied by the first Spaniards who had children by Indian women, and because it was used by our fathers as well as on account of its meaning, I call myself by it in public and am proud of it, though, in the Indies, if a person is told: "You're a mestizo," or "He's a mestizo," it is taken as an insult.)

The "fear" of mixture is also evident in this case given the high number of *mestizos* who are not appreciated by the Spaniards or the Andeans. From the conquistador's point of view, although they have white blood, it is "impure" for having been mixed with an inferior race. At the same time, the Andeans reject such a mixture because they see in it the loss of their cultural values. The narrator's defense of *mestizo* identity loses relevance because, if one keeps the preceding chapters in mind, what is of greater interest to him is the denouncement of Andean marginality. That is why the discourse on the abundance of *enxertos* has a counter-hegemonic purpose. According to Renato Barilli, in the passage from the Renaissance to the Baroque, writing was characterized by the use of "wit" to establish parallels between two different contexts in such a way that the discourse expressed one through the other (72). In Inca Garcilaso's chronicle, the narrator establishes a connection between two different situations in presenting the topic of the transplanted, marvelous vegetables throughout the three chapters that precede the chapter on "racial cross-breeding." Thus, the word *enxerto*, employed to describe fruits and vegetables, acquires a metaphorical meaning that alludes to the process of cultural "insertion" typical of the colonizing process (Covarrubias 527). This rhetorical strategy is directed toward the *lector avisado* of the Andean elite that resisted cultural domination and aimed to restructure the colonial social system.

If one studies this section on cultural *mestizaje* in the *Comentarios reales* with the narrator's marginal social position in mind, it is possible to infer that the variable nature of his identity represents a sociopolitical agenda that is trying to avoid the exclusion of Andean values from the identity of the colonized. This is achieved by inverting the hegemonic relationship established by the colonizer and strategically positioning himself in the border between Spanish culture and Andean culture. As a result, the narrator depicts the inconsistencies of viceroyal power that opened fissures through which the colonial subject was able to intervene. That is why he is able to speak Castilian while in the realm of the colonizer and *Quechua* in his own community. Similarly, the colonized regulate other cultural practices by adopting this "intermediate identity" as a strategy for challenging the hegemonic constrictions that exist in colonial society.

According to Antonio Cornejo Polar, colonial discourse "no quiere ver las tensiones irresueltas, los conflictos dramáticos y las desgarraduras sin remedio que corroen desde dentro, la tersura de ese discurso . . ." (72) (does not want to see the dramatic unresolved tensions, conflicts, ruptures that corrode, without remedy and from within, the smoothness of that discourse [my translation]). Contrary to the purely utopist and Neo-Platonist intentions that have been attributed to it, Inca Garcilaso's chronicle constitutes a premeditated counter-discourse that locates itself between both dominant and subordinate traditions. Thus, rather than promoting the idea of a harmonious encounter between two cultures and the subsequent fusion of values within the parameters of the monarchical-seigniorial culture of the sixteenth and seventeenth centuries, the *Comentarios reales* encourages the Andean reader to reconsider marginality as a strategy for change.

Along the same lines, Cervantes' last novel, *Los trabajos de Persiles y Sigismunda*, establishes a dialogue with Inca Garcilaso's chronicle in expressing dissonance with hegemonic culture. For Cervantes, the Aristotelian principle of verisimilitude explained by Pinciano in his *Philosophia Antigua Poética* (1596) became a defining element of his literary work. He believed that his stories had to follow nature's logic in order to develop in a coherent and believable way (Shepard 60). That is why, from a literary point of view, he demonstrates a tendency to enrich the text with nuances that, although forbidden by the canon, offer a more complex representation of reality. He writes *Los trabajos de Persiles y Sigismunda*, taking as a model Heliodorns *Aethiopica* (1534), one of the most successful adventure novels of the period, and narrates, with a didactic and moralizing intention, the story of a pair of lovers who, in spite of the misadventures that constantly separate them, succeed in getting married. However, Cervantes' critical attitude modifies this topic to produce a genre of "hybrid" adventure stories whose basic elements—stereotypical characters, the triumph of good over evil—are adjusted to the contingencies typical of the world of the *pícaro* (Sacchetti 29). That is to say, he depicts a society in which social position is not fixed or even the necessary requirement for obtaining status, so an individual's wealth and action are what makes social interaction dynamic. Therefore, a marginal subject can acquire social status through wealth, and a privileged subject can fall through the ranks if he/she loses his/her fortune. Accordingly, Cervantes' last novel transforms a hierarchical and static conception of the world to weave the "barbarous" and "non-barbarous" into the characters' identity.

In Renaissance Spain, the "barbarian" was defined in opposition to the "civilized man." Speaking Castilian and demonstrating proper manners and comportment with respect to food and clothing were attributes of the "civilized man." In contrast, a lack of intelligence ("reason") implied the absence of language and, thus, of civility ("policía") or the capability to control one's self and domesticate the environment (Pagden 24). Contrary to prevailing thought, Cervantes introduces a subject who is both "barbarous" and "non-barbarous" into his novel. In the first passage of *Los trabajos de Persiles y Sigismunda*, the narrator initiates his story by showing the hero Periandro's subjugation to the power of the "barbarian" characters as one of their captives. Although the language he speaks and the clothes he wears describe Periandro as a man with *civilitas*, he is not able to use his intelligence to reverse his unfortunate situation and, instead, finds himself defenseless. As they did with the others, the "barbarians" should kill him in order to complete a ritual that will help them find a new king. However, recognizing the young man's horror at their bows and arrows, they decide to spare his life. As a result, contrary to the Renaissance ideal of the "barbarous," these "barbarian" characters have a sense of *civilitas* because they want to live in a society ruled by a king and, at the same time, they are capable of compassion due to their capacity to discern between good and evil.

The use of language plays a decisive role in a situation that parodies the colonizer-colonized relationship. The first sentence of the story introduces the prevailing position of the "barbarian" Corsicurvo by signaling his capacity for speech. He is able to communicate thanks to the fact that he speaks Castilian perfectly, whereas Periandro barely knows this language. The hero's linguistic inability becomes apparent in relation to the importance placed on the Castilian language over the course of the novel and its status as the *lingua franca* recognized by the majority of the "non-barbarous" characters. The adoption of new clothing is also important to contradict the image that the Renaissance had of the "barbarian." Notwithstanding the establishment of a clear distinction between the clothes of the heroes and those of the "barbarian" characters, the narrator subverts this difference later on in the novel. In the middle of the pilgrimage, Periandro and Auristela begin to dress like Ricla and her children and, thus, to be perceived as "barbarians." When they enter Lisbon, Periandro notices that the people not only look upon them strangely but persecute them as well since they are astonished by the appearance of the couple. He becomes aware that his and Auristela's physical traits and good manners are inconsistent with the poor quality of the clothes they are wearing and immediately convinces her to return to their usual clothing. In light of the dominant values bearing down on them, they want to avoid being mistaken as "barbarians."

The social constraints depicted in Cervantes' novel reflect the weight of the ideal of pure-blood in Spain and its colonies. Despite the fact that the laws of the Indies, which were based on canonical law, promoted the protection and humane treatment of the Amerindian, their application depended primarily on the hierarchical conception of society. The desire to establish a warring caste that descended from old Christians who had not mixed their blood with any other "race" justified, according to the conquistadors, their superiority over the indigenous population and, consequently, their right to conquer them. For the same reason, many *encomenderos* and clerics felt disdain for the *mestizos* and demonstrated interest in marginalizing them by forbidding their presence in certain jobs and positions of honor in society. White skin "libre de mala raza" (free from a bad race) was synonymous with status (Konetzke 230). Given the rigidity of the principles on which this society was built, a dichotomy was maintained in the colonies between the "conquistadors" and the "conquered" that implied the association of stratification and social status with ethnic groups. From a legal standpoint, the Indians constituted the most important group second only to the Spaniards whereas, from a social standpoint, they found themselves in the lowest level of the hierarchy (Mörner *Estado, razas* 85–92). Therefore, before teaching Christian customs to the indigenous population, as ordered by the *encomienda* system established in 1503, the conquistadors forced them to work as personal servants and to pay monetary tributes they did not owe. Yet they did not favor a harmonious coexistence with the Amerindians but rather attempted to divide them in *repartimientos* in order to avoid the development of close relationships.

Society's belief in the superiority of the white man became a determining factor in social interaction in the colonies. Although the royal decrees favoring marriage between Spaniards and Amerindians were approved circa 1515, viceroyal authorities attempted to maintain ethnic division. According to the canonical law of the period, any person, European or Indian, had a right to free will and was able to decide whom s/he wanted to marry. In contrast, the secular authorities opposed mixed marriages because of ethnic prejudice, as demonstrated by the attitude of a viceroy of Peru in the eighteenth century who "used to receive white visitors in one room and Indians and mixed-blood people in a different one" (Mörner, *Estado* 94 [my translation]). Yet, social prestige did not only depend on the purity of one's blood but also on his/her honor and wealth. As a result, there were those who bought *gracias al sacar* documents to cleanse their ethnic origin and, consequently, their social status. However, in many cases it failed to have an impact on the society at large who continued to think of them as inferior.

In *Los trabajos de Persiles y Sigismunda*, Constanza and Antonio's social comportment reflects the complexity of social interactions in which colonized subjects were engaged because of the preeminence of caste values. In the "barbaric" universe of the novel, the Villaseñor family is the embodiment of the American colonial *mestizaje* problematic. The union between Antonio the "Spaniard" and Ricla the "barbarian" and the behavior of their *mestizo* children, Constanza and Antonio, are laden with significant traces of this process. On the one hand, the cultural exchange between Antonio and Ricla is presented as a colonizing process because it occurs between a "Spaniard" and a "barbarian." Lost on an island, Antonio the Spaniard is assisted by Ricla who, despite the fact that she speaks another language, tries to communicate with him and offers him food. That is why he begs her to return to see him. She agrees to bring him not only food and company on a daily basis, but also gold and pearls "abundant" in her land. However, Cervantes transforms the asymmetry of the cultural exchange process by materializing in Antonio the Spaniard the incorporation of "barbaric" cultural practices into his European culture. Consequently, even when both Antonio and Ricla privilege the use of the Castilian language, the fact that Antonio learned Ricla's native language and adopted some of her customs, like dressing in animal hides, eating with primitive utensils, or living in a cave, reflects an inversion of the colonizer-colonized relationship. If it is certain that one cannot assure his assimilation to the "barbarous" way of life, without civility (*policía*), neither can one ignore the security with which the narrator presents Antonio to us as a "barbaric Spaniard" (*Persiles* 1:161).

On the other hand, the way in which the "non-barbaric" characters perceive the *mestizos*, Constanza and Antonio the son, is significant. They admire them fundamentally for their "civilized" customs. Apparently, they are highly Hispanized subjects because they speak Castilian and there is not the slightest indication as to their knowledge of the "barbarous" language. Moreover, they practice the Christian religion and, according to Ricla, they aspire to live in a city because, for them, the island is a "prison" that does not allow them to practice Christianity freely (*Persiles* 1:168). In this sense, Constanza and Antonio's social conduct has been molded by the values of the dominant Spanish culture.

Cervantes collapses this cultural preeminence as he complicates the *mestizo* siblings' social identity later on in the novel. For example, despite the respect that they receive from those who recognize their moral integrity and the quality of their faith, they are always perceived as "barbarians." Thus, if no one doubts their social conduct, their ethnic origin—i.e. their mixed color—is what determines this perception. That is why, despite her extraordinary beauty, Constanza is still called "barbarous." Moreover, although she becomes the widow of a rich earl, the society considers her a person of low status. In mentioning her new condition, the narrator concludes that she is now "más cristiana que bárbara" (more a Christian than a barbarian) and, in doing so, points out the permanence of her inferior ethnic origins as an unequivocal characteristic of her social identity (*Persiles* 3:265). In any case, Constanza's attitude does not in any way reflect a questioning of the hierarchical principles of her society, but rather her decision to adapt them.

On the contrary, Antonio the son actively responds to the pressure of imposed hierarchical values. On the road to Rome, the group of pilgrims encounters an older woman, Zenotia, who immediately falls in love with the young "barbarian." However, when she tries to seduce him, he is offended and shoots an arrow at her. Zenotia and Antonio's father interpret this reaction as a reproachable act because of its brutality and its affinity with all that is "barbarous." Antonio comes to understand that the defense of his virility is seen by the "non-barbarous" culture as an irrational act. Thus, confronted with the need to maintain his own beliefs or to find a space for himself in society, he decides to adopt an "intermediate" identity that allows him to adapt the social demands of the dominant culture to the values of his own native heritage. When his father warns him that if he does not change his attitude he will be considered a "barbarian," he responds accordingly: ". . . procuraré enmendarme . . . de modo que no parezca bárbaro, por riguroso, ni lascivo, por manso" (*Persiles* 2:137) (I'll strive to be better from now on, trying not to appear as either barbarous by being severe or lustful by being passive). That is to say, his conception of bravery and virility in relation to physical strength remains intact, as it is a cultural value that he will only adopt in the context of the "non-barbarian" culture in order to avoid being a social outcast. Thus, when he writes an aphorism for Croriano's book, he signs his name "Antonio, el bárbaro" (Antonio the Barbarian) (*Persiles* 4:304).

In *Los trabajos de Persiles y Sigismunda*, Cervantes transforms an adventurous romance into a trip through the ambiguities of social reality. As he announces in the prologue to his *Novelas ejemplares* (1613), it is a ". . . libro que se atreve a competir con Heliodoro" (book that dares to compete with Heliodorus) (6). As in the case of the Greek author, he wishes to entertain the reader, but does so by revealing to them certain social contradictions that would have been impossible to find in Heliodorns' novel. Cervantes' stylistic innovations have as their objective the desire to give voice to the world that underlies a society molded by caste principles. From a literary point of view, the transgressive character of the Cervantine novel demonstrates in its structure that it is the result of genre hybridization. Thus, while Heliodoro's *Aethiopica* involves archetypical heroes in a series of adventures which culminate in a happy ending, *Los trabajos de Persiles y Sigismunda* destabilizes such an ideal.

From a sociopolitical standpoint, it may be said that Cervantes' novel incorporates those voices which, directly or indirectly, stood in opposition to many of the beliefs of those who were in a position of privilege. According to Maravall (*La cultura del Barroco* [1975], *La literatura picaresca desde la historia social* [1986]), Spanish society in the sixteenth and seventeenth centuries was molded by the socioeconomic interests of the monarchical-seigniorial segments. However, their predominance did not in any way imply the absolute subjugation of underprivileged sectors nor the complete adhesion of those who, as intellectuals, played an active role in that society. On the contrary, those cases that demonstrate the evident failures of state propaganda ratify this movement of forces in which power is constituted and reveal the active role assumed by those individuals who were from different sectors of society and demonstrated their discontent with the monarchical-seigniorial power (Elliott 77).

My study of *Los trabajos de Persiles y Sigismunda* in relation to the *Comentarios reales* attempts to explain the literary similarities between both texts by means of an interdisciplinary analysis. The examination of the literary discourse as well as its articulation in a particular historical context has served as the basis of an interpretation of the texts from the perspective of the colonized subject. I hope to have demonstrated that the structural connections between Cervantes' novel and Inca Garcilaso's chronicle are not merely a matter of intertextual influence, but rather express a profound coincidence in their respective approaches to certain aspects of the colonization of America. Moreover, in both cases they are looking to defy rhetorical and ideological molds by adopting the position of the marginal subject to reveal the tensions inherent in such molds. Cervantes and Inca Garcilaso found in writing a promising space in which to effect a cultural negotiation that led to, on the one hand, the renovation of the literary genre in which each one unfolded and, on the other hand, the formulation of an interpretation of *mestizaje* as a strategic cultural exchange directed by the same marginal subject who adopts an "intermediate," cultural identity.

The emphasis placed on the sociohistorical aspect of sixteenth- and seventeenth-century Hispanic culture in this study has also allowed me to outline a substantial difference in the formation of this transgressive tendency between both writers. Cervantes' approach to the topic of America from the perspective of the marginal subject is inspired, in part, by his social responsibility as an intellectual faithful to the "truth." For Inca Garcilaso, the contentious character of his writing is the result of his social condition as a marginal subject himself. Even still, the nexus between the *Comentarios reales* and *Los trabajos de Persiles y Sigismunda* resides in how Inca Garcilaso and Cervantes transformed writing into a space of free e xpression within the parameters of sixteenth- and seventeenth-century Hispanic societies. Both interpreted the American colonization process from the perspective of the colonial subject to whom they attributed an active role in the redefinition of social identity. In this sense, it is important to consider the early controversial stance undertaken by two icons in the actual discussion about what constitutes Latin American culture and, in particular, the question of identity.

Notes

1. The content of this essay is part of my forthcoming doctoral dissertation. My thanks to Professor Nicholas Spadaccini for his valuable insights and to Judy Colglazier and Gerardo Garza for their collaboration in the revision of earlier drafts of this article.
2. See the *Informe Final* from the *Comisión de la Verdad*.
3. I prefer to use the expression "intermediary identity," which combines the concept of "hybridity" with the notion of "diglossia" introduced by sociolinguists to explain the coexistence of two different languages within the same sociohistorical context. I want to emphasize the political dimension of the colonized subject's cultural production and, at the same time, the colonized subject's awareness of his capacity to alternate between two different cultures considered socially unequal: one imposed and prestigious, the other indigenous and inferior.
4. See Martin Lienhard, who argues that it is not appropriate to apply concepts such as *"mestizaje"* or "hybridity," created by the natural sciences, to the study of cultural practices.
5. I am referring to the laws about interethnic marriages that, in spite of having been approved by kings Fernando I, Carlos V, and Felipe III, were not observed by most of the authorities in the viceroyalties.
6. See Ann Twinam.
7. See Raymond Williams, *Marxism and Literature*.
8. The analysis of the drama *To Love One's Death* (1945) stresses the presence of Andean mythology as well as the leading role of women in defeating the monarchical power.

Works Cited

Barilli, Renato. *Rhetoric*. Minneapolis: University of Minnesota Press, 1989.

Cervantes, Miguel de. *The Trials of Persiles and Sigismunda, a Northern Story*. Trans. Celia Richmond Weller and Clark A. Colahan. Berkeley and Los Angeles: University of California Press, 1989.

_____. *Three Exemplary Novels*. Trans. Samuel Putnam. New York: The Viking Press, 1950.

Chang-Rodríguez, Raquel. *Hidden Messages: Representation and Resistance in Andean Colonial Drama*. London: Associated University Presses, 1999.

Comisión de la Verdad y Reconciliación. *Informe Final*. Lima: CVR, 2003.

Cornejo Polar, Antonio. "El discurso de la armonía imposible." *Revista de Crítica Literaria Latinoamericana* 38 (Segundo Semestre 1993): 73–80.

Covarrubias Horozco, Sebastián. *Tesoro de la lengua castellana o española, según la impresión de 1611, con las adiciones de Benito Remigio Noydus publicadas en la de 1674*. Ed. Martín de Riquer. Barcelona: Horta, 1943.

Crystal, David. *A Dictionary of Linguistics and Phonetics*. 5th edition. Oxford: Blackwell Publishing, 2003.

Elliott, John H. "La propaganda del poder en tiempos de Olivares." *Historia y Crítica de la Literatura española 3/1 Siglos de Oro: Barroco*. Barcelona: Editorial Crítica, 1992. 75-80.

García-Bedoya, Carlos. *Literatura peruana en el periodo de estabilización colonial (1580–1780)*. Lima: Universidad Nacional Mayor de San Marcos Fondo Editorial, 2000.

Garcilaso de la Vega, el Inca. *Royal Commentaries of the Incas and General History of Peru*. Part 1. Trans. Harold V. Livermore. Austin: University of Texas Press, 1984.

_____. *Comentarios reales de los Incas*. Ed. Ángel Rosenblat. Buenos Aires: Emecé, 1943.

Konetzke, Richard. "El mestizaje y su importancia en el desarrollo de la población hispanoamericana durante la época colonial (Conclusión)." *Revista de Indias* 24 (1946): 215–44.

Lienhard, Martin. "De mestizajes, heterogeneidades, hibridismos y otras quimeras." *Asedios a la heterogeneidad cultural. Libro de homenaje a Antonio Cornejo Polar*. Philadelphia: Asociación Internacional de Peruanistas, 1996. 57-80.

Maravall, José Antonio. *La cultura del barroco. Análisis de una estructura histórica*. Barcelona: Ariel, 1975.

_____. *La literatura picaresca desde la historia social (Siglos XVI y XVII)*. Madrid: Taurus, 1986.

Mazzotti, José Antonio. *Coros mestizos del Inca Garcilaso. Resonancias andinas*. Lima: Bolsa de Valores de Lima-Otorongo Producciones-Fondo de Cultura Económica, 1996.

Moraña, Mabel. "Introducción." *Relecturas del Barroco de Indias*. Hanover, N.H.: Ediciones del Norte, 1994. i-xiii.

Mörner, Magnus. *Estado, razas y cambio social en la Hispanoamérica colonial.* Mexico City: SepSetentas, 1974.

_____. *La corona española y los foráneos en los pueblos indios de América.* Estocolmo: Instituto de Estudios Ibero-Americanos, 1970.

Pagden, Anthony. *The Fall of Natural Man: The American Indian and the Origins of Comparative Ethnology.* Cambridge: Cambridge University Press, 1982.

Sacchetti, Maria Alberta. *Cervantes' Los Trabajos de Persiles y Sigismunda: A Study of Genre.* London: Tamesis, 2001.

Shepard, Sanford. *El Pinciano y las teorías literarias del Siglo de Oro.* Madrid: Gredos, 1962.

Twinam, Ann. *Public Lives, Private Secrets: Gender, Honor, Sexuality, and Illegitimacy in Colonial Spanish America.* Stanford: Stanford University Press, 1999.

Williams, Raymond. *Marxism and Literature.* Oxford: Oxford University Press, 1977

Zamora, Margarita. *Language, Authority, and Indigenous History in the* Comentarios reales de los incas. Cambridge: Cambridge University Press, 1988.

◆ **10**

Freedom and Containment in Colonial Theology: Sor Juana's *Carta atenagórica*[1]

Paola Marín

The tension between freedom and containment was inherent to the scholastic thought that dominated well-known debates in the humanities and sciences throughout the sixteenth and seventeenth centuries in both Spain and her colonies. Although Sor Juana was to state that theology was the "Queen of the Sciences," her work calls into question the then dominant conceptions of both knowledge and theology.

Sor Juana was a sharp social observer and had an extraordinary grasp of the predominant fields of seventeenth-century thought. Her reality as a poet, nun, and female theologian at a time when women were not allowed to discuss religious matters in public, was to weigh heavily on her writings, as was her identity as a Mexican Creole who straddled several cultures and sought out the relationship between several fields of knowledge. She moved easily between the cultures of the Old World and the New, and nothing was alien to her productive curiosity; Sor Juana's "reading" of the world is contextualized within the wider chain of knowledge, even if the immediate realities of her precarious existence were never far from her intellectual preoccupations. Her writing clearly underscores the tension between freedom and containment that were manifested in the cultural production of the Spanish-American Baroque.[2]

Sor Juana's *Carta atenagórica* (Letter Worthy of Athena) may be read as a critique of the colonial condition by an intellectual positioned in the periphery by virtue of her gender, religious status, ethnicity, and locus of enunciation. I will argue that she advances her critique by calling into question the foundations of both knowledge and theology. The author's position as a religious writer may be clarified through a discussion of the circumstances surrounding the publication of her letter.

The Bishop of Puebla published Sor Juana's *Carta atenagórica* with a prologue written by him under the pseudonym of Sor Filotea. In that prologue he urged Sor Juana to dedicate her talents to sacred matters. The topic of Sor Juana's letter was a refutation of a sermon on Christ's demonstrations of love by a famous theologian, the Portuguese Jesuit Father Antonio Vieira. The Bishop, astounded by the solid and carefully crafted arguments that Sor Juana had presented orally on a lively afternoon in 1690 at the convent's locutory, requested a written copy. By publishing Sor Juana's text without her knowledge or consent, his intention was to gain her talent and support for the Church's cause. Nonetheless, in her *Respuesta a sor Filotea de la Cruz (Answer to Sor Filotea of the Cross)*, Sor Juana emphasizes her impulse to write verses being a gift that God had bestowed upon her, a gift so strong that even in dreams she was not free of it. Therefore, she identifies herself primarily as a poet "porque una herejía contra el Arte no la castiga el Santo Oficio" (45) (for a heresy against Art is not punished by the Holy Office), and refuses to become a model of piety.

Taking into account that Vieira's sermon was published forty years before Sor Juana's commentary, Octavio Paz suggests that her letter had been published by the Bishop of Puebla in order to support his own point of view in a personal debate with another powerful prelate (Aguiar y Seijas). The real issue at stake was Mexico's archbishopric. A more recent and widely accepted hypothesis is that the real target of Sor Juana's critique was her confessor, Father Antonio Núñez de Miranda. He had also discussed the topic of Christ's greatest gift to humankind in his writings and his intellectual arrogance and excessive religious zeal proved painful for Sor Juana (see Marquet, Martínez and Trabulse, among others). The basis for this hypothesis is that in spite of her refutation of Vieira's ideas, she reasserts her admiration for the Portuguese prelate. Vieira expressed a deep and sincere respect for religious women writers, as is apparent in his panegyric addressed to María de Ataide (see Marquet).[3]

In spite of identifying herself mainly as a poet, Sor Juana's religious thought is not irrelevant. On the contrary, the *Carta atenagórica* is a significant example of how the author always moved along fragile borderlines as colonial woman, poet, and theologian. Besides, the *Carta* is Sor Juana's only extant theological commentary, which makes this document even more crucial in understanding Sor Juana's intellectual range. Consequently, I disagree with Octavio Paz when he states in his *Trampas de la Fe* (*Traps of Faith*) that this letter consists of nothing more than theological entelechy and that it is a scholastic construction with no connection to relevant philosophical inquiries. Perhaps as a result of this type of assessment, Sor Juana's arguments in the *Carta atenagórica* have barely been studied. While most scholarly works on this text deal with the circumstances and consequences of its publication, I would argue that it is important to read this text between the lines and consider the extent to which it sheds light on her religious thought vis-à-vis the colonial situation. For example, did she conceive Mexico as part of another history, with cultural values that differed from those of the Peninsula? Did she find any contradictions between such considerations and the cultural and religious horizon of the elite to which she belonged?

In this essay I will examine Sor Juana's positioning of herself as a woman theologian, and how a particular vision of religion is expressed in her theological disquisition, taking into account the arguments she presents to refute Vieira's sermon, in addition to three of her *loas sacramentales*, in which the author deals specifically with Amerindian religious practices.

One of the main tendencies in colonial Latin American literary studies is based upon the premise that the political unity of the Spanish Empire did not consequently imply uniformity in the field of cultural production. After the conquest, heterogeneous and culturally diverse voices began blossoming in the colonies, and their presence was to provoke a re-accommodation of Western frames of mind. This field of research is then defined by the need to recover and re-elaborate the history of Latin American literature by taking into account the perspective of colonial subjects, and their digression from Eurocentric discourse (see Jara and Spadaccini).

This scholarship concentrates mainly on two perspectives that complement one another. First, it focuses on a redefinition of what in traditional historiography has been called "modernity" and the ways in which this notion is related to colonialism (see Mignolo); and, second, it involves a reading of the literary productions of the colonial period as a means of shaping a Creole (or *criollo*) identity. This second perspective is well defined by Moraña, who states that these writings "interpelan al sujeto virreinal e impugnan el orden ideológico e institucional de la época" (32) (interrogate viceroyal subject constructions and question the ideological and institutional order of the time). It must be clarified that Spain itself was already a multicultural territory due to her own long history of migrations, conquests, and settlements coming from diverse regions. However, it was also the case that the imposition of religious uniformity and its denial of divergent viewpoints dominated most expressions of culture.

During the Counter Reformation, religion permeated all spheres of society and was inherently related to maintaining political and social control both in the Peninsula and the American colonies. Sor Juana's situation as a colonial woman writing on theology implied that she was simultaneously located on the political periphery of the Empire and on the periphery of gender models in religious discourse.

In considering the topic of women and theological thought, it is first necessary to trace its Western background. In Christian tradition from the Middle Ages to the Counter Reformation, the body had been conceived of as distinctly human. Upon being expelled from Paradise, human beings were now forced to bear the weight of their mortality, separating themselves from God who only appeared in the flesh when materialized in his son Jesus Christ. In studies about medieval feminine mysticism, it is clear this impacted the way in which religious men and women experienced the physicality of their bodies. Masculinity was identified with the rational and spiritual components of the human condition, while femininity was considered in terms of its carnal qualities (see Finke, Walker-Bynum). This meant that women were, by nature, more prone to identify with Christ's body and to experience direct union with God. Accordingly, most religious texts written by female authors had to base their authority on personal and even physical experiences of the Divinity. They were also seen as more prone to demonic influences due to their weaker biological condition, a conception based on Aristotle, and later, St. Thomas (see Maclean). Therefore, especially after the Council of Trent, they were forbidden from preaching and discussing theological matters. Women could not study Latin at a time in which translating the Bible into Spanish was not permitted, restricting their involvement in religious scholarship to an even greater degree.

As a result of these limitations, religious women's writings in the seventeenth century were primarily exemplary "lives" of sanctity. Colonial Spanish America was no exception. Several texts by nuns who had been forced to write under the supervision of their confessors were published, which showed the extent to which such writings were considered an ideological tool for enforcing orthodoxy (see Franco). Their works had to endure the harsh scrutiny of the Holy Office, as they were considered an essential part of the collective effort to counter heresy (i.e. Protestantism, Judaism, Illuminism, and in the New World, "pagan" native practices). While religious men were by no means free of danger, they enjoyed more freedom in accessing theological knowledge and writing on Divine matters.

Diverging from many other religious women in the Hispanic context, including figures such as Teresa de Jesús and Sor María de Ágreda, Sor Juana did not resort to her personal experience with the Divinity in order to write theological commentary. It is significant that the *Crisis of a Sermon*—which is the original title she gave to the *Carta atenagórica*—is a rhetorical armor completely removed from experiential matters. It is an astounding display of hermeneutic devices that Sor Juana justifies by stating "no lo digo yo, lo dicen las Santas Escrituras" (78) (it is not me, it is the Holy Scriptures that say so). She asserts that she is only an instrument in God's hands, and He is using her to punish the arrogance of learned men like Vieira who attempted to dispute and surpass the arguments of the Fathers of the Church. Consequently, in Sor Juana, the body as a basis for feminine theology has disappeared and is replaced by the intellect. Her mind is described as feminine only to the extent to which it makes the lesson in humility even more difficult for presumptuous men.

In this theological work, Sor Juana also chooses a solitary and opposed path vis-à-vis religious orthodoxy. She underscores freedom of will as a human need and even defines it as the quintessential gift of God to humankind. Such is the axis of my analysis of her position regarding the evangelization of Spanish America. As stated previously, in order to develop this idea I will draw from three *loas*, theatrical pieces which preceed three sacramental plays, in which she clearly presents the issue of free will along with native Amerindian religious practices. While Sor Juana makes no mention of her Mexican origins or the fact that she is writing on the margins of the Empire, her central argument in the *Carta atenagórica* is very close to the position she expresses in her *loas*. Rather than Christianization by force, she suggests establishing a dialogue between Catholicism and the religious views of the indigenous people.[4] She could not approach this topic in a sacramental play because this would imply a direct attack on the heart of the Empire's religiosity: the Eucharist. Therefore, she uses the festive and marginal nature of the *loa*, which was a minor genre as compared to the *Auto sacramental* (see Marín).

The topic of the greatest finesse (or gift) of Christ to humankind was at the core of the *Loa* to *El Divino Narciso* (*Divine Narcissus*). It also stood at the center of her *loa* entitled *Loa al Mártir del Sacramento, San Hermenegildo*, which precedes the sacramental play by the same title. In the *Loa al Divino Narciso*, Sor Juana portrays the God of Seeds as an Aztec deity and compares the rituals performed in his honor with those of Catholicism. I believe there is a specific historical reason for her doing so, which shows her awareness of failures in the spiritual conquest of the New World.

In spite of the continuous repression exerted by the Mexican branch of the Inquisition as a means of controlling the proliferation of heretical practices in New Spain (Colonial Mexico), propitiatory rituals related to agriculture were tenaciously kept alive. The enormous distance between rural regions and cities, which were the sites of Spanish colonial power, allowed for such rituals to be preserved with great fidelity. There were even Amerindian messiahs who tried to discredit the Spanish friars by accusing them of being incapable of bringing rain during drought season. In fact, this is the reason why the Virgen de los Remedios (Virgin of Remedies) ultimately substituted Tláloc (the God of Rain) in the Christian pantheon (see Lafaye).

To the extent that these practices show the impossibility of a thorough evangelization, Sor Juana points to the core of the religious colonial situation. It is true that she resorts to the sort of universalizing syncretism between Aztec religion and Catholicism keen to the Jesuits.[5] Nevertheless, she clearly establishes a difference between true Catholicism and institutional religion, namely the Inquisition. In the *loa* that precedes another of her sacramental plays (*El cetro de José*), an allegorical character representing Idolatry (dressed as an Indian woman) argues with another such character representing Faith. The first woman expresses discontent at the other's use of hymns and songs as a means of distraction to avoid answering her questions. At the end of the *loa* Idolatry recognizes that, upon seeing the *Auto*, she will be convinced of Faith's view of religion. Nonetheless, simply exposing the need for dialogue almost two centuries after the conquest of Mexico points toward the issue of an incomplete identity. It points to the fact that Spanish America possesses a different rationale, one that is still in progress and still in tension. Sor Juana suggests that evangelizing mechanisms will never be effective if they are nothing more than *dulces consonancias* (sweet rhymes) and do not attempt to establish a dialogue with native America. This approach greatly diverges from Spanish canonical religious drama (see Ynduráin on Calderón de la Barca, Sor Juana's most admired playwright).

The *Carta atenagórica* and the *loas* mentioned above were written close in time (the three *loas* were written between 1680 and 1688, and the letter in 1690). While her letter does not mention explicitly anything related to the colonial situation, the text itself is a critique of the same insofar as it is questioned not through allegorical characters, but by challenging the exegetical parameters for the interpretation of the Scriptures. In this manner, she represents the need to reexamine the current mechanisms used to establish the legitimacy of knowledge.

Sor Juana's document begins by exposing the causes of her *crisis* (critique). She goes on to describe the theses concerning Christ's greatest gift to humankind according to three Fathers of the Church, followed by Vieira's refutation of each. In general terms, St. Thomas stated that Christ's greatest gift was remaining in the Eucharist. Saint John Chrysostom, on the other hand, argued that it was His washing of the Apostles' feet, while St. Augustine believed it involved His dying on the Cross. Sor Juana continues with her objections by responding to each one of Vieira's arguments in the same order. Next, she focuses on Vieira's own thesis and his statement "que no habría quien le diese otra fineza igual, con que cree el orador que puede aventajar su ingenio a los de los tres Santos Padres y no cree que puede haber quien le iguale" (812) (that nobody could give it similar finesse, with which the orator thinks his ingenuity surpasses those of the three Saint Fathers and does not believe anybody can equate him). She concludes with her own opinion regarding the supreme gift of the Savior to humankind.

In spite of her admiration for Vieira, Sor Juana asserts that God gave freedom to individuals, who may decide where the truth lies. She defines the human intellect as "potencia libre y que asiente o disiente necesario a lo que juzga ser o no ser verdad" (812) (a free power that agrees or disagrees according to what it deems true or untrue). This is why—in comparison with Vieira, who dared to question three patristic figures—her critique lacks relevance: "Pues si sintió vigor en su pluma para adelantar en uno de sus sermones (que será solo el asunto de este papel) tres plumas, sobre doctas, canonizadas, ¿qué mucho que haya quien intente adelantar la suya, no ya canonizada, aunque tan docta?" (812) (Because, if he felt his quill so vigorous as to overcome in one of his sermons—which will be the only issue of this paper—three quills canonized on top of learned, what matters if somebody tries to overcome his, not canonized yet, though equally learned?). She explains that her commentary is a self-defense mechanism based upon three figures of Christian philosophical tradition. Shielded by the deep garments of scholastic propositions, her final goal is to present her own thought: "mi asunto es defender las razones de los tres Santos Padres. Mal dije. Mi asunto es defenderme con las razones de los tres Santos Padres. (Ahora creo que acerté)" (813) (because my affair is to defend the reasons of the three Saint Fathers. Badly said. My affair is to defend myself with the reasons of the three Saint Fathers. [Now I think I got it right]). Simultaneously, Sor Juana develops a critique of the foundations of both knowledge and theology. In my opinion, the main concern of Sor Juana involves interpretation. Vieira (and, indirectly, Núñez de Miranda) is unable to capture the subtleties of meaning, not only in the three Fathers of the Church, but also in the Bible itself.

The ingenuity of the writer is manifested in the manner in which she ratifies each one of the propositions of St. Thomas, Chrysostom, and Augustine. Sor Juana does so by using a rigorous syllogistic method and by adding numerous biblical references. In fact, her impressive display of knowledge prefigured the strategy that she used later on in her *Respuesta a sor Filotea*. Regardless of the solidity of her arguments, her attempt to demonstrate the impossibility to neither monopolize nor simplify meaning in the field of theological interpretation proves to be of ultimate concern.

In reference to Vieira's refutation of Chrysostom's position, Sor Juana asserts: "Dice el autor: que no fue la mayor fineza lavar los pies, sino la causa que le movió a lavarlos" (The author says that the greatest finesse was not [for Christ] to wash the [Apostles'] feet but the cause that moved Him to do so). She explains that cause and effect are inseparable; neither can be more relevant than the other. Sor Juana supports her critique with biblical examples and concludes: "luego es el efecto el que prueba la causa" (then is the effect what proves the cause). She questions the fact that Vieira tried to separate cause from effect, but most importantly, that he is not able to capture the complexity in the Saint's proposition: "el Crisóstomo quiere que infiramos de él [el efecto] lo grande de las causas, sin expresarlas, porque no pudo hallar más viva expresión que referir tan humilde ministerio en tanta soberanía" (814) (Chrysostom wants us to infer from it [the effect] the magnitude of the causes, without expressing them, because he could not find a more charged expression than to tell of such a humble ministry in so much sovereignty). Separating cause from effect implies separating acts from consequences, creating a world of abstract law disconnected from our experience—a dogmatic world very similar to the one promulgated by the Counter Reformation.

From the Middle Ages until the sixteenth century, both ethics and religion were based upon the same premise: a single God. After the Reformation, this unity no longer existed, and therefore, the tradition guaranteeing revealed truth also collapsed. The split between churches is apparent, and this situation is accentuated by the discovery of the New World (see De Certeau). Religious fragmentation had already manifested itself in Europe through the blossoming of heretical sects and magical practices. Further intensified as a result of encounters with regions of the New World that could not be located according to current epistemological parameters, fragmentation brought about many changes characterizing modernity: "En ese período en el que se derrumba un

viejo sistema y se construye otro, De Certeau advierte la emergencia de nume-
rosas expresiones simbólicas de marginamiento como el ateísmo o la mística"
(Arriarán and Beauchot 129) (In this period in which an old system crumbles
and a new one is born, De Certeau notices the emergence of numerous marginal
symbolic expressions like atheism or mysticism). It is possible to add to De
Certeau's list another symbolic expression: a Creole consciousness present in
writings like those of Sor Juana. I should clarify, however, that I am neither
using the term Creole in the sense of a prefiguration of independence (which
would be an anachronism), nor am I referring to the sense of belonging to a
group possessing common political interests.

De Certeau's ideas allow us to better understand the greater implications
of the *Carta atenagórica*, as this text is mainly a defense of the need to dissent.
At the end of her letter, before stating her own point of view, the author justifies her audacity by stating that God is using her in order to give learned men a
lesson in humility:

> Creo cierto que si algo llevare de acierto este papel, no es obra de mi entendi-
> miento, sino sólo que Dios quiere castigar con tan flaco instrumento la, al parecer,
> elación de aquella proposición: que no habría quien le diese otra fineza igual [. . .]
> Que cuando yo no haya conseguido más que el atreverme a hacerlo, fuera bastante
> mortificación para un varón tan de todas maneras insigne; que no es ligero castigo a
> quien creyó que no habría hombre que se atreviese a responderle, ver que se atreve
> una mujer ignorante, en quien es tan ajeno este género de estudio, y tan distante de
> su sexo; pero también lo era de Judit el manejo de las armas y de Débora la judi-
> catura. Y si con todo, pareciere en esto poco cuerda, con romper V.md. este papel
> quedará multado el error de haberlo escrito. (816)

> (I think that if this paper has something right, it is not the work of my ingenuity,
> but that God wants to punish with this puny instrument the apparent elation of that
> proposition: that nobody could give it similar finesse [...] even if I achieve not more
> than daring to do it, it would be mortification enough for a man notable in so many
> ways; because it is not light punishment to him who believed that no man would
> dare to answer him, to see dare an ignorant woman, for whom this type of study is
> so alien and apart from her sex; however, it also was alien to Judith handling the
> arms and to Deborah being a judge. And if, after all, I appear here hardly sane, it is
> enough that Your Mercy tear this paper apart.)

Therefore, an important part of her final argument is a diatribe against envy,
also a central component of the *Respuesta a sor Filotea*. This aspect works as
a self-defense mechanism regarding her exceptional intelligence: "Envidiamos

en nuestros prójimos los bienes de fortuna, los dotes naturales. ¡Oh, qué errado va el objeto de la envidia, pues sólo debía serlo de la lástima el gran cargo que tiene, de que ha de dar cuenta estrecha!" (816) (We envy in our neighbors the goods of fortune, the natural gifts. O, how wrong the object of envy is, it should be only the object of pity because of the heavy load it carries, for which he must give detailed account!). In this manner, she is able to tacitly establish a parallel between her own audacity and what God does in order to offer His greatest gift to humankind. According to Sor Juana, it is harder for God not to give humans benefits than to do so. Consequently, "mayor fineza es el suspenderlos que el ejecutarlos, pues deja Dios de ser liberal—que es propia condición suya—porque nosotros no seamos ingratos—que es propio retorno nuestro—y quiere más parecer escaso, porque los hombres no sean peores" (817) (stopping them is a greater finesse than exercising them, because God stops being liberal—which is a noble condition of His, so we do not become ungrateful—which is our proper tendency; and He prefers to appear sparse, so men do not get worse).

The Mexican exegete clearly identifies her text with God's will and, therefore, her own intellectual abilities as well. This aspect ultimately allows the Bishop-Sor Filotea to criticize her for writing profane literature rather than dedicate her life to pondering sacred matters. As expressed in the previous quotation, the parallel between Sor Juana and Divine Will emphasizes the unlimited nature of God's goodness regarding what he refrains from doing for individuals. By limiting good so that they are not spoiled, much room is left for human freedom. While her emphasis on the need to dissent has been pointed out by several critics and identified as a consequence of her fragile state as a woman writing on theology, I believe it also possesses a greater dimension, namely questioning the religious situation in the Spanish American colonies. Sor Juana is aware of what may be called an epistemological crisis. The dogma is no longer the source of answers, as it cannot provide the absolute certainty of the Divine presence. In fact, this is the topic of the aforementioned *loas*.

The arguments expressed through the voices of two allegorical characters (America in *Loa al divino Narciso* and Idolatry in *Loa al Cetro de José*) concerning the survival of pre-Hispanic religious practices focus on the imposition of Catholicism as a religion that admits no reply, and also on its lack of correspondence between discourse and praxis. The vast rhetorical display of the *Carta atenagórica* points toward this problematic issue. In a sort of theological puzzle, Sor Juana arranges various arguments in order to conclude that freedom of will is the greatest gift of God to humankind.

The distance between theology and real life conditions was even more pronounced in the Colonies than in the Peninsula. This degree of separation is seen
in her closing commentary, as she states that it is essential "que el ponderar sus
beneficios no se quede en discursos especulativos, sino que pase a servicios
prácticos" (817) (that extolling His benefits does not limit itself to speculative
speeches but goes into practical services). This could be easily compared to
the lines of the oldest character (Sor Juana's alter-ego) in her *Loa al Mártir
del Sacramento*. In this play there are three students discussing the greatest of
Christ's finesses. The wisest and oldest of the three sustains the thesis that remaining in the Eucharist is the maximum gift of the Savior. This character uses
a sort of magical artifice to show the other two the moment at which Columbus
arrived into the so-called New World. At this point in the *loa*, the Chorus addresses Spain: "¡Más Mundos hay, más Imperios, / que tus armas avasallen"
(469) (There are other Worlds, more Empires for your weapons to subdue!).
The play points to the fact that the notion of "non-plus ultra" regarding world
boundaries—as symbolized by Hercules—was proven wrong by Columbus'
action (see Sabat de Rivers). When asked by the two other characters why he
resorted to Columbus in demonstrating his thesis, the Chorus makes reference
to Christ in their reply: "Échese su Amor al agua y verá que hay más que hacer"
(469) (Let His love throw himself into the sea and He will realize there is more
to be done). For Sor Juana, the salvation of the Spanish colonies by virtue of
Christianity is far from over. At first, this may seem contradictory with her
final argument in the *Carta atenagórica,* because she states that God's greatest
finesse is precisely to refrain from benefiting human beings. She sustains that
this is an ontological characteristic of God as God, however, and as such, it is
different from Christ's gift when He sacrificed His life for humanity:

> Como hablamos de finezas, dije yo que la mayor fineza de Dios, en mi sentir, eran
> los beneficios negativos; esto es, los beneficios que nos deja de hacer porque sabe
> lo mal que los hemos de corresponder. Ahora, este modo de opinar tiene mucha dis-
> paridad con el del autor, porque él habla de finezas de Cristo, y hechas en el fin de
> su vida, y esta fineza que yo digo es fineza que hace Dios en cuanto Dios, y fineza
> continuada siempre; y así no fuera razón oponer ésta a las que el autor dice, antes
> bien fuera una muy viciosa argumentación y muy censurable. (816)

> (In speaking of finesse, I said that God's greatest finesses, in my opinion, are the
> negative benefits; this means the benefits He fails to give us because He knows how
> badly we are going to correspond to them. Now, this opinion carries large disparity
> with that of the author, because he speaks of Christ's finesses, those made toward

the end of His life, and this finesse I say is a finesse God makes as God, an always continuing finesse: and thus it would not be reasonable to oppose this to those the author says.)

I want to highlight the idea of God's unfinished work as it pertains to what the author terms His "negative benefits." This idea implies a constant search regarding the individual's quest for truth and presents an interesting parallel with the end of *Primero sueño* (First Dream), her most precious piece of work according to the *Answer to Sor Filotea*. In this philosophical poem, Sor Juana portrays the human quest for knowledge as a cosmic journey. The soul tries to encompass the immensity of the universe and decipher its conundrums. At the end, it realizes the impossibility of such a venture, which coincides with a hermetic conception of scientific knowledge (see Trabulse, *El círculo roto*). In this respect, another connection exists with the religious situation of New Spain. In spite of the repression, the co-existence of Spaniards and Creoles with indigenous peoples necessarily implied the resistance of the latter to a complete catechization. As a consequence, another side emerged within the spiritual conquest of the New World. Several Spaniards and Creoles who witnessed the abuses committed in God's name against Amerindian populations were to take distance from the Church and, in some cases, even slide into atheism (see Lafaye). I do not wish to suggest such was Sor Juana's situation, but taking into account her sharp and inquisitive intellect, it is quite possible that she had doubts about the viability of Christianizing the New World, or at least, about the totalitarian model that dominated the colonization process.

In the *loas*, by means of allegorical characters, Sor Juana describes the Amerindian world vision as distinguished by "una Potestad Antigua" (an ancient power or law) in *Loa al Divino Narciso*. She portrays its conception of knowledge as one based on concrete and palpable practices and, therefore, divergent from the European proliferation of Christian scholastic discourse. This is exemplified in a previously mentioned excerpt, when Idolatry tells Faith "y en vez de responder, cantas himnos que no entiendo yo" (*Loa al Cetro de José*) (instead of answering, you reply with hymns I do not understand). In a period in which the spectacular nature of mass, sermons, the worshipping of saints, autos-da-fé, and public prayers were all ideological tools to enforce indoctrination and social control, this example proves to be a significant response to the Counter Reformation (see Barnes-Karol). It relates to the *Carta atenagórica* in that she does not discuss the topic of Christ's greatest finesse in terms of origins or final ends. Instead, Sor Juana focuses on matters concerning cause and effect. Consequently, she takes distance from scatological goals in order to finally underscore the importance of the individual's present-day actions. González Echevarría mentions as a defining characteristic of Latin American Baroque "the uneasy relationship between representation and that which is being represented or expressed [so that] belief or theological cogency is no longer at the center, leaving a gap that is filled with the proliferation of figures" (205). According to him, as the seventeenth century progresses, the co-existence of pagan and Christian mythologies and deities "may very well lead to Enlightenment instead of impeding it" (205). While the *Carta atenagórica* does not make reference to the survival of pagan gods, I do find an element that symbolizes the uneasy relationship between representation and that which is being represented: silence. For Sor Juana, the only component of God's actions to which humans have access are external signs (or "finesses"):

> ¿Es fineza, acaso, tener amor? No, por cierto, sino las demostraciones del amor: ésas se llaman finezas. Aquellos signos exteriores demostrativos, y acciones que ejercita el amante, siendo su causa motiva el amor, eso se llama fineza. Luego si el Santo está hablando de finezas y actos externos, con grandísima propiedad trae el Lavatorio, y no la causa: pues la causa es el amor, y el Santo no está hablando del amor, sino de la fineza, que es el signo exterior. Luego no hay para qué ni por qué argüirle, pues lleva el Santo supuesto lo que después le sacan como Nuevo. (813)

> (Is it finesse, perhaps, to harbor love? No, indeed, but the demonstrations of love: those are called finesses. Those external demonstrative signs and actions the lover exercises, love being the motive cause, that is called finesse. Then, if the Saint is talking about finesse and external acts, very properly he brings about the Lavation, and not the cause: because the cause is love, and the Saint is not talking about love but about finesse, that is the external sign. Then, there is no reason to argue for it, because the Saint has implicit what they put in the open as new.)

In her *loas*, she underscores the centrality of concrete practices for the indigenous world vision, and in her commentary about Christ's greatest finesse, she points toward the importance of listening to the text. For Sor Juana, reading is an exercise consisting of deciphering "finesses." A few years earlier, in her sacramental play entitled *El Divino Narciso*, she presents the world as a divine book to be deciphered by men. In this *Auto*, Sor Juana utilizes Narcissus to portray Christ, who in the play dies after becoming one with Human Nature. In this manner, His gift to humankind becomes a cosmic book in which each written line returns to Him, Creator of the World.

This aspect coincides with *Carta atenagórica* when the author emphasizes the higher value of that which goes unmentioned and remains hidden behind words. For her, such concealed meaning must be the focus of exegetics. For instance, with respect to Christ's greatest finesse, she writes that pain suffered alone is even more valuable because it expresses a greater love. On the contrary, Vieira asserts that it was a greater finesse for Christ to be absent rather than dead, pointing to the fact that Mary Magdalene cried at His tomb but not at His crucifixion. Sor Juana replies that based on Mary Magdalene's actions, "no se infiere que sea mayor el dolor de la ausencia que el de la muerte: antes lo contrario" (816) (it is not possible to conclude that absence implies the highest pain over death, on the contrary). She supports this assertion by explaining that while inferior pain causes a flood of tears, supreme pain restricts such crying. Next, she makes reference to Christ, who cried for Lazarus' temporary decease but did not for Judas' eternal death (condemnation). Consequently, the author attempts to prove she is a better reader than Vieira. The authority of her interpretation comes from the text itself as opposed to an "obedient" knowledge.

For Sor Juana, human freedom is an individual gift of God, a point that also proves central to her *Respuesta a sor Filotea*. Such freedom should be transferred into actions,

y que el ponderar sus beneficios no se quede en discursos especulativos, sino que pase a servicios prácticos, para que sus beneficios negativos se pasen a positivos hallando en nosotros digna disposición que rompa la presa a los estancados raudales de la liberalidad divina, que detiene y represa nuestra ingratitud. (817)

(so that extolling His benefits does not limit itself to speculative speeches but goes into practical services, in order for His negative benefits to convert to positive, finding in us a worthy disposition that breaks down the dam for the stalled torrents of the divine liberality.)

In other words, truthful love of God can only begin when human beings are free to enter in this relationship. This notion coincides with her view of evangelization as expressed in the *loas* and also implies that salvation only becomes possible when faith goes hand-in-hand with good actions. Her simultaneous emphasis on the freedom of the human mind and on the pragmatic significance of Christian acts leads to a questioning of purposeless charity.[6] Therefore, she indirectly challenges those primarily concerned with theological entelechy rather than concrete realities. This may be read as a critique of the colonial religious situation regarding the divorce between representation and that which was being represented.

As a playwright, Sor Juana resorted to the plasticity and festive nature of theater in order to exemplify the conflictive relationship between evangelization and Amerindian beliefs. In the *Carta atenagórica*, she positioned herself as a theologian and exegete. As such, she underscored the need for a dialogue that proved unrealized between Catholic doctrine as proclaimed from the pulpit, and the religious reality of the New World.

Notes

1. All quotations from the *Carta atenagórica* (*Letter Worthy of Athena*) were translated by Humberto Marín. I also wish to thank my assistant Megan Schliep for her valuable editorial suggestions.

2. See Jara and Spadaccini for a detailed discussion of this issue in colonial writing (particularly in Sor Juana's *Loa al Divino Narciso*), and Spadaccini and Martín-Estudillo for a comprehensive treatment of this tension in the Hispanic Baroque.

3   Among these studies I must mention the one by Antonio Marquet. His hypothesis is based upon Sor Juana's recently found *Letter to Seraphine of Christ* (1690), published for the first time by the Mexican scholar Elías Trabulse and likely written before her *Answer to Sor Filotea* (1691). According to Marquet ("De Sor Juana a Serafina"), in this epistle Sor Juana praises Vieira and indirectly attacks Núñez de Miranda by being sarcastic about his poverty and fake intellectual humility. She also deals with his constant harassment and envy toward her intelligence.

4. It is important to clarify that Sor Juana was not free of ideological incoherence. For instance, in her *Auto* about a Catholic Visigoth saint (San Hermenegildo), she disqualifies the *comunero* revolt in Spain by establishing a parallel between Arrian heresy and the political demands of this revolt. Clearly, this may seem contradictory with the liberating view expressed in her *loas*.

5. Most of the priests who were close to her—including her confessor Father Núñez de Miranda—belonged to the Jesuit order.

6. Charity and self-punishment were taken to absurd extremes by prelates like the Bishop of Puebla and Sor Juana's confessor, Antonio Núñez de Miranda (see Benítez).

Works Cited

Arenal Electa, and Amanda Powell, eds. *The Answer/La respuesta*. New York: The Feminist Press at The City University of New York, 1994.

Arriarán, Samuel, and Mauricio Beauchot, eds. *Filosofía, neobarroco y multiculturalismo.* Mexico City: Editorial Itaca, 1999.

Barnes-Karol, Gwendolyn. "Religious Oratory in a Culture of Control." *Culture and Control in Counter-Reformation Spain.* Ed. Anne Cruz and Mary Elizabeth Perry. Hispanic Issues 7. Minneapolis: University of Minnesota Press, 1992.

Benítez, Fernando. *Los demonios en el convento: sexo y religión en la Nueva España.* Mexico City: Ediciones Era, 1985.

Brescia, Pablo A. J., and K. Josu Bijuesca, eds. *Sor Juana y Vieira, trescientos años después.* Santa Bárbara: Center for Portuguese Studies, Department of Spanish and Portuguese, University of California, 1998.

Bynum, Carolyn Walker. *Fragmentation and Redemption.* New York: Zone Books, 1991.

Calderón de la Barca, Pedro. *El gran teatro del mundo.* Ed. D. Yndurain. Madrid: Alhambra, 1981.

Cruz, Sor Juana Inés de la. *Obras completas.* Ed. Alfonso Méndez Plancarte. Mexico City: Fondo de Cultura Económica, 1956.

De Certeau, Michel. *La fable mystique.* Paris: Gallimard, 1982.

Finke, Laurie. "Mystical Bodies and the Dialogics of Vision." *Maps of Flesh and Light.* Ed. Ulrike Wiethaus. Syracuse: Syracuse University Press, 1993.

Franco, Jean. *Las conspiradoras.* Mexico City: Fondo de Cultura Económica, 1993.

González-Echevarría, Roberto. "Colonial Lyric." *The Cambridge History of Latin American Literature I: Discovery to Modernism.* Ed. Roberto González-Echevarría. Cambridge: Cambridge University Press, 1996.

Jara, René, and Nicholas Spadaccini. "Introduction." *1492–1992: Re/Discovering Colonial Writing.* Ed. René Jara and Nicholas Spadaccini. Hispanic Issues 4. Minneapolis: University of Minnesota Press, 1989.

Lafaye, Jacques. *Quetzalcoatl and Guadalupe.* Chicago: University of Chicago Press, 1976.

Maclean, Ian. *The Renaissance Notion of Woman.* Cambridge: Cambridge University Press, 1980.

Marín, Paola. "El ser y el parecer criollo en tres loas de Sor Juana." *Romance Languages Annual,* 1999.

Marquet, Antonio. "Para atravesar el espejo: de Sor Juana a Serafina de Cristo." *Sor Juana y Vieira, trescientos años después.* Ed. Pablo Brescia and Josu Bijuesca. Santa Bárbara: Center for Portuguese Studies, Department of Spanish and Portuguese, University of California, 1998. 113–26.

Martínez López, Enrique. "Sor Juana, Vieira y Justo Lipsio en la Carta a Sor Filotea de la Cruz." *Bulletin of Hispanic Studies* 64.4 (1987): 111–17.

Mignolo, Walter. *The Darker Side of the Renaissance.* Ann Arbor: University of Michigan Press, 1995.

Moraña, Mabel. "Apologías y defensas: discursos de la marginalidad en el barroco hispanoamericano." *Relecturas del Barroco de Indias.* Ed. Mabel Moraña. Hanover, NH: Ediciones del Norte, 1994. 31–57.

Paz, Octavio. *Sor Juana Inés de la Cruz o la trampas de la fe*. Barcelona: Seix Barral, 1982.

Sabat de Rivers, Georgina. "Apología de América en tres loas de Sor Juana." *Revista de Estudios Hispánicos* 19 (1992): 267–91.

Selke, Angela. "El iluminismo de los conversos y la inquisición." *La inquisición española.* Ed. Joaquín Pérez. Madrid: Siglo Veintiuno, 1980. 617–36.

Spadaccini, Nicholas, and Luis Martín-Estudillo. *Libertad y límites. El Barroco hispánico.* Madrid: Ediciones del Orto, 2004.

Trabulse, Elías. *El círculo roto: Estudios históricos sobre la ciencia en México.* Mexico City: Fondo de Cultura Económica, 1982.

_____. "El silencio final de Sor Juana." *Sor Juana y Vieira, trescientos años después.* Ed. Pablo Brescia and Josu Bijuesca. Santa Bárbara: Center for Portuguese Studies, Department of Spanish and Portuguese, University of California, 1998. 143–56.

◆ **11**

Sleeping with Corpses, Eating Hearts, and Walking Skulls: *Criollo's* Subjectivity in Antonio de la Calancha and Bartolomé Arzans de Orsúa y Vela[1]

Leonardo García-Pabón

There is a peculiar building in Evora, Portugal: a chapel built with human bones. In the seventeenth century, the cemeteries of the area had run out of space and were overflowing with human remains. Three Franciscan monks thought that to recover burial space and, at the same time, preserve these osseous remains they could build a chapel with the bones. This architecture of skeletons and skulls—a relocated cemetery, a virtual space for the afterlife—was conceived as a place where we could enter and feel, for a few but intense moments, how ineluctably we are headed to become bones and skulls, similar to those in the walls and ceiling of the chapel. So this chapel was built as a place of prayer and meditation on our ephemeral life. "Nós ossos que aqui estamos pelos vossos esperamos" (We, the bones in here, for your bones, are waiting) reads the legend at the door of the chapel. This may well be one of the most extreme examples of the Catholic Baroque's particular obsession with death as the final reality of human life.

Approximately a century later, in the Andean area, a narrative was being developed: the legend of the Manchay Puytu (the pot of fear). The legend tells the story of an Indian or a *mestizo* priest who has a love relationship with a Creole or Indian woman—the protagonists' ethnic belonging changes according to the version of the legend. When she unexpectedly dies, he refuses to accept her death. Blinded by pain and grief, he digs up her body, carries the corpse to his bedroom, and tries to bring her back from the kingdom of death. When he discovers that this is impossible, he removes one of her leg bones to make a *quena* (an Indian flute), and then composes a most sad and disturbing melody on the *quena* that he plays inside a *cántaro* (a pot).[2] The corpse of the loved one must be metonymically treated to become a residue, a relic—not of saintliness, but of the unsolvable conflict between desire and death, and its cultural inscription/sublimation in art. In this macabre tale, love, death, Catholicism, and art are mixed, creating another extreme moment of the Baroque—the Baroque created in Latin America, with its particular take on death.

These two examples of the views and understandings of death in the seventeenth and eighteenth centuries are representative moments of the baroque that spread from Spain and Portugal to the New World. Both examples show a similar mechanism: they put on stage that which is supposed to be buried. Bones and corpses surface to remind us of those attractions—such as death or love—that we cannot escape. In different contexts and with different goals, the unburied is placed in front of our eyes to let us see what we are really made of—dust, shadows, nothing—and confront it with some of the most powerful life forces: our loves and desires.

I mention these examples because they are the borders that demarcate a symbolic field in which the *Criollos* of the New World, caught between the culture of the Old World and the realities of the New, developed a philosophy about death. On the one hand, following one of the dominant types of Christianity developed in Europe, which emphasized the ephemeral, miserable, and vane aspects of life (Caro Baroja 135), the *Criollos* perceived death as the ultimate reality of life. This perception of death was strongly emphasized by artists and thinkers in the European seventeenth century as well as in the seventeenth and eighteenth centuries in the Spanish colonies. It became one of the most representative aspects of the Baroque in both Spain and the New World. As Sor Juana put it in her best-known sonnet, life and beauty were seen as "un engaño colorido" (a colored treachery) that in reality, "bien mirado" (rightly seen) was "cadáver, polvo, sombra, nada" (corpse, dust, gloom, nothingness).[3]

On the other hand, the eighteenth century witnessed a powerful resurgence of Indian population and a cultural renaissance, which lead to the rebellions of Tupac Amaru and Tupac Katari. This Indian renaissance was accompanied by an inquiry into both the historical reasons for the fall of the Incan empire and the emotional consequences of the conquest.[4] For example, the play *Tragedia del fin de Atahuallpa* shows the emotional and political conflicts that arose upon the rethinking of Atahuallpa's death. This play was conceived in the context of the *Inkarri* myth, which tells of the coming together of the Inca's dismembered body that had been buried in different places of the viceroyalty.[5] What the Manchay Puytu shows is how the indigenous conceptions of death changed in order to adjust to the imposed and dominant Catholic religion. In general, the Indian's question may have been: which system of beliefs—the Spanish or the indigenous—helps me most to understand and overcome the immense pain that comes with the loss of the beloved (be it the Inca Atahuallpa or a treasured consort)? The answer seems to be: neither. Instead, the response came in the form of an art that, being Spanish at the core but indigenous in many essential aspects, could only speak through a baroque style.

Caught between these different articulations of death, religion, and art, while consciously or unconsciously aware of their own ideological and cultural situation, the *Criollos* developed narratives that attempted to give their own response to the intersection of life and death. They seem to have found particularly useful the baroque attitude that does not accept opposing terms in their exclusivity, but rather displaces their opposition to another level, in which the conflict is not eliminated but somehow transcended (Echeverría 176). To explain the *Criollos*' perspective on death, I have chosen two tales written by *Criollos* that are illustrative of their attitude toward death and its relationship to their own subjectivity.

Corpse and Desire: De-Territorializing the Subject in Antonio de la Calancha's *Corónica*

The first story comes from the *Corónica moralizada*, published in 1638, by Friar Antonio de la Calancha (1584–1654), a *Criollo* born in Charcas (what is today the city of Sucre in Bolivia). The *Corónica moralizada* has served mainly as a document to study the religious life in the Viceroyalty of Peru, and its importance in understanding the *Criollo* mentality has not yet been fully appreciated.[6] In fact, Calancha outlines an illuminating representation of the *Criollo* as a subject standing in the intersection of cultures and ideological tensions by telling exemplary lives of Augustinian priests, innumerable miracles by the Virgin Mary, angels and demons populating the Andean landscape, Indians switching from one set of religious beliefs to another, and long digressions about good and evil that are full of erudite references to the Greco-Roman tradition as well as to the Bible. Calancha constructs his narrator and his characters as beings living in a hallucinatory reality, in which the fight between good and evil takes place all around them. The villages, towns, and cities of the New World, as well the souls of Spaniards and *Criollos*, are the battlefields of this war, and the trophies are usually the Indians' souls.

Perhaps no other exemplary story in the *Corónica moralizada* is more illustrative of how the text shows the *Criollo*'s subjectivity than the life of Friar Francisco Martínez de Biedma. This Friar, born in Granada, came to the New World with the Augustinian order. The vigor of his sermons made him, from the beginning of his stay in Lima, a most respected priest; however, after a while, he became a scandalous sinner. But God's grace opened his eyes, and upon realizing the wrongfulness of his sinful life, he again became a very pious priest. His continuous practices of mortifications as a sign of his repentance gave him the reputation for being a holy man, but the Devil still found ways to tempt him, especially with carnal desires. To stop these temptations, Biedma thought that the best solution was to dig up a corpse, bring it to his bed, and sleep with it, as a reminder of how beauty hides the horrors of death. After this peak moment on his path to exemplary virtuosity, he realized that he was not accomplishing his mission in the New World, and felt a pressing need to start converting Indians. Biedma left the city, and went to convert Indians. While living in Indian communities, he had to confront innumerable demons that appeared in fantastical forms. After a few years, he returned to Lima, and decided to continue his evangelical mission in the Philippines, where he died.

Biedma's story is that of a Friar who comes to America to fight the devil but has to face, first, his own demons, which are unleashed by his immersion in a new social context. He needs to restructure his personality in the context of the new social spaces that the New World offers to those coming from Spain. He has to adjust to this new social and cultural context that ignites in him an irreversible process of *criollización*, his transformation into a *Criollo*. The beginning of this change happens in the context of his social reception: his fame as a preacher. It is as if his success releases him from the vows and beliefs he brought from the Old World, allowing him to be "himself." It would seem that there was no punishment for this behavior in the colonial context. The other members of the order can only advise him to return to his godly ways. It is only by his own will (and God's help, no doubt) that he decides to abandon his sinful life. However, what has been revealed inside him during his period of licentiousness does not easily go away: his own desires which remain with him from then on. This is the turning point in his *criollización*. Haunted by his desires, he turns to the strongest bastion of defense that Spanish culture provides him: the Catholic perception of death. In a gesture similar to that of the priest in *Manchay Puytu*, he brings a corpse to his bed, in hopes that this aberrant act will put an end to the temptations by providing him an intimate reminder of the proximity of death.

Biedma actively follows the advice found in many piety treaties of the time. As Luis de Granada—one of the most widely read authors of this type of book—advises readers in their fight against lust, "Primeramente considera en qué para la flor de toda la hermosura del mundo; esto te dirá qué es aquello que deseas. Dice Sant Isidoro: Ninguna cosa más aprovecha para domar la fuerza de los apetitos carnales, como la consideración de cual será después de la muerte aquello que tanto amamos vivos" (Granada 1849, 3:123) (First of all, consider where does all the beauty of the world end: this will tell you what is that that you desire. Saint Isidoro says: Nothing is more beneficial to tame the force of carnal appetite as to consider what will happen, after death, to that that we love so much). Biedma follows this advice to the extremity of having a corpse in his bed in order to avoid forgetting "cual será después de la muerte aquello que tanto amamos vivos" (what will happen, after death, to that that we love so much). The importance of this act must be stressed. Although it has a religious aim which would justify it, it is a clear violation of Church norms. In the Andean world of the colonial period, the Catholic norm of burying corpses is an even more indispensable rule, because it opposes the Incan tradition of mummifying the dead rather than burying them (Gisbert, MacCormack). There is an echo of the indigenous tradition in Biedma's action that would have hardly escaped Calancha's eyes, but the breaking of the norm seems to imply also that some order inside Biedma is transgressed, as well. Perhaps the boundaries between the realm of his desires and the colonial context in which he lives get blurred. As a result his own demons come to inhabit the space where the Indians live. By bringing the corpse to his bed it is as if he brings the whole society into his psyche, and at the same time, he makes the social (and, not casually, that "social" is the indigenous one) the mirror of his own desires. However, no matter how radical this action is, the corpse does not prevent the flow of lust in Biedma's blood; it only changes the object of his desire by suddenly making his interest in the conversion of Indians a compelling need. The corpse seems to re-route part of his libido (to use Freud's terminology) to a new object, the Indians, while repressing another part that later will surface in a hallucinatory manner.

We can think of the corpse as a mirror in which Biedma sees death as part of himself. As the iconography that was created in the Andes region during the seventeenth and eighteenth centuries suggests, skeletons and skulls were often used to depict the baroque conception of death. Teresa Gisbert mentions, for example, a painting in Cuzco, in which a gentleman is portrayed with a normal face, but his body is already a skeleton. Another significant example mentioned also by Gisbert refers to two paintings located in Ayacucho (Perú) representing Juan Palafox y Mendoza, bishop of Puebla, that show the bishop's reflection in mirrors as a skull (Gisbert 205–20). Thus, Biedma brings a corpse to his bed to remind him of his death and to protect him against the sins of the flesh, but also as a way (unconsciously, perhaps) to look at the reality of his own desires in the context of his Catholic beliefs.

However, the corpse does not return Biedma's psyche to its original state. Some changes are now irreversible. The corpse brings some kind of order to his interiority but a precarious one that will require a different kind of mirror to stabilize it. The skull/mirror is replaced by the Indian-demon/mirror that better secures Biedma's self. The calling to convert Indians is nothing but this necessity to see himself reflected in a new mirror: Indians and demons. Although what he sees is still the real "enemy," it is not the Devil, but his own soul suddenly inhabited by demons and angels. As Calancha writes:

En breve conoció [Biedma] que su pelea era no tanto con egércitos de Indios infieles (que avía entonces gran número de Indios en aquellos contornos) como con legiones de espíritus infernales, que como en barrios del infierno asistían de asiento, i continuavan su abitación en aquellos pueblos. (1413)

(Soon, [Biedma] realized that his fight was not so much against armies of infidel Indians [at that time, there were big numbers of Indians in those regions] as against legions of infernal spirits who settled there as in hell's neighborhoods, and continued to have their habitat in those towns.)

These infernal spirits, as real for him as the Indians themselves, engage him in a major battle. But these demons are also a projection of those desires and temptations that he is trying to get rid of. Not surprisingly, Calancha recounts that the first Indian sorcerers Biedma finds are the "striges" or "lamias," creatures taken from biblical references. The narrator explains that "lamias" are demons in the shape of beautiful women, who eat children and young men. At this point, Calancha's narrative takes on a new direction. It is worth recalling that in the prologue to his *Corónica moralizada*, Calancha states that he has two main goals in writing this book:

La quarta advertencia es, que al aver moralizado esta Corónica, tiene dos intentos; el primero querer introducir quanto en este Reyno a sucedido desde años antes de conquistado, para que quien leyere este tomo, sepa por mayor quanto en lo temporal (así en conquista, como en fundaciones) sucedió en esta Monarquía, i en lo espiritual quanto a sucedido en estas indias; i el segundo, porque moralizando con lugares de Escritura, con dichos de Santos, i con sentencias de Filósofos, los acaecimientos, las virtudes, los vicios, pondere el libro lo que no se a de parar a ponderar el lector . . . Yo escrivo, para que se aprovechen las ánimas, i no para entretener a ociosos: mi estado no pide escrivir Corónicas que se queden en la esfera de la istoria, sino Corónica que suba a provecho de ánimas. (6)

(The fourth guidance is that to have made this a moralized Chronicle has two purposes; the first is the wish to introduce in it everything that has happened in this Monarchy since before the conquest, in order that who reads this volume knew at length what happened in the temporal [both in conquest and foundations] in this Monarchy, as well as what happened in the spiritual in these Indies; and the second is that by moralizing with Biblical references, with Saint's words, and with philosopher's statements, about facts, virtues, and vices, the book may evaluate what the reader may not. . . . I write for the benefit of souls, and not to entertain lazy people: my condition does not ask to write Chronicles that remain in the realm of history, but Chronicle that rises to benefit souls.)

Calancha makes it clear that he is writing a history as well as a moral book. More importantly, the moral part is supported by the authority of the classical and Catholic written word of Western civilization. When Calancha starts explaining who the "lamias" are, his intervention as a *letrado* narrator prevails over the narrative of Biedma's life. His authority and erudition are staged as a moral reference and an exhaustive explanation of Biedma's actions. With this purpose, the narrator fills several pages with long explanations—taken from biblical and Christian sources—about all kinds of demons, who may appear as animals, monsters, or grotesque beings. It is as if this discourse suddenly takes on a life of its own; and instead of being a detached reference, it invades and interlaces itself with the narrative of Biedma's life to the point where textual reference and historical life become one surface full of *plies* (Deleuze) and curves defining the texture of the *Criollo*'s Baroque. It does not matter much that the discourses are only juxtaposed, not intertextually produced; the effect is that they are intimately weaved into a singular surface that allows passage from one discourse to the other without running into any discontinuities.

The *Criollo*'s baroque narrative blurs the borders between a textual imagination, an exemplary life, and a social context. In its baroque texture, this limited yet, at the same time, open space, is the stage where the *Criollo*'s subjectivity is deployed. Here, Biedma's desire can freely travel from his inner self, to classical and biblical references, and then to Indian towns and lives. In their errant displacement, his desires, dislocated after the exhuming of the corpse, look for a new articulation. Calancha's story shows us a subject in the process of *criollización*, which is the process of his desire being de-territorialized and territorialized again.

We can now see the whole process of Biedma's *criollización*. Biedma's itinerary of transformation starts with the exacerbation of his desires upon his arrival to the New World. To stem these desires he undertakes an extreme action: the exhumation of a corpse. This act, however, does not reverse the flow of his desire: it redirects it to the indigenous realm. In trying to explain the incursion of Biedma into the Andean world, Calancha introduces the textual imagination of a *letrado Criollo*. Biedma's desires, now, freely move around these three spaces. From these spaces come the elements through which the *Criollo*'s subjectivity is being developed. The *Criollo*'s desire will acquire different forms and names, the most remarkable being that of the demons. This is why he needs so badly to fight the Devil among the Indians.

But not only a Friar has to suffer this process. *Criollos* in general have to follow and fight their own demons, incarnation of their desires, who hide and live side by side with the Andean indigenous. Likewise, it is not only Calancha's writing, but all *Criollo* writing that has a corpse floating between its lines, waiting for the appropriate conditions that will send it back to its grave. In the meantime, *Criollo* writing will wander among Indians, cemeteries, unleashed passions, and accounts of sins and offenses against God in the process of articulating *Criollos* subjectivities, as Arzáns's text shows extensively.

Hatred Beyond Death:
An Absolute Representation of the *Criollo*

The *Historia de la Villa Imperial de Potosí* by Bartolomé Arzáns de Orsúa y Vela (1673–1736)[7] can be seen as a compendium of details of the *Criollo*'s subjectivity. History, chronicle, book of exemplary tales, catalogue of miracles (many of them taken from Calancha's writing), and a permanent celebration of the Imperial Villa of Potosí, the wealthy mining city of the sixteenth and seventeenth centuries, the *Historia* provides some of the most extraordinary examples of the baroque conception of death as an integral part of *Criollo*'s subjectivity.

One of the most striking of Arzáns' tales is the story of a Creole who is, apparently, a hermit. For twenty years, the protagonist, Juan de Toledo, walks the streets of Potosí dressed in ragged clothes and carrying a skull in his hands. This attitude gives him the reputation for being a mystic hermit. He is seen as a man meditating on death while living in penitence, one who looks forward to

230 LEONARDO GARCÍA-PABÓN

seeing God after his death. When he dies, people find a letter inside the skull, which is a confession of the reasons for his behavior of the last twenty years. The letter tells that he is not really a saint but a horrible sinner. All these years he has been carrying the skull of a former acquaintance, Martín de Salazar, a Spaniard whom he killed because the man offended him. The letter continues by saying that after Salazar was buried, Toledo went to his tomb one night, opened it up, extracted the heart of the corpse, and devoured it. He then cut off Salazar's head and took it with him. Toledo so hated Salazar that he wished every day that he would come back to life, so he could kill him again: "y me pesaba en gran manera de verlo muerto, que si mil veces resucitara, otras tantas se la volviera a quitar [la vida]" (Arzáns de Orsúa y Vela, *Relatos* 115–17) (and I was sorrowful to see him dead, for had he risen again a thousand times I would have killed him again as many times).[8]

The same baroque conception of death that we have used for Calancha's story serves as a reference for Arzáns's tale. At first sight, the protagonist's appearance fits with the view of a man dedicated to thinking about death as the only certainty of life. However, these appearances hide a most sinful life, and even worse, an emotional drive that knows no repentance. This inversion of appearance and reality suggests already that we face a very complex baroque thought in this writing. In terms of the story's narrative structure, the use of several levels of representation is remarkable. First, we have the false representation of the protagonist as a hermit. Second, we have a calcified stage for a hidden confession: the letter inside the skull. And third, there is the content of the letter, the truth about the protagonist's life, which deconstructs the previous structures. These layers of representation point to the use of an important characteristic of political praxis in the Baroque, the *dissimulazione*,[9] as the moral digression about hypocrisy that opens the story already suggests. Although the tale seems to be set in an apolitical context and concerned only with the individual story, it has a strong though implicit political component, as we shall see.

Through his use of layered representations, Arzáns subverts the traditional moral purpose of the tale, opens a political dimension in the story, and produces a purely baroque writing. Thus, the text gains an autonomy that allows the representation of the writing subject, the Potosinian *Criollo*, as "el más malo de cuantos en el mundo ha habido" (the worst of those who have existed ever).[10] This powerful use of representation in baroque times has been defined as "absolute representation," by Bolivar Echeverría, who builds on Adorno's definition of the Baroque as "*decorazione assoluta*" (212). For Echeverría, absolute representation means that "lo que el arte propiamente reproduce al perseguir la forma perfecta de los objetos que produce no es la realidad de los mismos, sino el sentido del *ethos* desde el cual ha elegido cultivar la singularidad o mismidad de la vida social en la que se encuentra" (213) (what art properly reproduces by searching the perfect form of the objects that produces is not their reality, but the meaning of the *ethos* from which it has chosen to cultivate the singularity or sameness of the social life in which it occurs). The baroque *ethos*, as Echeverría explains, aims to transcend the contradiction inherent to modernity without having to accept or refuse any of the opposing terms. In the colonial period, a good case in point is the mixed cultural forms produced in the New World, the so-called cultural *mestizaje*. For Indians and blacks, for example, "la persistencia en su modo peculiar de simbolización de lo real, para ser efectiva, se vio obligada a trascender el nivel inicial en el que había tenido lugar la derrota y a jugarse en un segundo plano: debía pasar no solo por la aceptación, sino por la defensa de la construcción de mundo traída por los dominadores, incluso sin contar con la colaboración de éstos y aun en su contra" (Echeverría 54) (the persistence in their peculiar way to symbolize the real, to be effective, was forced to transcend the initial level in which the downfall had taken place, and commit themselves to a second level: it should pass not only by the acceptance, but by the defense of the construction of the world brought by the conquerors, yet without their collaboration, and even against them). As a political strategy, the defeated cultures not only accepted but defended the imposed Spanish culture while maintaining their own cultural identities. The same can be said for the *Criollos*. Although they were part of the dominant social class, and did not feel the Spanish culture as an imposition, they still had to construct their own identity as different from Spanish culture. The *Criollos* had to affirm themselves as part of the Spanish culture, and at the same time defend themselves against it. This is what the *Criollo* Espinosa Medrano's famous *Apologético* (a treaty in defense of Luis de Góngora's poetry against attacks from Spaniard intellectuals) perfectly shows.[11] Similarly, Arzáns' writing, through the interplay of representations, aims to create a space of absolute representation, where the baroque *ethos* allows the writing subject—the *Criollo*—to affirm and reject the culture that originally constitutes him. Thus the *Criollo* can represent himself as "el más malo" but also as "the best" of *Criollos*, the one that can speak by/for himself.

However, what is represented in this manner is not something that can be held fast. Like a mirage, the reflected image cannot be grasped, or even clearly seen; indeed it can only be located between the levels of representation. Arzáns's "truth" is not in his letter/confession; it has to be found between the representations, and in what makes possible the production of levels of representation as masks that aim to create an absolute representation. And that "truth"—that essential something, that goes from the *Criollo* Toledo to the Spaniard Salazar, and tries to reach him even beyond death, that goes from his life to the skull and to the text that explains his life, and that ultimately goes from the text to the reader with the pedagogical goal of moralizing about hypocrisy—is an unsolvable emotional conflict conveyed as hatred. This unrepentant hatred flows all over the story and overflows the individual and pedagogical—weak containers for such a hunger for emotional reparation. Even more, this hatred seems the resonance in an individual of a social malaise that cannot find yet a resolution.

It is highly significant that the *Criollo* kills a Spaniard, not an Indian, not another *Criollo*, and not a woman. From this perspective, Toledo's story is emblematic of a dominant theme in Arzáns' book: the rivers of blood that the fights between *vicuñas* (*Criollos* and Andalusians) and *vascongados* (Basques) brought to the city. Arzáns calls these fights one of the three plagues with which God punished Potosí for its sins. The function of hypocrisy becomes clear now: it is a form of *dissimulazione*, a form of political praxis. Under a tale of hypocrisy lies a tale of social malaise; and the tale's moralizing intention is just a veil that, instead of hiding, accentuates the political situation that confronts *Criollos* and Basques. Thus, by the creation of an absolute representation, the emotional conflict of the *Criollo* subject is revealed in its individual dimension as well as in its social and political ones. Killing the Spaniard, eating his heart, and carrying his skull for twenty years are symbolic moments that refer to a social conflict that will not be solved until the end of colonial days. Of these episodes, perhaps the most eloquent is the eating of the heart because of its cultural connotations.

Cannibalism is an act full of connotations about the relationship between the Old World and the New World. It was a mark of the American savage and a justification for colonization.[12] Toledo, by this act of cannibalism, infringes upon the norms of Western civilization, and brings an indigenous differential to his subjectivity equation. This is the necessary step to establish a difference that would put the *Criollo*'s identity beyond the realm of Spanish culture. It makes the decision to belong to a tradition that opposes *essentially* European culture. It is also an attempt to mark his origin beyond any cultural and historical determination: a beginning before humanity, still in the animal world. It is the invention of a pure origin. After this differentiation, a process of identity formation can be initiated. Toledo, as *Criollos* in general, initiated this process through a mechanism of primal identification with Spanish culture. Following classical psychoanalytical theory, we must recall that cannibalism is an act under the field of primitive oral impulses. To eat or not eat something is related to the separation between the ego and the outside world, and to what part of the latter can be made part of the ego. As Freud wrote:

> Expressed in the language of the oldest, that is, of the oral, instinctual impulses, the alternative runs thus: 'I should like to eat that, or I should like to spit it out'; or, carried a stage further: 'I should like to take this into me and keep that out of me.' That is to say: it is to be either *inside* me or *outside* me... The original pleasure-ego tries to introject into itself everything that is good and to reject everything that is bad. From this point of view what is bad, what is alien to the ego, and what is external are, to begin with, identical. (quoted by Kilgour 4)

This dialect between ego and external world, which is at the center of cannibalism, can be extended to the interaction between the social subject and its context. Thus cannibalism as representation produces, contests, and negotiates subjectivity and identities (Guest 1).[13] By eating the heart of a Spaniard, Toledo is performing an act of incorporation that aims to break the individual as well as the social boundaries between himself and an object that is not (and refuses to be) part of the *Criollo*.

The incorporation of the Spaniard has, however, a twist of its own. We should not forget that the heart does not come from a distinctive Other (an Indian, for example) but from his likeness and cultural brother. It is noteworthy that it is not strangeness that needs to be made part of the *Criollo*. It is the internalization of something that already exists in himself. After all, he belongs, culturally speaking, to the Spanish culture as much as Salazar himself. This is especially relevant if we think that part of the taboo of cannibalism "relies not in its participation in differential systems of meaning but rather on its recognition of corporeal similarity . . . . Indeed, the idea of cannibalism prompts a visceral reaction among people precisely *because* it activates our horror of consuming others like ourselves" (Guest 3). Consuming the one that is the most similar to the *Criollo*, the Spaniard, brings out all the horror of the act of cannibalism. "¡Oh terribilidad mía!" (oh, my enormity!) calls the main character to his act, and he calls himself "la más terrible bestia" (the most terrible beast) and "más fiero que las fieras mismas" (more bloodthirsty than the very beasts) (117). There is a double bind in this cannibalism: on the one hand, to make the external, the different, part of oneself; on the other hand, to incorporate something that is already in himself. Two different processes take place at the same time: an incorporation and a profound self-affirmation. It would seem that his cannibalism tries to cover all the space between the traditions that inform the

Criollo: the mark of the American savage, the incorporation of the Other, and the reidentification with Spanish culture.

Now, if cannibalism is the performance of an act strongly associated with Native Americans, the eating of the heart ties Arzáns's story to a not less powerful symbolic tradition but of European fabrication. The eating of the heart is a topic that is strongly associated with love in Western literature. The cultural representation of the heart as the seat for love, life, and energy begins with Greek culture, as Milad Doueihi has studied. For example, in Italy, the theme of the *cuore mangiato* (the eaten heart) has a high incidence in its literature.[14] The same topic can be traced in French or Spanish literature. Thus eating the Spaniard's heart is not only an act of cannibalism associated with American cultures, it is also a symbolic representation of love and hatred in the tradition of Western cultures. This is another way of looking at the conflictive relationship that the *Criollo* has with Spain: his love and hatred for the culture that supports its own cultural identity. But this love and hatred is also aimed at himself. As several other stories by Arzáns suggest, the relationship between two main characters is usually one of love and hatred.[15] In fact, Toledo's relationship with Salazar is a reflection, in many aspects, of the relationship with himself. The severity with which the protagonist judges his acts in his letter attest to his self-hatred, while the pride with which he reacts to the offenses perpetrated against his *honor* speaks of his love for himself.

How much more complex can an identity formation be? The *Criollo,* caught between extreme separations and identifications, has to rip out his heart as well as that of the others with whom he lives in order to be able to represent himself. But only within the framework of a baroque culture, within absolute representation, can this self-representation be performed. The flow of skulls, eaten hearts, rivers of blood, and obsessions with mirrors in Arzáns' texts carries its writing subject into a vacuum, where, for an instant, a *case* can be apprehended. It is a case in the sense that Arzáns puts it as the final line of Toledo's story: "¡Ved, cristiano lector, qué caso!" (117) (Take note, O Christian reader, of this terrible case!). In fact, the story seems to have been written for the *Criollo* to see the case: the judiciary, religious, political, and textual case of the *Criollo* writing and reading himself in the absoluteness of a baroque representation.

Changing the Mirror (and the Subject)

Both Calancha and Arzáns narrate death as a presence that detains or should detain the flow of life and desire. It is not so much an imaginary or internalized presence but a physical presence: the corpse or the skull. The corpse that should stop Biedma's desire or the skull that should bring relief to Toledo's hatred are objects with a powerful religious charge. They should bring to existence a symbolic order in which a Spanish subject could be. However, this is not the case as I have tried to show. On the contrary, the human remains that both protagonists live with exacerbate a deconstruction and a restructuring of their subjectivities. It is as if by looking at those relics in search of a cultural reaffirmation of what they thought they were, they would only find an image that does not correspond with it. But the change is not only inside themselves, or better, the change in themselves happens, and it is realized because the whole image in the mirrors (subject and context) has changed. A reference to the classic article by Lacan on subjectivity formation during infancy, "Le stade de miroir comme formateur de la fonction du jeu," may prove useful here. In Lacan's article, for the child to recognize his image in a mirror he needs the reference of the mother next to him, so he can realize that the image in the mirror is he, and not somebody else. But what if the mother changes? What if the mother, instead of being what the Spanish culture had codified and established as the parameter to define subjects in this culture, is suddenly altered? This is what may have happened to the *Criollos* in the initial steps of their identification as such. The references in the mirror were changed, therefore the subject itself had to learn again who he was. It was a realization that came with a failed expectation and a surprising revelation. The *Criollos* were expecting to see themselves as Spaniards, but they saw *Criollos*, who were as similar and identical to Spaniards as twins can be, but that had a differential, an essential one (that almost imperceptible indigenous tint), that made the whole difference. This was the source of such a conflictive and painful subjectivity formation.

There was only one symbolic space through which the *Criollos* could carry out this recognition of themselves: the baroque. The *letrado* narrator as well as the play of representations unfolded desires that were attracted and repelled by the absolute nothingness of death, while providing a mirror for the mirrors of the *Criollo*. The attempt of these American baroque texts to be absolute representations was the attempt also to construct a mirror that would not only give an identity to the *Criollos* but that would do it in a less conflictive manner. In fact, the disturbed souls of Biedma and Toledo would only find the peace and harmony they looked for in the stories of their lives as told by a *Criollo* writer. Through baroque writing taken to the extremity of an absolute representation, Calancha, Arzáns, and many others were building a new (b)order between life and death. This will not be a public building made out of human bones, nor a private space to worship a cadaver, but a cemetery where the name (the subject), the corpse (the image), and the tomb (the American space) are finally in conformity.

Notes

1. I want to acknowledge the editorial help of Lillian Darwin.
2. The Manchay Puytu tune has survived to this day, and it has become a traditional song both in Latin America and Spain. The modern name of the song is "Dos palomitas" (Two little doves).
3. The translations to English from Spanish in this work are all mine, except when noted. The translation of Sor Juana's lines is by Alix Inberg.
4. After the seminal study by Nathan Wachtel, several works have shown the importance of this play for the understanding of indigenous thinking in the eighteenth century. Among other works, we can mention those by Burga, Cornejo Polar, and García Pabón ("Comunicación," "Duelo").
5. The myth of the Inkarri, of the Inca Rey (King Inca), states that the body of a mythological Inca is growing under the earth. One day the body will come together, and this will signal the rebirth of the Inca Empire. The myth is born out of the history of rebellious Incas such as Tupac Amaru who were dismembered and buried in different places of the viceroyalty of Peru.
6. A recent and interesting study of Calancha as a *Criollo* is the one by Santa Arias: "Escritura disidente: agencia criolla, vidas y Milagros in la *Corónica moralizada de la Orden de San Agustín en el Perú* de Antonio de la Calancha." Arias also summarizes well other studies about Calancha.
7. The complete edition of the *Historia de la Villa Imperial de Potosí* was published in 1965. I quote from the anthology of tales prepared by myself, titled *Relatos de la Villa Imperial de Potosí*.
8. The translation of Arzáns' texts is by López-Morillas, and was published as *Tales of Potosi*.
9. Echeverría mentions *dissimulazione* as an aspect of the Baroque used by the *Criollos* in the New World, and reminds us that the same phenomena happened in Italy and other places of Europe. Echeverría says: "El planteamiento de la *dissimulazione* . . . aconseja hacer concesiones en el plano bajo y evidente, como maniobra de ocultamiento de la conquista en el plano superior e invisible; como instrumento para poner en práctica una política de oposición efectiva dentro de un espacio político dominado por la dictadura y la represión" (183) (The proposition of *dissimulazione* . . . advises to make concessions in the lower and evident level, as a maneuver to hide the conquest in the superior and invisible level, as an instrument to put into practice a politics of effective opposition inside a political space dominated by dictatorship and repression).
10. This would be the *Criollo* male counterpart to Sor Juana's "yo la peor de todas." (I the worst of them all).

11. See the excellent study by González Echevarría for an illuminating explanation of Espinosa's defense of Góngora.
12. In the New World, the cannibal became an essential mark of it. Columbus' writings associated cannibalism with Native Americans from the very beginning (entries in the first diary). For a study of representations of American cannibals in Western culture, see the work by Lestringant and Morris.
13. Since the seminal work by Kilgour, cannibalism has been rethought as an important topic in the production of ideological critique. The production of a substantial critical literature on cannibalism has helped to "advance our understanding of how cannibalism has historically 'enforced' and 'dissolved' the boundaries of identity of forms of representation and to suggest how cannibalism emerges as a useful focal point for ideological critique" (Guest 2).
14. Mariella di Maio has traced this topic since the twelfth century to the nineteenth century for Italian literature.
15. I have discussed the love/hatred relationship in Arzáns's tales in my introduction to the anthology of his work (García Pabón "Introducción").

Works Cited

Arias, Santa. "Escritura disidente: agencia criolla, vidas y milagros de la *Corónica moralizada de la Orden de San Agustín en el Perú* de Antonio de la Calancha." *Colonial Latin American Review* 10, no. 2 (2001): 189–208.

Arzáns de Orsúa y Vela, Bartolomé. *Historia de la Villa Imperial de Potosí*. 3 vols. Ed. Lewis Hanke and Gunnar Mendoza. Providence, R.I.: Brown University Press, 1965.

_____. *Relatos de la Villa Imperial de Potosí*. Ed. Leonardo García Pabón. La Paz: Plural Editores, 2000.

_____. *Tales of Potosí*. Trans. Frances M. López-Morillas. Providence, R.I.: Brown University Press, 1975.

Burga, Manuel. *Nacimiento de una utopía: Muerte y resurreción de los incas*. Lima: Instituto de Apoyo Agrario, 1988.

Caro Baroja, Julio. *Las formas complejas de la vida religiosa: religión, sociedad y carácter en la España de los siglos XVI y XVII*. Madrid: Akal, 1978.

Cornejo Polar, Antonio. "El comienzo de la heterogeneidad en las literaturas andinas: voz y letra en el 'diálogo' de Cajamarca." *Revista de Crítica Literaria Latinoamericana* 26, no. 3 (1990): 155–207.

Cruz, Sor Juana Inés de la. *She tries to refute the praises inscribed on her portrait by Truth, which she calls passion*. Trans. Alix Ingber. http://sonnets.spanish.sbc.edu/.

Deleuze, Gilles. *Le pli. Leibniz et le baroque*. Paris: Les Éditions de Minuit, 1988.

Doueihi, Milad. *A Perverse History of the Human Heart*. Cambridge: Harvard University Press, 1997.

Echeverría, Bolivar. *La modernidad de lo barroco*. Mexico City: Era, 2000.

García Pabón, Leonardo. "Comunicación, escritura e imaginario social en la *Tragedia del fin de Atahuallpa*." *Caravelle* 59 (1992): 225–40.

_____. "Duelo y melancolía en *La tragedia del fin de Atahuallpa*." *Memorias. Jornadas Andinas de Literatura Latinoamericana 1995*. Tucumán, 1997.

_____. "Introducción. Los relatos de la *Historia de la Villa Imperial de Potosí* de Bartolomé Arzáns Orsúa y Vela." *Relatos de la Villa Imperial de Potosí*, by Bartolomé Arzáns De Orsúa y Vela. La Paz: Plural Editores, 2001. xii–xxiii.

Gisbert, Teresa. *El paraíso de los pájaros parlantes. La imagen del otro en la cultura andina*. La Paz: Plural, 1999.

González Echevarría, Roberto. *Celestina's Brood: Continuities of the Baroque in Spanish and Latin American Literatures*. Durham: Duke University Press, 1993.

Granada, Luis de. *Obras de V.P.M. Fray Luis de Granada*. Ed. José Joaquín de Mora. Vol. XI. Madrid: Biblioteca de Autores Españoles, 1849.

Guest, Kristen. *Eating Their Word: Cannibalism and the Boundaries of Cultural Identity*. Albany: State University of New York Press, 2001.

Kilgour, Maggie. *From Communion to Cannibalism: An Anatomy of Metaphors of Incorporation*. Princeton, N.J.: Princeton University Press, 1990.

Lacan, Jacques. "Le stade de miroir comme formateur de la fonction du jeu." *Écrits 1*. Paris: Éditions de Seuil, 1966. 89–97.

Lestringant, Frank, and Rosemary Morris. *Cannibals: the Discovery and Representation of the Cannibal from Columbus to Jules Verne*. Berkeley: University of California Press, 1997.

MacCormack, Sabine. "Demons, Imagination and the Incas." *New World Encounters*. Ed. Stephen Greenblatt. Berkeley: University of California Press, 1993. 101–26.

Maio, Mariella di. *Il cuore mangiato: Storia di un tema letterario dal Medioevo all'Ottocento*. Milan: Guerini e Associati, 1996.

Part V
The Baroque and Its Transgressive Recyclings

12

Baroque/Neobaroque/Ultrabaroque: Disruptive Readings of Modernity

Mabel Moraña
(Translated by Gerardo Garza)

My song shall be a flood.
—Francisco de Quevedo

Allegories are, in the realm of thought,
what ruins are in the realm of things.
Hence, the baroque cult of ruins.
—Walter Benjamin

I am dressed in baroquism.
—Jacques Lacan

It seems to me that the laboratory of the future
is in Latin America, and that it is there
where one ought to think and experiment.
—Félix Guattari

From Colonization of Imaginaries to the Post-Auratic Era: The Baroque Disruption

1. Accidentalism, *Difference*, and the Origin Myth

As it is known, attempts to explain the term *baroque* etymologically have coincided in a double derivation of its meaning: one aspect recovers the name assigned to one of the argumentative forms (the baroque syllogism as "the prototype of absurd formalistic and scholastic reasoning" [Corominas 88]) while the other refers to a deformity, to an unfinished desire. As an allegorical introduction for a characterization of the American Baroque, this duality could be condensed in the following image, always brought to mind: A foreign particle becomes implanted into the corporeal substance of a mollusk, and it is slowly surrounded by layers of nacre that develop into a pearl. Nevertheless, if in the process of its formation, the emerging jewel finds irregularities in the interior walls of the oyster, its potential circularity is disrupted. Imperfect, pathological, that deformed pearl evokes a sphericity never achieved: its slightly monstrous body is affirmed in the nostalgia of totality and perfection.[1] The baroque pearl is a melancholic, transubstantiated, impure being, saturated by matter. It is, at the same time, hybrid and palimpsest, a deformity conceived through the transgression of its own limits—something new, that results from the defensive struggle exercised by the body that receives the challenge of heterogeneity. As the product of a contradictory dynamics of absorption and resistance, the baroque pearl combines, in its process of formation, both the norm and its exception. This product, which is appropriated and deterritorialized by culture, is extracted from its natural habitat, turned into sumptuous merchandise, and integrated, in its doubly symbolic and real character, in the elites' imaginaries as well as in their spaces of social and material exchange.

The syllogistic meaning, as well as the one that refers to the imperfect pearl, includes the inescapable detonator of conflict: the irresistible, vainly hyperbolic, and not totally achieved rationality; and the logic of a formal existence that evokes precisely what "it lacks," sinks into its limits, and explores its own borders.

From this initial etymological digression I am interested in recovering what might be called *the logic of baroque disruption*, that is, its epistemological operational capacity with respect to the discourses that accompanied the entrance of Latin America to the successive instances of globalized modernity.[2] This implies, in the first place, the understanding of the constitutive paradox of baroque aesthetics: the one that marks it as one of the principal mechanisms in the processes of transculturation implemented in America by Spanish colonialism, and that, at the same time, recognizes in the Baroque a fundamental piece in the process of construction of differentiated cultural identities in overseas territories. Thus, power and resistance, identity and difference, rationalist excess and sensorial extravagance are articulated, from the beginning, in the overcodified registry of baroque aesthetics, which was imposed on American territories as an instrument of domination and colonization on colonial imaginaries. Secondly, my research seeks to ascertain the cultural, historical, and ideological transformations of the baroque paradigm hat extends, through continuities and ruptures, from the humanistic enclaves of the viceregal period up to what might be called the post-auratic—postmodern, postcolonial—era, one that would correspond to the establishment of the Ultrabaroque.[3]

In this sense, I propose to read the Baroque as the allegorical reproductibility of the struggles of power that are inherent in the process of insertion of the American world in the context of Occidentalism. Elsewhere I have referred to the processes of appropriation of the baroque code in the colonies, as well as the functions it assumes with respect to the processes of emergence of Creole consciousness in the "New World."[4] In that analysis I mainly emphasized the way in which the Baroque, which is introduced in America with the propagandistic, mass-oriented, and popular dimension analyzed by José Antonio Maravall for the case of Spain, is co-opted by the Creole agenda. In effect, in the same manner in which the materials of construction and the climates of America imposed onto the architectural Baroque lines, colors, and structures that were alien to European models, the residue of pre-Hispanic cultures colonized the visual and linguistic spaces of metropolitan Baroque with images, words, and messages that transcended and re-signified the canonical norms. In this sense, one might say that the Baroque of the Indies implements, more than the mimesis, the mimicry of hegemonic imaginaries.[5]

The adoption of the Baroque in America is not, therefore, just a moment of appropriation or recycling of the imperial aesthetics, but a process of cannibalization in which the sumptuous, symbolic merchandise of the colonizers turns into a *barrueca* anomaly—deformed pearl—in its contact with the social body that receives it. The anomalous or monstrous is the mark of an American *difference* that resists the perfection of the sphere, and, in addition, refutes the universality of its aesthetic value restoring in its place its singularity and contingency. In this way, American "accidentalism" opposes the modernizing and Eurocentric "Occidentalism" and reverts it. The prestigious wit of Sor Juana turns her into someone who must assume a masculine appearance in order to survive: "me obligaron a malear la letra porque decían que parecía letra de hombre" (they forced me to corrupt my handwriting because they said that it looked like masculine handwriting), she says in the so-called "Carta de Monterrey" (de la Cruz 17). Juan Ruiz de Alarcón's hump visualizes his hybrid identity, one that is impacted by deterritorialization. The purple facial blemish that characterizes the *mestizo* Juan de Espinosa Medrano, *El Lunarejo*, underscores the anomaly of his sermons, which were preached in Quechua from the pulpit of Cuzco, and the disruptive value of his complaints about the relegation of the learned Creole that he includes in his brilliant study of the Gongorine aesthetics. These symbolic marks of American *difference*—to which critics have conferred an iconic importance, understanding them as signs of a conflicted socialization—point to the understanding of America as a space of contaminating and transformative exchanges, where the cultural logic of the dominator acquires new meaning as it is reformulated from, and in spite of, the positions of subalternity and marginalization imposed on Creole subjects by the practices of colonialism.[6] The "deformation" that takes place in the American Baroque—its *ab-normality*, its anamorphous nature, its *monstrosity*—is, therefore, *"de-monstration"* ("[in the Baroque] the monster is essentially a visual entity: monster, 'mostrar' (to show), demonstrate" [González-Echeverría, *Celestina's Brood* 165]).

In this way, an art like the Baroque, which is exported from the metropolis as a mechanism of homogeneization in accordance with the unifying plans of imperial Spain—"One God, one king, one language"—becomes, in its colonial re-production, a hybrid product, refolded upon the heterogeneity that it seeks to reduce, and unfolded from the parameters of "high" culture toward the popular horizons of the American difference and heterogeneity. It would be impossible to recognize the countercultural meaning that the appropriations of the Baroque acquire in the colonies without the recognition of this *agency* from which colonial subjects appeal not just to the re-*production* of imperial protocols, but above all, to the-proactive-*production* of a performativity that carries those models to the extreme in the process of their reconversion. Consequently, without the recognition of that cultural and political agency, it will also be impossible to evaluate in depth this foundational instance of the process of identity formation, both in itself and in relation to the development of Latin American culture in later centuries.

In its Latin American formulations, the baroque aesthetics appears to reformulate in multiple ways *the myth of origin*. In fact, we can ask ourselves: Where does America's consciousness begin? Where can one locate the traditions that feed the production of meanings that modernity sets in motion in order to legitimize the legacies of colonialism and domesticate the resistances to it? Are they in the pre-Hispanic cultures or in the discovery, in the classical and post-Renaissance traditions, in Counter-Reformation thought, in the emancipation and emergence of national cultures, or in the influences of Enlightenment and the establishment in Latin America of liberal, bourgeois modernity? Which contents become incorporated and which are displaced by the postcolonial subjectivity in the processes of formation of social identities? Which cultural contents are articulated in this process, and in what hierarchical order? But, above all, how do the voices that do not find representation in discourses of power speak in the imaginaries of the various Latin American modernities? And in that significant symbiosis, how does the neocolonial condition of Latin America play in imaginaries that constantly evoke both the violence originated by the conquest and the violence that is also inherent to European domination in postcolonial, transnational settings? In which way and to what degree does the baroque aesthetics play a role in the construction of emancipatory projects in Latin America? How is the baroque model articulated to the agendas of gender, to antiauthoritarian and re-democratizing thought, and to the vindication of marginal subjects? How do historical variations as well as political and cultural circumstances become incorporated in scenarios of symbolic representation in which the Baroque prevails as a constant referential focus of postcolonial subjectivity, "like the building principle governing the behavior and social objectives that in the midst of their heterogeneity reveal a co-membership among themselves, a diffuse but unmistakable parentage" (Echeverría, *Modernidad, mestizaje cultural* 14, my translation)?

For Octavio Paz, the Baroque—a style that is conceived as a transgression of the Renaissance and as an essentially paradoxical form—is situated in the origins of American expressivity, because it is assimilated from the colony to the "existential anxiety" of Creole subjects. According to Paz, "there was a profound psychological and spiritual correspondence between Creole sensibility and the baroque style. It was the style that [the Creole society] needed, the only one that could express its contradictory nature" (26). For Carlos Fuentes, the Baroque is also an inescapable style, though for different reasons: it provides the possibility of disguising the face and expressing ambiguous identities, trapped by the imperial domination and sheltered through the Baroque in the "art of abundance based on need and desire; an art of proliferations founded on insecurity, rapidly filling all the gaps of our personal and social history." Fuentes adds: "the Baroque is the art of displacements, similar to a mirror in which we are constantly able to see our mutant identity" (206). The Baroque is the gaze that focuses on itself but discovers, at the same time, *another* look, in the process of that original *de-monstration* that reveals the first instances of individual and social (self-) recognition.

When examining in detail this kind of genealogical analysis that has guided an extensive part of studies on the Baroque, Carlos Rincón notices that, in some cases, the appropriations or re-productions of the Baroque constitute an attempt to find in this consecrated aesthetics roots that could render prestige and authenticate subsequent cultural developments in Latin America. For instance, according to some critics (e.g., Pedro Henríquez Ureña, Luis Alberto Sánchez) the Baroque would be a historical antecedent of the modern Latin American narrative. The relapses of the Baroque are read, then, as transhistorical recurrences. In other cases (e.g., José Lezama Lima, Alejo Carpentier), the baroque tradition allows us to understand the cultural history of Latin America in a more integrated and global manner, thus overcoming restrictive models such as those of identity, culture, or the *national* literary canon (the Baroque is interpreted, then, as an American phenomenon, that is, as a migrant, totalizing, and transnationalized model of symbolic representation).[7]

As part of his project to identify the foundations that give rise to an expressive form that we could recognize as *specifically Latin American*, Alejo Carpentier conceptualizes the Baroque as a style that is bound to the expressive requirements of *American* elements. The Baroque constitutes, therefore, a *necessary*—inescapable—style that explains and projects into the future the adoption of those specific forms of aesthetic codification, thus naturalizing a tradition that continues to feed and legitimize literary forms in the twentieth century. For Carpentier, the expansion of the baroque phenomenon not only manifests itself at the geo-cultural level, but also at the transhistorical, temporal level:

> Barrocos fuimos siempre y barrocos tenemos que seguirlo siendo, por una razón muy sencilla: que para definir, pintar, determinar un mundo nuevo, árboles desconocidos, vegetaciones increíbles, ríos inmensos, siempre se es barroco. Y si toma usted la producción latinoamericana en materia de novela, se encontrará con que todos somos barrocos. El barroquismo en nosotros es una cosa que nos viene del mundo en que vivimos: de las iglesias, de los templos precortesianos, del ambiente, de la vegetación. Barrocos somos y por el barroquismo nos definimos. (cited by Rincón, "La poética" 176)

> (We were always baroque and we have to continue being baroque, for a very simple reason: in order to define, paint, determine a new world, unknown trees, incredible vegetation, immense rivers, one is always being baroque. And if you take the Latin American production in matters of the novel, one will find that we are all baroque. For us, the baroque style is something that comes to us from the world in which we live: from the churches, from the pre-colonial temples, from the ambience, from nature. We are baroque and by the baroque style we define ourselves.)

In this way, for several authors, either in a historicist reflection or in one of a geo-cultural character, the Baroque is re-signified through interpretations that bind this aesthetic model to multiple strata: to the qualities of the American nature, to the conformation of the bourgeois culture (urban and liberal), or to the hybrid and fragmented continental identity. This identity, which although it is often essentialized by liberal criticism, takes part in processes of sociocultural (self-) recognition that were affected, from the colony to modernity, by the material and symbolic violence of European colonization and the subsequent modernizing instances. The problem is how the Latin American artist manages to assume, from his/her peripheral and dependent circumstance, that foundational violence, and how he/she represents, in a symbolic manner, all subsequent stages of American coloniality. Finally, this also poses the question of how baroque reappearances can be understood, as the Baroque continues to appeal, from the symbolic locations that were once occupied by the old Empire, to the aesthetics of saturation and proliferation, in order to reshape the utopia of definitive emancipation.

The interpretations of the Baroque and its more current manifestations in Latin America constitute, therefore, the history of the re-appropriations and re-significations of the European model, both from an aesthetic and an ideological perspective. From this point of view, Carpentier's quote takes on a new meaning, one that suggests a much more programmatic and complex significance than the one that might have inspired the Cuban author at the moment of his reflections. Perhaps it is precisely the perpetuation and the recycling of the Baroque that is the most clear proof of the persistent dialogue between Latin American postcolonial cultures and the "perverse modernity" imposed in overseas territories both in colonial and in contemporary times, which has resulted, then and now, in the configuration of heterogeneous, peripheral, and hybridized models of symbolic representation. And perhaps it is precisely from the residue of colonization and the subsequent reality of a perpetuated or surviving coloniality ("colonialidad supérstite") mentioned by Mariátegui in his *Seven Essays*, that the implication of the process of absorption and implementation of the Baroque in America could be thoroughly analyzed, both in the colonial and contemporary eras. In this sense, Bolívar Echeverría indicates that the baroque model puts forward, even in its more current forms, "an original dramaticity" (*Modernidad, mestizaje cultural* 25) that would explain its transgressive mode, its constant symbolic and ideological influence, and its functional character, within so many diverse cultural contexts. In my opinion, this is also why it is necessary to historicize its constant reappearances, without being tempted to explain the relapse of the Baroque as a merely mechanical survival of the remote, but better yet as a *return of the repressed*, that is, as the obsessive resurgence of a sensibility that the narratives and practices of modernity have suppressed, marginalized, and turned invisible.

Aside from the foundational moments that would correspond to the first stages of Westernization in the colonial period, and concentrating now on the more current critical revisions of the legacies of Enlightenment and modernity, the question regarding the reasons that would explain the recurrences of the Baroque (that "cultural operator," according to Rincón) within so many different cultural and historical contexts acquires new validity.

2. Toward a Baroquization of Latin America?

It is obvious that the phenomenon of the reappearances of the Baroque has gone beyond the geo-cultural territories that we traditionally identify as the primary sites of baroque production in the Hispanic world. For many authors, the expansion of this aesthetic model already constitutes a transnational process of "baroquization without borders." In his study titled "La curiosidad barroca," José Lezama Lima acknowledges that in the twentieth century, once the neoclassic moderation that opposes the decorative excess of European Baroque as a superficial and degenerative form is overcome in America, the baroque aesthetics is reinstated at many different levels:

> Se amplió tanto la extensión de sus dominios, que [el Barroco] abarcaba los ejercicios loyolistas, la pintura de Rembrandt y el Greco, las fiestas de Rubens y el ascetismo de Felipe de Champagne, la fuga bachtiana, un barroco frío y un barroco brillante, la matemática de Leibniz, la ética de Spinoza, y hasta algún crítico excediéndose en la generalización afirmaba que la tierra era clásica y el mar barroco. Vemos que aquí sus dominios llegan al máximo de su arrogancia, ya que los barrocos galerones hispanos recorren un mar teñido por una tinta igualmente barroca. (Lezama Lima 302)[8]

> (The dominions of the Baroque extended so much that they included the exercises of Loyola, paintings by Rembrandt and Greco, the festive representation in Rubens, and the asceticism of Felipe de Champagne, the Bachian fugue, a cold but also a brilliant Baroque, Leibniz's mathematics, Spinoza's ethics, and even a critic who, exceeding himself in the generalization of the term, stated that the earth was classical and the sea was baroque. There, we see that its dominions reach highest degrees of arrogance, since the Hispanic baroque galley covered a sea tainted by an equally baroque ink.)

In a similar radical sense, Adolfo Castañón sees the Baroque—"a cabalistic word that suggests both magic and enchantment"—as a stylistic symptom that crystallizes in artistic manifestations which are very dissimilar, both historically and culturally.

> [E]n el árbol de Navidad del barroco encontramos suspendidas la Contrarreforma y los sonetos, la poesía metafísica inglesa (inspirada directamente en el sermón hispánico y portugués, según hace ver José Ángel Valente), la poesía desengañada y fría de un Quevedo, pero también la letrilla mordaz y salaz de Góngora y sus imitadores como el brasileño Gregorio de Matos, la pintura flamenca y los artistas

del claroscuro, la máquina de guerra jesuita y los claustros, el hedonismo y el ma-
soquismo, la monarquía autoritaria y la semilla de los imperios de papel que hoy
llamamos burocracia. (Castañon 1644–45)

(We find, hanging from the Christmas tree of the Baroque, the Counter Reformation as well as the sonnet, the English metaphysical poetry (directly inspired by
the Hispanic and Portuguese sermon, as it has been shown by José Angel Valente),
the cold and disenchanted poetry of Quevedo, but also the scathing and salacious
writing of Góngora and his imitators, like the Brazilian Gregorio de Matos, Flem-
ish painting and the artists of chiaroscuro, the Jesuit war machine and the cloisters,
hedonism and masochism, the authoritarian monarchy and the seed of administrative Empires that today we call bureaucracy.)

Serge Gruzinski has spoken about the "baroque planet," whose very extensive specter would embrace, in a unifying and significant gesture, the grotesque and the sublime, the original centrality and its peripheral modalities, the
manifestations of Humanism and the hybridity that characterizes the processes
of transculturation. Gruzinski locates the baroque phenomenon within the extensive framework of "world transculturations" that in America's case are initiated with the "discovery." The artistic nomadism, connected to the imperial
expansions of the sixteenth and seventeenth centuries, is part of the processes
of transculturation that constitute early stages of globalization: "This premodern order, that has made us forget the triumph of the nation-states, is the origin
of the baroque planet, its paradoxes and ambiguities" (Gruzinski, "El planeta
barroco" 116). Hybrid and *mestizo* elements, which act as cultural interventions of Eurocentric modernity, create "the appearance of a planetary language"
(Gruzinski, *El pensamiento mestizo* 40) that baroque reappearances reaffirm
and reformulate through the epochs.

In this direction, the critics have persisted in identifying the lines of expansion of the Baroque which, aside from its canonical manifestations, extends
transgressively through the most diverse mediations, creating a series of endless
cultural flows that run across different media.[9] The Baroque appears in many
different forms of symbolic and cultural production that converge on the global
market. It can be seen in representations as diverse as the visual proliferation
of Peter Greenaway and the compositive pastiche of Cindy Sherman, liturgical
rituals and religious festivities, the representational exuberance that saturates
public spaces and the decorative twists and turns that configure modern urban
life and bourgeois intimacy. Other scenarios that have also been catalogued as
baroque are, for instance, the dense settings of Luchino Visconti, the churrigueresque language—the horror of silence—of Cantinflas, Hollywood extrava-

ganzas, magical realism, kitsch—which Calinescu recognized as one of the "five faces of modernity"—and the "Eden-like industry" (Monsiváis) where tapestries and folkloric artifacts offer to the consumer of the "popular" the aesthetic value of what is *dissimilar* as the paradigmatic expression of what in every culture is, in a final analysis, *differential* and not transferable. Finally, in the settings of postmodernity, the Baroque is inserted in the virtuality of cyberspace, which saturates with the obscenity of over-representation and extreme availability of messages, and with the multiple temporalities that modernity had ordered in a historical, linear, progressive, teleological course, and that now are displaced and endlessly rearticulated in a communicative carnivalization.

My research turns away, nevertheless, from the mere registry of the epiphenomenal dispersion of the Baroque in the diversity of cultures. In a study that follows a direction different to the one I am proposing here, Omar Calabrese, for example, illustrating the aforementioned interpretations of the Baroque, has analyzed the ample field of formal and compositive moments that would make it possible to understand the Neobaroque as a "sign of the times." In *Neobaroque: A Sign of the Times*, Calabrese alludes to the Neobaroque as an "aesthetic of repetition" that would characterize the "contemporary taste binding objects and phenomena that go from the natural sciences up to phenomena of mass communication, from art products to everyday habits" (xi). The Neobaroque covers, in his analysis, an ample specter that includes from chaos theory and the theory of catastrophe to the experiences of consumption and some specific philosophical elaborations of contemporary times. Therefore, all the fields of knowledge and cultural phenomena would be united, according to Calabrese, by a recurrent *motif* that confers to them an *air of familiarity* supported on the common traits of instability, polydimensionality, and change (xii). Calabrese calls *neobaroque* that substantial *form* that underlies the representational disparity of culture, and that functions as a principle of "abstract organization of phenomena, governing the system of its internal relations" (xiii).[10] The suggestive study of Calabrese dismisses, in a radical manner, the historicity and contingency of all cultural production in order to establish a transmediatic and transcultural perspective that approximates phenomena and fields of knowledge that, in fact, are only related by their semiotic behavior and their contemporaneity. It is as if the advent of postmodernity had resulted in the spontaneous reappearance of formal and conceptual reactivations that, for some reason never explained, became particularly popular and efficient in the task of capturing and re-presenting the spirit of the times. Calabrese distances himself explicitly from all possible historification of the (neo) Baroque, indicating that the adoption of the term is just conventional, a "label" that allows him to qualify his analysis, and to differentiate the phenomena he focuses on the characteristics that have been adjudicated to postmodernity, in the attempt to understand culture, even now, as an organic totality. He clarifies, in this sense, that "it is not a question of going back to the Baroque" (xii). He is, instead, identifying a recurrence (a relapse or *retombée* in the sense used by Sarduy and recovered by Calabrese [11]).[11] He refers, then, not so much to a *style* or a form of *sensibility*, but to a *cultural behavior* that interconnects, in diverse contexts, varied and heterogeneous textualities, from science to art. The interpretative strategy of Calabrese is only possible from the total abstraction and universalization of the features that he identifies as inherent traits of baroque aesthetics (which he characterized as a "spirit of the epoch"). He does not propose to problematize the ideological value of those operations of aesthetic reappropriation—just to register and interpret them synchronically.

My intention here is, rather, to understand baroque relapses taking into consideration the processes by which American societies were introduced to the dominant paradigms of Occidentalism during the first modernity, which corresponds to the period of viceregal consolidation in the "New World," when a *differentiated* social consciousness crystallized within Creole society. It is clear that the case of the Baroque challenges the critical strategies that associate established forms of collective sensibility and symbolic representation with the particulars of a specific historical-political moment. The dissemination of the Baroque confronts us, rather, with the challenge of interpreting transhistorical reappearances of representational paradigms that connect with foundational cultural and ideological matrices of historical consciousness. In this sense, the history of the Baroque implies an unfinished series of aesthetic accounts, an always renovated succession of symbolic and allegorizing narratives that cover the cultural history of Latin America with an obsessive recurrence. From that highly formalized repertory which, at the same time, presents an overflowing abundance of subject matters and formal representational strategies, these *accounts* interrogate—interpellate—the different stages of continental development. These *accounts* pose questions that point to the relation between subject, power, and representation, to the *possible* agency that neocolonial subjects can develop in the context of modernizing projects, and to the possibilities of articulation of utopian and emancipatory spaces within diverse social and political contexts characterized by the fragmentation of the public sphere.[12]

Starting with a critical revision of what we could call *the question of the Baroque*, this study attempts, then, to provide some basis for an understanding of the proliferating disseminations of the Baroque: its aesthetic and ideological ubiquity and its constant processes of re-signification at different symbolic and

cultural levels. In fact, we could begin by posing a series of critical interroga-
tions: What parameters of aesthetic and ideological evaluation should one turn
to in the effort to understand the tormented art—the "creative leprosy"—of
Aleijadinho, or the artistic syncretism of the mulatto Juan Correa, or the Indian
Kondori, generally quoted as examples of subaltern appropriations of baroque
aesthetics? How does one explain, from the perspective of postcolonial theory,
and in the particular case of Latin America, the reappearances of an aesthetic
style of imperial origin that reemerges in the context of the Cuban Revolution,
is reaffirmed in the settings of the post-dictatorships in the Southern Cone, and
is reinstalled in the fragmented settings of postmodernity, with all the formal
and ideological variations that correspond to these diverse historical contexts?
What sense does one assign to the reinscriptions of that particular art of writing and imagery in projects so dissimilar like the ones by Alejo Carpentier,
José Lezama Lima, Severo Sarduy, Luis Rafael Sánchez, Néstor Perlongher,
Marossa di Giorgio, and Pedro Lemebel? How does one read the innumerable
gravitations of the critics toward the baroque paradigm? How does one interpret the Peronist and Lacanian Osvaldo Lamborguini who "turns into Baroque
or messes up" ("embarroca o embarra," Perlongher 27) the preserved space of
Argentinean writing by reterritorializing in it an archaic, dissonant, and remote
literary style? How does one understand current trends that transfer to the visual scenarios of our globalized postmodernity, techniques already explored by
American artists since the seventeenth century, now recovered with the purpose
of channeling, for instance, the sensibility of an "anomalous"—*in-between*—
Latin culture in the United States, thus representing a transnationalized, decentered, *out of place* post-identity—which will be, in turn, reterritorialized as
simulacrum and pastiche in the allegorizing and symbolic space open by the
Ultrabaroque?

Obviously, the heterogeneity presented by these cultural products requires
an updated and flexible concept of art and culture. In this sense, it is worth
remembering that since the works of Alejo Carpentier, the conception of the
Baroque as utopian convergence of heteroclite elements resulted, in the first
place, in the relativistic reevaluation of Eurocentric and humanistic centralism,
and, secondly, in the vindication of America as an-*other* nucleus of the Western
civilization, which was supposed to generate new meanings and incorporate the
idea of *difference* into the concept of cultural identity. This is a nucleus, then,
that generates forms of expression and representation that reveal new epistemologies constituting an alternative to the dominant ones, which have survived
the ups and downs of modernization since the beginning of colonial times. A
second effect resulting from this conception of the Baroque as a space of ar-

ticulation of dissimilar elements was the redefinition of both the concept of art and the notion of originality and aesthetic transcendence that are traditionally associated with it. All production is in the Neobaroque—*re*-production—and every art product is an artifact. Severo Sarduy acknowledged in his definition of the *Baroque*, that in this style, author and work are refunctionalized. In the process of de-auratization of art, *the copy* (which has been seen as one of the characteristic procedures present in the formation of neocolonial imaginaries) is not inferior to the original, but is rather situated in its own self-supporting epistemological space.[13]

The Neobaroque is not, in this sense, a *creative* art, but an *art of citation*. Recycling, pastiche, fragmentation, and simulacrum intervene the territory of cultural and historical memory, and reactivate it in combinations that are, at the same time, evocative and parodic. The Neobaroque gives momentum to the expansion of the concept of art, until it covers from textures and monuments of nature to the mobile sculptures by Alexander Calder and the *ready-made* by Marcel Duchamp, as it was noticed by Carlos Rincón in his studies on the genealogy of magic realism. Both pre-Hispanic art and Orientalism, the popular craftwork as well as "high" bourgeois culture, ecological elements as well the legacies of "ethnic" cultures, are not organized in the Neobaroque from the perspective of an *aesthetic of shock* which is typical of surrealism, but through processes of articulation that explore the conditions of possibility for the vindication of *dissimilarity*, i.e., of art products where the constituting elements interconnect in productive and unseen simultaneity. This new function of the aesthetic product that the "dialectic sensibility" of Carpentier recognizes (Rincón, "La poética" 28) makes it possible to explore, from another perspective, the relations between dominant and dominated cultures or, in other words, the dynamics between hegemony and subalternity. It also allows us to understand the production and reception of art as a tense process of continuous rediscovery and re-appropriation of imaginaries that coexist and struggle in the heterogeneous modernity of Latin America.

3. Modernity, Negativity, and the Baroque "Machine of Subjectivization"

Facing the challenge that the recurrences of the Baroque present to us—and referring here to both the representational persistence of this style and the constant gravitations of literary and artistic criticism toward this concept—it has been frequently suggested that the term *Baroque* has experienced, with time, a semantic erosion. According to some critics, the term should be reserved to refer to the "purest" content of the word, the one that closely attaches it to post-Renaissance historicity and artistic production. Consequently, posterior reappearances of the Baroque are considered a banal and ludic perpetuation of an archaic aesthetics. In some cases, the Baroque is associated also with the ideas of decadent affectation, expressive depletion, and representational crisis. Jorge Luis Borges, for example, points out: "I would say that the Baroque is that style that deliberately exhausts (or wants to exhaust) its possibilities and that verges on its own caricature [. . .] I would say that the Baroque is the final stage of all art when this art exhibits and dilapidates its means" (9). The Baroque—or rather, here, the baroque style—is the expression of the limit: an expressivity situated at the abyss of irrepresentability, a language that looks toward silence.

In any case, it is obvious that the cultural-historical expansion of the Baroque and its capacity for aesthetic and ideological reformulation have constituted, through the centuries, a phenomenon that has put to the test—and sometimes, has gone beyond—traditional interpretative strategies that explore the correspondences—both punctual and mediated—between certain historical periods and specific aesthetic expressions. It is exactly that excessive quality which has made the critics gravitate toward the imperial imaginaries of the seventeenth century, suggesting that the new versions of Baroque aesthetics can only be understood as the result of vacating original models of their cultural and historical meaning. The Neobaroque would constitute, thus, from this perspective, a parodic, mannerist, and anachronic gesture traumatically fixed in the transcultured origin of societies dominated three centuries ago by European imaginaries.

In my opinion, the recurrences of the Baroque would require an analysis that, without de-historizing the processes of symbolic production and without sacrificing its various degrees and forms of socio-cultural materiality, would allow for an understanding of the continuous dialogue that the baroque aesthetics establishes not just with specific historical-political moments within the processes of consolidation of political and cultural power in Latin America, but rather—as I pointed out before—with wider and more basic cultural and ideological matrices that run across different periods of continental history. I am thinking, in particular, about the categories of *modernity* and *coloniality*, that could provide a solid point of departure for an exhaustive diachronic study of Latin America's cultural history.[14]

Concurrently, when bringing up the concept of *negativity* in relation to the processes of modernization and with respect, also, to an aesthetics that, like the one of Baroque/Neobaroque, is associated with diverse stages of development in Latin America, I not only refer to the effects of inhibition and cancellation of subaltern imaginaries that derive from the transculturating practices in colonial times. I also refer to the photographic *negative*, which reveals in a preliminary and ghostly manner the object of representation.[15] In respect to the first point, Maravall himself points out aspects of negativity in multiple manifestations of the peninsular Baroque. He makes reference, for instance, to social scenarios characterized by urban development and massive populations, where cities are the generating and disseminating nuclei of modernity. He alludes, for example, to the forms of urban and massive anonymity in the seventeenth century and to the loss of individual freedom (to the correlative acquisition, for example, of forms of *"negative* freedom or exemption of controls" [257, my emphasis]) that lead individuals to experiences of violence and feelings of melancholy. In the colonies, one could find innumerable examples of "negative freedom" and cultural devastation, which are the obvious consequences of the colonizing experience. With respect to the second point, in America the appropriations or co-optations of the Baroque, which result from processes of re-signification of hegemonic models of representation and social recognition, constitute a productive instance in which, as in a photographic *negative,* the existence of peripheral imaginaries is gradually revealed.

My suggestion here is that in America the Baroque channels through its belligerent, emancipatory, and vindicative quality—which I have analyzed in my studies on the Baroque of the Indies—forms of *disjunction* and *disruption* of modern consciousness. In this sense, I believe that the archaic quality channeled through the aesthetics of the Neobaroque functions as an efficient interrupter of the discourses that regulate and express the "incomplete" emancipation of modernity—if we want to adopt here, provisionally, a Habermasian perspective—through the different stages of integration of Latin America in globalized modernity. *Interruption*, but also *interpellation*—through the strategies of verbal and visual allegorization—de-naturalize the series of mass-produced messages that modernity administers as part of the plan of homogenization and centralization instituted in America since the so-called period "of viceregal stabilization" to the present.

This interpretation would require, at some point, a critical exploration of the applicability that sociohistorical analysis would have nowadays, in the particular case of Latin America. As it is well known, these positions efficiently canonized, at some point, the Hispanic Baroque as a hegemonic, aesthetic and ideological paradigm—as an *organic* model—of Spanish monarchical absolutism in its peak of imperial expansion in the seventeenth century. From this perspective, critics are prone to perpetuate a historicist—and diffusively *dependentist* interpretation—of the Neobaroque in the post (or neo) colonial context that corresponds to an "emancipated" Latin America. It is worth remembering that José Antonio Maravall himself, the highest exponent of that critical orientation—perhaps in order to preserve the purity of his centralist cultural analysis—never incorporated in his studies on the "culture of the Baroque" its colonial manifestations. Nevertheless, he recognizes the incorporating capacity of the baroque paradigm. In his opinion, the Baroque behaves as a hegemonic ideology with the capacity to celebrate the established power as well as to integrate its "outlying areas" and channel, in several ways, the resistances that imperial power generated on "the ones down below." As indicated by Maravall when analyzing the eminently urban (and in its way, modernizing) orientation of "the culture of the Baroque," in Spanish seventeenth century:

> los poderosos habitan [en la ciudad] y desde ella promueven el desarrollo de una cultura barroca en defensa de sus intereses; los de abajo se incorporan al medio urbano, los unos porque favorece sus posibilidades de protesta [. . .], los otros porque es allí donde los resortes culturales del Barroco les presentan vías de integración. (267)

> (those in power lived in the city and from there, promoted the development of a baroque culture in defense of their own interests; those down below were incorporated into the urban milieu, some because it favored their possibilities of protest [. . .], others because that was where the cultural mechanisms of the Baroque presented them with means of integration.)

It will be precisely that incorporating capacity—that Maravall registers even though he does not foster it as a possible form of countercultural agency—that will allow the heterodox appropriation of the Baroque in America, as well as the factor that will catalyze, through the crevices of dogma and the fissures of its monumentalizing exhibitionism, the co-opting of the canonical model in the colonial world.

In its Janus-like character, the American Baroque constitutes precisely the *performance* that is correlative to the complex network of negotiations that take place in America between hegemony and subalternity, between autochthonous cultures and European traditions, between mimesis and mimicry, between power and desire, exploring—and exploiting—the *negative productivity* of that dominant representational aesthetics from the perspective of stratified subalternization. It is interesting to note how the reappearances of the Baroque after the colonial period will obsessively return to that *negativity* that already exists in the foundational stages of formation of Creole identity, re-presenting the contradictions that accompany the rising of American societies from the beginning. It is precisely from the point of departure of this conflictive dynamics that is inherent to situations of colonial and neocolonial domination—which the Neobaroque tirelessly re-presents—that the American subject articulates itself to the successive modernizing instances that have been imposed, with reiterated alternation of promise and disenchantment, all throughout the cultural history of Latin America.

In the effort to make sense of the insistent reappearances of this imperial aesthetics in the scenarios of Latin American modernity, critics have attempted to interpret baroque recurrences in different ways. In some cases, they have essentialized the phenomenon; in other cases, they have interpreted it in a romantic, stereotypical, and individualistic manner. Nevertheless, these readings have been able to discover in the syncretic, radical nature of the Neobaroque, a creative response to the Eurocentric homogenizing drive that has characterized Latin American neocolonial history. Let us make reference to some of the landmarks of that elaboration.

In his studies on the American Baroque, mainly in *La expresión americana* (1957), José Lezama Lima reflects on the topic of continental identity taking as a point of departure the poetics of Góngora—which Lezama incorporates into his own creative style—that is, following in the footsteps of the Hispanic tradition and its transatlantic reverberations. He begins with the experiences of appropriation of the Baroque by Creole *letrados* who, by conquering the technologies of baroque representation, achieve a participating insertion in the dominant culture. Lezama proposes the image of the "señor barroco" (American baroque gentleman) as a paradigm of the transculturating instances that run across—and counteract, in their own way—the "tumult of the conquest" (230). For Lezama, the "triumph of the city" is, as for Maravall, the social and political phenomenon that creates the conditions of possibility for the installation of a symbolic "order." Lezama assimilates this order with the American capacity of overcoming through culture, the irrationality of the colonialist depredation. For the Cuban writer, the protagonists—or we could say, perhaps, the agonists of that order—are, on one extreme, the Creole artist or *letrado*, that appropriates the instruments that metropolitan culture provides, and then subverts them by converting them in identitary technologies who allow him/her to represent, with the language of the colonizer, American *accidentalism* (e.g., Sor Juana, Sigüenza y Góngora, Domínguez Camargo, etc.). In the other extreme, and following an impulse of culturalist romantization, Lezama turns his focus toward the American "plutonism" that merges the *organic* fragments of European repertories into the metamorphozised, anomalous, hybrid, *Barroco mestizo*.[16] The Indian Kondori represents, for Lezama, the "Hispano-Incaic" side of this production. In an exercise of Quechua-Spanish syncretism, Kondori installs in the facades of the churches of Potosi his hieratical figures of Incaic princesses that colonized the visual archive of the Peninsular missionary Baroque. In Brazil, the "creative leprosy" of the Afro-Brazilian Aleijadinho illustrates in turn the "Hispano-Negroid" synthesis (Lezama Lima 245) with sculptures and altars that populate stealthily the city of Ouro Prêto and its surroundings, during the mythic nights in which the creating spirit triumphs over the body corroded by sickness and colonial marginalization. The American Baroque is, then, according to Lezama, a repository in which the living forces of an inexpugnable cultural spirit are lodged. In this scenario, baroque aesthetics constitutes an alternative time-space, a "puro recomenzar" (pure starting over, Lezama Lima 232), a "plenary" form that although emerges from an original negativity, is not a "degenerative" modality but an efficient combination in which *tension* and *plutonism* are conjugated (meaning, *tension* as the expression of conflicts of power and epistemic struggle but, for Lezama, also *plutonism* as the synthesis that unifies, through the creative fire, dispersed fragments of meaning [229]). In his reading of the origin of American consciousness, Lezama considers the saturation of signs as a phenomenon of fusion that exceeds the underlying indigenous, African, or Peninsular traditions, in order to propose in its place a synthesis that is much more than the sum of its parts. Nevertheless, in this exercise Lezama discovers, on the one hand, a teleology ("an impulse turned toward the form, in search of the finality of its symbol" [Lezama Lima 231]) and, on the other hand, "the effort, as Dionysian as dialectic, of incorporating the world, of making the exterior world his own, through the transmutative furnace of assimilation" (235). But the Cuban writer takes just a marginal look at the conflictive political nature of those operations, at the economic structures that make those operations possible, and at the cultural matrices through which the symbolic and material domination of the American world are exerted. He sets aside, then, the agency of the colonized subjects who exist in several degrees of marginality (Creole, Indian, or Afro-American) and who are able, each one of them from his/her own specific epistemological and socio-cultural *locus*, of carrying out the appropriation and re-signification of acquired models as part of the dynamics of transculturation.

In any case, for Lezama Lima, the "counterconquest" of the American Baroque—that takes up again Weisbach's idea of the "baroque as art of the Counter Reformation"—consists of reversing the constitutive negativity of the *Barroco de Estado* (Baroque of the State) referred to by Maravall. But, what is more important, Lezama Lima notices in the reappearances of the Baroque renovated attempts to establish a dialogue with the Eurocentric *grand nar-*

ratives taking precisely, as a point of departure, the archaic, transhistorical, and disruptive impulses of colonial Baroque.[17] The (Neo)baroque is proposed, then, paradoxically, not only as a mimetic impulse, but also as the aesthetics of (dis)integration: an expressive form that is essentially agglutinative and hybridized, and, at the same time, an art that, by evoking the origins of the imperial appropriation, explores the drama of colonialism and the possibilities of dis-aggregation and divergence—of de-totalization and fragmentation—of the models that represent absolute power and dogmatic truth.

Alejo Carpentier would undertake, on his part, a similar and at the same time differentiated search from the one that Lezama Lima carries out in *La expresión americana* and in his narrative, particularly in *Paradiso* (1966). The telluric and "ontological Baroque" of Carpentier (Moulin-Civil 1650 n. 5) persists, in the footsteps of Eugenio D'Ors, in the attempt to vindicate a beginning without origin, a continuity that farther away from the catastrophes of colonization, would allow a reading of the continental history as universal history or, better yet, as the history of multiple convergent universes, truthfully transnational and wishfully transhistorical:

> Nuestro arte siempre fue barroco: desde la espléndida escultura precolombina y el de los códices, hasta la mejor novelística actual de América, pasando por las catedrales y monasterios coloniales de nuestro continente [. . .] No temamos, pues, al barroquismo en el estilo, en la visión de los contextos, en la visión de la figura humana enlazada por las enredaderas del verbo y de lo ctónico, metida en el increíble concierto angélico de cierta capilla (blanco, oro, vegetación, revesados, contrapuntos inauditos, derrota de lo pitagórico) que puede verse en Puebla de México o de un desconcertante, enigmático árbol de la vida, florecido de imágenes y de símbolos, de Oaxaca. No temamos al barroquismo, arte nuestro, nacido de árboles, de leños, de retablos y altares, de tallas decadentes y retratos caligráficos y hasta neoclasicismo tardíos, barroquismo creado por la necesidad de nombrar las cosas. (Carpentier, "Problemática" 32–33)

> (Our art has always been baroque: from the splendid pre-Columbian sculpture and that of the codices, to the best current Latin American novel, through the colonial cathedrals and monasteries of our continent. [. . .] Let us not fear, then, the use of the Baroque in different styles, in the vision of scenarios or human figures bound by the bindweeds of the verb and of what is *ctónico*, fitted in the incredible angelic concert of a certain chapel (white, gold, vegetation, intricate, unprecedented counterpoints, defeat of all that is Pythagorean) as it can be seen in Puebla, Mexico or in an enigmatic, disconcerting tree of life, flourished in images and symbols from Oaxaca. Let us not fear the baroque style, an art that is ours, born out of trees, out

of wood, out of retables and altars, out of decadent carvings and calligraphic portraits and even late neoclassicism, baroque style created by the necessity to assign a name to things.)

In *Concierto barroco* (1974), a work inspired on the opera by Antonio Vivaldi titled *Motezuma,* first performed in Venice in 1733, Carpentier puts in practice those theoretical principles, creating in the spectacular setting of language and phonetics, an impossible alliance where music and words, literature and history, modernity and pre-modernity are conjugated vertiginously. The text synchronizes and juxtaposes the cultural times and spaces of America and Europe, to exhibit the products of the bourgeois modernity saturated with merchandise and melancholy. Vivaldi's operatic Moctezuma overcomes the dimension of myth, becoming only an anachronistic mask (a sign *out of place*) that the Baroque convokes in order to explore the crossroads between "high" and popular culture, between the pre-Hispanic and the modern, emphasizing a utopian unity of heteroclite elements that supports Carpentier's uncompromising Americanism. *Concierto barroco* proposes a harmonious combination of dissimilar elements, a *"pluri*versality" (as opposed to *"uni*versality") that makes it possible to integrate times, spaces, and cultural forms-epistemologies-in order to establish a Latin American utopia that is summarized in the words that the author puts in the Master's mouth, at the end of the work: "The future is fabulous."

In a more complex way, in Severo Sarduy, the neobaroque carnivalization becomes simulacrum, transvestism, and an affirmative performance of *difference*. It constitutes, at the same time, a process that transforms the negativity of what is missing—the lack, the desire, the abnormality—in original impulse, in the *locus* of the initial suppression/repression that can be hyperbolically filled with meaning and saturated with signs.[18] In his cosmological-linguistic conception of the Baroque as the Big-Bang—the explosion from which a new universe is created out of primordial emptiness—the image of the ellipse is recovered. This image suggests a deformed circle with two centers, one of which looks displaced, challenging the perfection of circularity, of an organized world that rotates around one unique nucleus that capitalizes the production of energy and meanings. This elliptic image could evoke the diagram of an imperial culture that is projected, in imperfect duplicity, in overseas peripheries, i.e., it could be interpreted as an allegorical—baroque reflection on that which is created in America departing from an initial emptiness: a movement of expansion and replica, mimesis and mimicry that inscribe in an irregular-differential-manner and dominant imaginaries in the imagination of dominated subjects. In this way the baroque word and imagery hide and at the same time attract attention on the silence that precedes them. The whiteness of the page challenges and frames the writing that occupies it. The baroque object hides and ratifies the subject that creates it. The explosion of the sign gives origin to a new focus that packs space and time with meaning. The Baroque is a "proliferating focus" of infinite expansion that metaphorically names what lacked denomination and qualifies the indescribable. The baroque *meaning* is figurative, catachrestic, transitional, spurious, and anamorphic.

But in the theorization and in the writing practice of Severo Sarduy, the materiality of the baroque language reaches the transvestite materiality of the body and its attires. In the metamorphoses of his characters and in the eternal return of their intertwined and fragmented vicissitudes, the subject is deterritorialized (it loses its "existential territories" [Guattari 20], its identity of gender, its cultural, primordial roots), articulating unknown subject positions—that we could call *post-identitary*—in a pastiche that resembles the definitive exile of the subject from the certainties provided by modernity. "Poetics of deterritorialization, the Baroque always clashes and runs a preconceived and subduing limit" (Perlongher, "Prólogo" 20). In *Cobra* (1972) the simulacrum forever loses its contact with the original. The body is tortured and forced, an exceeding and insufficient evocation of an "original" form lost forever. *Maitreya* (1978) and *Cobrí* (1988) are also abundant in deformity and excess. The tortured, tattooed, monstrous bodies are in constant metamorphosis; they are vainly sacrificial and conceited (in this sense, they are at the same time excessive and residual, as the baroque pearl). Sarduy's essay writing as well as his narrative (characterized by Castañón as "erotic summary" [1647]) are an organized effort to counter Eurocentric universalism with a "pluriversal" vision. As Castañón puts it, "the body of the universe demands an integral reading that is also sensible and intellectually faithful to its essential polyformism" (1647). Heterogeneity and plurality are articulated in a constant process of rewriting, where the word questions itself and is constantly reformulated, dispersing and multiplying its meanings, canceling all possible forms of consensus and epistemological stability. The Neobaroque no longer encircles, as the copy/original of seventeenth century, "a buried truth" (Picón Salas 123), but dramatizes uncertainty and dis-identity; the word is neither a symbol nor yields to metaphorical strategies or mutations of meaning: it is only sign, impulse, and sound. What greater disbelief than this could have been orchestrated with respect to the supposed transparency and communicability of language as the rational instrument that allows to structure the social experience in the liberal and dependent modernity of Latin America? What greater dissidence with respect to the project of creating a "new" language (for a "new man"), one that could socialize and regulate the traffic of meaning as part of the Cuban socialist alternative? What more punctual effort could have been carried out from the trenches of literature to vindicate the *difference* in the categorized world of modernity, a world based on mechanics of exclusion and on the perpetuation of coloniality, based on the application of reductive binaries (subject/object, feminine/masculine, private/public, power/desire)?

With "cosmological" and Lacanian support, Sarduy's concept of the Baroque defends the idea of plural and polyphonic post-identities, but locates these constructions outside of history and beyond the specificity of culture, that is to say, beyond all referentiality and beyond all organized social projects. As González-Echevarría concludes in a final analysis, for Sarduy, "Cuba is a text" (*Celestina's Brood* 237). Modernity operates, then, as an initial, primordial explosion, that by exposing its negativity, leaves an open and infinite space for the manifestation of subjectivities that exist "in a relation either of contiguity or delimitation with respect to an alterity that is also subjective" (Guattari 20) The Baroque is re-functionalized, then, as a "machine of subjectivization" that counteracts the "war machine" of postcolonial modernity: subjectivity is polyvocal and composed of multiple strata that cover and exceed language, and that propose "collective agencies," *ritornellos*, and "small social rhythms" that exist disseminated in *the social*—in the social *body*. In other words, those dispersed and fragmented forms of collective subjectivity have found an alternative habitat eluding the settled, institutionalized existence within the regulated and structured spaces of *society* (Guattari, "La producción de subjetividad" 9).

In one way or another, the topic of the crisis of modern subjectivity run across all elaborations related to the Neobaroque. This aesthetics is interpreted then, as a proposal of *utopian,* non-programmatic nature, where the saturation of signs would point to a reconstitution of matrices that generate meanings that could promote unknown forms of perception of social and *political* levels. In an attempt to define the "conditions of a desiring cartography"—of the kind that could derive from the poetics of the Neobaroque—Néstor Perlongher alludes to post-identitary phenomena that exceed the limits of modernity, characterizing them as "Dionysian groupings [that exist] in the lustful darkness of the metropolis" ("Los devenires" 14), and remind us of the settings and anecdote that appear, for example, in the urban chronicles of Pedro Lemebel. According to Perlongher, those minority movements—related to conflicts of race, class sexuality, etc.—constitute phenomena that could be interpreted "from the point of view of the mutation of collective existence [since] they would be indicating launching, experimenting 'counter-cultural,' dissident, alternative ways of subjectivization" (Perlongher, "Los devenires" 15).

The Neobaroque renders a diagnosis on the crisis of modern processes of subjectivization and depletion of its correspondent identity politics and, at the same time, proposes a proliferating expansion of *difference* (even if we face the risk, as Jameson warned some time ago, that *difference* may turn into the new postmodern *identity*). As a "desiring cartography," the aesthetics of the Neobaroque does not attack either the profound structure of the social order or the epistemological models that legitimize it, but it effectively breaks down its logic and disarticulates its principles. The poetics of the Neobaroque subverts; it does not revolutionize. It is informed, as we mentioned before, by a utopian principle, where the simultaneities of multiple cultural times open a space full of potentialities and common grounds. As the desire that guides it, the poetics of the Neobaroque cannot be prescriptive, nor can it propose to exhaust in its accumulation of signs the infinite possibilities included in the global design of modernity. It proposes, nevertheless, on the basis of the ghostly presence of symbolic commodity that freely circulates in the plural market of cultures, exposing intersections, superimpositions, and reminiscences. From this perspective, the poetics of the Neobaroque could be understood, as Sarduy suggested, as an aestheticized form of *diagnosis*. In this sense, that poetic can only "be a map of the effects of surface, since depth is nothing [. . .] but a fold and a wrinkle of the surface" (Perlongher, "Los devenires" 14). The neobaroque sign does not *re-present*, then, in the sense of *presenting again*, but in the sense of dramatizing, and converting the world in spectacle, performance, and scenography. Society and politics—as defined by modernity—lose thickness and materiality. In their place, the opacity of the linguistic and visual sign suddenly appears, and the proliferation of the signifier calls attention to itself as the last horizon of social (self-) recognition. The Neobaroque sets up in this manner the dissidence, the *difference*, and the fold, saturating the void to make it visible.

4. *Difference*, Ruin, and the Neobaroque "De-Artification"

Paying attention to the countercultural quality of the American Baroque, Irlemar Chiampi proposes that "[i]f the Baroque is the aesthetics of the effects of Counter Reformation, the Neobaroque is that [of] countermodernity" (144–45). For Chiampi,

> [l]os desastres y la *incompletud* de[l] modelo modernizador [implementado a través de la reforma religiosa, la revolución industrial, la revolución democrático-burguesa y la difusión de la ética individualista] [. . .] se ha revelado sobre todo

en su incapacidad para integrar lo "no occidental' (indios, mestizos, negros, proletariado urbano, inmigrantes rurales, etc.) a un proyecto nacional de democracia consensual. No es casual, pues, que sea justamente el Barroco—preiluminista, premoderno, preburgués, prehegeliano—la estética reapropiada desde esta periferia, que sólo recogió las sobras de la modernización, para revertir el canon historicista de lo moderno [. . .] Este contenido ideológico—motivación cultural específica e insoslayable—torna precario todo intento de reducir el neobarroco a un manierismo "retro" y reaccionario—un reflejo de la lógica del capitalismo tardío, conforme sugiere Jameson al mentar el modismo de los "neo" en el arte posmoderno—Tampoco cabe diluirlo en la "atmósfera general," en el "aire del tiempo," como un principio abstracto de los fenómenos [Calabrese], y menos aún tomarlo como la salvación de una modernidad crepuscular, tras la supuesta "muerte de las vanguardias" mediante la "impureza generalizada" con que las culturas que relegaron al Barroco al ostracismo, con su buen gusto clasicista, desean renovar la experimentación y la invención. (145–46)

([t]he disasters and incompleteness of [the] modernizing model [implemented through the religious reform, the industrial revolution, the democratic bourgeois revolution and the diffusion of the individualistic ethics] [. . .] has disclosed above all in its capability to integrate the "non-Western" (Indians, *mestizos*, Blacks, urban proletariat, rural immigrants, etc.) to a national project of consensual democracy. It is not by chance, then, that it is precisely the Baroque—preilluminist, premodern, pre-bourgeois, pre-Hegelian—the aesthetics that is reappropriated from the periphery, that only gathered the scraps of modernization in order to revert the historicist canon of what is modern. [. . .] This ideological content—a specific and inescapable cultural motivation—makes all intent of reducing the Neobaroque to a "retro" (and reactionary) mannerism—look like a precarious attempt, a reflection of the logic of late capitalism, in keeping with the suggestion made by Jameson, when he mentions the idiom of the "neo" in postmodern art. It is neither possible to dilute it in the "general atmosphere," in the the air of time, as an abstract principle of the phenomena [Calabrese], and much less take it as the salvation of a crepuscular modernity, after the supposedly "death of the vanguards" through the "generalized impurity" with which cultures that relegated the Baroque to ostracism, with its good, classicist taste, wish to renovate the experimentation and invention.)

If modernity can be characterized as a model that functions from "hard" identitary concretions, (such as national subject, citizenship, disciplining, progress, gender roles, institutional order, etc.), that dismisses, regulates, or relegates the existence of the *Other*, the baroque or neobaroque intervention would introduce strategies of alteration and detachment in the modernizing imaginaries. I would propose, based on the opacity of languages and representational strate gies, *anomalous* contents (in the etymological sense of *irregularity*), that is to say, an *anti-normativity* that invites to a dismantling—a deciphering—from a new perspective, of aesthetic norms and communicative normativeness.

I propose, in consequence, to think about the Baroque through the notions of *difference* and *ruin* that have been frequently associated with the interpretation of modern aesthetics, and that should be placed at the very center of an aesthetic and ideological deconstruction of baroque paradigms, particularly in its peripheral formulations.

I understand *difference* not only as *qualification of the other with respect to the same*—of alterity with respect to *identity*—(that is, not only as "variety among things of the same species") but also, in the mathematical sense, as *residue* or *remainder* (Corominas 498). Related to this second meaning, the concept of *ruin* refers also to the differential: to what survives and remains in a ghostly existence, out of time and out of place. I refer to *ruin*, then, in the Benjaminian sense in which the illusion of perdurability and the notion of deterioration are combined (ruin, in its primary, etymological meaning of "demolition, collapse," and also in the meaning by which the primitive is recognized as "ruinous, *gone bad*" [Corominas 516, my emphasis]).[19]

For Benjamin, modernity is precisely an experience of loss and collapse, an experience of mourning that recognizes that in the post-sacred world there is no place for ancient monumentalities, which can only exist vainly, as melancholic vestige, as relic that evokes completeness from loss.[20] Art, then, loses—*ruins*—its value of worship, and de-secularizes its transcendence: it realizes its ephemeral quality—its temporary nature—and ritualizes, in the context of modernity, new forms of spectral presence. Alienated from the "here and now" that were conferred to the work of art (from its legitimacy and "organic" functionality), art—to use here an expression of Adorno—de-artificates itself, and becomes artifact, symbolic operator, simulacrum.[21]

In this sense, the baroque codification would be constituted not only as allegorical reproductibility of the conflicts that characterize the insertion in modernity in the post-auratic era, but also as a re-signifying machine of cultural, social, epistemological alterity, and as *performance*—collection of choreographed and allegorical behaviors—of border subjectivities. In some sense, recovery of the Baroque would renovate then in the post-illuminist modernities and the symbolic impulse of the counterconquest alluded by Lezama Lima, finding in the recourse of formal saturation a way of channeling the elements that were never fully absorbed by the narratives of Occidentalism. The Baroque and the Neobaroque are proposed in this way as systems of codification that, through the articulation of several divergent temporalities, cultures, and representational means, concretize—materialize—the constitutive hybridity of the colonial and (neo)(post)colonial subjectivity, inserting that productive—*barrueca*—anomaly of American elements, in the variegated and multilayerd mixture of language or imagery. It is in that sense that Carpentier indicated that "every symbiosis, every *mestizaje* engenders a Baroque style," and that in an interpretation no just culturalist but materialist, Bolívar Echeverría speaks of the *baroque ethos* as a specific *way*—a social behavior, a semiotics—that makes it possible "to internalize capitalism in the spontaneity of everyday life" (*Modernidad, mestizaje cultural* 20). In this way, he conceives this aesthetics as a constructing principle that does not accept or join "the capitalist fact," but keeps it always as "unacceptable and alien" (20). Therefore, the Baroque, as the first manifestation of the modern *ethos,* emerges and re-functionalizes itself "in the tendency of modern civilization to revitalize, time and again, the code of the Western European tradition after each destructive wave coming from the capitalist development" (21). According to Echeverría, "it is Baroque the manner of being modern that makes it possible to experience the destruction of what is qualitatively produced by capitalistic productivism, by converting it in the access to the creation of another dimension, challengingly imaginary, of what is qualitative" (21). In this way, even though the baroque *ethos* constitutes, from these positions, a "strategy of radical resistance" it is not, in any way, *revolutionary*. In the words of Echeverría,

> La actualidad de lo barroco no está, sin duda, en la capacidad de inspirar una alternativa radical de orden político a la modernidad capitalista que se debate actualmente en una crisis profunda; ella reside en cambio en la fuerza con que manifiesta, en el plano profundo de la vida cultural, la incongruencia de esta modernidad, la posibilidad y la urgencia de una modernidad alternativa. (*La modernidad de lo barroco* 15)

> (The current standing of the Baroque is, without a doubt, not based on its capacity to inspire a radical alternative to political order in capitalist modernity which is currently undergoing a profound crisis; it resides, rather, in the strength with which it expresses, in the profound level of cultural life, the incongruity of this modernity, the possibility and the urgency of an alternative modernity.)

The specific *type* of baroque radicality is concentrated, then, at the level of the imaginaries, providing not a direct attack to the social, political, and economic foundations of the modern system, but a peformative *exposé*—dramatized, carnivalized—of the discursive and representational staging of modernity, a parody of its language and gestuality. According to Sarduy:

Ser barroco hoy significa amenazar, juzgar, parodiar la economía burguesa, basada en la administración tacaña de los bienes, en su centro y fundamento mismo: el espacio de los signos, el lenguaje, soporte simbólico de la sociedad, garantía de su funcionamiento, de su comunicación. (Quoted by Echeverría, *La modernidad de lo barroco* 16)

(To be baroque today means to threaten, judge, parody the bourgeois economy based on the stingy administration of goods, at its very center and foundation: the space of signs, the language, the symbolic support of society, guarantee of its functioning, of its communication.)

The notion of the baroque *ethos* as a form of alternative representation of modern subjectivity is reintroduced and reinforced also from the sociological perspective. Boaventura de Souza Santos associates narrowly the baroque *ethos* with what he recognizes as the two central crises of modernity: the "crisis of the practice and thought of social regulation" and "the crisis of the practice and [emancipatory] thought"(313). According to the Portuguese sociologist, modernity has led to the convergence of these two *critical* forms that he explains in the following manner:

Por ejemplo, la soberanía del Estado nacional—fundamental para la modernidad después de 1648—el derecho estatal, el fordismo, el estado de bienestar, la familia heterosexual separada de la producción, el sistema educativo, la democracia representativa, la religión institucional, el canon literario, la identidad nacional, todo esto son formas de regulación social que hoy están en crisis. Pero al mismo tiempo, y en eso reside la originalidad de la situación actual, hoy están igualmente fragilizadas, desacreditadas, debilitadas las formas de emancipación social que le correspondieron hasta ahora a esa modernidad: el socialismo, el comunismo, el cooperativismo, la socialdemocracia, los partidos obreros y el movimiento sindical, la democracia participativa, la cultura popular, la filosofía crítica, los modos de vida alternativos, etc. Mientras que antes, como señalaba, las dos crisis no coincidían, hoy coinciden y, por tanto, esta crisis doble nos muestra que hoy en día la crisis de regulación se alimenta de la crisis de emancipación. (314)

(For example, the sovereignty of the national State—fundamental for modernity after 1648—State law, Fordism, the welfare state, the heterosexual family separated from production, the educational system, the representative democracy, the institutional religion, the literary canon, the national identity, all these are forms of social regulation that today are in crisis. But at the same time, and here lies the originality of the current situation, today the forms of social emancipation that corresponded until now to that modernity are made equally fragile, discredited, debilitated: socialism, communism, cooperativism, the social democracy, the labor parties and union movement, participative democracy, popular culture, critical philosophy, alternative life styles, etc. While before, as I have indicated, the two crises would not coincide, today they do coincide and, therefore, this double crisis shows us that nowadays the crisis of regulation is fed by the crisis of emancipation.)

If social regulation and social emancipation are, as indicated by de Souza Santos, the two pillars of the modern project, and they should have a harmonious development, the convergent crisis of both axes places current societies in what this sociologist calls a "paradigmatic transition," similar, somehow, to the one that is produced in the seventeenth century—in the baroque century—in which epistemological struggles are settled (between Aristotelians and Galileans, Aristotelians and Newtonians, for example, in the field of science), leading to a questioning more and more profound of the certainties that sustained the colonialist, monarchical, and theocentric world. The "diversion," "dramatization," "hyperitualization" of the Baroque would operate as mechanisms through which modern subjectivity would pace the path toward postmodernity.[22]

But there is more. De Souza Santos perceives in the question of the Baroque a conflicting dialogue between South and North, observing in his aesthetics not only a particular and joyful form of representation, but also a transgressive search that re-functionalizes ideological monumentalities, rationalities, and forms of authority and representational authorization, creating from the peripheries of the great systems and through the irreverent appropriation of their codes, an alternative *way of looking*. That "madness of looking" of which Buci-Glucksmann speaks constructs reality from a new perspective, subverting the same canons that served to systematize an image of the world from the platforms of modernity. The baroque *ethos* would function, thus, as a utopian proposal oriented "toward suppressed traditions, subaltern experiences, the perspective of the victims and the oppressed, toward the margins, the peripheries, the borders, toward the South of the North, toward forbidden languages, toward the un-recyclable garbage of our mercantile well-being" (quoted by Echeverría 322). Concepts—the one of Baroque, in this case—migrate and are relocated, temporarily and spatially, defying *from the ruin* (from what remains, from the *differential*) the hard nuclei of historical origin and regulated subjectivity, in a centrifugal flight from the centers of elaboration of mass-produced epistemologies, theories, and symbolic practices, toward utopian horizons of liberation and desire.

The cultures that emerged from the colonizing processes implemented from "weak colonial centers" as Spain and Portugal were at that time, exist, above all, as *border cultures*—Janus-like, *in-between*—and they are characterized by the fluidity, exchanges, and contaminations between diverse cultural paradigms, social projects, and epistemological models, that is, by the hybridity and overcharge of representations that collide and negotiate in the configuration of social practices and cultural imaginaries. The baroque *ethos* de-theorizes reality in order to reconfigure it as utopia. It extremes the limits of colonizing and neocolonial projects, exposes the processes of appropriation and cultural cannibalism in which national cultures are based, and destabilizes the solidity of "strong epistemologies" working from the residual and ruinous—from vestige, from *difference*, from loss and grief, from pastiche and simulacrum—in a disjunctive and disruptive direction with respect to the principles and legacies of modernity. If the *epistemicide* of which de Souza Santos speaks marked mercilessly the colonial and postcolonial history of Latin America, the *codephagia* of which Echeverría refers to (that is, the process "through which the code of the masters transforms itself through the assimilation of the ruins in which the destroyed code survives")[23] opens another avenue for the study of forms of social consciousness and cultural practices in the subcontinent and in its migrant imaginaries.

Then, it would be precisely that utopian matrix that would support and explain, according to the proposals of the Portuguese sociologist, the recurrences of the baroque code and its capacity of re-functionalization, as a response to the contradictions of capitalism and the exclusions of modernity. As de Souza Santos indicates, "if it is true, as Hegel said, that the patience of concepts is great, obviously, the patience of utopia is infinite" (de Souza Santos quoted by Echeverría 331).

5. Ultrabaroque and Globalization

Based on the scenario we have been outlining thus far, the recovered notion of *Ultrabaroque* constitutes a new twist in the history of reappearances of this aesthetics in Latin America. Utilized to designate extreme forms of baroque style, "rococo" or "churrigueresque" mostly in the European context and then mainly in Mexico in the seventeenth century, the notion of "Ultrabaroque" refers to the syncretic phenomena of ornamental oversaturation, evocative of the Peninsular Baroque, which manifests itself mostly in religious art.

In *Divine Excess: Mexican Ultra-Baroque* (1995), Ichiro Ono indicates:

Fused with native American sensibility while absorbing other influences from the sea-trading world that collected in Mexico, the baroque style evolved and commenced to tightly pack the architecture with so much ornamentation that we could describe it as a kind of "gap-ophobia." This is "ultra-baroque," meaning, in other words, the baroque of the baroque. (83)

Some Latin American art historians have preferred, in some instances, rather, denominations that underscore the hybridized and *differential* character of the American forms that penetrate with their cultural uniqueness the imaginary and representational protocols of the master in a kind of visual "counter-conquest." In this way, for example, Teresa Gisbert and José de Mesa choose a nomination that rescues the multicultural and syncretic character of this art form when referring to the Andean Baroque:

Creemos que la arquitectura barroca desarrollada en América se independiza de los moldes europeos a principios del siglo XVIII [. . .] Las palabras "*ultrabarroco*" y "churrigueresco" son insuficientes porque indican formas extremas del barroco europeo, pero no concepciones diferentes. Por esta razón hemos usado el término "mestizo" que [. . .] es el más propio para denominar a una *arquitectura estructuralmente europea, elaborada bajo la sensibilidad indígena.* (Gisbert and de Mesa 255, my emphasis)

(We believe that the baroque architecture developed in America becomes independent from the European molds at the beginning of the eighteenth century [. . .] The words *ultrabaroque* and churrigueresque are insufficient because they indicate extreme forms of the European baroque, but not different conceptions. For this reason, we have used the term *mestizo* that [. . .] is the most appropriate one to designate a *structurally European architecture, elaborated under the indigenous sensibility.*)

Nevertheless, I am interested in focusing here on the reappropriation of the term in current contexts, in which the word "ultrabaroque" acquires new strength through its insertion within *other* contexts, linked to forms of cultural hybridity related to postmodern scenarios. These scenarios are characterized, as it is well known, by the decline of the epistemological certainties that were articulated around concepts of nationhood, identity, citizenship, consensus, progress, and subjectivity, and that guided modernizing projects since the Independence until the decade of the 1980s. Without getting into a radical dissemination of the processes of contemporary "baroquization" nor in the idealization that would attribute this new relapse of the Baroque to a renovated "spirit of the epoch," the Ultrabaroque has been characterized in these new contexts not as a form of expression that abides by definite formal or thematic traits, but as a *disposition* from which it is possible to re-present (to expose, to make intelligible) the processes of transculturation and hybridization that characterize contemporary culture.

Elizabeth Armstrong and Víctor Zamudio-Taylor, curators of the itinerary exposition titled *Ultra Baroque. Aspects of Post-Latin American Art*, and editors of the corresponding catalogue, describe the concept in the following manner:

> [W]e suggest that the baroque is a model by which to understand and analyze the processes of transculturation and hybridity that globalization has highlighted and set into motion. Given this approach, we propose that the baroque, in all its conflictive reception and reinterpretation, *is pertinent today more as an attitude than as a style* and is interdisciplinary (sic) in nature and not restricted to architecture, music, and visual arts, the fields to which it has traditionally been confined. The designation "ultrabaroque" is itself a self-conscious (and intentionally playful) [. . .] [and] suggests a very contemporary, postmodern, exuberant visual culture with inextricable ties to a historical period, style, and narrative. It plays off of the Cuban writer Alejo Carpentier's idea of a "New World Baroque," in which *the European baroque encountered indigenous forms that were also baroque*. The mingling of European and American forms produced an intensified baroque, "a baroque to the second power"—an ultrabaroque. (3, my emphasis)

In the introduction to *Ultra Baroque*, Elizabeth Armstrong characterizes the trans-historical extensions and the reterritorializations of the Baroque as postnational aesthetics: not only as the aesthetic codification that is transferred from European societies to colonial territories—as it happened, at other levels, with the deterritorialized practices of Christianity, mercantilism, or the slave trade—but also as a product that, in its modern and postmodern modulations, appears definitively emancipated from its historical specificities. In this sense, Armstrong refers to the final twist of the Ultrabaroque as a post-Latin American art, which beyond the limitations imposed by national borders and political identities, is inserted in the most current settings, combining local and global impulses:

> [We want] to emphasize our interest in art from Latin America characterized by a postmodern approach to cultural production that is no longer determined by geographical borders and identity politics. Informed by other critical positions engaged in a revision of theory and practices (which are linked to specific rubrics, such as "postfeminist" and "post-Chicano"), this provocative nomenclature reflects the

production of a discourse that can account for artistic expressions driven by local as well as global impulses, that are grounded in historical specificities yet that seek to go beyond them. (Armstrong 5)

The allegorical nature of the Neobaroque convokes in its exacerbated expressivity the politics of citation and the experience of fragmentation, bringing forth as a result products that in its strong syncretism provide "the key to the interpretation of hybridity in the visual culture" and the comprehension of cultural products that reveal the systemic *mestizaje* of Latin America (Zamudio-Taylor 141).

For Serge Gruzinski, the adoption of the Baroque is bound to the internationalization of cultural markets, an effect of the colonizing processes. But what is important is not so much to register that effect as a *necessary* result of European history, but to perceive the significance of cultural hybridizations as counter-Western channels through which new forms of sensibility and new agencies are expressed. The preference for "exotic and novel forms, a taste for the unusual, what is original and what is amazing" (Gruzinski, "El planeta barroco" 117) not only characterizes the Baroque as an *organic* aesthetic and ideological product of the Spanish monarchy and as one of the most prominent expressions of the cultural hegemony of Occidentalism (as a rationalist, bourgeois, and Christian cultural model). It also opens the doors through which subaltern subjectivities colonize dominant imaginaries, while they remain, at the same time, in a constant state of resistance and differentiation. Without a doubt, the negotiations between these new forms of cultural *agency* and the general market of symbolic commodities constitute a complex and frequently contradictory universe of historical and social dynamics. As Gruzinski himself acknowledges, given the current evaluation of the work of American artists, like the Mexican mulatto Juan Correa (c. 1645/1650–1716) or the Afro-Brazilian sculptor Aleijadinho (1738–1814), who are producers of great creations of ecclesiastic Baroque, one is forced to understand their works as a form of submission to the power of the Church and, in general, to the colonizing forces that devastated pre-Hispanic cultures ("El planeta barroco"). Nevertheless, it is in the process and projections of those subaltern appropriations that one should look for the ultimate cultural meaning of the transcultural dynamics. In fact, "[e]ach time that the European paganism allowed the indigenous artist to introduce elements from the Amerindian pantheon, it opened the spaces for the recovery of the indigenous memory" (Guzinski, "El planeta barroco" 120). In that sense, the history narrated by the American baroque production is not only one of colonialization and transculturation, but also one of reciprocal interactions that give place to the expression of *other* epistemologies that force their entrance in the solid, symbolic system of colonialist domination, hybridizing its dogmatic uniqueness.

Evocative and attached to the present, the Ultrabaroque constitutes the most current inflection of a semantics that challenges the rational regulation of art, as well as the representational equilibrium, and the hermeneutic disciplining that go with it. The strategy of the Ultrabaroque is, for the most part, the recovery, de-centering, and re-contextualization of elements that remit to epistemological fractures associated with the crisis of modernity, and with the advent of cultural forms of subjectivization affected by mass-media transformations and de-auritization of humanistic discourses. If the Baroque is defined by its nomadism and its constant aesthetic and ideological re-functionalization, that is, for its constant re-settlement in new existential territories, the Ultrabaroque would constitute the symbolic enclave of our time and our circumstance, where the borders between the two Americas are gradually diluted in processes of exchange and identity reformulation. At the same time, the Ultrabaroque pretends to bear witness to—to *re*-present—the fact that this porosity of borders does not invalidate, but in fact accentuates and tends to naturalize not just the existence of cultural *differences*, but the social inequalities that continue to be imposed, from North to South, in the context of neo-liberal postmodernity.

In this context of fluid territorialities, reinforcement of hegemonies and cultural resignifications, the Ultrabaroque explores anew the limit of aesthetic codification and representability of transnationalized subjectivities—of post-identities—saturating the global space in an irreverent gesture of counter-conquest of consecrated imaginaries. Zamudio-Taylor considers that this new re-functionalization of the Baroque "offers today, in the era of globalization, the key to the interpretation of hybridity in the visual culture" (141), because it acts as an intervention of the (post)modernizing protocols that have been developing since the colony:

> The legacy of the Iberian colonialism forced the emergent Latin American colonies, particularly Brazil, Cuba and Mexico to negotiate conditions of modernity fed by mannerist and baroque cultures, that translated, transformed and circulated to the European metropolis. In this sense, the baroque problematized the negotiation of modernity in Latin America, and offered a conduit from which its values in conflict and its language were filtered and spilt to postmodernity. (Zamudio-Taylor 141)

In current settings, the Ultrabaroque dramatizes the weakening of the "hard" contents of individual and collective identity: territoriality as the natural site of national cultures; the notion of consumption as principle of democratization and as a privileged form of personal realization and social integration; the belief in the transparency of language as a vehicle of political and social consensus; the pedagogical role of art; and the conception of the work or art as a finished, harmonious, and complete symbolic product. Without ritualism, in the post-sacred era, the Ultrabaroque vindicates the materiality and reproducibility of the work, exerts and maximizes the art of citation (the contents *out-of-place*, the minimization of contextual memory), and puts forward the fragmentation and the impurity of cultural signifiers as some of the basis for post-identity representation. The poetic art of the Ultrabaroque maintains, nevertheless, a historic memory that becomes evident in the appeal to elements that remit to the original violence and that make continuous references to colonialism through the almost obscene exhibition of dismembered bodies or overwhelming spaces, saturated by objects. In other cases, the Ultrabaroque creates ephemeral and melodramatic settings—melancholic, in their own way—which do not resemble the monumentality of the great catafalques or the triumphant arches of the first (baroque) modernity. In fact, as an alternative to the consecrating and museistic orientation that characterizes the canonization of art in that and subsequent modernities, the Ultrabaroque operates, rather, from a more immediate, nontrascendental approach to symbolic representation, emphazising the capacity of art of expressing in a performative manner, fragmentary and even provisional aspects of individual and collective subjectivities.

The Ultrabaroque minimizes the authorial subject but emphasizes the positionality of the gaze, as the principle that organizes experience and self (recognition), in the terms defined by Lacan: "Le baroque c'est la regulation de l'âme par la scopie corporelle" (*Le Seminaire* XX, 105). It is as if from the perspectives of globalization and postmodernity, the irreverent symbolic commodity of the Ultrabaroque would interrogate rhetorically traditions and legacies, analyzing the balance of progress from the savage instances of late capitalism, saturating the transnational space with a *gap-ophobia* that reveals the horror of silence that has followed the death of the *grand narratives*, offering in its place micro-histories that have renounced to philosophic totalization and revolutionary epics. The Ultrabaroque dramatizes, in this manner, in its own way, in times of globalization, neoliberal triumphalism, as well as the reformulation of hegemonies, the realization of having trespassed beyond an epistemological, civilizatory, and representational limit. Its utopia does not consist on the capacity or on the desire of articulating concrete propositions, but in still believing in the efficacy of deconstruction and de-sublimation through art. History is neither circular nor progressive. History is residual; it is *difference* and ruin: it is a fold that returns onto itself, a refolding, and an unfolding; it is *retombée*.

Notes

1. The definitions that reintroduce the idea of the Baroque as pathology of the form give evidence, above all, of the expository place, and the epistemological positionality from which the baroque aesthetics is evaluated. Bolívar Echeverría has indicated in his definition of the baroque *ethos* that "in effect, only from the formal, *classical* perspective, what is baroque can appear as a de-formity; only in comparison to the *realist* form it can result in-sufficient and only with respect to formal *romantic* creationism, it can be seen as conservative." He adds that: "It deals, therefore, under those three groups of descriptors that the post Renaissance art has received, three definitions that, taken in themselves, *tell more about the theoretical place from which it is defined than about what is baroque*, what is mannerist, etcetera. They are definitions that only indirectly make it possible to see what can be constituted as 'baroque'" (Echeverría 23; my emphasis).

2. This work is part of a major project, and for this reason it does not develop in depth some of the proposals that are outlined in this introductory section.

3. I use here the concept of "Ultrabaroque"—that I will discuss later in this piece—in its more current retake to designate practices of reappropriation of the baroque aesthetics in the context of postmodernity, and following the designation suggested in the catalogue titled *Ultra Baroque: Aspects of Post-Latin American Art*, edited by Elizabeth Armstrong and Víctor Zamudio-Taylor.

4. See, in this respect, my *Viaje al silencio. Exploraciones del discurso barroco*, particularly the first part, in which I study the specific characteristics of the Baroque of the Indies.

5. On the concept of the "Baroque of the Indies" the studies by Mariano Picón Salas and Leonardo Acosta, among others, are indispensable. For more current perspectives on the topic, see my *Relecturas del Barroco de Indias* and *Viaje al silencio*. On the concept of "mimicry" in relation to the representation of the colonial subject, see Bhabha.

6. In *Celestina's Brood*, in the chapters dedicated to Calderón and to Espinosa Medrano, González-Echevarría refers to the theme of monstrosity in the Baroque relating it to the problem of identity ("monstrosity as identity"). He interprets monstrosity as a form of catachresis (trope that makes it possible to give a name to something that does not have it yet, through a procedure of figurative re-signification). According to González-Echevarría, "Monstrosity appears in the Baroque as a form of generalized catachresis, one that affects language as well as the image of self, and that includes the sense of belatedness inherent in Latin American literature" (5). The baroque "mon-

strosity" is associated, in this way, with the proper hybrid quality of the Creole society (of Peninsular ancestry but of American origin and roots), and with the coexistence of contradictory attributes of colonial *letrados*, of the kind that we indicated, emblematically, in the cases of Sor Juana, Espinosa Medrano, etc. As it is suggested by González Echevarría, monstrosity indicates the transitional state of these identities which appear equipped of a two-faced quality, from a cultural perspective and also from the point of view of gender. The symbolic transvestism that is associated with the figure of Sor Juana and that the Neobaroque will take up again, reminds us of the speech of Rosaura in *La vida es sueño*, where she appears, in the eyes of Segismundo—as Gonzalez Echevarría points out—as a "monstruo de una especie y otra" ("monster of one and another species"; as a man, or as a woman, or as a combination of both), creating an epistemological ambiguity and a saturation of visual and verbal signs that are characteristic of baroque aesthetics. Concerning the relation between monstrosity and colonialism, see also Zavala.

7. For Carlos Rincón, certain interpretations of the Baroque, like the one of Alejo Carpentier, for example, are looking precisely to establish a cultural genealogy that makes it possible to set certain historical, cultural roots from which the narrative of the 1960s would have developed. Then, for example, according to Rincón, "[t]he recourse to the *Auctoritas* of the Baroque as a myth allows to unify the contradictory and refractory reality of the contemporary novel, and paves the way for the one which will be written in the future: it has created an ennobled stereotype. What is presented as a 'hermeneutic' process of approximation to the Baroque is an operation to authenticate a cultural myth of origin and legitimate the 'originality' of the new narrative. Forged on the base of that cultural *corpus*, it 'expressed' and assured a community of consciousness, tradition and language" (*Mapas y pliegues* 192; my translation).

8. Nevertheless, even though Lezama Lima appears to satirize the expansion of the Baroque, it will be precisely this aspect which will guide his assertion that the Baroque "is not a degenerescent (*sic*) style, but a plenary one, which in Spain and America represents acquisitions of language, that are perhaps, unique in the world, as well as furniture for housing, ways of living and curiosity, mysticism that adheres to new modes for prayer, ways of taste and handling of delicacies, that exhale a refined and mysterious way of life, theocratic and self-absorbed, errant in form, and deeply rooted in its own essences" (*Confluencias* 229).

9. When studying the genealogy of the American Baroque and its connections with modernity and postmodernity, Rincón also makes reference to the manifestations of a *virtual* Neobaroque present in the configuration of the global "hypermarket of cultural and aesthetic signs" (*Mapas* 157).

10. The use of the term "neobaroque" is attributed to Gustavo Guerrero, who uses it in his studies of the works of Severo Sarduy.

11. In a section in the form of a poem. At the beginning of *Barroco* (1974), the word *retombée* is "defined" in the following manner:
    Retombée: a-chronic causality

non-contiguous
isomorphism
or
consequence of something that has yet not been produced,
similar to something that does not exist yet. (Sarduy 1196)
Sarduy, then, indicates in 1987: "I called *retombée*, for lack of a better term in Spanish, to all a-chronic causality: the cause and consequence of a given phenomenon may not be successive in time, but coexist; the 'consequence,' can even precede the 'cause'; both can be shuffled, as in a game of cards. Retombée is also a similarity or likeness in what is discontinuous: two distant objects, without communication or interference, can reveal themselves as analogous; one can function as the *double* of the other—the word also taken in the theatrical sense of the term: there is no hierarchy of values between the model and the copy" (Sarduy 1370).

12. According to Rincón, "Given the paradoxical condition of Latin American societies as part of the history of decolonization, and given the position occupied by the Baroque in some of its cultures, the deciphering of the Baroque and the issue of the relation mimesis-/alterity tends to be situated and oriented today, in the direction of the new cultural and transdisciplinary criticism and the historization of issues of identity it undertakes" (*Mapas y pliegues* 190).

13. With respect to debates on originality and copy in connection with national cultures, see Schwarz.

14. In fact since the establishment of the so-called "culture of the Baroque" in the seventeenth century, the problems of colonial power, and much later, what Aníbal Quijano has called "the coloniality of power"—that is registered, in diverse modalities, all along the modernizing process and is distinguished, epistemologically, from the historial phenomenon of colonialism—suggest the necessity to integrate these paradigms of social-political structure in Latin America, basic (modernity, coloniality) to the interpretation of cultural and ideological forms. In this case, the same can be used as matrix from which to think about the (neo) baroque aesthetic, which the residues of the imperial monumentality and the subversion of those same canons are combined, which we could call areas of influence of peninsular Hispanic studies.

15. The idea of *negativity* used here is certainly not alien to the concept popularized by Theodor Adorno in *Negative Dialectic* (1973), since the term articulates notions that make it possible to approach a general comprehension of socio-cultural phenomena of post-national or multinational character, as far as it proposes the anti-utopian conception of modernity as an instance that is implemented, not overcome, but rather to reconcile social contradictions.

16. "Lezama wields the Baroque as an already original anxiety of creation and innovation—Lezama's Baroque is a romantic Baroque, a Baroque endowed with the fundamental features of German Romanticism" (González-Echevarría, *Celestina's Brood* 218).

17. According to Irlemar Chiampi, Lezama liberates the Baroque from the flux of con-

tinuous history, in order to produce "a leap" toward what is incomplete and unfinished in that aesthetics, revealing to us how that metahistorical fragment is constituted in a "form" that *situates us in modernity through dissonance*" (140, emphasis mine).

18. Lack and excess are the interchangeable inversion and reversal of Sarduy's metaphoric system (González-Echevarría, *Celestina's Brood* 220).

19. On the baroque obsession with the ideas of transience and decadence, and the elaboration of these topics made by Walter Benjamin, see Buci-Glucksmann, *La raison baroque*.

20. Nevertheless, it would be useful to remember that in Benjamin, the loss is not pure negativity but also *production* (in the economic sense, but also in the theatrical one): an encounter of the being with that which lies concealed, awaiting, in order to manifest itself, an instance from which an *other* plenitude can be reached: "Contemplated from the side of death, life consists on the production of the cadaver" (Benjamin 214).

21. In this elaboration I follow the work of Buci-Glucksmann on Walter Benjamin. See mainly chapter 4, "The Aesthetics of Transience," in *La raison baroque*.

22. It is worth noting that de Souza Santos separates baroque *ethos* and postmodernity. According to him, "what is baroque is not postmodern, what is baroque is an integral part of modernity; his own digression, in my opinion, is a transgression within modernity. It is a centrifugation from a center that can be, more or less, weak, but that exists and makes itself known. The postmodern, on the contrary, in either one of its two versions, does not have a center, it is a-centric, from which it gets its 'post' character" (Echeverría, *Modernidad, mestizaje cultural* 324).

23. Echeverría clarifies the semiotic process of "codephagia" in the following manner: "The sub-codifications or singular and concrete configurations of the code of what is human do not seem to have another way of coexisting among themselves that is not of consuming each other; the way of beating destructively in the center of constitutive symbolization which they have in front and appropriating and integrating within themselves, submitting themselves to an essential alteration, the remains still alive that are left of it afterwards" (Echeverría, *Modernidad* 32).

Works Cited

Acosta, Leonardo. *Barroco de Indias y otros ensayos*. La Habana: Casa de las Américas, 1985.

Adán, Martín. *El más hermoso crepúsculo del mundo. Antología*. Ed. Jorge Aguilar Mora. México: Fondo de Cultura Económica, 1992.

Adorno, Theodor. *Negative Dialectic*. New York: Seabury Press, 1973.

Armstrong, Elizabeth. "Impure Beauty/Belleza impura." *Ultra Baroque. Aspects of Post Latin American Art*. Ed. Elizabeth Armstrong and Víctor Zamudio-Taylor. San Diego: Museum of Contemporary Art, 2000. 1–18.

Armstrong, Elizabeth, and Víctor Zamudio-Taylor, eds. *Ultra Baroque. Aspects of Post-Latin American Art.* San Diego: Museum of Contemporary Art, 2000.

Badiou, Alain. "Gilles Deleuze, The Fold: Leibniz and the Baroque." *Gilles Deleuze and the Theater of Philosophy.* Ed. Constantin V. Boundas and Dorothea Olkowski. New York and London: Routledge, 1994. 51–69.

Baudrillard, Jean. *La transparencia del mal. Ensayo sobre los fenómenos extremos.* Barcelona: Anagrama, 1991.

Benjamin, Walter. *El origen del drama barroco alemán.* Madrid: Taurus, 1990.

Bhabha, Homi K. "Of Mimicry and Man: The Ambivalence of Colonial Discourse." *October* 28 (1984): 125–33.

Borges, Jorge Luis. "Prólogo." *Historia universal de la infamia.* Buenos Aires: Emecé, 1954.

Buci-Glucksmann, Christine. *La raison baroque. De Baudelaire à Benjamin.* Paris: Galilée, 1984.

_____. La *manera* o el nacimiento de la estética." *Barroco y Neobarroco.* Ed. Francisco Jarauta and Christine Buci-Glucksmann. Madrid: Cuadernos del Círculo de Bellas Artes, 1993. 23–31.

Calabrese, Omar. *Neo-Baroque. A Sign of the Times.* Princeton: Princeton University Press, 1992.

_____. "Neobarroco." *Barroco y Neobarroco.* Ed. Francisco Jarauta and Christine Buci-Glucksmann. Madrid: Cuadernos del Círculo de Bellas Artes, 1993. 89–100.

Calinescu, Matei. *Five Faces of Modernity. Modernism, Avant-Garde, Decadence, Kitsch, Postmodernism.* Durham: Duke University Press, 1987.

Carpentier, Alejo. "Problemática de la actual novela latinoamericana." *Tientos y diferencias.* La Habana: Casa de las Américas, 1966.

Castañón, Adolfo. "Severo Sarduy: Del Barroco, el ensayo y la iniciación." *Obra completa* by Severo Sarduy. Ed. Gustavo Guerrero and François Wahl. 2 vols. Madrid: Ediciones UNESCO, Colección Archivos, 1999. 1644–48.

Chiampi, Irlemar. "El neobarroco en América Latina y la visión pesimista de la historia." *Sobre Walter Benjamín. Vanguardias, historia, estética y literatura. Una visión latinoamericana.* Ed. Gabriela Massuh and Silvia Fehrmann. Buenos Aires: Alianza Editorial and Goethe-Institut, 1993. 137–49.

Corominas, Joan. *Breve diccionario etimológico de la lengua castellana.* Madrid: Gredos, 1987.

Degli-Esposti Reinert, Cristina. "Neo-Baroque Imaging in Peter Greenaway's Cinema." *Peter Greenaway's Postmodern/Poststructuralist Cinema.* Ed. Paula Willoquet-Maricondi and Mary Alemany-Galway. Lanham, MD, and London: The Scarecrow Press, Inc. 2001.

Deleuze, Gilles. *The Fold: Leibniz and the Baroque.* Minneapolis: University of Minnesota Press, 1993.

De Campos, Haroldo. "Barroco-ludisme deleuzien." *Gilles Deleuze. Une vie philosophique.* Ed. Eric Halléis. Paris: Institut Synthélabo, 1998. 545–53.

280   MABEL MORAÑA

De la Cruz, Sor Juana Inés. *Carta de Sor Juana Inés de la Cruz a su Confesor. Autodefensa espiritual.* Ed. Aureliano Tapia Méndez. Monterrey: Impresora Monterrey, 1986.

De Souza Santos, Boaventura. "El Norte, el Sur, la utopía y el *ethos* barroco." *Modernidad, mestizaje cultural, ethos barroco.* Ed. Bolívar Echeverría. Mexico City: UNAM/El equilibrista, 1994. 311–32.

Echeverría, Bolívar, ed. *Modernidad, mestizaje cultural, ethos barroco.* Mexico City: UNAM/El equilibrista, 1994.

_____. *La modernidad de lo barroco.* Mexico City: Era, 2000.

Fuentes, Carlos. *El espejo enterrado.* Mexico City: Fondo de Cultura Económica, 1992.

Gisbert, Teresa, and José de Mesa. *Arquitectura andina: 1530–1830. Historia y análisis.* La Paz: Colección Arzans y Vela; Embajada de España en Bolivia, 1985.

González-Echevarría, Roberto. *La ruta de Severo Sarduy.* Hanover, NH: Ediciones del Norte, 1987.

_____. *Celestina's Brood. Continuities of the Baroque in Spanish and Latin American Literature.* Durham and London: Duke University Press, 1993.

Gruzinski, Serge. *El pensamiento mestizo.* Barcelona: Paidós, 2000.

_____. The Baroque Planet/El planeta barroco." *Ultra Baroque: Aspects of Post Latin American Art.* Ed. Elizabeth Armstrong and Víctor Zamudio-Taylor. San Diego: Museum of Contemporary Art, 2000. 111–26.

Guattari, Félix. *Caósmosis.* Buenos Aires: Manantial, 1996.

_____. "La producción de subjetividad del capitalismo mundial integrado." *Revista de Crítica Cultural* 4 (Noviembre 1991): 5–10.

Guerrero, Gustavo. *La estrategia neobarroca. Estudio sobre el resurgimiento de la poética barroca en la obra narrativa de Severo Sarduy.* Barcelona: Edicions del Mall, 1987.

Hanssen, Beatrice. *Walter Benjamin's Other History: Of Stones, Animals, Human Beings, and Angels.* Berkeley: University of California Press, 1998.

Jarauta, Francisco, and Christine Buci-Glucksmann, eds. *Barroco y Neobarroco.* Madrid: Cuadernos del Círculo Bellas Artes, 1993.

Lezama Lima, José. *Confluencias: Selección de ensayos.* Ed. Abel Prieto. Havana: Letras Cubanas, 1988.

_____. *La expresión americana.* In *Obras completas, Tomo II.* Madrid: Aguilar, 1997.

Lyotard, Jean-Francois. *La condición postmoderna.* Buenos Aires: REI, 1989.

Maravall, José Antonio. *La cultura del Barroco.* Barcelona: Ariel, 1980.

Marcus, Laura, and Lynda Nead, eds. *The Actuality of Walter Benjamin.* London: Lawrence & Wishart, 1998.

Mariátegui, José Carlos. "El Anti-soneto". Lima: *Amauta*, año III, 17 (September 1928): 76.

Monsiváis, Carlos. "Neobarroco y cultura popular." *Modernidad, mestizaje cultural y ethos barroco.* Ed. Bolivar Echeverría. Mexico City: UNAM/El Equilibrista, 1994. 299–309.

Moraña, Mabel. *Relecturas del Barroco de Indias.* Hanover, NH: Ediciones del Norte, 1994.

_____. *Viaje al silencio. Exploraciones del discurso barroco.* Mexico City: UNAM, 1998.

Moulin-Civil, Françoise. "Invención y epifanía del neobarroco: excesos, desbordamientos, reverberaciones." *Obra completa* by Severo Sarduy. Ed. Gustavo Guerrero and François Wah. 2 vols. Madrid: Ediciones UNESCO, Colección Archivos, 1999. 1649–78.

Ono, Ichiro. *Divine Excess: Mexican Ultra-Baroque.* San Francisco: Chronicle Books, 1995.

Paz, Octavio. "Voluntad de forma." *Esplendores de treinta siglos.* New York: Metropolitan Museum of Art, 1990. 24–26.

Perlongher, Néstor. *Prosa plebeya. Ensayos 1980–1992.* Buenos Aires: Colihue S.R.L., 1997.

_____. "Prólogo." *Medusario: Muestra de poesía latinoamericana.* Selection and notes by Roberto Echavarren, José Kozer, and Jacobo Sefamí. Mexico City: Fondo de Cultura Económica, 1996. 19–30.

_____. Los devenires minoritarios." *Revista de Crítica Cultural* 4 (November 1991): 13–18.

Picón Salas, Mariano. *De la conquista a la independencia.* Mexico City: Fondo de Cultura Económica, 1982.

Quijano, Aníbal. "Colonialidad del poder, cultura y conocimiento en América Latina." *Anuario Mariateguiano* 9 (1997): 113–21.

_____. "Colonialidad del poder, eurocentrismo y América Latina." *La colonialidad del saber: eurocentrismo y ciencias sociales. Perspectivas latinoamericanas.* Ed. Edgardo Lander. Buenos Aires: FLACSO, 2000. 201–46.

Rincón, Carlos. *Mapas y pliegues.* Bogotá: Colcultura, 1996. 151–266.

_____. "La poética de lo real maravilloso americano." *Alejo Carpentier.* La Habana: Valoración múltiple, 1977. 123–77.

Sarduy, Severo. *Obra completa.* Ed. Gustavo Guerrero and François Wahl. 2 vols. Madrid: Ediciones UNESCO, Colección Archivos, 1999.

Schwartz, Robert. "Brazilian Culture: Nationalism by Elimination." *Misplaced Ideas. Essays on Brazilian Culture.* Ed. John Gledson. London: Verso, 1992.

Zamudio-Taylor, Víctor. "Ultra Baroque: Art, Mestizaje, Globalization/Ultra Baroque: arte, mestizaje, globalización." *Ultra Baroque: Aspects of Post-Latin American Art.* Ed. Elizabeth Armstrong and Víctor Zamudio-Taylor. San Diego: Museum of Contemporary Art, 2000. 141–60.

Zavala, Iris. "Representing the Colonial Subject." *1492–1992: Re/Discovering Colonial Writing.* Ed. René Jara and Nicholas Spadaccini. Hispanic Issues 4. Minneapolis: University of Minnesota Press, 1989. 323–48.

◆ Afterword: Redressing the Baroque

Edward H. Friedman

Like most literary and theoretical issues, approaches to the Baroque have changed over the last decades. Students traditionally—a word that also changes according to context—have been exposed to the concept of the Baroque as mediated through the world of the plastic arts. Baroque cathedrals and architecture adorned to the maximum catch the eye and affect the senses. One may think of gold on silver trimmed with colored tiles, topped by the richness of paintings, each of which holds a complex treasure of symbols and associations. The Baroque seems to aspire to more than the eye can behold and more than the mind can synthesize. Complexity and obscurity, arguably, are its driving forces. Eva Perón sums up the baroque attitude in the song "Buenos Aires" from *Evita* when she proclaims, "All I want is a whole lot of excess." The emphasis on excess can be contemplated, and defended, in several ways. The richness of texture adds depth. Rhetoric, when heightened, gains formal and conceptual strength. The more that the artist can work (and play) with the tools of the trade, be they words or another medium, the more room for creative expression. The more difficult the process of comprehension may be, the more involved and engaged the reader, listener, or spectator. The Baroque tends to raise the bar for the artist and for the consumer of art, and this may be seen as good or bad, challenging or elitist. The playwright Lope de Vega's interest in pleasing the general public, the *vulgo*, stands in stark contrast to the poetic aims, and the implicit politics, of Luis de Góngora or Francisco de Quevedo, who sought a readership of educated and subtle thinkers and who brought the social and theological politics of ostracism to bear on literature. In this essay, I would like to look at the Baroque from the perspective of the methodologies and focal points of the contributors to this volume and from my own reading of the Baroque, the term and the texts classified as such, as a means of continuing the dialogue. One conclusion, which I will reveal at this early juncture, is that the Baroque used to be far simpler, and more contained, and that, appropriately, the theoretical boom of recent decades has opened the doors for further investigation of a phenomenon already marked by open doorways. The fact that I also believe that the Baroque as a label has become so overdetermined as to render it flexible to a fault does not nullify its appeal or, ultimately, its value as a means of access to the intersections of art and life.

To a degree, baroque sensibility is predicated on the idea that the medium is the message. The Baroque can be seen, although debatably, of course, as a victory of form over content, or of form as content. Poetry, as the predominant genre of the early modern period, certainly accentuates verbal proficiency and inventiveness, but the rhetoric of baroque poetry honors imaginative gifts in language and wit. The baroque style combines floridity, embellishment, ardor, and mental acuteness; *culteranismo*, *conceptismo*, and *agudeza* figure among its operative terms. As David Castillo underscores, the Baroque pursues the extreme. *Culteranismo* realizes the objective through ornamentation on the formal level, whereas *conceptismo* seeks the density of the conceit through brevity. The categories obviously are not mutually exclusive, given that rhetoric, in its multiple manifestations, lies at the center of each. The Baroque may seem to convey an illusion of emptiness, of form for its own sake, but that was never the case, and one may note, in a Borgesian (or Pierre Menardian) fashion, that it is less so in the new millennium. Perhaps the most lasting and the most steadfast lesson of poststructuralism—and some may attribute this to other sources—is that every statement and every set of signs have an ideological thrust and a broad array of subtexts, often contradictory. By virtue of its intricacy, its intensity, and its innate sense of competition, what might be called the nature of the Baroque hinges on the topos of rivalry, enacted at every stage of the act of creation and replicated in critical and theoretical discourse.

It is possible, and fairly conventional, to cast baroque art as a response to the Renaissance. The moderation, symmetry, and attention to proportion of the Renaissance ideal cede to violent oppositions, distortion, and calculated imbalance. In literature, words have an almost palpable presence; one can feel the effort behind their construction. Centuries before the Russian formalists, Góngora and Quevedo were masters of defamiliarization. Their experiments in the realm of the figurative invite the reader to confront a barrage of linguistic obstacles on the path toward comprehension, which consists of the search for the signified behind the verbal artifice or the concept behind the display of ingenuity. Making a show of difference and often of irreverence, the baroque artist deliberately seems to defy expectations and established norms. Within the baroque aesthetic, and paradoxically, less is more, conceptually speaking, and, more is more, tropologically speaking. Theology is a regulating factor, but hardly stable in the baroque mindset. Spiritually oriented writers feel that they are dying as they wait impatiently for the eternal life, but in the age of the Inquisition the soul of a poetic speaker may insist that love remains constant and burning in the cold waters of the Lethe, beyond the limits of death. Seventeenth-century Spain offers exquisite examples of writers and other artists who share an interest in complication, radical antitheses, metaphorical representation, consciousness of process, audience involvement, and rivalry—key features of the Baroque—as they endeavor to detach themselves from the past and from their contemporaries. I will cite textual examples to illustrate the particular anxiety of influence that comes across in the transition from the Renaissance to the Baroque, the self-referentiality and the dialectics of author and public in baroque works, and variations on the theme of baroque structure. My goal here is not so much to submit new readings as to set forth a general framework for the artistic production in Spain from around 1600 to 1650, and then to move beyond the Iberian Peninsula and beyond the first half of the seventeenth century. It may be noted that the label *baroque* is similar to the label *picaresque*, and other labels, with regard to precedence of object and tag. Recalling the dilemma of the chicken and the egg, we are not always sure which came first, and it is frequently the case that the two develop simultaneously.

Two often-quoted *carpe diem* sonnets—Garcilaso de la Vega's "En tanto que de rosa y azucena" and Góngora's "Mientras por competir con tu cabello"—help to provide a succinct comparison between Renaissance and baroque technique in Spanish poetry. The two sonnets are intertextual gems, part of a trajectory that goes back to Ausonius, Petrarch, and an illustrious gallery of poets. Garcilaso's sonnet epitomizes both the elegance of his writing in general and his ability to convert the poem into a parable, or paradox, on the consistency of change. Like many of his predecessors, Garcilaso frames seduction in a warning about the brevity of youth, the impermanence of beauty, and the inevitability of old age that comes too swiftly and surprises those who ignore the signs around them. Garcilaso's source for describing the beloved lady is nature. The highest compliment is that her beauty equals that of nature, which also foreshadows the imminent loss of her physical gifts. Góngora's strategy is different. His lady "competes" with nature and wins. Moreover, the poetic speaker refuses to stop his argument at old age, making the end of the line a crescendo of "earth, smoke, dust, shadow, nothingness." The addition is fascinating in at least two ways. By transforming nature into a competitor, Góngora acknowledges, and allegorizes, his own poetic rivalries and rivals, notably Garcilaso. His lady outshines nature, and, as a corollary, she outshines Garcilaso's lady, and the poet likewise outshines his adversary (and his forebears). The sonnet concludes with the word *nada*, but Góngora is hoping for everlasting fame. Ironically, in his attempt to persuade the object of his affection of the ravages of time, the poetic speaker forgets Christian theology and the promise of eternal life. In the sonnet, Góngora immortalizes poetry as he secularizes immortality. His vision, or version, of love and of poetic composition is obsessive, and the implied center—allurement—proves misleading, ceding to art itself and, with that, to the place of the artist. In the same vein, Góngora's *Fábula de Polifemo y Galatea* is an extended exercise in figural discourse. The cyclops's pursuit of the nymph has a simple and familiar story line: the mighty Polifemo woos Galatea and crushes his enemy Acis. Reading becomes synonymous with decoding a system of figures and conceits geared to show the overwhelming strength, power, and possessions of Polifemo, against the attraction and attractiveness of Galatea and Acis. Metaphor and hyperbole join forces to stress abundance and plenitude. Once more, the motif of rivalry covers the poetic and the extrapoetic: the contest for Galatea, the battle to supersede the intertext, and the quest for critical recognition, for victory over one's peers. Within the poem, Polifemo has his own voice, roaring and awe-inspiring but noticeably, and studiedly, less eloquent than his creator's.

Quevedo's sonnets foreground *conceptismo*, built around elaborate conceits that elevate and exalt the authority of the word. The images are precious, consolidated, and fresh. Although they may carry moral messages, they are more oriented toward verbal resourcefulness and gamesmanship than toward ideology, and ultimately more about metapoetics than metaphysics. Quevedo and his fellow (and, more rarely, sister) baroque poets strive to find innovative ways to refashion age-old topics such as *memento mori* or the deceptive brevity of life; it is their uniqueness as poetic vehicles that sets them apart. For a number of years, Quevedo's venture into the picaresque genre with *La vida del Buscón* led to a critical debate about priorities, that is, whether the writer uses the picaresque format to showcase his linguistic and conceptist skills or whether the story line and the antihero warrant the stronger scrutiny. What is clear is that Quevedo makes his protagonist more notorious, more outrageous, and more articulate (especially in the opening chapters of the narrative, when his voice is barely distinguishable from the author's) than Lázaro de Tormes, Guzmán de Alfarache, and their ilk. In the picaresque, commonly garbed in first-person narration, there is a struggle for discursive dominance between the narrator and an implied author, purveyor of irony, most discernible perhaps in the feminine variations written by men. Quevedo's social status and agenda are so far removed from Pablos's that a rare brand of literary determinism takes over. The manipulation is so unmistakable that the underling's standing in society is mirrored in the text, granting him a modicum, or more, of sympathy, despite his character flaws and despite his lack of respect for the social hierarchy (a quality that might, in fact, endear him to latter-day readers). The push-and-pull aspect of the text, exemplified in the combat for narrative control, captures the pronounced dynamics of oppositions emblematic of the Baroque. The picaresque formula of pseudoautobiography, which consists of single authorship plus a supplementary, and contradictory, layer of discourse, automatically situates the reader as arbiter of the proceedings. Correspondingly, three works that I would consider as the primary manifestations of the Spanish Baroque—*La vida es sueño*, *Las meninas*, and *Don Quijote*—are, at once, dialogical and interactive.

In *La vida es sueño*, Calderón explores to the fullest the implications of the metaphor of the title. His characters come to realize that the eternal order is the umbrella under which all else falls, but that the earthly order parallels and influences one's destiny. Segismundo's decision to concentrate on salvation comes after experiencing the trials and learning the lessons of this world. The playwright uses *theatrum mundi* as the subject matter and as the structuring agent of his poetic design. Metaphor becomes a rhetorical device, a decoration—a thing of beauty—and a conceptual axis. Calderón opens the play with metaphors strung together and metaphors within metaphors, to be recalled as the speeches progress. The aesthetic object is also a philosophical, theological, political, social, and dramatic object, and it is metaphor that unites the elements. The ornateness and density of the language—an exaggeration of sorts of Lope's practice—connect *La vida es sueño* to the Baroque, as do the interrelated angles of vision. Calderón's sense of theater, inseparable from his sense of metatheater, guides the play, as characters script their actions and those of others, as plays within plays confuse and illuminate, as the protagonists move from the monstrous to the princely and from dishonor to earthly redemption, and as plot and subplot blend to support the analogical plan. The brilliance of the metaphorical shifts, however, cannot conceal the innate failure of metaphor to be exact. Metaphors depend on equivalence, which favors similitude but cannot elide difference. Calderón seems to indicate this difference by eschewing perfect symmetry and by leaving certain issues, such as determinism versus free will, unresolved or open.

The spectator (or reader) should be able to identify with the plight of the characters while contemplating the actions at a distance, spatial and emotional. Poetry is a means to an end and a performance, at times natural and at times contrived speech within the context(s) of the play. This is composite art, copious and overflowing, and, in turn, demanding on its producer and its audience.

The same is true, needless to say, of *Don Quijote*. While one can speak of the subtly, and justifiably, flawed symmetry of *La vida es sueño*, Cervantes in *Don Quijote* relishes inconsistency and discontinuity of expectation and signification. He adheres to many of the same recourses as Calderón, but with a poetic license facilitated by the properties of prose. Narrators, narratees, writers, and readers—real, implied, and in-between—are as enigmatic as they are abundant. Madness suggests a lack of harmony with the protocols of the world, and *la razón de la sinrazón*, reason upended, prevails. Opting for theory through praxis, Cervantes reconfigures the Aristotelian distinction between history and poetry by fusing and confusing the two in a ludicrous *verdadera historia*. He satirizes the plots of chivalric romance on one plane and allegorizes reading, writing, and criticism on another. Not only does he present in Part 1 the metafictional protagonist par excellence, but in Part 2 he introduces characters who have read the book and who emulate and preempt the anachronistic knight errant. Apparently concerned with literary idealism, Cervantes brings in the evolving realism of the Italian *novella* and the Spanish picaresque, but unlike eighteenth- and nineteenth-century European realism, *Don Quijote* flaunts its devises, its self-referentiality. A corps of narrators would seem to mask the historical author, but Cervantes, in various guises and sometimes as pure abstraction, is conspicuously at the heart of the matter, gaining control as he pretends to yield to others.

It is not unsual to see comparisons between *Don Quijote* and Diego Velázquez's *Las meninas*, and one would be hard-pressed to find a more suitable visual correlative to Cervantes's narrative. The artist is in the work, at work. A group of observers witnesses a work of art in progress. The walls are covered with framed paintings and with other objects of framed reality, including a doorway and a mirror. The rendering of the reflection in the mirror permits the artist to include what is not included in the literal space of the frame, the subject of the unseen part of the artist's canvas, namely, the king and queen of Spain. They displace the young princess and her attendants to occupy an ironic center. One set of spectators faces another, and, although decentered, they may be deemed the de facto base of interest. Velázquez positions himself as a metonym for art and for the practitioner of art, but he allots even more room for the spectator, without whom art would have no meaning. The dimensions of reality and the dimensions of the creative act cross and repeatedly redefine themselves. History enters the art object, and the art object reimagines history. Perspectivism functions as a sign of perception in flux. Velázquez builds upon Cervantes's insights and transfers them into his own medium. He seems as bound as Cervantes not to treat art and life as discrete entities but rather to look at them as parts of a mutable whole. Velázquez unquestionably wants to cultivate an individual style, and he dissociates himself from the Renaissance and even from those artists, like Caravaggio, who most keenly have influenced him. His chief adversary, nonetheless, may be social custom, which habitually judges the painter as an artisan, a craftsman, and which fails to see the production of high art as a noble calling. That is one of the reasons why Velázquez places himself alongside royalty, to bask in the aura of their superiority and sublimely to argue that he belongs in the frame. Cervantes, on the other hand, is motivated by literary history and the intertext, by a yearning for success, and by an intrusive and elusive rival.

The publication in 1614 of a continuation of *Don Quijote* by the pseudonymous Alonso Fernández de Avellaneda had a profound impact on Cervantes, whose second part was published the following year, with concessions to the spurious sequel. What initially will have unnerved the authentic author contributes, via the emendations, to a more polished, more sophisticated, and more ironically charged narrative. The "true history" is now legitimately true, and the Arab historian who chronicles the adventures ceases to be an obstruction, given that Cervantes must align himself with everyone and everything that pertains to the genuine account. The precipitous closure allows Cervantes to come to terms with his protagonist's fate and with his template for the novel. Part 1 interrogates historiography, the limits of fiction, idealism, truth, point of view, sanity, etc., not to mention reading, writing, censorship, and critique. Its tone is comic and satirical, although Cervantes takes his project, and himself, seriously while maintaining his distance from Don Quijote and Cide Hamete Benengeli. Part 2, before Avellaneda, brings reader response into the scheme, through the discussion of the errors and omissions of the first part and through characters such as Sansón Carrasco and the duke and duchess, who usurp the knight's metatheatrical space. Don Quijote is relegated to the role of actor in the dramatic scenarios of others, until the appearance of the false sequel provokes and invigorates him, and prompts him into a passionate defense of his authenticity. He reclaims his authority, in a double sense, through decisive action and through a somewhat desperate campaign to declare and to certify his preeminence over the impostor (and, by extension, his creator's contempt for the invasive Avellaneda). The real world inserts itself into fiction in a magical way. It would have been impossible for Cervantes to have fabricated a more suitable ploy or a more convincing rival than the false continuation, which proves the relativity, and malleability, of perception and perspective. The ending closes one door but opens others. It removes *Don Quijote* from an always appreciated—and always present, in one form or another—literary past while breaking new ground for the developing novel.

Self-consciousness, impenetrability, ingenuity, studies in contrast, unstable centers, competition: the Baroque seems to equate the mysteries of the world with the mysteries of the word, but with a respect for and faith in art and letters. Its poetic triumph notwithstanding, *La vida es sueño* addresses theology, politics, and semiotics. *Don Quijote* is without question a narrative tour de force, but Cervantes manages to survey not only the literary climate of his day but also the society that produces and consequently is reproduced in literature. The *Persiles* may satisfy his desire to reach classical heights, but *Don Quijote* embraces his philosophy of everyday life, a reflection of a society in which the quotidian translates as anything but simple. If Góngora and Quevedo erect linguistic edifices that challenge comprehension, Cervantes purports to "make" history through a labyrinthine route, starting with archives, informants, mystifying data, lacunae, reliable and unreliable storytellers, and a manuscript written in the tongue of the Muslim enemy. Within the comic and absurdist panorama— an important shield against watchful censors—he incorporates blood purity, class divisions, racism, gender politics, the instruments of justice, and other topics into the text. He comments, directly and indirectly, on the institutions of a unified Church and State, sparing not even the Inquisition, for example, in the scrutiny of Alonso Quijano's library. As in the case of the picaresque, the historical present is embedded in *Don Quijote*. Art and current events commingle and coalesce, often in understated commentaries by authors who need to protect themselves but who specialize in circumlocution and pregnant silences. Love (social practice), honor (rules of conduct), and religion (faith in theory and practice) are said to be the ruling themes of Golden Age drama, and one may add political thought, since so many plays deal with ancient, biblical, and medieval kings whose problems would seem to be bound to early modern monarchs. In short, one does not have to force reality onto the texts, for, while the writers create consummate art, they do not do so in a vacuum, and their works show an awareness of the world around them. In what follows, I will use literary history as a lead-in to cultural history and its ties with the Baroque.

A number of scholars approach the Baroque by way of the Renaissance, and some of them credit *Mannerism* as an intermediary mode. Transitions are crucial, of course, and poststructuralism hails the mediating space in which meaning is negotiated. Rather than try to define or defend the category, I will submit that it is fruitful to recognize the texts "in the middle" which clarify the form and content of the works at either extreme, works such as the poetry of Fernando de Herrera (between Garcilaso and Góngora), the plays of Tirso de Molina (between Lope and Calderón), and Mateo Alemán's *Guzmán de Alfarache* (between *Lazarillo de Tormes* and *La vida del Buscón*). There are many other possibilities, among them, arguably, the Avellaneda *Quijote* and the lesser-known but equally weighty (and mortifying) spurious sequel to *Guzmán de Alfarache*. Here, as with labels as a whole, the catch-terms are valuable not for their durability but for their elasticity. Labels are frames, and, as Jacques Derrida would have it, they are fundamental but never indestructible. We can applaud their usefulness and overlook their vulnerability to reframing, to deconstruction. Frames fall victim to what one might characterize as the teleological fallacy or the false sense of an ending. What may seem to be the end of the road is rarely that. Góngora, for example, stands at the end of a tripartite continuum that includes Garcilaso and Herrera, but he may be placed in the middle of another that moves from Garcilaso to Sor Juana Inés de la Cruz.

Drawing on three representative poems, one can note that the distance from Garcilaso's *Égloga primera* to Góngora's *Polifemo* is great, as is that from the *Polifemo* to Sor Juana's *Primero sueño*. Garcilaso achieves a balance of discourse and emotion; grief is profound, yet beautiful and controlled. As their names signal, the two shepherds represent phases of the author's own life and of his own sadness, but the human side cannot separate itself from the poetic side, and suffering is made poetic. Góngora's vision is convoluted by design. The very choice of the cyclops denotes disproportion, aberration, exaggeration; the love triangle is completely out of kilter with normalcy and moderation. The structure and language of the poem become analogues of the monster who knows no bounds and whose voice rises above all others. Figures and conceits abound, and the reader is left to decipher the verbal puzzles and to reduce the plot to its ordinary (standardized) elements. Even with its generous dose of *conceptismo*, the *Polifemo* is first and foremost a conduit for poetic largesse, a sterling paradigm of *culteranismo*. And this is where Sor Juana outdoes Góngora, by placing the *Primero sueño* at the service of language, philosophy, and theology. When the reader, doubtlessly with difficulty, can manage to conquer the linguistic and rhetorical barriers, there remain conceptual and ideological hurdles to overcome. Sor Juana adds a stage, or more, to the process of decoding or deciphering. She amplifies the base by penetrating the oneiric and spiritual planes, and, thus, with complexity as the criterion, she can be said to best her (Spanish, male, and elitist) rival as a baroque artist. Similarly, she sets herself up to vie with Calderón through the feminist and New World inflections of her play *Los empeños de una casa*.

The writings of María de Zayas offer an alternative version of the Baroque. Her two collections of novellas, *Novelas amorosas y ejemplares* and *Desengaños amorosos*, published some thirty to forty years after Cervantes's *Novelas ejemplares* and the second part of *Don Quijote*, highlight and attempt to remedy the absence of a wide-ranging feminine perspective. In his short novels, Cervantes reorganizes the conventions of idealistic and incipient realistic fiction, through unusual and striking combinations and permutations. As in *Don Quijote*, he summons the intertext only to deviate from its form and spirit. Zayas, for her part, summons the *Novelas ejemplares* as points of reference for herself and her readers, and then enacts her own deviation from the model. Genre-bending may be the salient feature of Cervantes's novellas, while Zayas's major concern seems to be the representation of the sensibility and psychology of women, in all their complexity. Zayas exposes the patriarchal and authoritarian system and the biases under which women must live. She is wise enough to make her characters nuanced, more realistic than heroic, and flawed; some are resigned to their subordinate status, while others resist, but neither option brings happiness. By placing women in vastly different settings and situations, Zayas demonstrates patterns of abuse and injustice. There is a definite method to the progression of the texts, a movement that gives women narrators increased space and control within the literary space and that foreshadows an exodus from society to the convent as a refuge from male oppression. The decision to depict women from meek to defiant, from martyr to monster, and from grandiloquent to silent grants Zayas an authority over the social landscape. She registers her point of view, by proxy, in the constant stream of editorial comments of the female storytellers. It may be the structure of her novellas, however, that most "rival" their Cervantine counterparts.

Like Cervantes in *Don Quijote*, Zayas puts forward a revisionist history, but of a totally different nature. Hers is a feminist inscription as both writing and gap-filling, and it does not deal just with women in society but with psychology and sexuality, as well. Gender is at the root of the narratives, but so is the cross of the feminine imagination and intelligence with disillusionment.

Until the end, female characters maintain a ray of hope even when mistreated and betrayed, but Zayas concludes by conceding to the reality principle of male domination. Adroitly, she softens the retreat by making it an escape to a higher order of peace and spirituality, a locus of God the Father. It may be a bit ironic to see a parallel between the ending of *Don Quijote* and the dénouement of the frame story of the *Desengaños amorosos*, but the death of Alonso Quijano and the sanctuary of the convent share an uneasy closure. For *Don Quijote*, the specter of Avellaneda unwittingly advances the evolution of the novel; a character dies, but an idea lives on and its author is inspired to clarify his fantasies. In Zayas's novellas, society never ceases to be the backdrop, because all women cannot withdraw from the world. Zayas understands this, and she beseeches men to see themselves in her works and to modify their behavior. She reaches out to her audience by dividing them, as she divides the narrators in the *Novelas amorosas y ejemplares*, into two camps and into two sets of narratees. She breaks the equilibrium—which was only tenuous, at best—in the *Desengaños amorosos*, by awarding the full narrating space to women.

In the collections, Zayas surpasses Cervantes, in my opinion, on the psychological level, and her dedication to probing the desires and fears of women shapes the narrative in a manner that may be termed baroque. She must depend on feeling, intuition, experience, and observation. She has the intellectual depth and the imaginative drive to tell her stories, which are, of course, pre-Freudian and, for some, prefeminist. She is missing a frame of reference, a modern science of the mind, and a vocabulary. As a result, she needs to reach out to what is available to her; that is, she must compensate for what she lacks as a woman and as a writer. This complicates her private and public lives, and it complicates the structure of her narratives. An ordered arrangement of materials—a conscious *dispositio*, as it were—conjoins with the disorder of the unconscious. Secret rituals, black magic, incantations, sleepwalking, pacts with the devil, unmitigated cruelty, violent acts, coincidence, and eerie doublings disrupt logic and order. They also become metafictional, indicators of an artist grasping for unity under illogical conditions, amid chaos. While Zayas may be, *stricto sensu*, unsuccessful in this regard, the analogue of disarray among the constituent parts and personae bestows a paradoxical uniformity and internal logic on the narrative blueprint. The oppositions include the obvious one of men versus women, but Zayas's women are as regularly antagonists as protagonists, as regularly irrational as rational, and as regularly selfish as selfless. They can be instigators as well as victims of violence. One of Zayas's points is that, while women may not be innately superior to men, society treats them as if they were innately inferior, and its statutes and customs sustain the prejudice. Zayas writes from the heart, and with a mental agility that may startle, rouse, and enlighten readers of various persuasions, but that probably will not leave them disinterested.

Because the Baroque is associated with the politics and the policies of early modern Spain—imperial Spain in its glory and decline—there is a tendency on the part of some scholars to see complicity when the texts themselves may disclose strategies of nonconformity. The picaresque, for example, inverts center and margin, and even though the *pícaro* (or *pícara*) rarely thrives, idealistic literature and society at large are as much the objects of satire as the roguish antiheroes, who more often than not have distinctive voices and souls. The verbal meanderings of a Guzmán de Alfarache, a fully drawn character in his own right, bespeak a Mateo Alemán tortured by a legacy that forces him to pass as an Old Christian. Neither serves as an emblem of imperialism. Even Pablos, poles apart from Quevedo in class and modus operandi, carries, for better or worse, the social and moral weight of the *Buscón*. Despite the dominating presence of his master, Pablos contributes to a radicalization of the lower depths. In the dramatic interlude "El retablo de las maravillas," Cervantes veils critique in farce as he lambastes the national obsession with blood purity. *Don Quijote* brings together a marginalized protagonist whose enterprise consists of removing his fellow characters from the center and whose chronicler resides in the margins of Spanish history and of Christianity. María de Zayas's women are also defined by their isolation from the centers of authority. In contrast, Góngora, Quevedo, and other baroque poets recoil from the popular, and from the *vulgo*, in their intentionally obscure works, and their cultural elitism has social and political implications. The Polifemo of the *Fábula*—in his bulk and in his pride of possession—may symbolize the Spain of Góngora's day, but it would seem that he more credibly symbolizes a devotion to language and a devotion to competition on the part of the poet. Góngora indeed evokes the center, but it is a center that requires qualification and that belongs to a system of erratic and ironic centers.

There is an oddly transgressive air to baroque art. The break from Renaissance principles of symmetry and beauty through constancy and moderation yields to exaggeration, intensity, and excess. Baroque production self-consciously seeks to improve on its models poetically and intellectually. It redefines elegance and eloquence to advocate a new approach to beauty, bereft of restraint, classical discipline, and unobtrusive rhetoric. The baroque artists are perfectly aware of the Renaissance intertext and of an unwritten challenge to outdo precedent. One would be hard-put to identify a baroque work that did not render homage to earlier texts and traditions. In the literary domain, the movement from the Renaissance to the Baroque might be encapsulated by the shift from nature as the source of beauty to words as the source of beauty. This might be deemed a victory for artifice, but I would classify it as a transposition of the Renaissance paradigm, wherein nature is the macrocosm and verbal representation is the microcosm. Words add thought to vision. The notion of surplus is negated, for one cannot have too many words, images, figures, displays of wit, or ideas. The *Polifemo* is emblematic in this context, because Góngora confidently deploys the monstrous to reference beauty. The cyclops cannot be contained, and Góngora reproduces him through a type of verbal overload. The subject is overly aggressive, and the poet responds in kind. Nevertheless, the rhetoric of excess becomes a thing of beauty, with tropes and conceits that transform and poeticize the grotesque, and that distract readers from the brutal acts by encoding obscurity into the text. The method raises the level of poetic intensity and ensures the participation of the reader, co-opted by the decoding process and by the contest of interpretation.

The transgressive, or potentially subversive, aspect of *Don Quijote* begins in the prologue to Part 1, when the friend of the author—alter ego, twice-removed from the historical Cervantes—advises him to ignore convention and to make up the requisite quotations and allusions. The theme of novelty and innovation is evident, and the proposal has serious implications, despite the parodic tone. Defiance of authority in early modern Spain, whatever the context, cannot be taken lightly. Reading, writing, and criticism are, perhaps, the farthest-reaching frames of the narrative; each is a function of Counter-Reformation and Inquisitorial doctrines of propriety. Cervantes breaks one rule after another, with verve and boldness. He queries the very concept of representation by having his narrators insist on the veracity of fictional devices and by blurring the lines between the historical and the imaginary. The baroque movement of *Don Quijote* is most prominent in the polyphony of voices that posit and continually redirect the story, in the play of contrasts that stubbornly refuses to draw to a close or to stabilize, in the amorphousness that seems to promise irresolution but never quite admits chaos, and, finally, in the dual ending that gives special worth to Don Quijote's life. The motifs of translation and mediation energize and enrich the discourse and, with singular and remarkable force, shore up the story of the errant knight. Like the onlookers in *Las meninas*, the textual and extratextual readers in and of *Don Quijote* are assured of a space in the story and in history. They stand witness to a narrative performance that takes history and reality to new heights. *Don Quijote* debunks the myth of objectivity and reveals an alternate reality, that is, an alternative to the association of realism with verisimilitude. Both Don Quijote and *Don Quijote* are metafictional. They approach the world from literary bases. They suggest, as the baroque poets suggest, that words enhance and encompass phenomena, that they incline, refine, and modify vision. Cervantes anticipates poststructuralism and its aftermath, but, to a degree, he has an advantage over later skeptics, for he lives in an age of faith. His brand of renunciation is less severe than Alonso Quijano's repudiation of the romances of chivalry and the mad adventures that they have triggered. While Cervantes's targets are broad and deserving of judgment, he does not succumb to cynicism nor does he remove himself from his time and place in history.

María de Zayas's novellas "naturally" involve an ironic form of transgression derived from the gender shift. Their baroque qualities may be most obvious in the juxtaposition of aggression and defenselessness exhibited in the behavior of men against women and of women against women. Zayas recreates these patterns on the discursive level by contrasting eloquence and silence on the part of her characters, and by using her own eloquence—and that of her narrators—to point to the figurative silence imposed upon women by society. In his prologue to the *Novelas ejemplares*, Cervantes uses the phrase *mesa de trucos*, roughly equivalent to "a bag of tricks," to describe his unique contribution to the narrative art. Zayas's table, plate, or, *con perdón*, pantry is filled with an exceptional larder of narrative devices, whose common denominator is feminine psychology. In one sense, Zayas takes steps to break a longstanding silence. In another, the overdetermined discourse, which results in a paradoxical underdetermination, validates the silence by exposing the gaps in the social and expressive orders. Zayas has the instincts but, given the historical moment, has neither the scientific nor the lexical skills fully to articulate her feelings and the desires of her characters. This works to the benefit of her cause. Her eloquence stems from her intelligence, from her grasp of human nature, from her willingness to present her arguments in bold strokes, from her uncanny ability to engage male and female implied readers, and from her efforts to resist an imposed silence.

The most transgressive of baroque subgenres is, likely, picaresque narrative, which records—usually through first-person narration accompanied by an ironizing voice-over—the failed life of a social outcast. The plot is comprised of attempts to ascend the social ladder in an environment that only sanctions upward mobility after death. Whether part of an original authorial plan or not, the picaresque tenders morsels of vicarious pleasure as it lampoons both the misfit and his or her alleged superiors. Picaresque narratives are, to borrow Stanley Fish's term, self-consuming artifacts. The narrator's discourse self-de(con)structs, as the implied author takes pains to trick the trickster. The laying bare of recourses (in the parlance of Russian Formalism) makes the discourse of the picaresque distinct and double-edged, and it parallels the sweeping deconstructions wrought by the rogues' narratives, which take aim at literary idealism, Renaissance humanism, the spiritual confession, clergymen who do not practice what they preach, and the divide between words and actions. Because *pícaros* cannot prosper in the long run—since happy endings are few and far between—transgression occurs, and entertains, before the just desserts collide with the antiheroes' unseemly pretensions. As in the model set forth in the *Libro de Buen Amor*, negative exemplarity can establish the tone of a text and can override didacticism until the end, when the prescribed lesson is due. There is a saturnalian flavor to the picaresque. The reader can take pleasure in the barbs on both sides of the satirical spectrum without feeling guilty, since social crimes will be punished and upstarts put in their place. This sort of poetic license allows the author—speaking for the character—to bend the rules, in most cases, without alienating the censors. As views on the relation between the individual and society change, so may the reading (and the more blatant objects) of the satire.

The Spanish *comedia nueva*, whose sire is Lope de Vega, has been denounced—by neo-Aristotelian preceptists and by Cervantes, in *Don Quijote*, I, 48—for failing to respect the classical heritage, but more recently critics have emphasized its conservatism and its allegiance to the values of an authoritarian State. Because plays revolve around dramatic conflict, personal transgressions routinely become the raw material of plots, but that in itself does not translate into subversive behavior or subversive writing. There are several theories regarding the ideology of the Comedia. I believe that some dramatists and some plays take a conservative stance regarding the social hierarchy and questions of gender, ethnicity, and theology, among others. I also believe that many plays and their protagonists, male and female, do transgress the boundaries of approved conduct. The discrepancy between the two rests on endings that may be considered reasonable conclusions to the dramatic action and character motivation and that, alternatively, may be read as concessions to censorship. In the second instance, the conclusion is less a wrapping-up than strategy of concealment, detectable through cracks in the textual structure, which Alan Sinfield has called faultlines.

When, in early modern Spanish plays, peasants kill abusive noblemen, for example, something in the end negates the act of rebellion. King Fernando in Lope's *Fuenteovejuna* makes it clear to the townspeople who appear before him that the murder of the Comendador is indefensible, even though the king and queen will not punish the village as a whole. (Lope even has the assassins shout "Long live the Catholic Monarchs!" as they cry "Death to tyrants!") Husbands can find justification in killing their wives to protect their honor, because honor is sacred and dishonor is tantamount to death. Kings and princes can, in their way, and by virtue of their royal blood, get away with murder. When women determine their marriage partners over the objections of their fathers and brothers, the audience is aware that the play is a comedy, and thus not bound to portray society as it is, but rather as it might be. Because marriage endings, in comic and serious works, often produce multiple pairings, some men and even more women must take the hand of suitors who have snubbed or betrayed them. In the rigid and obsessive codes of honor and love, and in theological and social polemics woven into the *comedias*, playwrights have the opportunity to convey multiple perspectives, to make their dramas profoundly dialogical, and to grip their audience on the affective and conceptual levels. In the plays, the language that communicates complex ideas can be decidedly ornate, and the writers call upon the spectator to see, hear, reflect, and make choices. The semiotics of the Comedia is a product of proscription and fear, and forms of resistance can be almost imperceptible. The authorial point of view may not be as evident as one may suppose, and the response may place the dramatist and the public off-center.

The Baroque, initially at least, lies chronologically between classicism and neoclassicism, and its dates in Spain might be approximately the first half to three-quarters of the seventeenth century. To say that elitism is at its core is both correct and incomplete, since the literature and the plastic arts of this time span appealed, on numerous fronts, to the members of society at large, the majority of whom were illiterate and all of whom were candidates for Counter-Reformation practicums. If complexity, decoration, contrast, self-consciousness, parody (and self-parody), underlying rivalries, games of illusion, the celebration of process, open-endedness, and mediation mark baroque style, the backdrop of Habsburg Spain itself serves to mediate the composition and analysis of texts. The artistic products of the period may demonstrate that the lack of creative freedom is not a deterrent to brilliance, and that the need for subtlety, camouflage, and restraint can, in fact, lead to sublime invention. Yet it must be understood that the practitioners of art—masters of the frame—were subject to frames from the outside. The intertext, official and unofficial critics, and the push to succeed were factors that influenced creation, as was censorship in its various forms. The power of the imagination was subordinated to the power of the State. The pursuit of art was precarious, and so was life; instability was a literary device whose origins were nonfictional. The strength of Spain in the world was informed by its policies of unity, its drive for expansion, and its mechanisms to keep operative structures in place. Baroque art venerates and exploits consumers by defining a space for them but compromising that space. As Louis Althusser and others have shown, subjectivity can be irretrievably linked to indoctrination. The individual is conditioned, aesthetically and ideologically, as a reader, observer, or listener (and as a "private" citizen). Instruction in prudence and wit—from teachers such as Baltasar Gracián, who excelled in both areas—favors the emergence of thinkers who are independent-minded yet pragmatic, attuned to the precious and the practical, and aware that art has real-world referents and exigencies.

The Baroque thrives on oppositions, and it is hardly surprising that its most renowned art objects are laden with ambiguity as well as with adornments. When Cervantes, Calderón, and Velázquez bring self-referentiality and multi-perspectivism into their works, the renderings acquire an implicit awareness of extended horizons and, as would follow, an awareness of difference, of alterity. In *Don Quijote*, one may think of Cide Hamete Benengeli, Zoraida, Ricote, and Ana Félix as obvious examples, and of Marcela and Don Quijote himself, as well. In *La vida es sueño*, Segismundo and Rosaura figuratively (and thematically) stand outside themselves before their final, and authentic, transformations, and, in *Las meninas*, viewers may count a minimum of five sets of spectators, including themselves. Art in art (narratives within narratives, plays within plays, and paintings within paintings), history in fiction (the captive's tale and the allusion to the expulsion of the *moriscos* in *Don Quijote*, and the princess, her parents and Velázquez in *Las meninas*, for example), and theology in drama (the debates on determinism in *La vida es sueño*, for example) designate a type of self-absorption, an internal movement. As fundamental as this inwardness, or self-reference, is to baroque production, it is so because of its combination with an equally strong external movement, an association with the outside world in all its projections, low and high. To argue that the Baroque is mimetic *and* self-referential is to juxtapose imitation and the simulation of imitation, that is, reality approached directly and indirectly, suppressing or uncovering the seams of production. The two extremes meet, in a manner of speaking, in the *desengaño*, or disillusionment, that has been considered an essential quality of the baroque outlook. Not only do reality and appearance confuse, but they become intertwined and inverted. As illustrated in the Calderonian honor plays, appearance replaces—devalues—reality as the criterion for judgment, and what is true matters less than what is perceived to be true. Fernando R. de la Flor discusses a world of appearances accepted as real, citing the sermons of Antônio Viera as one of his sources. He relates the Baroque to an "epochal anxiety," in which the skeptics who dominate cultural production impose "their own psychological economy of sadness." The notion of manipulation applies to art as process and to the realpolitik of the era. Baroque sensibility entails a knowing complicity—an agreement on interpretive conventions—among the participants in the creation, appreciation, and efficacy of art.

Early modernity is mediated by a past that runs from classical antiquity to the Renaissance and by our past and present, our current parameters. We read the Baroque through the lens of the modern and the postmodern. The result is not so much a theoretical movement as a theoretical *motion* that avails itself of the intertext as a moment in time and as a moment in space, as a paradigm and as a pretext for new paradigms. Thus far we have looked at the Baroque in context, but the premise of a Neobaroque and an Ultrabaroque would call for a review of the construct *out of* context. The impressive field of associations might include the German Romantics, the *modernista* poets of Latin America and Spain, the Spanish poetic Generation of 1927, the Boom and post-Boom novelists and their counterparts in the genre of poetry, a large group of modernists and postmodernists, their respective followers and disciples, scholars of culture, and significant others. As the list would suggest, the recuperation of the Baroque takes many forms and can be used for diverse, and not necessarily complementary, purposes. Each linking presupposes, formulates, or reformulates a set of elements on which judgments, analyses, and agendas are based. The appropriation and modification of the signifier *Baroque* will have a bearing on the interrelation—never quite synchronic and newly diachronic—of form and ideology. There has been, as one would expect, greater agreement on the formal properties per se of baroque texts than on ideological issues and, accordingly, more intense interest in the ideology (including the rhetoric and ideology of form) of early modern Spain, as a channel or mediating agent of integrated, and updated, discourses. Whatever the ramifications, the Baroque—often concerned with transcendence of one kind or another—transcends its original, albeit proudly tentative, frames, to craft new borders, hypotheses, and sites of contention.

In David Lodge's *Small World* (1984), the protagonist Persse McGarrigle, who as the novel opens is unfamiliar with structuralism, truly enters academia—and loses his theoretical virginity—when he gains the insight to refer to his scholarly project as "The Influence of T. S. Eliot on Shakespeare." Patricia Waugh's *Metafiction: The Theory and Practice of Self-Conscious Fiction*, published the same year, "deliberately" focuses on contemporary texts. *Tristram Shandy* is the source of the first epigraph, and Laurence Sterne is listed eight times in the index. Cervantes does not appear in the index, although page 70 contains the following sentence: "Cervantes' *Don Quixote* (1604) parodied the outmoded conventions of the Romance." One may accuse this otherwise

fine study of lacking a sense of history (or a sense of Hispanism) and of attach-
ing metafiction to postmodernism a bit too liberally. The link is valid, but the
order may be troubling, even for detractors of strict causality and *cervantistas*
accustomed to faulty chronology. Something similar can happen when the exami-
nations of the Baroque are inflected by the theoretical and ideological preoccupations of the present. The blend can be illuminating and exciting. In the richly
titled "Shakespeare, Cultural Materialism, Feminism and Marxist Humanism"
(*New Literary History* 21.3 [1990]: 471–93), for example, Jonathan Dollimore
discusses (1) the idea of an alliance between cultural materialism and the new
historicism; (2) attacks on cultural materialist and new historicist approaches;
(3) overlaps in cultural and gender politics, and the impact of the tendency to see
identity as socially constituted; (4) feminism and recent readings of *King Lear*,
Hamlet, and *Measure for Measure*; (5) the distinction between the flexibility of
interpretation and misinterpretation or misrepresentation (built around the case
of the silent prostitutes and "heterosexual economy" in *Measure for Measure*);
(6) the "constructionist view" of gender and sexuality; (7) the positing of a
"new humanism"; (8) the social and theoretical implications of cross-dressing;
and (8) a synthesis of the elements listed above in an "imagined production" of
Anthony and Cleopatra. Dollimore concludes his serious and ingenious reflection by agreeing with Leslie Fiedler's comment that the only actress equipped
to play the part of Cleopatra is Mick Jagger and by nominating three candidates
of his own for the role of Anthony (Peter Stallybrass, Gary Taylor, and Mar-
jorie Garber). It would not be unusual to see references to Queen Elizabeth,
Queen Mab, Margaret Thatcher, and Judith Butler (or to Francisco de Quevedo,
Francisco Franco, Francisco Rico, and Frank Lentricchia) in the same soundly
argued and balanced essay, because advances—some might prefer *new developments*—in theory have taught us to read, respond, and synthesize differently.
My point here is to signal, first, the transition from *literary* theory to cultural
studies and to a more general concept of theory which freely admits interdis-
ciplinarity, and, second, the possibility that a concept such as the Baroque can
lose its historical determinacy while accommodating new or revised theoretical
objectives.

   The genres of the Spanish Baroque—poetry, drama, narrative, the sermon, and, one may add, history—meet in the performance of linguistic and
perspectivist feats and in the production of open and polemical spaces, spaces
apportioned for argument and counterargument. Imprecision and a dependence
on irony are conducive to conflicting and even antithetical judgments. When
the plasticity of baroque art is filtered through contemporary theory and political stances (and spin), critical commentary may become intriguingly, if some-

times perplexingly, free-floating. Baroque artists have been accused of creating monsters, in one way or another, and it could be noted—without a negative aim—that theorists who have reimagined the Baroque have done the same, by allowing ample room for interpretation and interpolation. Traditionally, there have been advocates of moderation (Renaissance values), placed against those who revere beauty in volume. There are those who, following Heinrich Wölfflin, Wylie Sypher, and others, attempt to codify the qualities of the Baroque; they begin with form, but realize that formal choices imply meaning. They are the guides of Walter Benjamin, José Antonio Maravall, and a group of illustrious scholars who are concerned with defining the sensibilities and ideologies of the age. Maravall's *The Culture of the Baroque*, first published in 1975, is a decisive critical tool for its treatment of what Nicholas Spadaccini and Luis Martín-Estudillo refer to in the introduction to this volume as "the 'containment' side of the Baroque," itself a highly suggestive and complex concept. Maravall accentuates the role of the State in the control of—along with everything else—discourse and the institutions of art. (The reader of this volume will note that the dialectics of freedom and containment are alluded to in a number of the essays, whether their authors refer to peninsular or transatlantic topics.) The extraordinarily influential thought of Michel Foucault on power relations and of Fredric Jameson on "the political unconscious," to cite but two models in a broad field, provides new ways to chart culture and social practice. As cultural history, postcolonial theory, and transatlantic studies have developed, the Baroque has become a factor, and often a starting point, in the analysis of the countless facets of Latin American literature and society. The process is mediated by writers of early modern Spain and by the *barroco de Indias*, in a line that moves from Sor Juana Inés de la Cruz to Carlos de Sigüenza y Góngora to Alejo Carpentier, José Lezama Lima, Severo Sarduy, Octavio Paz, and well beyond. As in Europe, questions of style, identity, and power direct the commentary on the New World, and the duplicity of the Baroque—its contradictory doubleness—remains intact.

Spadaccini and Martín-Estudillo stress "the reciprocities of power" and "the discrepant voices that are raised against [the] conservative programs of the Spanish State." The subversion of dominant discourses is part of a progression that originates on home ground. In scrutinizing the contact between Spain and its colonies, it is crucial to take into account the tensions, the prominence of the margins, and the multiplicity of voices in picaresque narrative, *Don Quijote*, María de Zayas's novellas, and the Comedia (with the *corrales* and the palace as stages), as well as the popular and the patently obscure strains (by the same writers) in poetry. The strategies of survival from Lazarillo de Tormes to Gracián presuppose the need for such strategies, on the street and in the court. The introduction cites Elizabeth Armstrong, who in *Ultra Baroque* compares the baroque era, "where people could choose a different faith, a different occupation, even a different part of the world to live in," with the profusion of "'lifestyle' options" in the present, without differentiating between those decisions that are forced upon one, or are acts of desperation, and those that emanate from the freedom of choice. As Spadaccini and Martín-Estudillo state, Armstrong's allusion to "eroding borders" is applicable to both levels, but not for the same reasons.

Not long ago, French was in the center of departments of Romance (or foreign) languages in U.S. universities and Spanish was in the margins, and, within the Hispanic curriculum, Spain was in the center and Spanish America in the margins. Literature and theory, in general, were seen as compatible yet often as separable entities, and so, at times, were form and content. The Baroque referred almost exclusively to a style and to Spain, with Sor Juana and a few others, under the influence of Góngora and Calderón, as exceptions. In the heyday of structuralism, historical approaches were anathema to those devoted to a ("scientific") method of identifying not meaning, but how meanings are produced. Maravall's study signifies a return to—and a modification of—history, falling as it does in the transition from structuralism to poststructuralism and between dictatorship and democracy in Spain. As scholars such as Hayden White were looking at history (and historiography) rhetorically and with a revisionist bent, Latin American intellectuals—including novelists and other writers—were examining national and individual identity, and related matters, from a number of vantage points and with depth, acumen, and variety. The ensuing discourse is a discourse of textuality, a mixture of fiction, social science, and philosophy. Present-day aesthetics, politics, and morality collaborate to look at modernity and postmodernity (and poststructuralism) with an eye on the Baroque, and vice versa, disregarding disciplinary and thematic boundaries. This is why studies of the Baroque, among them those included here, go all over the literary and ideological map, in the best sense of the phrase. In his well-known essay "The Historical Text as Literary Artifact," from *Tropics of Discourse* (Johns Hopkins University Press, 1978), White applies the term *emplotment* to speak of the configuration of events into narrative form, be it for historical or imaginative purposes. White is essentially echoing Cervantes on the encoding and the decoding of perspective; the writer's will—will power, one might insist—is forever etched onto the document. The openness of the Baroque, as period and (again, *con perdón*) as punctuation, permits the emplotter to use it in seemingly limitless, and certainly contradictory, ways, in deference to paradigm shifts, shifting centers, and shows of conscience.

Knowing that some readers will dispute this observation, I would submit that the unifying elements and guiding forces of the essays in this collection are, equally, the Baroque and poststructuralism (and its aftereffects, which are formidable). Both are defined by a facility for and a dependence on repositioning strategies. Both operate dialectically, confusing and rotating priorities. Both assimilate and pay tribute to the audience (observer, listener, reader, narratee, the general public, the social superior), apparently, and altruistically, ceding interpretive and analytical power while clinging protectively to the rights of authorship. There is, then, a paradoxical decisiveness to the Baroque and to poststructuralism(s), paradoxical because all sides are potentially viable and mutable, and because artists give their consumers a freedom that they themselves do not enjoy. That is why the products of each are unvaryingly open and why the relative is dominant in an age of absolutism. Recognition of the adaptability and applicability of the baroque plastic arts to other spheres becomes the first stage in the ideological transfer that takes place when the term enters standard usage. The Baroque, with its inherently cumbersome baggage, is a supreme signifier and a self-consciously artificial construct. It calls attention to itself, to the vastness of its reach, and, I believe, to its ripeness for deconstruction. Its objects and formulations lead us up, down, and around. One example, of many, is the path that takes Mabel Moraña from "the logic of baroque disruption" to "allegorizing reproducibility" to a "process of cannibalization," although not irrefutably in that order. Another is Hernán Vidal's narrative of baroque angst, felt in the movement from the awkward union of seventeenth-century Spanish artistic production and the government of the Habsburg State to discomforting historical anecdotes of social transgression which waver between the symbolic and the trivial, the paradigm and the fleeting image. And the list could go on.

Just as Pierre Menard's *Don Quijote* would have to be different from Cervantes's (con)texts, the readings of the Baroque register difference through the elements of mediation selected by the essayists. I remember a time when I thought that the Spanish Baroque was monstrously beautiful and magnificently self-referential, but somehow limited in scope. Years of reading— and innovations in theory—have shown me otherwise, to my great delight. The essays assembled in this volume are, in true baroque spirit, ambitious, moving, demanding, unreserved, and controversial. I have found it pleasurable and instructive to reflect on each of them, to try to figure them out and to refigure them in my mind. They have kept me busy and will keep on doing so. I admire the coeditor of this collection, Nicholas Spadaccini, and his colleagues in the Department of Spanish and Portuguese at the University of Minnesota for linking ideologies and literature in Hispanic and Luso-Brazilian studies before it was fashionable to do so. Even more, I admire their dedication to training graduate students and to serving as mentors to young scholars in the field. There is an "icing on the cake" feel to the collection, in which a good number of those former graduate students are represented and acquit themselves superbly. They are well educated *en toda la extensión de la palabra*, rigorously prepared and taught in the end to follow their own course of research and investigation. This may be deemed a baroque inversion, a reversal of expectations, and a demystification of Harold Bloom's now classic conceit, for it enacts the anxiety of influence on the high road.

◆ Contributors

David R. Castillo is Associate Professor of Spanish at the University at Buffalo. He is the author of *(A)Wry Views: Anamorphosis, Cervantes, and the Early Picaresque*. He has also written articles on Baltasar Gracián, Miguel de Cervantes, Renaissance and baroque Spanish narrative and theater, questions of nation-building, identity formation and cultural theory. At the present time he is working on a book project tentatively titled "Baroque Gallery of Horrors and Curiosities" and an edited volume on the topic of "Reason and Its Others in Early Modernity."

William Egginton is Associate Professor of Romance Languages and Literatures and Comparative Literature at the University at Buffalo, and teaches courses in literary history, literary theory, and philosophy. He is author of *How the World Became a Stage: Presence, Theatricality, and the Question of Modernity*; translator and editor of Lisa Block de Behar's *Borges: The Passion of an Endless Quote*; and editor of *The Pragmatic Turn in Philosophy: Contemporary Engagements between Analytic and Continental Thought* (forthcoming).

Edward H. Friedman is Professor of Spanish and Comparative Literature at Vanderbilt University. His books and essays center on early modern Spanish literature, with special emphasis on Cervantes and the picaresque. He is the author of *Wit's End*, an adaptation of Lope de Vega's *La dama boba*, and he recently published an edition of Lope's *El caballero de Olmedo*. He is editor of *Bulletin of the Comediantes* and immediate past president of the Cervantes Society of America.

Leonardo García-Pabón is Associate Professor of Spanish-American literature at the University of Oregon, where he directs the Latin American Studies Program, and the Oregon Consortium of International and Area Studies. His publications include *La Patria íntima. Alegorías nacionales en la literatura y el cine de Bolivia*, and editions of *Relatos de Potosí. Antología de la Historia de la Villa Imperial de Potosí* by Bartolomé Arzáns Orsúa y Vela, and Óscar Cerruto's *La muerte mágica y otros relatos*. Currently, he is working on a book on *mestizaje* and Andean literature since the colonial period.

Carlos M. Gutiérrez is Associate Professor of Spanish at the University of Cincinnati and has formerly taught in France (Strasbourg) and Spain (Soria, Valladolid). He has published creative fiction and several studies on Spanish Golden Age. His most recent work is *La espada, el rayo y la pluma. Quevedo y los campos literario y de poder*. He is presently working on a book-length study about Cervantes' *Viaje del Parnaso* and has recently finished a volume of short stories (*Recurso al método*). His research focuses on the seventeenth-century Spanish literary field.

Paola Marín is Assistant Professor of Spanish and Women's Studies at Gustavus Adolphus College. Her areas of concentration include Spanish Golden Age and Colonial Latin American literature and culture. She has published articles in *Romance Notes, Universitas Humanistica, Romance Languages Annual*, and is the author of a book on Sor Juana Inés de la Cruz, *Teología y conciencia criolla*.

Luis Martín-Estudillo is Assistant Professor of Spanish Literature and Cultural Studies at the University of Iowa. He has published several articles on Spanish literature and cultural history in American and European journals and is co-author of the book *Libertad y límites. El Barroco hispánico*. His research interests include the relationships between early modern and contemporary aesthetics and epistemologies. He is co-director of *Ex Libris, Revista de Poesía*.

Mabel Moraña is Professor of Spanish American Literature at the University of Washington and Director of Publications of the Instituto Internacional de Literatura Iberoamericana. She is the author of *Literatura y cultura nacional en Hispanoamérica, 1910-1940*; *Memorias de la generación fantasma*; *Políticas de la escritura en América Latina: de la Colonia a la Modernidad*; *Viaje al silencio: Exploraciones del discurso barroco*, and *Crítica impura*. She has edited a number of volumes, including *Relecturas del Barroco de Indias* and *Ideologies of Hispanism*. She has also coordinated special volumes on colonial literature for the *Revista de Crítica Literaria Latinoamericana* and the *Revista Iberoamericana*. In recent years, she has coordinated multiple volumes on indigenism, Latin American cultural criticism, modernity, and postcolonialism.

Bradley J. Nelson is Associate Professor of Spanish at Concordia University in Montreal, Quebec, Canada. His research interests include early modern symbolic culture in its theatrical, festive, and emblematic forms in Spain and Colonial Latin America. His recent and forthcoming essays include studies of Cervantes's theater and prose, Lope de Vega's *auto sacramentales*, and emblematic studies of Sigüenza y Góngora and Sor Juana Inés de la Cruz. He is currently completing a book-length study of the emblematic mode of representation in Spanish Golden Age literature.

Fernando Ordóñez is Graduate Instructor at the University of Minnesota, where he specializes in early modern Spain and colonial Latin America. He has taught in Uruguay and has held research fellowships in Italy. He is co-author of *Estudios socio-religiosos en el Uruguay* and has participated in many research projects dealing with social and cultural issues in Spain and Latin America. He is the former executive director of the OBSUR social science research center in Montevideo, Uruguay.

Fernando R. de la Flor is Professor of Spanish Literature at the University of Salamanca, Spain, and associate member of the Real Academia de Bellas Artes de San Fernando. His research deals with the philosophy of the Baroque, about which he has published several books, among them *Atenas castellana: estudios sobre cultura simbólica*; *Teatro de la memoria. Estudios sobre mnemotecnia española de los siglos XVII y XVIII*; *Política y fiesta en el Barroco*; *Emblemas: lecturas de la imagen simbólica*; *Barroco. Representación e ideología en el mundo hispánico*; and *La península metafísica: arte, literatura y pensamiento en la cultura española del Barroco*. His next book is titled *Pasiones frías. La cultura del secreto en el barroco hispano*.

Nieves Romero-Díaz is Assistant Professor at Mount Holyoke College, and specializes in Golden Age literature and culture. Along with articles on María de Zayas's *comedia* and the novellas of Céspedes y Meneses, Mariana de Carvajal and Andrés del Prado, she has also published a monograph entitled *Nueva nobleza, nueva novela: Reescribiendo la cultura urbana del Barroco*. She is currently working on a critical edition and translation of María de Guevara's political writings.

Nicholas Spadaccini is Professor of Spanish and Comparative Literature at the University of Minnesota. He has published books, editions, and collective volumes, with an emphasis on early modern Spain and Latin America. His most recent study (co-authored) is *Libertad y límites. El Barroco hispánico* and he is currently completing a book on Cervantes and the culture of crisis of Baroque Spain. He is editor in chief of the Hispanic Issues series.

Silvia B. Suárez is a doctoral candidate in Spanish American Literature at the University of Minnesota and is currently writing on transatlantic relationships in the early modern period. She has published articles on Cervantes and el Inca Garcilaso and has recently completed a monograph on *Comentarios reales de los Incas*.

Hernán Vidal is Professor of Latin American Literature, Comparative Literature, and Cultural Studies at the University of Minnesota. His research, teaching and publications are oriented towards a definition of a poetics of Human Rights based on the International Bill of Human Rights proclaimed by the United Nations and the Humanitarian Law of Armed Conflict. He is the author of numerous books on early modern and contemporary Latin American culture stressing socio-historical approaches.

Index

Compiled by Alyssa Sanan

323